Francis Marshall

Football

The Rugby Union Game

Francis Marshall

Football

The Rugby Union Game

ISBN/EAN: 9783742877017

Manufactured in Europe, USA, Canada, Australia, Japa

Cover: Foto ©ninafisch / pixelio.de

Manufactured and distributed by brebook publishing software (www.brebook.com)

Francis Marshall

Football

CONTENTS.

CHAPTER I.
The Origin of the Game 1

CHAPTER II.
A Bigside at Rugby. By Arthur G. Guillemard . . 15

CHAPTER III.
Eton Football. By Sydney R. James 23

CHAPTER IV.
The Harrow Game. By an Old Harrovian . . . 37

CHAPTER V.
The Winchester Game. By an Old Wykehamist . . . 44

CHAPTER VI.
Rugby Football in Scottish Schools. By H. H. Almond, M.A., LL.D., Head-master of the Loretto School . . 51

CHAPTER VII.
The Foundation and Progress of the Rugby Football Union from 1870 to 1880. By Arthur G. Guillemard . . 67

CONTENTS.

CHAPTER VIII.

PROGRESS OF THE RUGBY FOOTBALL UNION FROM SEASON 1880-81 TO THE PRESENT TIME. BY G. ROWLAND HILL, *Hon. Sec.* . 94

CHAPTER IX.

PAST DEVELOPMENT IN RUGBY FOOTBALL AND THE FUTURE OF THE GAME. BY ARTHUR BUDD 115

CHAPTER X.

INTERNATIONAL MATCHES AND PLAYERS, 1871-1880. BY ARTHUR G. GUILLEMARD 139

CHAPTER XI.

INTERNATIONAL MATCHES AND PLAYERS, 1881-1892. BY A. BUDD 167

CHAPTER XII.

INTERNATIONAL FOOTBALL: SCOTLAND. BY R. W. IRVINE . . 198

CHAPTER XIII.

INTERNATIONAL FOOTBALL: IRELAND. BY J. J. MACCARTHY . 222

CHAPTER XIV.

INTERNATIONAL FOOTBALL: WALES 249
THE FOUR THREE-QUARTER SYSTEM. BY W. H. GWYNN . 259

CHAPTER XV.

RUGBY FOOTBALL AT OXFORD. BY H. VASSALL, late Captain of the Oxford University Football Club 266

CHAPTER XVI.

RUGBY FOOTBALL AT CAMBRIDGE. BY C. J. B. MARRIOTT, late Captain of Cambridge University Football Club . . . 300

CONTENTS.

CHAPTER XVII.

METROPOLITAN FOOTBALL. BY A LONDONER . . 323

CHAPTER XVIII.

COUNTY FOOTBALL: THE COUNTY CHAMPIONSHIP . . . 352

CHAPTER XIX.

COUNTY FOOTBALL: LANCASHIRE. BY A. M. CROOK . 373

CHAPTER XX.

COUNTY FOOTBALL: YORKSHIRE . . . 409

CHAPTER XXI.

COUNTY FOOTBALL: RECOLLECTIONS OF NORTHUMBERLAND FOOTBALL. BY WILLIAM CAIL 447

CHAPTER XXII.

COUNTY FOOTBALL: CHESHIRE, by J. W. H. THORP. CUMBERLAND, by R. WESTRAY. WESTMORLAND, by G. WEBSTER . 464

CHAPTER XXIII.

COUNTY FOOTBALL: THE MIDLANDS, by E. B. HOLMES. GLOUCESTER; AND SOMERSET 476

CHAPTER XXIV.

FOREIGN TOUR . . . 499

LIST OF ILLUSTRATIONS.

	PAGE
"Old Crocks" *Frontispiece*	
The Close, Rugby School	1
A Bigside at Rugby	17
Mixed Wall Eleven, 1890	24
"A Bully in Bad Calx"	28
St. Andrew's Day, from "Bad Calx"	30
"Six-and-Six"	45
A "Hot"	46
"Six-and-Six"	48
Canvas as Arranged to Commence Six-and-Six	50
Fettes-Loretto Fifteen	52
H. H. Almond	55
"A Drop Out"	60
H. B. Tristram	63
A. R. Don Wauchope	64
A. G. Grant Asher	65
E. C. Holmes	67
F. Stokes, L. J. Maton, A. Rutter, C. D. Heatley, A. G. Guillemard	69
E. H. Ash	71
The Kick-off—After the Kick	74
E. Rutter	78
C. S. Dakyns	79
Ball out of Scrummage: Passing from one Halfback to the Other	85
The Calcutta Cup	89
A Try: The Place Kick at Goal	91
F. I. Currey, L. Stokes, J. Maclaren, A. Budd, E. T. Gurdon	95
G. Rowland Hill	96
Lord Kingsburgh and Major Marindin	101
A Free Kick: Placing the Ball	106
The Kick-off : Ready for the Kick	112
A Line-Out : Waiting for the Ball	118
A. Rotherham	123
Loose Play	125
A Tight Scrummage	130
Loose Game: Forwards Following up	136
English Team *v.* Scotland: Edinburgh, March, 1871	142
J. F. Green	143
F. Luscombe	145
M. W. Marshall	147
W. E. Collins	149
Putting the Ball into a Scrummage	158
H. T. Twynam	162
Charles Gurdon	163
English Team *v.* Scotland: Manchester, Feb. 28, 1880	164
C. Hutton Coates	166
W. N. Bolton	170
A Forward Rush	173
R. S. F. Henderson	175
English Team *v.* Scotland: Blackheath, March 1, 1884	177
A. E. Stoddart	183
Forming the Scrummage	185
English Team *v.* Scotland: Edinburgh, March 1, 1890	190

LIST OF ILLUSTRATIONS.

	PAGE
Percy Christopherson	195
R. W. Irvine	199
Scottish Team v. England: Edinburgh, March 27, 1871	201
L. M. Balfour	203
J. H. S. Grahame	206
W. E. Maclagan	207
W. A. Peterkin	208
R. T. Ainslie	210
A Free Kick: Taking a Punt	213
J. Gordon Mitchell	214
C. Reid	215
Scottish Team v. England: Richmond, March 7, 1891	218
H. G. Cook and E. McAlister	223
R. M. Peter	225
Irish Team v. England, 1875	228
A. P. Cronyn	229
The Brothers Moore	231
J. H. Taylor	237
Irish Team v. England, 1887	238
J. C. Bagot and R. B. Walkington	242
R. G. Warren	244
R. W. Hughes	246
G. Scriven	247
R. Mullock and C. H. Newman	250
W. D. Phillips and D. Gwynn	251
John Henry Bowen	252
H. S. Lyne and A. J. Gould	254
C. J. Thomas	255
David and Evan James	256
C. B. Nicholl	257
W. H. Gwynn	259
Welsh Team v. England, 1890	262
Oxford University Rugby Union Fifteen	268
A Dribble	273
H. Vassall	278
W. M. Tatham	280
A. M. Evanson	281
A. R. Patterson	284
G. C. Wade	285
C. S. Wooldridge and R. S. Kindersley	288
E. J. Moore and A. Court	289
Passing the Ball	294

	PAGE
Cambridge University Rugby Team, 1886-7	302
R. T. Finch	304
A Line-Out	305
C. P. Wilson	307
H. G. Fuller, John H. Dewhurst, Chas. J. B. Marriott, W. R. M. Leake, and G. L. Jeffery	313
Middlesex Team v. Somerset, 1889	324
Surrey County Rugby Football Team v. Yorkshire, 1890	328
A. Spurling	332
John F. Hammond	334
W. G. Clibborn	339
W. W. Hewitt	344
Yorkshire (Champion County) Team v. England, 1889	353
Yorkshire (Champion County) Team v. England, 1890	362
Lancashire (Champion County) Team v. England, 1891	368
Yorkshire (Champion County) Team v. England, 1892	370
William Bell	374
Lancashire Team v. Middlesex, 1887	379
A Place-Kick	385
A. N. Hornby, W. H. Hunt, and R. Walker	398
E. Kewley and R. Hunt	399
J. T. Hunt	400
C. M. Sawyer	401
H. C. Rowley	402
H. H. Springmann	403
J. H. Payne	404
A. T. Kemble	405
James Valentine and Tom Kent	406
The Yorkshire Presidents	410
J. B. Ogden and T. Glover	414
J. G. Hudson	417
Fred Bonsor, J. L. Hickson, Gilbert Harrison, E. Holmes, W. F. Bromet	419
W. H. H. Hutchinson	422
F. S. Tetley	424

LIST OF ILLUSTRATIONS.

	PAGE
Bradford: Winners of the Yorkshire Challenge Cup, 1884	425
The Brothers Robertshaw	427
J. J. Haweridge	429
C. W. L. Fernandes	431
The Brothers Huth	432
E. Woodhead and J. Dyson	433
Huddersfield: Winners of the Yorkshire Challenge Cup, 1890	434
G. T. Thomson and H. Wilkinson	438
Wakefield Trinity: Winners of the Yorkshire Cup, 1879	440
A. Newsome	443
R. E. Lockwood	444
Donald Jowett	445
Northumberland Team v. Yorkshire, 1891	449
W. M. Scott, M. T. Scott, T. L. Bell, C. H. Sample, E. B. Brutton	454
Durham Team v. Yorkshire, 1891	459
C. H. Elliot, H. E. Kayll, T. M. Swinburne, F. H. R. Alderson, P. B. Junor, and W. Yiend	461
Cumberland County v. Lancashire, 1880	468
R. Westray	469
"Kendal Hornets": Winners of the "Northern Counties Challenge Cup," 1888	474
J. H. Rogers	478
F. Evershed	479
Midland Counties Team v. Yorkshire, 1892	482
Hiatt C. Baker and J. D. Miller	486
Gloucester County Team v. Lancashire, 1891	487
Somerset Team v. Yorkshire, 1891	489
F. H. Fox, H. Fox, S. M. J. Woods, F. E. Hancock, and P. F. Hancock	494
Shaw and Shrewsbury's Australian Team, 1888	501
New Zealand Native Football Team, 1888-9	505
The Cape Team, 1891	509
England v. Cape Colony, at Cape Town	512
England v. S. Africa, at Kimberley	515

THE CLOSE, RUGBY SCHOOL.

RUGBY FOOTBALL.

CHAPTER I.

THE ORIGIN OF THE GAME.

IT is not within the purpose of the present work to give a detailed and exhaustive record of the ancient games of football or to compile a history of the game as played in this country for so many centuries. The ancient records have been so exhaustively searched into by Mr. Montague Shearman, and embodied by him in the Badminton Series, in addition to a work by the same author in conjunction with Mr. James E. Vincent—" Football: its History for Two Centuries"—that to attempt to go over the same ground again would be a work of supererogation. The present work is intended to treat of Rugby Football only, and the present chapter will be devoted to an endeavour to trace the origin of that game, and that game alone.

Rugby football is the modern scientific development

of an ancient game at ball. It can therefore lay claim to
be the most ancient of British sports, and in its present
form is the legitimate refinement of the rough and crude
games which in their main features are undoubtedly the
source from which the Rugby game and the Rugby
game alone is the true issue. It is often urged as a
charge against the Rugby game that the title "football"
is singularly inappropriate, inasmuch as the distinctive
features of the game are the handling and carrying of
the ball. And this charge has some foundation as
regards the nomenclature of the game, which has certainly, as will shortly be shown, been known under other
titles than that of football. In the Western Counties it
has been designated as "hurling," whilst in Norfolk and
the Eastern Counties it has been styled "camp-ball." But
under whatever name the game may have been known,
it is possible to trace back for many centuries the
existence of a game at ball which in its general features
has been unmistakably the precursor of the modern
Rugby Union game.

Without going so far back as the days of ancient
Greece, there was a game of ball amongst the Romans
called *harpastum*, which both from its name and
the description given of it was clearly a somewhat
similar sport to the Rugby football of the present
day. Very probably this same Roman game *harpastum*
was introduced from Greece, and, if so, the antiquity
of the game can be traced back still further than
Roman times. The name *harpastum* is derived from
the Greek ἁρπάζω, signifying "to seize," and the game
was so called from the efforts of the players to seize
or carry the ball from their opponents. The game
was therefore a "carrying" rather than a "kicking"
game, and in this respect is exactly in accord with
the Rugby game. But the similarity is not confined
to the act of carrying the ball. The description of
the game, as given by an ancient writer, affords
reasonable ground for assuming that the *harpastum*
may have been the parent source from which sprang
those games which afterwards became developed into
the Rugby game. From this description it may be
gathered that in the *harpastum* the players were
divided into two bands: that the game was started
by the ball being thrown up on a line in the middle

between the two sets of players, whilst behind the
players at the two ends there were marked two other
lines (corresponding to our goal lines), and that the
players tried to *carry* the ball beyond these lines,
which they were unable to accomplish without pushing
one another backwards and forwards. Here are distinctly described the two acts which are most strongly
characteristic of the Rugby game, viz., the scrummage,
and the carrying of the ball.

The Romans may, or may not, have introduced the
harpastum into Britain. There is no historical evidence
to show that they actually did so; but only one
conclusion can be arrived at from the above description
of the *harpastum*, viz., that amongst the Romans there
was a game of ball strangely similar in its chief characteristics to the game now played under Rugby Union
rules.

But though there is no record of the introduction
of the *harpastum* into Britain, yet it is possible to infer
that the game may have been known in this island
during the Roman occupation, for there is evidence
that at this period there was some such game in
vogue. Needless to remark that we allude to the
traditions of the games played at Chester and at
Derby. A Chester antiquary mentions a practice
which prevailed in that city "time out of mind, for
the shoemakers yearly, on Shrove Tuesday, to deliver
to the drapers, in the presence of the Mayor of
Chester, at the ball of Rodehee, one ball of leather,
called a football, of the value of three shillings and
fourpence or above, to play at from thence to the
common hall of the same city"; and it is likewise
chronicled that the first ball used was the head of a
Dane, who had been captured and slain, and whose
head was kicked about for sport. Here, then, at a
period little later than the Roman occupation, we
have an indication that some game at football was
played at Chester, a city which owes its origin and
name to the Romans themselves. With respect to the
character of the game we can glean nothing further
than that it must have been of a somewhat rough nature,
for it was "productive of so much inconvenience that
the ball was afterwards changed into six glayves of
silver of the like value as a reward for the best runner

of the day upon the Rodelice." Glover, in his "History of Derby," in referring to the celebrated match played annually in that town on Shrove Tuesday, mentions a legend that points unmistakably to the connection of the game with Roman times. He says, "The origin of this violent game is lost in antiquity, but there exists a tradition that a cohort of Roman soldiers, marching through the town to Derwentio, or Little Chester, were thrust out by the armed populace, and this mode of celebrating the occurrence has been continued to the present day." It is even added that this conflict occurred in the year 217, and that the Roman troops at Little Chester were slain by the Britons. Whatever the character of the game played at Derby in ancient times may have been, the game as played at that town in more modern times was certainly more of a "carrying" than a "kicking" game, as will be gathered from an account which is given later.

So in the two most ancient games to which we have any allusions we are met with two indisputable facts, viz., that at or about the period of the Roman occupation, there are traditions that some game at football was played at the two centres of Derby and Chester, and that such games were of a character to warrant the not unreasonable inference that the *harpastum* had been played by the Romans in Britain, and had suggested the method of play, if it had not actually been the model itself upon which the game was formed. Shrove Tuesday, in each instance, is the day appointed for the game, and it is not a little singular that this day was also the one set apart for many games at football, which, it is well known, have been in vogue at different times in this island. Thus the great game at the Cross of Scone, in Scotland, was played upon Shrove Tuesday. On Shrove Tuesday there is still played the Corfe Castle game, which can be traced as far back as the year 1553. This game is a curious custom of the Company of Marblers at Purbeck, who, to preserve an ancient right-of-way which they claim, kick the ball from Corfe to Owre-quay on Shrove Tuesday. This company is a most ancient body, and in its articles, the earliest extant copy of which bears the date 1553, provision is made for the game as follows:—"That any man in our companie the Shrovtewsdaie after his marriage shall paie unto the Wardings, for the use of and benefit of the companie, twelve pence, and the last married man to brynge a footballe according to the custom of our companie." In the counties of Northumberland and Cumberland the inhabitants have from time immemorial been accustomed to celebrate the sport annually. Special mention may be made of a game at Alnwick Castle, where, on Shrove Tuesday, the porter of the castle threw out a football to the young men assembled at the castle gate. This was not so much a game at football as a struggle to obtain and keep possession of the ball itself, which became the prize of the person who could carry it off. At Bromfield, in Cumberland, the scholars of the Free School obtained the privilege of a football match in a very peculiar manner, by barring out the master. If the boys succeeded in keeping the master out for three days, they claimed the right of honourable capitulation on certain conditions, which were duly written out, and subscribed to by both parties. Amongst these conditions was the privilege of immediately celebrating a football match, and a cock fight. The cock fight was indulged in first, and then the football was thrown down, and each side strove to *carry* the ball to the house of their respective captains, generally some two or three miles distant. In the "Statistical Account of Scotland" it is mentioned "that in a certain parish in Midlothian it was the custom for the married women to play the single yearly, on Shrove Tuesday"; and it is added that the married women always won.

So far we have dealt with traditions only, and, as far as can be gathered from those traditions, it is certain that whatever football was played in ancient time, it was more of the carrying and running game than any other, and was very nearly allied to the Rugby game of the present day. We shall now make some reference to written evidence concerning the game, still, as before, with no intention of writing a history of the game and its antiquities, but rather with the view of further strengthening the grounds for the assumption that the Rugby game is the legitimate descendant of the football of former times. The first mention of football in English history is made by FitzStephen, who wrote in the thirteenth century. Speaking of the various games played by London schoolboys, he says:—" Annually, upon Shrove Tuesday, they go into the fields immediately after dinner and play the celebrated game of ball." The allusion is somewhat vague, and from the passage itself it cannot be absolutely deduced that the game mentioned was football. Indeed, Stowe and other writers explain the game as having been tennis, and Strutt is also of the opinion that it is very doubtful if the reference was to football. But inasmuch as Shrove Tuesday, as we have already shown, was the day specially set aside for games of football, it may reasonably be inferred that the game played by these London boys was football.

Strong evidence as to the universality and popularity of the game can be drawn from the various edicts of several monarchs prohibiting it. The earliest prohibition dates as far back as the reign of Edward III., in the year 1349. That monarch did not object to the game of football in itself, but because the playing of the game tended to distract the youth from cultivating skill in archery. At that period of our country's history the military strength of England depended upon the skill of its archers, who pre-eminently were the cause of England's great military achievements in that age. The edict of Edward III. conclusively proves that in his time football was sufficiently popular, and so widely indulged in, as to be a serious hindrance to the practice of archery. In modern times the rulers of both the Rugby and Association games have found it necessary to forbid the playing of football during the summer months, because it encroached upon the game of cricket, and caused less interest to be taken in that game. The prohibition of Edward III. was followed by similar interdicts in the reigns of Richard II. and Henry IV. In the Tudor period Henry VIII. and Elizabeth also issued prohibitions, but there is no absolute proof that the statutes suppressing the game were ever put in force or recognised, except where fatal results had occurred, or where a riot had arisen from the game.

And so, without quoting the many allusions to the game of football by Shakespeare and other writers, we have clear evidence of the continuance of the game till Elizabethan times. Then we get a description of an actual game played under distinct rules, and those rules bearing a curious resemblance to the Rugby Union laws of the present day. The game mentioned is not called football, but "hurling," and the chronicler is Carew, in his "Survey of Cornwall," published in 1602. Though the game is styled "hurling," the description is clearly that of a game at football with very little kicking, and very much carrying of the ball and running with it.

Carew describes two games, one of which he calls "hurling to goales," *i.e.* playing the game within prescribed limits of space, and the other, "hurling over country." We will quote his description of the latter first. In this game the goals were three or four miles apart, and were houses or trees or some other conspicuous landmark. Carew's description of the game is as follows:—"Two or three parishes agreed to hurl against two or three other parishes," and so the number of players was practically unlimited, and in this respect the game would correspond to Bigside at Rugby School. It was essentially a "carrying" game, for "that company which could catch or carry it (the ball) by force or slight (*i.e.* stratagem) to the place assigned gaineth the victory. Such as see where the ball is played give notice by crying 'Ware East,' 'Ware West,' as the same is carried. The hurlers take their way over hilles, dales, hedges, ditches, yea, and thorow bushes, briars, mires, plashes, and rivers whatsoever, so as you shall sometimes see twenty or thirty lie tugging together in the water, scrambling and scratching for the ball." We can also gather that the players were assigned particular positions in the game, for there were "companies laid out before, on the one side, to encounter them that come with the ball, and of the other party to succour them in the manner of a forewarde." Is this the origin of the term "forward" in modern football? If so, the main idea conveyed in the term is that of being in the van to bear the brunt of the first attack.

Passing over for a moment the game of "hurling to goales," we find that a game very similar to hurling was played in the Eastern Counties. There it was styled as camp-ball. This was also a game at football, and evidently took the name by which it was known from being played in the open country (Latin *campus*, a plain or open country). To this camp-ball there are many references in documents of the fifteenth century, and in an old comedy of 1649 one of the characters describes himself as "Tom Stroud of Hurling, and I'll play a gole at camp-ball"; but we get no actual description of the game till a much later date. In the Badminton Series there is quoted a description of this game as given by a writer named Moor in the year 1823: "Each party has two goals, ten or fifteen yards apart. The parties stand in a line, facing each other, about ten yards distance midway between their goals and that of their adversaries. An indifferent (*i.e.* neutral or impartial) spectator throws up a ball about the size of a cricket ball midway between the confronted players, and makes his escape. The rush is to catch the falling ball. He who can first catch or seize it speeds home, making his way through his opponents and aided by his own sidesmen. If caught and held, or rather in danger of being held—for if caught with the ball in his possession he loses a snotch—he throws the ball (he must in no case give it) to some less beleaguered friend more free and more in breath than himself, who, if it be not arrested in its course or be jostled away by the eager and watchful adversaries, catches it; and he in like manner hastens homeward, in like manner pursued, annoyed, and aided, winning the notch or snotch if he contrive to carry or throw it within the goals. At a loss or a gain of a snotch a recommencement takes place. When the game is decided by snotches, seven or nine are the game; and these, if the parties be well matched, take two or three hours to win. Sometimes a large football was used; the game was then called 'kicking camp'; and if played with shoes on, 'savage camp.'"

From these descriptions we can see that the "hurling over country" was of the same character as the celebrated games played at Scone and Derby, and that "camp-ball" was a game that differed very little from the "hurling" described by Carew. Indeed, "camp-ball" might very well be the same game as "hurling to goales," the description of which game as given by Carew we will now quote. "For hurling to goales there are fifteen, twenty, or thirty players, more or less, chosen on each side, who strip themselves to their slightest apparel, and then join hands in ranks one against another; out of these ranks they match themselves by payres, one embracing another and so passe away, every of which couple are especially to watch one another during the play. After this they pitch two bushes in the ground some eight or ten feet asunder, and directly against them, ten or twelve score paces off, other twain in like distance, which they term goales, where some indifferent (*i.e.* neutral or impartial) person throweth up a ball, the which whomsoever can catch or carry through the adversaries' goales hath won the game."

"Camp-ball" and "hurling" were clearly games at football, though not actually so called, and they contained the germs and essential features of modern Rugby football. For we can recognise the scrummage of the Rugby game, notice that the goals are much the same distance apart, and in the "matching of the players in payres" are at once reminded of the present practice of every player marking his man at the line out. But, from the rest of the description of "hurling to goales," it is evident that not only was the play under definite rules, and with orderly and systematic tactics, but these rules and tactics only emphasise the similarity of the game to modern Rugby football; thus we find it forbidden to "but or handfast under the girdle," *i.e.* in modern phraseology, "to charge or collar below the waist." Now, though this is not forbidden in the modern game, the feeling that to "leg" a man is not exactly fair play is exemplified by the chorus of dissent with which such proceeding is greeted from the lungs of the observant spectators. Tripping is absolutely forbidden, and tripping may well be described as "charging below the waist." But, further, there is strong presumption that the rules of onside were already formulated, for it was distinctly prohibited to "deal a foreballe," *i.e.* "to pass forward." So that Vassall and his famous Oxford team, in perfecting the system of judicious and scientific passing, were but copying the example of the "hurlers" in Cornwall, who, like the modern tacticians, were equally restricted as to the direction in which the ball might be passed.

We cannot refrain from quoting the description of the game as given by Joseph Strutt, the great historian of English sports, who, writing in 1801, thus describes the game :—

"When a match at football is made, an equal number of competitors take the field and stand between two goals placed at a distance of eighty or an hundred yards the one from the other. The goal is usually made with two sticks driven into the ground about two or three feet apart. The ball, which is commonly made of a blown bladder and cased with leather, is delivered in the midst of the ground, and the object of each party is to drive it through the goal of their antagonists, which being achieved the game is won. The abilities of the performers are best displayed in attacking and defending the goals; and hence the pastime was more frequently called a 'goal at football' than a 'game at football.' When the exercise becomes exceedingly violent, the players kick each other's shins without the least ceremony, and some of them are overthrown at the hazard of their limbs."

With the same object still before us, viz., the tracing of resemblance between the ancient games at football and that of the modern Rugby game, we will now quote descriptions of some renewals of the ancient games. One of these took place at Scone, in Perthshire, and is minutely and graphically described by Sir Frederick Morton Eden, in his "Statistical Account of Scotland," which description is as follows :—" At the parish of Scone, county of Perth, Scotland, every year, on Shrove Tuesday, the bachelors and married men drew themselves up at the Cross of Scone on opposite sides. A ball was then thrown up, and they played from two o'clock till sunset. The game was this: He who at any time got the ball in his hands, ran with it till he was overtaken by a player of the opposite party, and then, if he could shake himself loose from those who were holding him, he ran on; if not, he threw the ball from him, unless it was wrested from him by one of the other party, *but no person was allowed to kick it*. The object of the married men was to hang it; that is, to put it three times into a small hole on the moor, which was the 'dool' or limit of that side; that of the bachelors was to drown it, or dip it three times into a deep place in the river which was the limit of the other; the party who could effect either of these objects won the game; if neither won, the ball was cut into equal parts at sunset. In the course of the play there was some violence between the parties; but it is a proverb in this part of the country 'All is fair at the ball of Scone.'"

The following is the account of the Derby game given

by Glover, in his "History of Derbyshire," published in 1829:—"The contest lies between the parishes of St. Peter's and All Saints, and the goals to which the ball is taken are Nun's Mill for the latter, and the Gallows balk, on the Normanton road, for the former. None of the other parishes in the borough take any direct part in the contest; but the inhabitants of all join in the sport, together with persons from all parts of the adjacent country. The players are young men from eighteen to thirty or upwards, married as well as single, and many veterans who retain a relish for the sport are occasionally seen in the very heat of the conflict. The game commences in the market place, where the partisans of each parish are drawn up on each side, and about noon a large ball is tossed up in the midst of them. This is seized upon by some of the strongest and most active men of each party. The rest of the players immediately close in upon them, and a solid mass is formed. It then becomes the object of each party to impel the course of the crowd towards their particular goal. The struggle to obtain the ball, which is carried in the arms of those who have possessed themselves of it, is then violent, and the motion of the human tide heaving to and fro without the least regard to consequences is tremendous. Broken shins, broken heads, torn coats, and lost hats are amongst the minor accidents of this fearful contest, and it frequently happens that persons fall, owing to the intensity of the pressure, fainting and bleeding beneath the feet of the surrounding mob. But it would be difficult to give an adequate idea of this ruthless sport. A Frenchman passing through Derby remarked that if Englishmen called this playing, it would be impossible to say what they would call fighting. Still the crowd is encouraged by respectable persons attached to each party, who take a surprising interest in the result of the day's sport, urging on the players with shouts, and even handing to those who are exhausted oranges and other refreshment. The object of the St. Peter's party is to get the ball into the water down the Morledge Brook into the Derwent as soon as they can; while the All Saints' party endeavour to prevent this and urge the ball westward. The St. Peter's players are considered to be equal to the best water spaniels, and it is certainly curious to see two or three hundred men up to their chins in the Derwent continually ducking each other. The numbers engaged on both sides exceed a thousand, and the streets are crowded with lookers-on. The shops are closed, and the town presents the aspect of a place suddenly taken by storm."

This, though an amusing extract, does not throw much light upon the connection between the Rugby game and former games at football, save in the one respect that there could have been little kicking of the ball-in such a struggle as that which took place annually at Derby. But this same game at Derby is the survival of the ancient game which, according to tradition, originated as a memorial of the triumph over a detachment of Roman troops; and though the thread of connection is long drawn and through many centuries, we are met with two undisputed facts, viz., that the *harpastum* of the Romans was essentially a game of "carrying" the ball, and that in the game at Derby, which is traditionally connected with Roman times, the carrying of the ball is the specific feature of the play.

Uniting the extracts, references, and descriptions as above, we can summarise the history of football as played in this island as follows, viz.:—That the Romans, who occupied this island during the first four centuries of the Christian era, played at a game of ball called *harpastum*, which game presented the special features of carrying the ball and the scrummage, found in no other modern game of football save in the Rugby game; that it can be traced back to Roman times that a game of football was played in Britain; and that, as far as can be gathered from tradition, all games then played were characterised by much carrying and little kicking of the ball. It can also be concluded that a game of ball—passing under various names of "football," "hurling," "camp-ball," and the like—has always been a popular sport of the lower orders of society: and though such games have differed somewhat from each other, they have all concurred in being "carrying" games. Indeed, little or no trace of kicking the ball can be found, and in some cases there has been an actual prohibition of kicking altogether. Further, other distinctive features of the Rugby game can be traced, as, for instance, the forbidding of the passing forward of the ball, which clearly demonstrates that the game as at present played under the Rugby Union Code is the legitimate refinement of the rough and crude games of our ancestors. Nowhere can there be found any trace whatever of a game assimilating, however remotely, to the kicking game of the Association Code. In making this assertion we have no intention of indulging in disparagement of the Association game. If the name of football can in the strict meaning of the word be applied to any game, the Association game can legitimately claim an almost exclusive right to be termed football; but if it be a reproach, as is often so alleged, against the Rugby game, that it contains much handling but little kicking of the ball, it is, on the other hand, the glory and privilege of Rugby Unionists to know that the game which they so dearly love, and which they have spent so much time in developing and perfecting, is in its main features the *same game* that has been played in this island for centuries. The Rugby game is, in fact, *the* most ancient of all popular sports of the present day.

But modern football has been evolved from the schoolboy games of our great English schools. Modern Rugby football, in particular, has been modelled upon the game played at Rugby School. The game will always be known by the name of the school which gave it birth. But the great schools of Eton, Harrow, Winchester, Charterhouse, Marlborough, Westminster, Uppingham, Shrewsbury, and others, have had a large share in the development of the game of football. From the chief schools the game, in either the dribbling or the handling form, has spread to the smaller schools, and from the schools to the public at large. Our schools have been the *fons et origo* of modern football. It is well to emphasise this fact in these days when the enthusiastic supporters of the game in the North of England are apt to forget the source from which the game has sprung, and are ready to imagine that all interest in the game and development of the same are the peculiar prerogatives of the sport-loving public of Yorkshire and Lancashire. It should never be forgotten that the schools taught the game, and that old schoolboys created football clubs.

As regards the Rugby game, no record would be complete that did not include some account of the famous school, and the game as played there. But other schools cannot be passed over. They have done good work in developing the game of football. At the present time there are practically only two codes of rules in existence for clubs, viz., the Association and the Rugby Union. Both styles owe their origin to the public schools. At these schools, with few exceptions, any peculiarities in their games have been put aside, and either Association or Rugby football is now played at them; but Eton, Winchester, and Harrow have still remained constant to old traditions, and at those schools their own time-honoured games are played.

The next five chapters will, therefore, be devoted to a slight sketch of football as played at the great English and Scotch schools. Eton, Harrow, and Winchester are included (though they have no direct connection with the Rugby game)—first, because the distinctive features of the games played at those schools are interesting in themselves; and secondly, because it cannot be too strongly insisted that the schools of England have been the founders of modern football.

CHAPTER II.

A BIGSIDE AT RUGBY.

By Arthur G. Guillemard.

WHAT stirring recollections of bygone days do the words which head this chapter bring to the mind of many an Old Rugbeian: what visions of hard-won victories, of still more stoutly-contested defeats, of moments when the gaining of a foot of ground seemed worth a kingdom, and the honours of Best House hung on the issue of a long and difficult place-kick, flit fresh and clear before his eyes! A picture forms itself: a cold, bright November afternoon; the shadows of the noble old elms lengthening over the Close: the long line of school buildings standing out in strong relief against the pale blue of the wintry sky; crowds of boys in the Pontines hard at work at punt-about with innumerable balls; a solitary "pink" trotting home from Dunchurch; and in the foreground two bodies of "caps" straggling leisurely across Old Bigside to hang up their coats previous to standing up for kick-off.

The above sentences, written by me five-and-twenty years ago, I venture to reproduce by way of introduction to the few notes which I have been asked to write upon the famous description of the match School-house *v.* School in "Tom Brown's School Days."

More than fifty years have gone by since the day when the great match, so graphically described by Mr. Thomas Hughes, was supposed to have taken place. Half a century is a period long enough to work material changes in most things terrestrial, and not only the style of play, but even Old Bigside itself, has undergone considerable alteration since Pater Brooke led the School-house forces. The field of play, however, is still of the same dimensions—about 130 yards long by 80 yards in breadth: the aged elms, though more gnarled and rugged, still stand in serried rank behind the lines of touch and goal; and descendants of the rooks of Tom Brown's days claim the old home in the windy tree-tops. One only of the Three Trees remains standing, and no trace is left of the Roller Tree which trespassed on the field of play on the Barby Road side of the ground. The steep slope between the Three Trees and the Island goal-line was levelled in 1887, but there is still a very slight incline towards the Pontines. Up to the year 1858 or thereabouts all the school who were not "caps" had to stand in goal during Bigsides; for the next twenty years goal-keeping was limited to the three great matches, Sixth v. School, Old v. Present, and Two Best Houses v. School; and in or about 1877 it was abolished altogether. Truth to tell, standing in goal for a couple of hours on three afternoons during the season was no very great hardship; there was always some grand football to be watched, and in a gathering of four hundred and fifty boys there are enough lively ones to create plenty of fun, the more mischievous of the crowd snatching a fearful joy from attempts to attach lighted crackers to the coat-tails of unpopular præpostors.

A perusal of the appended extracts from "Tom Brown's School Days" (which we are enabled to include by kind permission of Messrs. Macmillan & Co., the publishers of the work) will show that the game as played in those days did not differ materially from the present style as regards the placing of the players, the three divisions of forwards affected by Old Brooke corresponding with the centre and wing players of modern times, the "dodgers" being our half-backs, and the boys "in quarters" the three-quarter-backs and full-backs. Nor from the account of the struggle do we judge that the leading principles of the game have been in any way altered. The fact that the ball is not now brought out after a try in the manner in which Crab Jones received it from the toe of Old Brooke is of no moment; fifty changes of such-like minor character have taken place in the fifty years; but the game still remains the same manly, rough-and-ready, give-and-take struggle, in which science, pluck and endurance, unselfishness and good-temper, all have leading parts. I may add that the school waived all their old idiosyncrasies and adopted the Rugby Union laws in October, 1890.

A BIGSIDE AT RUGBY.

SCHOOL-HOUSE v. SCHOOL.

"Hold the punt-about!" "To the goals!" are the cries, and all stray balls are impounded by the authorities; and the whole mass of boys moves up towards the two goals, dividing as they go into three bodies. That little band on the left, consisting of from fifteen to twenty boys, Tom amongst them, who are making for the goal under the Schoolhouse wall, are the School-house boys who are not to play-up, and have to stay in goal. The larger body moving to the Island goal are the School boys in a like predicament. The great mass in the middle are the players-up, both sides mingled together; they are hanging their jackets, and, all who mean real work, their hats, waistcoats, neck-handkerchiefs, and braces, on the railings round the small trees; and there they go by twos and threes up to their respective grounds. There is none of the colour and tastiness of get-up, you will perceive, which lends such a life to the present game at Rugby, making the dullest and worst-fought match a pretty sight. Now each house has its own uniform of cap and jersey, of some lively colour; but at the time we are speaking of plush caps have not yet come in, or uniforms of any sort, except the Schoolhouse white trousers, which are abominably cold to-day. Let us get to work, bare-headed, and girded with our plain leather straps—but we mean business, gentlemen.

And now that the two sides have fairly sundered, and each occupies its own ground, and we get a good look at them, what absurdity is this? You don't mean to say that those fifty or sixty boys in white trousers, many of them quite small, are going to play that huge mass opposite? Indeed I do, gentlemen; they're going to try, at any rate, and won't make such a bad fight of it either, mark my word; for hasn't old Brooke won the toss, with his lucky halfpenny, and got choice of goals and kick-off? The new ball you may see lie there quite by itself, in the middle, pointing towards the School or Island goal; in another minute it will be well on its way there. Use that minute in remarking how the Schoolhouse side is drilled. You will see, in the first place, that the sixth-form boy, who has the charge of goal, has spread his force (the goal-keepers) so as to occupy the whole space behind the goal-posts, at distances of about five yards apart; a safe and well-kept goal is the foundation of all good play. Old Brooke is talking to the captain of quarters; and now he moves away. See how that youngster spreads his men (the light brigade) carefully over the ground, half-way between their own goal and the body of their own players-up (the heavy brigade). These again play in several bodies; there is young Brooke and the bull-dogs—mark them well—they are the "fighting brigade," the "die-hards," larking about at leap-frog to keep themselves warm, and playing tricks on one another. And on each side of old Brooke, who is now standing in the middle of the ground and just going to kick-off, you see a separate wing of players-up, each with a boy of acknowledged prowess to look to—here Warner, and there Hodge; but over all is old Brooke, absolute as he of Russia, but wisely and bravely ruling over willing and worshipping subjects, a true football king. His face is earnest and careful as he glances a last time over his army, but full of pluck and hope, the sort of look I hope to see in my general when I go out to fight. The School side is not organised in the same way. The goal-keepers are all in lumps, anyhow and no-how; you can't distinguish between the players-up and the boys in quarters, and there is divided leadership; but with such odds in strength and weight it must take more than that to hinder them from winning; and so their leaders seem to think, for they let the players-up manage themselves.

But now look, there is a slight move forward of the School-house wings: a shout of "Are you ready?" and loud affirmative reply. Old

Brooke takes half a dozen quick steps, and away goes the ball spinning towards the School goal—seventy yards before it touches ground, and at no point above twelve or fifteen feet high—a model kick-off; and the School-house cheer and rush on: the ball is returned, and they meet it and drive it back amongst the masses of the School already in motion. Then the two sides close, and you can see nothing for minutes but a swaying crowd of boys, at one point violently agitated. That is where the ball is, and there are the keen players to be met, and the glory and the hard knocks to be got; you hear the dull thud, thud of the ball, and the shouts of "Off your side," "Down with him," "Put him over," "Bravo." This is what we call "a scrummage," gentlemen, and the first scrummage in a School-house match was no joke in the consulship of Plancus.

But see! it has broken: the ball is driven out on the School-house side, and a rush of the School carries it past the School-house players-up. "Look out in quarters." Brooke's and twenty other voices ring out; no need to call though; the School-house captain of quarters has caught it on the bound, dodges the foremost School boys, who are heading the rush, and sends it back with a good drop-kick well into the enemy's country. And then follows rush upon rush, and scrummage upon scrummage, the ball now driven through into the School-house quarters, and now into the School goal; for the School-house have not lost the advantage which the kick-off and a slight wind gave them at the outset, and are slightly "penning" their adversaries. You say you don't see much in it all— nothing but a straggling mass of boys, and a leather ball which seems to excite them all to great fury, as a red rag does a bull. My dear sir, a battle would look much the same to you, except that the boys would be men and the balls iron; but a battle would be worth your looking at for all that, and so is a football match. You can't be expected to appreciate the delicate strokes of play, the turns by which a game is lost and won— it takes an old player to do that—but the broad philosophy of football you can understand if you will. Come along with me a little nearer, and let us consider it together.

The ball has just fallen again where the two sides are thickest, and they close rapidly around it in a scrummage: it must be driven through now by force or skill, till it flies out on one side or the other. Look how differently the boys face it! Here come two of the bull-dogs, bursting through the outsiders; in they go, straight to the heart of the scrummage, bent on driving that ball out on the opposite side. That is what they mean to do. My sons, my sons! you are too hot; you have gone past the ball, and must struggle now right through the scrummage, and get round and back again to your own side before you can be of any further use. Here comes young Brooke; he goes in as straight as you, but keeps his head, and backs and bends, holding himself still behind the ball, and driving it furiously when he gets the chance. Take a leaf out of his book, you young chargers.

* * * * * *

Then the boys who are bending and watching on the outside, mark them—they are most useful players, the dodgers, who seize on the ball the moment it rolls out from among the chargers, and away with it across to the opposite goal; they seldom go into the scrummage, but must have more coolness than the chargers: as endless as are boys' characters, so are their ways of facing or not facing a scrummage at football.

Three-quarters of an hour are gone; first winds are failing, and weight and numbers beginning to tell. Yard by yard the School-house have been driven back, contesting every inch of ground. The bull-dogs are the colour of mother earth from shoulder to ankle, except young Brooke, who has a marvellous knack of keeping his legs. The School-house are being penned in their turn, and now the ball is behind their goal, under the Doctor's wall. The Doctor and some of his family are there looking on, and seem as anxious as any boy for the success of the School-house. We get a minute's breathing-time before old Brooke kicks out, and he gives the word to play strongly for touch, by the Three Trees. Away goes the ball, and the bull-dogs after it, and in another minute there is shout of "In touch!" "Our ball!"

Now's your time, old Brooke, while your men are still fresh. He stands with the ball in his hand, while the two sides form in deep lines opposite one another: he must strike it straight out between them. The lines are thickest close to him, but young Brooke and two or three of his men are shifting up further, where the opposite line is weak. Old Brooke strikes it out straight and strong, and it falls opposite his brother. Hurra! that rush has taken it right through the School line, and away past the Three Trees, far into their quarters, and young Brooke and the bull-dogs are close upon it. The School leaders rush back, shouting "Look out in goal," and strain every nerve to catch him, but they are after the fleetest foot in Rugby. There they go straight for the School goal-posts, quarters scattering before them. One after another the bull-dogs go down, but young Brooke holds on. "He is down." No! a long stagger, but the danger is past; that was the shock of Crew, the most dangerous of dodgers. And now he is close to the School goal, the ball not three yards before him. There is a hurried rush of the School fags to the spot, but no one throws himself on the ball, the only chance, and young Brooke has touched it right under the School goal-posts.

The School leaders come up furious, and administer toco to the wretched fags nearest at hand; they may well be angry, for it is all Lombard-street to a china orange that the School-house kick a goal with the ball touched in such a good place. Old Brooke of course will kick it out, but who shall catch and place it? Call Crab Jones. Here he comes, sauntering along with a straw in his mouth, the queerest, coolest fish in Rugby: if he were tumbled into the moon this minute he would just pick himself up without taking his hands out of his pockets or turning a hair. But it is a moment when the boldest charger's heart beats quick. Old Brooke stands with the ball under his arm motioning the School back; he will not kick-out till they are all in goal, behind the posts; they are all edging forwards, inch by inch, to get nearer for the rush at Crab Jones, who stands there in front of old Brooke to catch the ball. If they can reach and destroy him before he catches, the danger is over; and with one and the same rush they will carry it right away to the School-house goal. Fond hope! It is kicked out and caught beautifully. Crab strikes his heel into the ground, to mark the spot where the ball was caught, beyond which the School line may not advance; but there they stand, five deep, ready to rush the moment the ball touches the ground. Take plenty of room! Don't give the rush a chance of reaching you! Place it true and steady! Trust Crab Jones—he has made a small hole with his heel for the ball to lie on, by which he is resting on one knee, with his eye on old Brooke. "Now!" Crab places the ball at the word, old Brooke kicks, and it rises slowly and truly as the School rush forward. Then a moment's pause, while both sides look up at the spinning ball. There it flies, straight between the two posts, some five feet above the cross-bar, an unquestioned goal; and a shout of real genuine joy rings out from the School-house players-up, and a faint echo of it comes over the Close from the goal-keepers under the Doctor's wall. A goal in the first hour—such a thing hasn't been done in the School-house match these five years.

"Over!" is the cry. The two sides change goals, and the School-house goal-keepers come threading their way across through the masses of the School; the most openly triumphant of them, amongst whom is Tom, a School-house boy of two hours' standing, getting their ears boxed in the transit. Tom indeed is excited beyond measure, and it is all the sixth-form boy, kindest and safest of goal-keepers, has been able to do to keep him from rushing out whenever the ball has been near their goal. So he holds him by his side, and instructs him in the science of touching.

* * * * * * *

The ball is placed again midway, and the School are going to kick off. Their leaders have sent their lumber into goal, and rated the rest soundly, and one hundred and twenty picked players-up are there, bent on retrieving the game. They are to keep the ball in front of the School-house goal, and then to drive it in by sheer strength and weight. They mean heavy play, and no mistake, and so old Brooke sees; and places Crab Jones in quarters just before the goal, with four or five picked players, who are to keep the ball away to the sides, where a try at goal, if obtained, will be less dangerous than in front. He himself, and Warner and Hedge, who have saved themselves till now, will lead the charges. "Are you ready?" "Yes." And away comes the ball, kicked high in the air, to give the School time to rush on and catch it as it falls. And here they are amongst us. Meet them like Englishmen, you School-house boys, and charge them home. Now is the time to show what mettle is in you—and there shall be a warm seat by the hall fire, and honour, and lots of bottled beer to-night, for him who does his duty in the next half-hour. And they are well met. Again and again the cloud of their players-up gathers before our goal, and comes threatening on, and Warner or Hedge, with young Brooke and the relics of the bull-dogs, break through and carry the ball back; and old Brooke ranges the field like Job's war-horse: the thickest scrummage parts asunder before his rush, like the waves before a clipper's bows. His cheery voice rings over the field, and his eye is everywhere. And if these miss the ball, and it rolls dangerously in front of our goal, Crab Jones and his men have seized it and sent it away towards the sides with the unerring drop-kick. This is worth living for; the whole sum of school-boy existence gathered up into one straining, struggling half-hour, a half-hour worth a year of common life.

The quarter to five has struck, and the play slackens for a minute before goal; but there is Crew, the artful dodger, driving the ball in behind our goal, on the Island side, where our quarters are weakest. Is there no one to meet him? Yes! look at little East! The ball is just at equal distances between the two, and they rush together, the young man of seventeen and the boy of twelve, and kick it at the same moment. Crew passes on without a stagger; East is hurled forward by the shock, and plunges on his shoulder, as if he would bury himself in the ground; but the ball rises straight into the air, and falls behind Crew's back, while the "bravos" of the School-house attest the pluckiest charge of all that hard-fought day. Warner picks East up lame and half stunned, and he hobbles back into goal, conscious of having played the man.

And now the last minutes are come, and the School gather for their last rush, every boy of the hundred and twenty who has a run left in him. Reckless of the defence of their own goal, on they come across the level Bigside ground, the ball well down amongst them, straight for our goal, like the column of the Old Guard up the slope at Waterloo. All former charges have been child's play to this. Warner and Hedge have met them, but still on they come. The bull-dogs rush in for the last time; they are hurled over or carried back, striving hand, foot, and eyelids. Old Brooke comes sweeping round the skirts of the play, and turning short round picks out the very heart of the scrummage, and plunges in. It wavers for a moment—he has the ball! No, it has passed him, and his voice rings out clear over the advancing tide, "Look out in goal." Crab Jones catches it for a moment, but before he can kick the rush is upon him and passes over him; and he picks himself up behind them with his straw in his mouth, a little dirtier, but as cool as ever.

The ball rolls slowly in behind the School-house goal, not three yards in front of a dozen of the biggest School players-up. There stands the School-house præpostor, safest of goal-keepers, and Tom Brown by his side, who has learned his trade by this time. Now is your time, Tom. The blood of all the Browns is up, and the two rush in together, and throw themselves on the ball, under the very feet of the advancing column; the præpostor on his hands and knees arching his back, and Tom all along on his face. Over them topple the leaders of the rush, shooting over the back of the præpostor, but falling flat on Tom, and knocking all the wind out of his small carcase. "Our ball," says the præpostor, rising with his prize; "but get up there, there's a little fellow under you." They are hauled and roll off him, and Tom is discovered a motionless body. Old Brooke picks him up. "Stand back, give him air," he says; and then, feeling his limbs, adds, "No bones broken. How do you feel, young un?" "Hah-hah," gasps Tom as his wind comes back. "Pretty well, thank you—all right." "Who is he?" says Brooke. "Oh, it's Brown; he's a new boy, I know him," says East, coming up. "Well, he's a plucky youngster, and will make a player," says Brooke. And five o'clock strikes. "No side" is called, and the first day of the School-house match is over.

CHAPTER III.

ETON FOOTBALL.

By Sydney R. James.

(1) THE "WALL" GAME.

EVERYONE knows, or Etonians think everyone ought to know, that there are two games of football played at Eton; but the average non-Etonian is apt to suppose that the "Wall" game holds the higher place in the affections of the school, whereas the fact is that practically every one of the thousand boys plays at the "Field" game several times a week, while the seventy Collegers, and perhaps thirty Oppidans, are all who ever play at the "Wall." But there is no doubt that the peculiar features of this game give it an interest which its enemies might say is not due to its merits, and it shall therefore have the precedence in this sketch.

Books about games invariably begin by giving a history of the origin and development of the games of which they treat, and the intelligent reader as invariably "skips that part." But the "Wall" game, like the game of tennis, owes its origin and development entirely to local circumstances; and in order to understand the main features of the game it is necessary to have some idea of the place in which it is played. A road runs from Windsor to Slough through Eton; when it has cleared the College and School buildings which line it for some way, it is bounded on the left by the palings which enclose the "School Field," known in summer as "Sixpenny" and to the geographer as "the Timbralls"; and on the right by a wall about eight feet high, though higher on the further side, where the "Wall" game is played. The road trends to the left, and there is a corresponding outward bend in the wall, which thus forms to the players a slight salient angle. Let us climb the wall by the iron staples let into it for that purpose on the road side, about half-way along it, and descend on the other side by the ladder which is there whenever no game is going on. We shall first notice a line cut out in the ground, roughly parallel to the wall, about six yards from it, technically called the "furrow." It is in the narrow space between this furrow and the wall that the game is played. Next we shall see, at about eighteen yards from

MIXED WALL ELEVEN, 1890.

either end of the wall, a white perpendicular line painted the whole height of the wall. Either space between these white lines and the ends of the wall is called "calx." As we look towards the wall we next observe that a garden wall runs at right angles to the "Wall" itself at the left-hand end. In this wall, about eighteen yards from the angle, is a door. That door is one of the goals. At the other end there is no corresponding wall. There the goal is a marked part of the trunk of a large elm, rather further off from the wall. It will be perceived, then, that neither goal is within the field of play, a circumstance which gives colour to the well-grounded belief that at one time the game was played on a much larger area than it is to-day, and that the limits were contracted for reasons now unknown. It should be mentioned that the "calx" at the garden end is known as "good," the other as "bad" calx; the reason for this distinction being that the side playing towards good calx have the advantage of the use of the right shoulder in pushing and the right foot in kicking out. Further, it is easier to score in good calx. So much for the field of play. The players are eleven a side, thus classified:— three "walls," two "seconds," three "outsides," known as "third," "fourth," and "line"; and three "behinds"— namely, "flying-man," "long behind," and "goals." The "walls" are protected by "sacks," which are padded "sweaters," and by padded caps, which are so constructed as to protect the head and ears; the "seconds" generally wear similar caps, and the rest of the players are dressed in ordinary football clothes. The ball is of the Eton species, much smaller than an Association ball, but of the same shape, and more stoutly made than the ball used in the "Field" game. It is the only football now in use which is lined with a bladder instead of india-rubber.

Let us suppose that it is St. Andrew's Day, when Collegers yearly meet Oppidans. This contest one might expect to be ridiculous, for the Collegers are but 70 and their opponents 930; but as the 70 Collegers all play the game from the time when they first come to Eton, and hardly any Oppidans ever try it till their last year or two, the odds are not so absurd as they seem. The space for play is kept free from encroachment by a line of posts and ropes, about forty yards from the wall. The partisans of College are gathered near good calx; the larger body who favour the other side are all down the rest of the line; some enthusiasts are seated on the top of the wall with their legs dangling; others are on the garden wall in which the goal is; the space between the furrow and the wall is thickly strewn with sawdust; all is ready for the fray, and it is nearly half-past twelve. The Collegers have won the toss, and in their colours of violet and white they take up their positions facing bad calx; their opponents, in purple and orange, play towards good calx first. Within the ropes stand the two umpires, the referee, and the "twelfth man" of either side. The "bully" is formed thus: the three "walls," usually big heavy fellows, are next the wall itself; they stand *half-*

facing the wall, one behind another. Their object is to hustle the ball along the wall, to turn it out from the wall, or to hold it, according to their captain's orders, so far as they can. Next to them, packed in the bully, but away from the wall, come the "seconds," usually short sturdy players, who are either to keep the ball in at the wall, to help to turn it out, or to kneel upon it and struggle on with it when it comes away from the wall, as policy may dictate. These five players make up the bully. Whenever the ball goes out they have to "form down" as at first, but in a certain rotation, "first wall" becoming "third wall," and so on, and the two sides taking it in turns to form "under" and "over"; the side forming "under" having a certain advantage in leverage.

Clear of the bully comes the "third"; his duty is to be on the ball like lightning as soon as it comes out of the bully, to go straight through the opposite "third," to charge the "flying-man" of the enemy before he can get his kick, to protect his own "flying-man" by stopping the opposing "outsides," and to kick the ball *out*. Be it understood that no "outside" can commit a more deadly sin than to kick the ball *in*, so that it comes "cool" to one of the opponents' behinds. Be it also understood that the ball is put in opposite the place where it stops, or is touched, or crosses the ropes, and not opposite the place where it crosses the furrow, so that much ground is gained by a well-directed kick-out. Occasionally, but rarely, an opportunity occurs for the whole bully, outsides and all, to make a dribbling rush down the wall, keeping the ball in; but this, though a fine piece of play when it comes off, is very seldom attempted because of the extreme risk and difficulty attending the manœuvre. The duties of "fourth" and "line" are of the same kind as those of "third"; but the latter must also run out to touch the ball when kicked out by an opponent. The "behinds" alone remain; their duty is to kick far and to kick out. "Flying-man," who stands just behind the bully, has often to stop an ugly rush of the opposing bully and outsides; he must have the power of kicking in any position and of lifting the ball quickly, and he must be equally good with either foot, for when playing to good calx his right foot usually has the kicking-out to do, and the left when positions are reversed. His is perhaps the most important, as it is the most attractive, place of all. Such are the duties of the various players before the ball gets into either calx. It is very unlikely that any score will be made without its doing so; but now and then a goal is *kicked* direct from some way down the wall, though this has never occurred on St. Andrew's Day. In ordinary cases the game proceeds somewhat as follows:—The bully is formed as previously described, and the ball put in by one of the umpires when the clock strikes the half-hour. It must touch the wall then, and on each occasion when it goes out; it is the policy of the side playing to good calx (in this case the Oppidans) to turn it out and let the outsides have a chance of driving it onwards; this is done two or three times, but not much ground is gained or lost, the outsides being fairly equal; next bully, however, a College outside sends a "cool runner" past the Oppidan "flying-man" to "long behind," who makes a fine kick-out nearly half the length of the wall, and the next bully is formed some eight yards out of good calx. To the spectator the game now becomes dull, for the College "walls" and "seconds" have orders to "hold it," and for a long time the superior weight of the three Oppidans against them fails to overcome their *vis inertiæ*, or to turn them out away from the wall. After about seven minutes the Oppidan "goals" is brought up, and slowly but surely the College bully is forced back and outwards, and at last the ball is freed; but in a moment a College "second" drops with his knees upon it, and, backed up by his colleague and the "walls," maintains a stubborn resistance, and actually gains a yard or two, crawling on his hands and kneeling on the ball. This, however, cannot last for ever; he is turned on one side and off the ball, and it is hustled in to the wall again by the Oppidans, who try to get it into calx that way. They nearly do so, but are stopped a yard outside; the ball once more is held, but only for a minute or two; it comes out to the outsides, and a loud Oppidan cheer proclaims that it has been kicked out well into calx. Now comes the chance for making a score, and now comes the difficulty of writing a description. The object of the attacking side is to gain a "shy"—that is, to get the ball up from the ground on the foot against the wall and to touch it when in that position, facing towards the goal to which they are playing. The ball must be "up," *i.e.* not touching the ground, and it must be in contact with the wall at the moment when it is touched.

The object of the defending side is, first, to prevent the ball being got up; secondly, to get it out of calx. For these purposes the bully is now formed in a different way: the attacking side have a "getter," who is to get his foot under the ball and raise it against the wall as soon as it is put in; a "second," who is to sling his foot in directly the ball comes in, so as to keep it in his own

"A BULLY IN BAD CALX."

side of the bully and impede the other side; a "furker," who turns his back to the bully and puts in his leg along the wall, knee bent, so as to come down and hook the ball along the wall towards his own goal; a "toucher," who is to help the "furker" and touch it when the chance comes; the rest form as directed to help "getter" and "second," or to act "outside" or "behind." The defending side have a "stopper," who is to stand on the ball and prevent it being got up; a "second" and a "furker," whose functions are similar to those on the attacking side; a "kicker-out," who stands in the angle of the wall to kick the ball out when his "furker" gives him the chance: the rest form in the bully and outside as directed. Three lines are roughly drawn at right angles to the wall on the ground, some six inches apart:

it is the duty of the umpire to roll the ball in along the centre line, having previously seen that neither "getter," "stopper," "second," nor "furker" has his foot nearer that line than the six inches indicated by the side lines, and that the "stopper's" knee is not over the middle line. When all are duly arranged, the umpire, having from prudential motives removed his hat, stoops down, and calling "Are you ready?—Coming!" rolls the ball in so as to touch the wall, and extricates himself as best he may. As soon as ever the ball touches the wall the "getter" tries to get it up, the "stopper" tries to stand on it, the "furkers" try to hook it out, each in his own direction, the "seconds" sling in their legs, probably kicking someone in the process, and everybody in the bully pushes with might and main; the "outsides" butt at each other aimlessly enough, as it would appear, and the excitement is intense. It usually happens that skill and experience are on the side of College, and strength on that of the Oppidans; the odds in calx are therefore rather on College. In the match which we are describing, however, the Oppidans possess a "furker" of great power and skill, with an invulnerable left ankle. Gradually he works the ball back, and it emerges on his side of the bully; he has time to whip round, get it up on his foot facing the proper way, and touch it, crying as he does so "Got it." The second umpire, who is looking along the wall, gives his decision—"Fair Shy" —the "outsides" run out, one of them rushing to defend the door goal; the successful "furker" throws the ball from within the furrow at the door, but his shot is not good: it neither reaches the door nor the hands of any of his own side, who might catch and throw it on. One o'clock strikes and ends are changed, with one shy to the credit of the Oppidans. It now is Oppidan policy to hold it, and the Collegers want to turn it out. Here the weight of the Oppidan "walls" comes in, and for a long time the game is very dull from a spectator's point of view, but at last the ball is extricated; the College "flying-man" gets a cool runner with his right foot and lands the ball in calx; the same proceedings take place, but the Oppidan "furker's" right ankle is a weak point, and he cannot manage to get the ball out. In a very short time College get two shies, and the game seems in their hands, but by a piece of carelessness or over-confidence the "getter" allows the ball to slip from him, and somehow it crawls out on the Oppidan side of the bully, and is passed to the "kicker-out," who lands it safely a long way down the wall. Nor is this all. Next bully the Oppidan "outsides" make a grand rush down the wall, run right through the College "behinds," and appear to have a "shy" in bad calx at their mercy, but through ignorance or eagerness they kick the ball too far: it goes behind and is touched by College "goals," who runs up just in the nick of time. Result: a kick-off to College.

ST. ANDREW'S DAY, FROM "BAD CALX."

But here a fatal error is made. Instead of kicking it out the "goals" kicks it in along the wall; the Oppidan "goals" makes a fine return, and the ball is landed in bad calx. The bully is formed as in good calx; the Oppidans at once get a "shy." The next bully the ball is furked out by College, taken behind, and touched. Time is now all but up. The kick-off on this occasion is a fine one; the last bully is formed not far from the middle, and the clock strikes as it comes out, and so the Wall match of 189- is over, with two shies to each side.

"It is impossible to convey any idea of the minutiæ of the game on paper; but the foregoing account may give some notion of the general features of a match at the Wall. It will be seen that the game affords opportunities

to the strong as well as to the skilful, to the small as
well as to the big. "Outsides" and "behinds" do not
get much exercise (except at times "third" and "flying-
man"), but "walls" and "seconds" have plenty. A
loose bully is a lively sight, when the ball comes away
from the wall, and everyone is kicking at it at once; but
little damage is usually done to shins; the worst injuries
inflicted are as a rule either strains or scrapes, and the
writer does not call to mind any case of serious or permanent harm done. In a word, it is a fine game, and full
of interest, though the peculiar circumstances in which
it is played make it impossible, even if it were desirable,
to establish it elsewhere. The weak points are: 1. That,
owing to the great advantage possessed by the side
attacking good calx, it is nearly always to the interest
of the other side to hold the ball, and it is easier to hold
it than to force it away from the holders; consequently
the play in the great match of the year is usually very
dull for spectators. 2. The existence of the goals, such
as they are, introduces an element of chance into the
game which might easily make the weaker side win, for
one goal outweighs any number of shies.

It may possibly be of interest to place on record the
fact that of the 47 matches played since 1845, the
Collegers have won 15 times, the Oppidans 16 times,
and the match has been left drawn on no fewer than
16 occasions.

No goal has been *kicked*; one was "bossed," *i.e.*
thrown, by W. Marcon for College in the early "forties,"
and one by H. Jete; by H. J. Mordaunt for College
in 1885; in 1858 H. Hollingworth is believed to have
done the same, but the claim was not allowed.

(2) The "Field" Game.

If the "Wall" game can never become popular away
from Eton, for reasons stated in the previous article, the
"Field" game is not likely to be practised elsewhere
(save at Oxford and Cambridge) because of the complete
hold now obtained by the Rugby Union and Association
games throughout the country. Were it not so, the
present writer, who has had a practical acquaintance
with both of these games for over twenty years, is
of opinion that the Eton "Field" game is on the whole

the best game of football yet invented. This assertion may be difficult to justify, and the following sketchy account of the game will probably convince as little as most special pleading does, but the attempt must be made.

The game may be played in any field of reasonable size. It happens that the "School field" at Eton is of large dimensions as compared with most Rugby Union or Association grounds, being no less than 150 yards long and 100 yards broad: but it is an open question whether grounds of a smaller size do not conduce to closer dribbling and better play. The goals are both low and narrow, being only seven feet high and eleven feet broad, with a cross-bar, under which the ball must pass. Consequently there is no need of a regular goal-keeper, though the third behind is called "goals." The ball is round, made like an Association ball, but very much smaller and lighter. The proper number of players is eleven a-side, but this number in ordinary games is often largely increased without spoiling the fun. There are eight forwards and only three behinds. The forwards are thus divided:—Four form the "bully"; "post" in the centre, "back-up post" to support him, and a "side-post" on either side. Behind the "bully" is "flying-man," usually the best player on his side, most important both in attack and in defence; level with the bully, though not in it, are three "corners," one on one side, two on the other. The bully is formed at the beginning of the game, at half-time, and, whenever the ball goes out at the side, opposite the place where it crossed the side-line and half-way to the middle of the ground; in certain cases a "bully" is the penalty for the infringement of a rule. The "behinds" are known as "short-behind," "long-behind," and "goals." They stand one behind the other, near enough to support each other easily. The great principle of the game is to keep the forwards together, backing-up, and on the ball. Consequently no player is allowed to touch the ball or to charge the behinds, or in any way to assist his own side or obstruct his adversaries, if he is either "sneaking" or "cornering." He is "sneaking" if he is behind the main body of his adversaries, and the ball is kicked to him or in front of him from behind him; he is "cornering" when he is away from the ball, and at the side of and apart from the rest of the players. The penalty for sneaking is a free kick; for cornering, a "bully." "Sneaking," it will be seen, roughly corresponds to "off-side" under Rugby Union rules, but with this exception, that the whole body of the forwards are not put out of action by the fact that the ball is kicked to them by one of their own behinds, but may charge under his kick. "Cornering" is forbidden because, if it were allowed, the forwards would soon become scattered over the field, passing sideways to each other as in the Association game, and the three behinds would be quite unable to do their work. No player is allowed to handle the ball wilfully; the penalty is a "bully."

Such are the main provisions of the rules for the general conduct of the game; they are fairly simple in practice, but there are occasions when the umpire has a difficulty in deciding questions of "sneaking" and "cornering." The really fine points occur when we come to the scoring.

We will suppose that it is the great day of the "Field" game—the final tie for the House Cup—an event which has furnished more matter for conversation than any other of the whole Football Half. It is a fine sunny morning; the field, in spite of a damp autumn, is in good condition: there is a thick line of spectators down either side-line, except some thirty yards at each end. Nearly all of the thousand boys are present; the "swells" with their "Pop" canes to keep the line; members of the School "Field" Eleven with their caps of scarlet and light-blue in quarters; members of the "mixed" (or School) Wall Eleven, with their caps of darker red and blue in hoops; boys who have their "house-colours" of every hue and pattern; boys who as yet boast no such athletic distinction and can only don the "scug-cap" of dull-blue or violet and black; old Etonians in large numbers, most of the masters, not a few ladies—even a reporter or two. Most of the two elevens are keeping themselves warm by kicking-about while they await the arrival of the one or two who always make a point of turning up late. Such is the scene; but now the laggards have come; the umpires take up their positions at either end; the two elevens hang up coats and scarves, and take up their positions

D

in the field; one eleven wear scarlet shirts, the other black and green. The bully is formed, the ball is put in by one of the "corners," and the game begins. The two bullies seem equally matched, and neither "post" can force his way through with the ball, so eventually it comes out at the side, and is pounced upon by one of the red corners—well backed-up by the rest of the forwards. He makes some ground, but is stopped by long-behind, and the ball goes out. Another bully is formed, but this time the ball goes out on the other side of the bully, and a black and green corner is off with it. He is one who trusts to his pace, and goes diagonally across the field; but kicking the ball too far in front of him he loses it to the red short behind, whose kick is too violent to be of real service to his side, for it goes "cool" to the "goals" of the other party; he returns it high and hard, so that his forwards charge under it and carry it on in an irresistible rush to the reds' goal-line, backing each other up well. They reach the line near the corner, and now comes in the peculiar feature of the game. Instead of running it along quickly and taking a shot at goal, they form a sort of phalanx and dribble it very slowly and cautiously along the line. Should the reds charge them and the ball go behind from the charge and be touched by one of the attacking side, a "rouge" will be scored. Now three rouges make a goal, and moreover a rouge may perhaps be turned into a goal, so that it resembles in some measure a "try" in the Rugby game. Well, they work slowly and cautiously along, till they are near the reds' goal, when a charge of the reds sweeps the ball away and the danger is averted. A second time it is brought down to the line; this time it goes behind and a rouge is claimed, but not allowed— one of the defenders has touched it first. The ball is kicked off, and carried past the centre; but yet a third time the reds' behinds fail them, and down come the black and green forwards; but as they take the ball along within a yard of the line it is allowed to stop, and a kick-off is given.

At last, however, a rash charge of the red "flying-man," unsupported, some thirty yards from the line, gives an unmistakable opportunity, for the ball goes diagonally out and behind from the charge, and the swiftest runner in Eton is after it and touches it before

the red "goals" can get there—an indubitable rouge.
Loud cheers greet the score, and a general rush is made
by the spectators towards the goal to see the rouge
played out. The ball is placed a yard from the line in
front of the centre of the goal ; the defending side "form
down" so as to prevent its being forced through. Some
of the attacking side "form down" at either side of the
bully, leaving a lane clear between them, and three or
four of the same party run into this gap, one behind the
other, to try and drive the ball through the opposing
phalanx. The black and green are the lighter side ;
they do not succeed in forcing it past their opponents,
and slowly but surely the bully is worked away from
the goal. At last the ball gets free and the reds rush
it away some two-thirds of the length of the field, when
it goes out, and "change" is called. It should be stated
that the game lasts an hour. The reds have now the
advantage of the wind, and begin to force the game.
Their policy when they get near the line is different
from that of their opponents, and they try to score by
taking the ball rapidly along and either kicking it
against an opponent, so that it may bound behind off
him and be touched, thus obtaining a rouge, or, if they
can, taking a shot at goal. Three or four attempts are
thus made, without success, and twice appeals for
"sneaking" are given against the reds, so that the game
is carried back past the middle from the kick-off. But
they are not to be denied, and charging under a fine
volley of their long-behind, one of the forwards succeeds
in baffling the opposing "goals" and shoots the ball
cleverly between the posts, amid deafening cheers. Nor
is this all ; a stronger puff of wind than usual happens
to arise just as the black and green "goals," already
nervous from his recent failure, gets a critical kick, and
the ball is caught by the wind and carried right off to the
left and behind the goal-line, where one of the reds gets up
and touches it almost before the other side have realised
what is happening. A rouge is a matter of course ; and
the jubilant reds proceed to their easy task of forcing it
through goal. This they do, and victory is well within
their grasp, for even if their rivals get a goal they will
still be two points ahead, and there are only ten
minutes left for play. No such catastrophe occurs,
however, and the custody of the House Cup passes

into the hands of the wearers of the red for the next year.

In the above account most of the ways in which a rouge may be obtained are described. They are defined at length in the rules of the game, but it is probably easier to comprehend them from a description than from a mere statement of the rule.

The finest points in the game are undoubtedly— (1) The behind play. With the small Eton ball the most extraordinary volleys and half-volleys may be made, and as a consequence of the rule against "cornering" a behind has not to cover the whole field at once. (2) The backing-up together of the whole of the forwards. It is a treat to see a well-balanced pack of players charging down the field together, backing each other up, yet not getting in each other's way. Again, the Eton ball is beautifully adapted for dribbling, and probably there is a far greater proportion of clever dribblers at Eton than at schools which employ the larger ball.

On the other hand, the slow play which is ordinarily seen along the line is a blot upon the game, and more shooting at goal would be a great improvement. If the goal were enlarged there would probably soon be a goal-keeper allowed to use his hands, which would be a pity; but without enlarging the goal it seems likely that the present plan will continue, to the detriment of enterprising play.

An advantage may fairly be claimed for the Eton game in the fact that it may well be played by more than eleven a-side. It is therefore peculiarly well adapted for House games, where three or four houses combine forces, and there may be three games going on with perhaps fifteen or sixteen a-side, well-assorted players, whereas the Association game is utterly spoilt if more than eleven a-side take part in it.

In conclusion, the writer's experience leads him to place the Eton game first *as a game for boys*, though only a little way above the Rugby Union form of football; both, in his opinion, *as games for boys*, are far superior to the Association game. But this is not the place for an elaborate discussion, and he will be satisfied if attention is called to the prominent features of an undoubtedly noble form of the national pastime.

CHAPTER IV.

THE HARROW GAME.

By an Old Harrovian.

THE origin of the Harrow game has not been recorded by any historian. All that need be said here is that the game is probably coeval with the school, and that it belongs to neither of the great football families, Rugby or Association. It is distinguished from the former by the fact that the ball, as a rule, may not be handled, that no player may be held, and that tries, drops, and place-kicks are unknown; and from the latter by possessing an absolute off-side rule, and the right, under certain circumstances, to catch the ball, if kicked from below the knee, before it has touched the ground and then claim a free kick. The Harrow game is, except in two respects, the simplest possible form of a game the object of which is to kick a ball between two posts. Its first peculiarity is that the ball is not round as in the Association, or oval as in the Rugby game, but more like a church hassock than anything else, flattened at the sides, and irregularly circular elsewhere. Whatever may have been the original reason for choosing such a shape, it is certain that the heavy uneven ball is admirably suited to the absolute sloughs in which, even in these days of improved drainage, the game has sometimes to be played. The other peculiarity is the right to catch the ball, as above-mentioned, if the player so catching it is not offside.

The best way to give a general idea of the game will be to record the experiences of a Harrow boy in his first house game, and his first house match. After dinner on a whole school day, he will at once change into football attire, consisting of his house cap and shirt, white duck knickerbockers (it used to be trousers for all not in the House Eleven), and long stockings. When the ground is reached the poles are erected as nearly as possible 150 yards apart, each base being 18 feet wide; a small trench cut each year marks the limits within which the ball is in play, the width of the ground not being allowed to exceed 100 yards. Then the players divide, the ball is kicked off by a punt from the middle of the ground, and the game begins. The main rules are quite simple: the ball may be kicked, headed, or breasted, but not touched with hand or arm, unless these are close to the side. A base can be obtained by sending the ball anywhere between the poles, which have no cross-bar, but extend in theory *usque ad cælum*. If the ball touches the pole and then goes through it counts a base, but not so if it passes over the pole. It is the duty of every forward to be behind the ball, never in front of it, as in that case he is technically " behind," or off-side, as it is now called. Good play consists in keeping the ball close to the feet, and dribbling it through the enemy, long kicks being left to the backs. We will suppose our new boy following after the ball which is being taken along by one of his own side, when suddenly a hostile back swoops down upon it and kicks it far away. Our hero turns to pursue, but in a moment his own back returns it, and it falls near his feet. Knowing the off-side rule, he stands waiting for one of his opponents to touch the ball, not perceiving that this has happened already, a rash player having vainly tried to catch it and so put the enemy between him and his goal on-side. " All on!" is the cry, and the ball is rushed into a corner of the field. " Give yards!" shouts the captain from behind, where he is playing back; " Here, yards!" shriek the players on the outside of the scrummage. Suddenly the player in possession of the ball turns round and lifts it daintily with his foot into the hands or arms of one of his own side, who is at the moment further from the enemy's base. " Yards!" shouts the catcher (it used to be " three yards "), and the play ceases for a moment. If " yards " were not called the ball might be dashed out of the player's hands and the fray would begin again. As it is the catcher may run unhindered for three yards in any direction and then either punt the ball, or drop it and dribble. If the catch was given near the base, the game is to punt; if far off to dribble, except in the case of a back whose duty, as a rule, is to kick from a catch. In the present case, however, the catch has been given in a corner, almost on the back line, whence it is impossible to kick a base. The catcher's duty is clear: he should at once kick the ball in front of the enemy's base, where anyone on his side, who was not off-side at the time of the kick, may catch it in turn and so have a clear shot. It is a good test of an unselfish player to see whether he will "middle" or try an impossible kick. If a player sends the ball out to the side it is thrown in again by one of his opponents in any direction, but not less than six yards. According to Mr. Thornton, the historian of Harrow, this is a return to the earlier practice, but in the writer's time the ball, if sent "straight in," as it is still called, was always kicked back, as the words imply, down a lane formed by the players, and might not be touched until it had reached the ground. If driven behind by an enemy it was kicked out by the back, and this is so still: if by a friend, it was kicked out gently by one of the other side, where now it is thrown straight out to any distance, but neither kick nor throw may be caught.

All these rules the new boy learns in time. His first day's play leaves him probably with three distinct ideas. One, that it is his duty to charge and be charged, however unequal the weight; secondly, that if he has the ball near the enemy's base he must "give yards;" and thirdly and chiefly that he must always "follow up." The history of these words bears striking testimony to the power of poetry. Some twenty odd years ago they were the shout of the driver to the slave; then Mr. E. E. Bowen, *quem honoris causa nominamus*, made them part of the chorus of the familiar "Forty Years On," and to-day they are a rallying cry wherever Harrovians meet.

Let us suppose now that our new boy is no longer "new," but in his third year, and a "choice" for his House Eleven. On the day of the match the players will move down the hill in a body. First the "fezzes," so called from the tasseled caps worn by actual members of the eleven, then the "choices," and then the rest of the house armed with lemons for the refreshment of their champions. On the ground the captains toss for ends, an important matter as there is a decided slope from the Harrow end of the school ground, and this, if assisted by a strong wind, often decides the fate of a match. The rule is to change ends after every base, or, if none has been obtained, at half-time. At 2.30 p.m. precisely the captain who has lost the toss kicks off from the middle of the ground, and the match begins.

The reader will perhaps have noticed that nothing has been said as to the number of players engaged in the Harrow game. As a matter of fact the number is indefinite, as it can be played with a hundred a-side or, as actually is done in a special competition, with only one! In matches, however, the players are always eleven a-side, and arranged nowadays as follows:—There are two backs, who divide the field between them longitudinally, each being responsible for his own side; two players on either wing, known as "top-side" and "bottom-side," and five others who play in the centre. In earlier days there was one half-back and one goal-keeper, but this is not so now. Consequently, if a player can get past the backs he has a clear opening to run a base. Personally the writer is inclined to think that this has led at once to larger scores and the giving of fewer catches. Many a kick which a goal-keeper could save has now a chance of rolling through, and the consciousness of this fact is apt to lead to playing for one's own hand, or more accurately, shooting for one's own foot, instead of giving "yards." Now to return to our match. The ball once started is being rushed from one end of the ground to the other by a series of "runs-up," but each time only to be returned by the watchful backs. Every now and again it goes "straight in," and as it is hurled out again towards the enemy's base, a devoted champion will occasionally head it, Association-wise, at the imminent risk, *experto crede*, of dislocating his neck. Then, again, the ball will lie exactly between two players, and a charge becomes inevitable. No handling, as before said, or tripping, is allowed, but charging with the shoulder is fair, in whatever direction the enemy may be going. Consequently, in a house match, with the blood at fever heat, it is not to be wondered at if charges are fierce and frequent. At least they were so in the old unregenerate days, when every boy in either

house, not actually playing, was standing by and cheering
in a state of wild excitement hard to explain to those
who have not experienced it. "Played, well played!"
shouted one house, as a quick runner took the ball
down the side, closely followed by the other forwards.
"Pick him up!" yelled the other savagely, as their back,
distrusting his power to stop the ball, hurled himself
upon the dribbler, and sent him crashing to the ground.
Thus it was when Plancus was consul; but, to quote
from a letter just received, "*Pick him up* and other
ancient cries are rare indeed now. So cultured are we!
Personal chaff is considered beneath the dignity of a
Harrow boy. Contrast this with your recollection of the
match between Butler's and Middlemist's in"—never
mind the year. Well, well, let us hope that it is a more
faithful study of the ingenious arts that, as Colonel
Newcome would say, *emollunt* the manners of the
present generation. Sooner or later, however, one side
will work the ball down into a corner, and then begins
the familiar "Yards! Give yards! Here!" till the shrill
cry proclaims that a catch has been held. The forwards
hurry in front of the base, for the ball will be middled,
and as it comes dropping down, they shoulder and
thrust one another away, and leap with uplifted arms to
make or prevent a catch. Well then for the tall player
whose hands can reach above the crowd and hold the
ball fast, no easy task at any time, and doubly hard
when, as is so often the case, the ball is slippery with
mud. It used to be, and perhaps is still, customary in
matches to wear rough white gloves to give a surer
grip. If a catch is obtained quite close to the base,
the player, after marking the spot, may retire for a run,
and try to carry the ball through the poles with a hop,
step, and jump. If he fails, he may return to the mark
and try a kick, when the other side may come as far as
the spot to which he jumped, but no nearer. If when
the ball is middled no one succeeds in holding it, a
desperate scrummage ensues in front of base, the assail-
ants trying for another catch, the defenders seeking to
work the ball away down the side; and so the fight
rages for "a long hour by Harrow clock," until the
sound of the school bell ends the fray. If a house match
results in a tie, it is played again with the distance
between the poles doubled; if, on the other hand, one

side scores five bases to none, the match is over at once.

The above description applies to the game as it has been played for many years past, but there are signs of approaching changes to be perceived. In 1883 there was some considerable correspondence in *Harrow Notes* on the advisability of altering the ball and the rules so as to bring Harrow football into closer conformity with the Association game. On that occasion the conservatives appear to have triumphed, and the proposed changes were not adopted. The question has, however, been raised again in *The Harrovian* (December 19th, 1891), where it is stated that there is a growing tendency to rely more upon passing and heading than on following up *en masse*. Those who deplore this suggest that heading should be discouraged, and that some steps should be taken to enforce the strict off-side rule. Their opponents would, as before, modify the rule and alter the shape of the ball.

As at present played, the Harrow game teaches chiefly how to dribble and how to charge, and its main requirement is that a player shall always be on the ball. The weight of this last makes it easier to keep it close to the feet, and though the irregular shape is at first very puzzling, a good player soon acquires a wonderful command over the ball, and takes it along with a speed and certainty that are marvellous to behold. The skill thus gained may be nearly as useful afterwards to the Rugby as to the Association player. In the latter game it can rarely be right to dribble for any distance instead of passing, whereas in the former, a running and tackling team may be considerably disconcerted by judicious play with the feet. In an England *v.* Ireland match some years ago, the defeat of the latter was largely due to the adoption by the former of these tactics in the middle of a hard-fought game. The off-side rule, and the consequent necessity of being behind the ball, calls for great endurance and long wind, and discourages lying-in-wait near the enemy's base, on the chance of getting a pass. There is no absolute rule against doing this, and, as has already been explained, a chance touch may put such a player on-side; but as a matter of fact, it is not the way in which the Harrow game is played, and any attempt in that direction would be promptly suppressed by the offender's captain with a sharp order to get behind the ball. On the whole, it may be claimed that such a game gives the best moral and physical training. If it be argued that Association passing promotes unselfishness, the answer is that it promotes selfishness still more on the part of the player who keeps forward, and that the surrender of personal interests is amply inculcated by the duty of giving catches and middling.

Finally, it may be asked, How long can a player hope to keep up the Harrow game? At Association, owing to the possibility of passing, a fair share of work can be done long after school has been left; but this is hardly so in the Harrow game, and on the whole it must be admitted that this last is not well adapted to the needs of the veteran. Brilliant instances might be cited of players deserving the praise of Cleopatra, of whom it is true that—

> "Age cannot wither *them*, nor custom stale
> *Their* infinite *agility*."

The name, for instance, of Mr. Bowen, will suggest itself to every Harrovian. But, as a rule, it is not possible to remain in the first rank for many years. Those who have left the school lose the old command over the ball, and the necessity of following up tells heavily on men who are

> "growing older and older,
> Shorter in wind as in memory long."

All the same, we hold that the present game is the best for the school, which is, after all, the chief thing; and if we ourselves can no longer follow up as of old, we can yet wish that younger generations should do so in our place, and learn the same lessons of daring, endurance, and unselfishness, as their predecessors did, when they formerly "drank delight of battle with their peers" on the fields beneath Harrow Hill.

CHAPTER V.

THE WINCHESTER GAME.

By an Old Wykehamist.

WINCHESTER football, like so many other details which belong to the ancient foundation of William of Wykeham, is a form of football peculiar to Winchester. Its origin is veiled in the mists of obscurity, and although some enthusiastic Wykehamists have been known to play it at the university, it has never obtained a foothold in any other place.

The first feature which strikes any visitor to either "Meads" or "New Field" is the curious method by which the football grounds are marked out, and which more resembles the wall of an aviary or a wild beast show than the boundary of a football arena. Two parallel walls of network, tarred for its better preservation and hung upon a framework formed of gas-piping screwed together, extend for 80 yards at a distance of 25 yards from one another. These walls are about 10 feet high, and possess meshes just so small as to prevent the passage of a full-sized football; but being by nature too weak to resist the rush of an impetuous player, a further barrier is erected inside them. About a yard from "canvas," as the network wall is technically called, is a line of stakes connected by a stout rope. These posts, eleven in number, are equidistant and form convenient landmarks during the game, while the rope is sufficiently stout to keep the players from pressing against "canvas." To complete the ground, the boundary at either end is indicated by a furrow cut in the ground, to which in Winchester parlance the name of "Worms" is given. Goals are scored whenever the ball crosses this line at any height fairly between and not over the terminal posts and untouched by the defending side, subject of course to the other rules of the game, which make this a feat far less easy to accomplish than might at first sight appear.

The present method of enclosing the ground is of comparatively recent adoption, and took the place of hurdles, while in earlier times the posts and ropes were considered sufficient to mark the limit of play, and a row of juniors outside the ropes formed the wall from which the ball rebounded into play. From this custom came the application of the term "kicking in," which denotes the duty of a number of small boys who stand beyond the canvas walls to throw the ball back into play when it has been kicked out, not that they ever dared to kick it, as such a proceeding would have ensured instant castigation.

"SIX-AND-SIX."

The number of players on either side varies between twenty-two and six, and gradually diminishes towards the end of November, when preparation is being made for the Six-and-six matches, of which more hereafter. The rules are somewhat puzzling to the uninitiated, but a summary of the leading points may not prove uninteresting to the student of comparative football.

The game invariably commences with a "hot." This somewhat resembles a Rugby Union packed scrummage, but is conducted upon strictly scientific principles, and the players take their places in a prearranged order. At a given signal they lower their heads and endeavour to butt through the phalanx of their opponents. In games where a large number take part this is a matter of considerable time and difficulty, a hot frequently lasting as much as ten minutes. A hot takes place not only at the commencement of the game, but on every occasion when the ball goes out of canvas anywhere except across the goal line; and it also follows any infringement of the rules.

The off-side rule is here extremely stringent, and divided into two parts, each with a separate name.

A "HOT."

Passing is illegal, and is called "tagging," and to pass on is probably the greatest offence against the rules. Lurking off-side is dealt with in another way. Theoretically, every player is supposed to be on the ball, following it as accurately as in Rugby Union, and when in advance of it is not permitted in any way to incommode an opposing player. In this he is said to be "behind his side."

The walls within which this game is confined must appear inadequate to keep in the ball, and it must seem ridiculously easy to kick a ball over a line 23 yards wide until the next rule is considered. By this it is illegal to kick a ball more than 5 feet high unless it comes to the player as a "flier"—*i.e.*, is bounding or rolling rapidly towards him; and if it touched one of his own side last, not even in this case, it being then what is termed a "made flier." Dribbling is strictly prohibited, the instructions being that the ball shall be kicked as hard as possible.

Owing to the variation in numbers, the game presents two entirely different aspects, and this will be best seen by an explanation of the school matches. In the early days of Winchester, up to 1868, the majority of the boys not on the foundation resided in Commoners, a few living in Tutors' houses outside. The school, originally divided into College and Commoners, was then divided into College, Commoners, and Houses, the name Commoners being applied to those boys who resided in the four new houses provided for their accommodation when Commoners ceased to exist. In the earlier days two matches only were played, one on the 5th of November called "Twenty-two," and the other "Six-and-six" in the first week of December. Later on, the twenty-two was reduced to fifteen a-side, and in consequence of the sub-division of Commoners six matches a year became necessary. The Fifteens were played on Tuesday, Thursday, and Saturday nearest to November 5th, and the Sixes were played in the corresponding week in December. College wore blue and white hoops, Commoners red and white, and Houses, who at first tried a sickly arrangement in green, wore blue and red.

The games were played from 12.15 to 1.15, lasting exactly an hour, half time each way, time being kept and all disputes decided by the two umpires, usually two of the masters, stationed at diagonally opposite corners of the ground. The ball, which is round and a trifle smaller than the present Association ball, was formerly made heavier and harder by treatment of the leather, but this custom is now fallen into disuse. During the whole hour the network walls were lined with the enthusiastic partisans of the players, who, except for the brief interval of "time to change," kept up a continuous yell of the name of their side.

Fifteens were apt to be a trifle slow and dull; hots lasted a very long time with ten ups in the hot, and very little opportunity was afforded to the two hot-watchers, who, like Rugby half-backs, stood ready to pounce on the ball when once clear of the hot. In addition to the necessary hot at the commencement of each half-hour, there was certain to be a large amount of under-ropes play when the ball escaped into the space between the ropes and stakes and the network. Here weight told; and if a maul in ropes was close down to a goal line, it was obviously to the interest of the defending party to prevent the ball from emerging towards their goal. Similarly, in a closely contested game,

"SIX-AND-SIX."

the side who happened to have got a goal in front were at times tempted to kick out—thereby causing a hot, or to prolong unnecessarily mauls in ropes. From this account it may be readily understood that goals in a Fifteen match were not numerous, and averaged about two to three. Practice for Fifteens consists in playing daily practices of about fifteen a side, varied at the last by playing the first six against the next sixteen. In addition to the fifteen chosen to play, five or six names were added as reserves, or "dress," and in the event of a player becoming disabled during the course of the match, one of the "dress" men was permitted to take his place—a custom which is peculiar to this form of football.

After Fifteens, every energy was devoted to the preparation for Sixes. Practice-sides of not more than six, or at most eight a-side, are the rule; the trial contest being the first six against the next nine. The possession of a place on Six roll is the one coveted position in Winchester football, and carries with it the right to wear a cap, and also the privilege of arraying one's limbs in knickerbockers instead of trousers. *A propos* of costume, it is odd, in the present modern fashion of almost universal wearing of leg-guards by Association players, to recall an effort made to introduce such things at Winchester, when a powerful, but decidedly rough, college "behind" appeared in canvas, in leathern gaiters, and was greeted with a roar of derision and hisses which lasted a considerable period, and gifted with the *sobriquet* of "Gaiters," which stuck to him for the remainder of his school life.

It is, naturally, in Sixes that the crowning pitch of football excellence is reached. In Fifteens, mere weight and brute strength not unfrequently were successful against the greater skill and equal pluck of lighter teams; but in a contest confined to four "ups" and two "behinds," speed and dash, combined with skill, were the essential qualities to victory. As a well-known Wykehamist has remarked, "If anyone wishes to learn how powerful, active, and enduring the human frame may be in the prime of its youthful vigour, he should look on at a game of Six-and-six."

In reviewing the essential features of the game, it cannot be denied that the prohibition of dribbling and passing resulted, rather more than a critic of Association football would approve, in an exhibition of kick-and-run football. However that may be, it has produced a race of forwards well worthy to maintain the reputation of Winchester in the Association football field. With the later development of Association, however, fewer Winchester names are associated, and those more in the back division or as goal-keepers. Unlike most Association backs, the Winchester behind is bound to kick in one direction. It is absolutely essential that (if the expression be permitted) he should be ambidextrous on his feet and should kick equally straight with both of them. He must also possess a power, which many backs of to-day would find useful when playing against the wind, of keeping the ball low as well as straight. It has already been remarked that no drop-kicking is permitted; but punting is an essential qualification. This becomes necessary either after a goal when the ball is punted out from the first post, or after a catch, when it is permitted to the ups to charge down the ball if possible, or at least to touch it, thereby saving a goal.

The work of Six-and-six is extremely heavy, and needs a perfect condition of wind and stamina. The comparatively small size of the ground is quite made up by the exacting nature of the off-side rule and the lack of passing; and it was calculated that in addition to the labour of the game the actual distance travelled by an up during the hour's game was more than eight miles. Among those who hoped to be included in the roll for either Fifteen or Six, training of a more or less strict character was observed: and there can be little doubt that the character of the work required in Fifteens was an admirable preparation for the different work required in Sixes.

Wykehamists have seldom been conspicuous in the carrying game, and the rare exception has been when the boy's home was a centre of Rugby Union football, such as Blackheath or Richmond, or one of the great provincial football centres. At the same time there is nothing to prevent a good Wykehamist at football from being a useful adjunct to any carrying team, more especially if he possesses a fair weight.

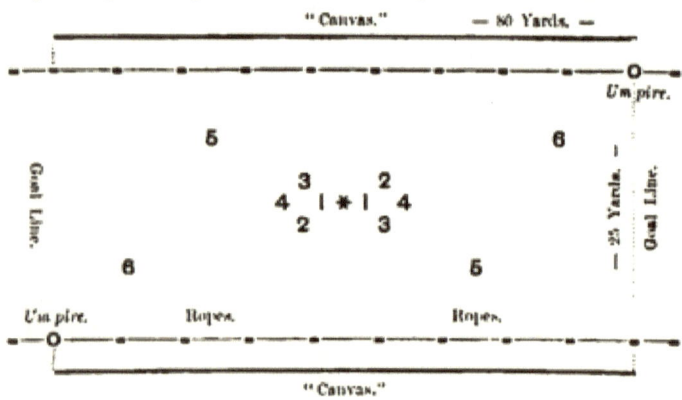

CANVAS AS ARRANGED TO COMMENCE SIX-AND-SIX.

CHAPTER VI.

RUGBY FOOTBALL IN SCOTTISH SCHOOLS

By H. H. Almond, M.A., LL.D., Headmaster of Loretto School.

SCOTCH public school cricket could hardly claim a chapter in a book on cricket. Even for the size of the schools it is seldom good except in respect of fielding, which is usually excellent. But Scotch school football is a very different thing. The only two schools which send up a fair proportion of their sixth form to the universities have within the last twelve years obtained between them thirty-five football "blues,"* whilst the two English schools which have been most successful in this respect have only obtained twenty-nine. And yet these two Scotch schools between them number only about 330.† Rugby football has, in fact, fitted in with the national genius, though it was utterly unknown in Scotland forty years ago. Not that there was no football. At school we used to play a game which we enjoyed very much; two walls, the whole breadth of them, were the "hails." It was said that the ball had once been kicked right across. Two good drop-kicks might have amused themselves by clearing both walls from the outside. At Glasgow College we had wider scope. The "hails" were about 400 yards apart. It was not a bad game we had there: the great beauty of it was that there were no rules.

So far as I know, Rugby football was introduced into Scotland in 1855 by a small knot of men connected with the Edinburgh Academy. Mr. Alexander Crombie, of Thornton Castle, may fairly be said to be the father

* Loretto 20, and Fettes 15.
† Fettes being nearly double Loretto in number.

of the game in Scotland, for he was the chairman and organiser of the club. The hon. secretary was Mr. William Blackwood, the well-known publisher. Neither of them had had any knowledge of the game as boys.

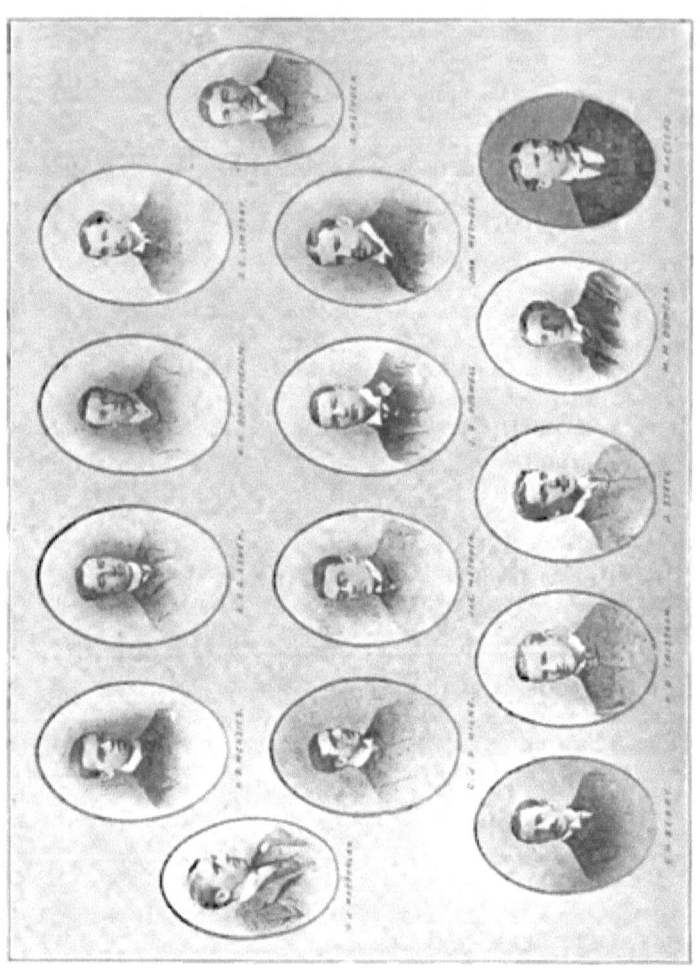

FETTES-LORETTO FIFTEEN.

Very slowly the game spread. There was a kind of mongrel "Rugby" at Merchiston in 1858. Some of the rules were very funny. "Off-side" was voted "rot;" but if a player lay on the ground with the ball, no one might touch him till he chose to move. A closer conformity to the game was, however, enforced by an approaching match with the Edinburgh Academy; but so little did any of us, masters or boys, then know about it, that I remember how, when Lyall ran with the ball behind the Merchiston goal, the resulting try was appealed against on the ground that no player might cross the line whilst holding the ball. The previous rule at Merchiston had been that he must let go of the ball and kick it over before he touched down. It must be said in excuse for this and other similar sins of ignorance, that the only available rules were those printed for the use of Rugby School. They were very incomplete, and presupposed a practical knowledge of the game.

Gradually, however, the game approached, with local variations and resulting disputes, to that then played at Rugby. Clubs were formed in the West of Scotland, at the Scotch universities, and at various schools, but for a long time, in fact until well on in the "'seventies," the only schools able to play each other on even terms were the Edinburgh Academy and Merchiston, and occasionally the Royal High School.

So far as I am aware, the first attempt anywhere made at concerted action was the meeting of a committee of three schools in Edinburgh to codify the rules. The "Green Book," which was the result of our deliberations, was assented to by the other then existing Scotch clubs. A committee on a somewhat similar basis challenged England in 1870, and, to our utter astonishment, the first national match was won by Scotland at Raeburn Place in 1870. And here let me make a personal confession. I was umpire, and I do not know to this day whether the decision which gave Scotland the try from which the winning goal was kicked was correct in fact. The ball had certainly been scrummaged over the line by Scotland, and touched down first by a Scotchman. The try was, however, vociferously disputed by the English team, but upon what ground I was then unable to discover. Had the good rule of the "Green Book" been kept, viz., that no one except the captains should speak in any dispute unless appealed to, I should have understood that the point raised was that the ball had never been fairly grounded in the scrummage, but had got mixed up among Scottish feet or legs. This I only learned afterwards, and my fellow umpire was at a distance from the scene of action. Indeed, when the game was played twenty a-side, the ball, at the beginning of a scrummage, was quite invisible to anyone outside, nor do I know how I could have decided the point had I known what it was. I must say, however, that when an umpire is in doubt, I think he is justified in deciding against the side which makes most noise. They are probably in the wrong.

At the end of the same year the English Rugby Union was formed; and soon after this the committee which had hitherto done all the work was hurriedly and unceremoniously displaced by the formation of the Scottish Rugby Union. This step was doubtless due to a misunderstanding as to the intentions of the committee, which was supposed to be too exclusive, although it was only taking time for the consideration of a rule about the admission of new clubs and the formation of a working executive. It was unfortunate, however, that the committee was superseded at that particular time, because it had arranged for a conference with England about the rules of the two countries, which differed in several respects—notably, about the important question of picking up. The new Union adopted the English rules and any changes in them subsequently made by England in bulk, and hence afforded a precedent for the claim on the part of England of a sole right to legislate, which caused such a stir some years afterwards. But a still greater evil was the exclusion of the schools from all share in legislation. The schools are the nurseries of the game; it began with them; it is perhaps, under all modern circumstances, their best instrument of "education," in the true and wide sense of that word; for I cannot conceive of any school making a good stand-up fight against the soft and self-indulgent ways of living in which town boys, at all events of the richer classes, are usually brought up, in which football is not a flourishing institution; nor is the Association game a possible refuge for Scotch schools. We are all Rugby, and Rugby, I hope, we shall remain; for the defect of the Association game is that it gives no exercise for the upper limbs, and thereby does not tend to the strengthening of the lungs, and the equal development of both sides of the person, as the Rugby game does, so that we are at the mercy of the club. And I am afraid that in their legislation they have not sufficiently in view what is really the great end of the game—viz., to produce a race of robust men, with active habits, brisk circulations, manly sympathies, and exuberant spirits. I don't think I am overstating my charge when I say that they regard it far too much as a means of attracting spectators. This is in itself an evil. When a man is past playing football, which is ten years sooner by the modern game than by the old one, he ought, as a rule, to be taking hard exercise in some form himself whenever he gets the chance, and not spending his Saturday afternoons as a stationary and shivering spectator. But putting aside this aspect of the question, I have no doubt that the tendency of recent legislation has injured football as a school game. By increasing the pace it has also increased its most serious danger, which is not to the limbs, but to the heart. Boys

H. H. ALMOND.

with even slightly weak hearts ought not to play the modern game, though they might safely play the old game. And all who know anything about schools are aware what a serious evil it is that many boys should be excluded from the chief school games. Further, the old game could be advantageously played at least four days weekly. I am convinced that the modern game should never be played, at least by big side, two days in succession, and certainly not within three days of a "big match." And, lastly, the discouragement of dropping would have been impossible had the voice of the schools been heard in the Unions. Dropping is one of our very best outdoor occupations for old times, and it is quite impossible to get boys to practise with the same keenness when a dropped goal, by an infatuation which I cannot understand, has been made to count less than a goal from a try. Let me hope that at least this monstrous innovation on the essential spirit of Rugby football may soon be repealed, not only in the interest of schools, but in that of the beauty and science of the game. My own belief is that some day legislation will retrace its steps still further. There is great danger in the practice of dropping on the ball to save, and already many serious accidents have happened from a player being kicked when falling on the ball. Schools will not be able to resist the outcry which will be caused by one boy killing another in this way, by mere accident or from momentary loss of temper. My own belief is, and always has been, that the worst change ever made in the game was the abolition by the English Union in 1872 (endorsed with all other English legislation by the then infant Scottish Union) of the old rule that the ball might not be taken into the hands except in the case of a free catch or when fairly bounding.

Holding, however, as I do, that recent legislation has both injured the game and made its position precarious, I believe that Rugby football, even as it is, is the best instrument which we possess for the development of manly character. In one point at least it is superior to the old game. The development of passing and of combined play generally has fostered unselfishness. A player used to play chiefly for his own hand; now, if he is worth playing, he plays for his side. Passing was, however, quite as consistent with the old rules as with the present. I tried to introduce long passing for years without much effect. I was told that it would "look like funking," etc. To the best of my belief its efficacy was first proved in the Fettes and Loretto match in November, 1880, and its introduction at Oxford by the old boys of the two schools was the chief cause of the football supremacy of Oxford a few years afterwards. But a still more important point even than passing appears to me to be combined play among forwards. In that art, one school—viz., Merchiston—has usually enjoyed an unquestioned pre-eminence. I have no hesitation in saying that in recent years I believe the best football in the world has been played at Merchiston. Few of its boys go to English universities, and they commonly leave school younger than is the case at Loretto and Fettes. Still, with only about one hundred and thirty boys in all, it has held its own in Scotch School championships against the far superior numbers and greater age of Fettes, and has completely distanced Loretto. Since 1880, when the three schools first began to play each other regularly, Merchiston has won the championship six times, Fettes thrice, and Loretto twice, the remaining year being a tie between Merchiston and Fettes.

It is a pity that the Scotch schools have no opportunity of measuring their strength against the great English schools. Rugby once invited Loretto to play them at Manchester at the beginning of the Christmas holidays, but there was an epidemic at Loretto which made it impossible. And I may add that I think all matches between schools ought to be played in term time and on the school grounds. Such intercourse between schools, to a limited extent, is well worth the time and money. The headmasters of the great English schools have, however, generally a great aversion to football matches between schools. I believe they are afraid of rough play. If so, their fears are groundless. No keener matches can possibly be played than those for the Scotch School championship. And they are usually played with the utmost fairness, and in a good-humoured, sportsmanlike spirit. In fact, I believe that house matches at schools are often played in far worse temper than any matches between well-disciplined schools are likely to be. I have seen the Fettes and Loretto teams standing by in silence, while some point was being discussed between captains and umpires about a disputed goal on which a match depended.

The facts as to "blues," however, given at the beginning of this chapter, when coupled with the fact that Merchiston scarcely enters into this competition, prove indirectly the great excellence of Scotch School football. This arises from several causes.

1. I think that North-countrymen in general are bigger-boned and more muscular than Southerners are. Also possibly, children are more hardily brought up in Scotland before they come to school than they are in England, though the extent to which modern softness of living vitiates family and nursery life everywhere is lamentable.

2. Our constantly playing against each other creates a great enthusiasm for the game. Besides the matches

mentioned above, an Edinburgh Day School championship and an entirely Day School match between Edinburgh and Glasgow are merely samples of what is going on in secondary schools in Scotland generally. There are also matches for 2nd and 3rd fifteens, played on the same days, twice each season, as the Fifteen matches. To get into one of the teams at once gives a boy a certain degree of school position. There are also matches for boys "under fifteen," which are as keenly fought as those for their seniors.

3. It has come to be understood, even by the smallest boys, that a place in any of the teams cannot usually be gained without a good deal of trouble and self-denial. Small schools also become aware that they cannot hope for football eminence unless they bring not only a select few but the whole mass of their boys into the fittest possible condition. The desire to do this therefore gives rise to sanitary rules of various kinds. Regular exercise in all weathers is insisted upon: boys are encouraged to sleep with open windows, and schoolrooms are kept fresh and airy. And perhaps above all, the importance of a proper dietary becomes evident; and the detestable and loathsome habit of "grubbing" all sorts of unwholesomes, even between meals, becomes warred against not only by masters, but by prefects and by public opinion. Why so many public schoolmasters permit unlimited "grubbing," and yet regard the less injurious vice of smoking as one of the gravest of school offences, is more than I can comprehend. I think also that it is becoming evident to the more far-sighted men in my own profession, that attention to matters of this kind produces benefits of a higher order than any football excellence. And this very fact serves to strengthen and perpetuate the foundations on which really good school football rests. On the indirect bearing of all this upon school morality I need scarcely enlarge to all who know anything about schools.

I subjoin the special system of training carried out at Merchiston during the football season. The particulars have been kindly supplied to me by Mr. Burgess, to whom Merchiston football has been so largely indebted for its vigour and excellence.

Boys are called at 7, when they turn out in flannels, and have a run or smart walk of about three-quarters of a mile, then a cold bath and rub down. Breakfast at 8; school from 9 to 12.

Monday, 12.30 to 1.30.—Big side (as often as possible a team of masters and old boys play the Fifteen on Monday).

Tuesday, 12.30 to 1.—The Fifteen look after the lower teams and make them play up. From 1 to 1.30 they practise drop and place kicking, and the halves and quarters practise passing.

Wednesday, 2.30 to 5.—Football match, or if before a school match, a cross-country run of from seven to ten miles, usually over the Pentland Hills.

Thursday, 12.30 to 1.30.—Big side.

Friday, 12 to 1.—Cadet corps drill; 1 to 1.30, kicking in field as on Tuesday.

From 3 to 6.—There are four periods, three of work and one of gymnastics, so that every boy gets about forty minutes gymnastics every day.

On Friday night they have in addition fencing and boxing. The Fifteen have also half an hour of this every night after preparation.

Every boy in the school must play football, unless exempted by the school medical officer.

All boys are accurately weighed and measured twice a term.

The bearing of the last particulars on football may not be obvious. But nothing makes a boy believe in a good physical system so soon as the increase of his measurements. They are the tangible outcome of the system under which he is being trained. And when you have once got his belief and will on your side, he is on the high road to becoming both a more vigorous football player and a better man. The system pursued at other leading Scotch schools does not differ materially from that of Merchiston. We, at Loretto, have rather less gymnastics. But "fives" are more prominent with us, and "shinty," or "hockey," as well as, occasionally, Association sides, are both a pleasing variety, and also, I think, an excellent and not too violent training. All training, however, should be carefully watched and studied. There is a great deal still to learn about general principles, and these ought to be applied with discrimination to particular cases by any schoolmaster

who knows his business. Training which would be
too severe for the rapidly-grown or anæmic boy is
the best possible discipline for the flabby, lazy, greedy
boy, or for the boy who prefers sitting over the fire with
a book to the free air of heaven. But by training I do
not mean special rules of life adopted for a short season
and then suddenly dropped. The greatest obligations I

"A DROP OUT."
(From an Instantaneous Photograph by E. Airy, Bradford.)

owe to any instructor are due to a certain Mr. Harrison,
who was a medical student when I was a master at
Merchiston. He fully persuaded me that training, in
its true sense, was that wholesome and vigorous condition in which we ought to try to live always, and
that boys or men who habitually, in this sense, live
in "training," are not only on the right road towards
usefulness and happiness in life, but that they need
no change, or, at most, a very slight change, in diet
or exercise, to make them most fit for athletic games
of any kind.

A word or two ought to be said as to the organisation
of football in a school. As it is obvious that the avail-

able players are not likely to be an exact multiple of thirty, there ought to be considerable elasticity, on the lower sides at least, as to the number playing on a side. The best practical plan for ordinary sides, as distinct from school matches, is to divide the number of available players into a number of nearly equal sides, "big side" being the smallest and having about thirty-four on its list. Two boys should be made heads of each side, and great care should be taken in their selection—knowledge of the game, and power of enforcing order and obedience being the most necessary qualities. They should have printed school lists, with the boys on their sides ticked off, and either the medical officer or some competent master should look through these lists to see that no boy is placed on a side for which he is too small or too delicate. It is easy for the captains to arrange exchanges, or to let boys who can be spared off to play fives or take some other exercise. The head boy of the school, or of the house, should of course be bound to see that those who for any cause are off football or other school games do not "slack," but have other sufficient exercise. A certain number of "crocks" or "slackers" are a necessary evil; but if not looked after they constitute a great source of danger. They are far more liable than football players to take any epidemic, and they are apt to get into lounging, lethargic habits, which are also a most infectious malady, if the "crock" or "loafer" is unfortunately a boy of any influence.

Great care should be taken that no favouritism is shown in choosing the school teams. My experience is that it is easy to show boys what a dishonest thing it is to use any public office, such as that of captain of a team, for private purposes; and surely any headmaster or school chaplain who gives his boys anything worth calling religious teaching, will speak often and strongly about the right use of responsibility of any kind. Certainly, to take the lowest ground, the excellence of school football greatly hinges on the certainty felt by every boy that he will get absolutely fair play, and that any mistake made about him will be one of judgment. One cannot aim at too high a standard of school morality in such matters. Another very important point is that of referees at sides. Masters who know the game will of course help in this way, and where the cricket professional resides refereeing should be part of his duties. Members of the Fifteen also, who are temporarily "crocked," should, if capable, be sent to referee, and at the same time to coach lower sides.

Much more, however, may be done to prevent "crocking" than is usually supposed. The most common cause of it is that a boy gets a slight sprain or twist about the knee or ankle, hobbles home with it, and thinks little more about it till the next morning, when the joint has swollen and water probably set in. He should have been carried home, and then immediately had the place fomented with water rather hotter than he can bear; he should then lay up until seen by the medical officer. About two-thirds of the ordinary sprains will be arrested at once if treated in this way. Boys should, of course, be frequently spoken to about these and kindred matters. They are a most important, but too often neglected, part of their education.

Lastly, no idle spectators should be allowed to stand looking on at school sides. The very sight of loungers takes the spirit out of players, and the loungers should be doing something else if they are too feeble for football. "Spectating" generally is, in fact, the greatest of all football dangers. When boys are allowed to look on at a big match they should all be sent a run of a couple of miles afterwards to quicken their circulations and to prevent that deadliest of dangers, "a chill."

THE FETTESIAN-LORETTONIAN CLUB.

The history of Rugby football in Scotland, dating from 1871, when the first international match between Scotland and England was played, is very closely associated with the history of the teams of old boys of one or other of the great Scottish schools. In the Scottish team of 1871 a very large proportion of the players were drawn from the Edinburgh and Glasgow Academical clubs, and throughout the 'seventies in a very marked degree, and during the 'eighties up to the present decade in a lesser degree, these clubs have been represented in the Scottish national matches. Scotland has owed much of her success in the field to such men as Hon. F. I. Moncrieff (the captain of the first Scottish team), R. W. Irvine, N. J. Finlay, J. H. S. Grahame, W. E. Maclagan, Charles Reid, and H. J. Stevenson, of the Edinburgh Academicals; and T. Chalmers, Malcolm Cross, D. Y. Cassels, W. A. Walls, and J. B. Brown, of the Glasgow Academicals. Merchiston Castle School was the training ground of at least three of those whose names are given —selected from giants of football.

About the year 1881 the prominence of old Lorettonians and old Fettesians in the International teams became noticeable, and up to the present time it is clear that players from Loretto School and Fettes College have assumed the lead over the other schools in the number of representatives in the Scottish teams. Many have also found places in the chosen teams of England. But not only in the national teams, but, in more pronounced fashion, in the University fifteens of Oxford and Cambridge have they been very prominent. During the unbroken record for three years held by Oxford, Loretto

H. P. TRISTRAM.
(*From a Photograph by J. Weston & Son, Folkestone.*)

had always several "blues," while at Cambridge Fettes has always had a noteworthy representation. The two schools have had eleven captains of Oxford and Cambridge in the last eleven years, but a record was reached in 1889-90, when exactly one-third of the two University teams were Fettesian-Lorettonians. The origin of the club was, however, on this wise. In the summers of 1880 and 1881, cricket teams of O. L.'s and O. F.'s went tours in Yorkshire and were very successful; and as a result the idea of the formation of a club took definite shape at an informal meeting at Lasswade in the autumn of the latter year. The original circular, signed by A. R. Paterson, a well-known Lorettonian and Oxonian, and by A. R. Don Wauchope, an equally well-known Fettesian and Cantab, called a meeting at which the club was duly formed; at first, chiefly as a football club, but during the eleven years of its existence it has developed several other branches of athletics.

The performances of the club in football are perhaps worthy of a brief sketch. During the season of 1881-2 five matches were played; the first three against the strongest clubs in Scotland, viz., West of Scotland, Edinburgh Wanderers, and University, and each match was lost by narrow majorities. But the visit to the North of England to play Manchester and Huddersfield can only be described as having created a sensation in the football world. Both matches were won easily, the first by three goals to a try, and the second by one goal and three tries to nil. The team in England comprised six Oxford and two Cambridge "Blues," as well as four Scottish and one English International players. The current issue of the *Athletic News* remarked: "Those persons who saw the doings of the Fettes-Loretto boys in Huddersfield and Manchester are willing to swear that a better team never existed, and a general wish has been expressed that Don Wauchope should bring his grand team into the North of England once more."

A. R. DON WAUCHOPE.
(From a Photograph by Hills & Saunders, Cambridge.)

These successes set the club on its legs, although they were nothing to what was to follow, for from that time, December, 1881, until January, 1888, the club won every match except three, which were drawn, viz., those against the Edinburgh Academicals in 1884, and Bradford in 1886 and 1888. The last three successive seasons have each seen the club narrowly defeated by the Bradford Club; in 1889-90 by a dropped goal to nil; in 1890-1 by a try to nil; in 1891-2 by a goal to nil, each match being productive of a splendid struggle.

Perhaps the most strikingly successful season of the club was during 1883-4, when eight matches were played, seven being won and the other drawn. The team that year was as follows—

H. B. Tristram (Oxford University and England) (back); D. J. Mac-Farlan (London Scottish and Scotland), G. C. Lindsay (Oxford University and Scotland), E. Storey (Cambridge University) (three-quarter backs); A. R. Don Wauchope (Cambridge University and Scotland), A. G. G. Asher (Oxford University and Scotland) (half-backs); A. Walker (West of Scotland, and Scotland), J. G. Walker (Oxford University, and Scotland), A. R. Paterson (Oxford University), C. J. B. Milne (Cambridge University), R. S. F. Henderson (Blackheath and England), W. M. Macleod (Cambridge University and Scotland), H. F. Caldwell (Edinburgh Wanderers), F. J. C. Mackenzie (Oxford University), C. W. Berry (Oxford University and Scotland).

E. Storey was the only player behind who did not secure his national cap. He would probably have gained it but for an accident which stopped his football altogether.

Of all the first-class men who have played for the F.-L.'s there is no one who stands out so prominently as A. R. Don Wauchope. His brilliant and consistent form through all those years, from 1881 to 1888, for his country, university, and club, dwarfs the performances of almost any other player one could name. Can any person forget the overwhelming excitement and even delight of the Yorkshire and Lancashire crowds when their favourite, "the great Don," got the ball: the shouts and cries from thousands of throats resounding round and round the enclosure as each opponent tried to tackle him and was left lying on the ground, until at last the ball was safely carried over the line? One of A. R. Don Wauchope's greatest triumphs happened in 1885 at Bradford, when he ran in behind twice—the only scoring in the game. In 1883 at Huddersfield his play was quite phenomenal; he ran and re-ran the whole of the opposing side time after time, to what might be called "a dead standstill," to the infinite delight of a huge crowd of genuine Tykes, who yelled in desperation, "Why, 'e's like a bloomin' eel; they can't 'old 'im nohow!" The great feature of his play was, of course, his running and dodging powers, but there was not a single point in half-

A. G. GRANT ASHER.
(From a Photograph by W. H. Wheeler, Oxford.)

back play in which he did not excel. Dropping at goal was perhaps a weak point—he always preferred to run—and it was in this particular that A. G. G. Asher, his companion half-back in many a struggle, was so strikingly good. H. B. Tristram in his best days has hardly been equalled as a full-back. He seemed to be able to get the ball away to a greater distance than any other back, and when he got the chance he *did* "down" his man. At three-quarters one must refer to such distinguished players as D. J. MacFarlan, G. C. Lindsay, M. F. Reid, P. H. Morrison, and P. R. Clauss. The first-named was the most consistent player of the lot, but Lindsay, Morrison, and Clauss were all brilliant at times, while Reid, if an unreliable player, used to drop a goal in the most unexpected way, just when badly wanted. He is one of the few who obtained his national cap when a schoolboy. In later days C. E. Orr and W. Wotherspoon have been among the most noticeable players in the club. It is difficult to discuss the form of all the better known forwards who have played for the F.-L.'s, but it can be safely asserted that, speaking widely, the forward teams of the last few years have not been of the same class as formerly. The preponderance of light men amongst them has enabled opponents to "shove them" in the scrummages; this has been specially marked in the late matches and defeats at Bradford. After all, however, the club will always hold, under existing circumstances, the same high position among Rugby football clubs of the United Kingdom. The members have all undergone the same vigorous training, at schools remarkable throughout the land by means of their intellectual and physical success. The best reason one can give for the uninterrupted prosperity of the Fettesian-Lorettonian club, is that teams who are chosen to represent it have considered it good enough to train for the tours and keep in good condition when away; in fact, there is a rule of the club which prevents the acceptance of invitations to football dinners. It is unnecessary to add more to this sketch, except perhaps to express the hope that the club, unique in many ways, may continue in the future as it has done in the past to play an honourable part in Rugby football, and be as often on the winning side.

CHAPTER VII.

THE FOUNDATION AND PROGRESS OF THE RUGBY FOOTBALL UNION FROM 1871 TO 1880.

By Arthur G. Guillemard.

IT was on the evening of the 26th January, 1871, that a party of thirty-two members of London and suburban football clubs following the Rugby School laws, assembled in solemn conclave at the Pall Mall Restaurant in Regent Street, London, under the presidency of E. C. Holmes, captain of the Richmond Club, resolved unanimously that the formation of a Rugby Football Society was desirable, and thereupon proceeded with all due deliberation to found the Rugby Football Union. The society was christened, a set of bye-laws drafted, and a president, a secretary and treasurer, with a committee of thirteen, elected, to whom was entrusted the drawing-up of the laws of the game upon the basis of the code in use at Rugby School. Everyone present was of one heart and of one mind that eventful evening, so that the labour was not protracted, and in the course of a couple of hours the bantling had been brought forth, a fund provided for maintenance, and the custody of the person assigned to Edwin H. Ash, the secretary of the Richmond Club, who, very proud of his charge

E. C. HOLMES.
(From a Photograph by T. Fall, Baker Street, W.)

and modestly conscious of his abilities as a dry-nurse, marched off home with "the person," in the shape of the minutes of the proceedings, safe in his great-coat pocket.

It will be well here to give the names of the clubs which were represented on this important occasion:— Blackheath, Richmond, Civil Service, Marlborough Nomads, West Kent, Wimbledon Hornets, Gipsies, Clapham Rovers, Law, Wellington College, Guy's Hospital, Flamingoes, Harlequins, Queen's House, King's College, St. Paul's School, Lausanne, Addison, Mohicans, and Belsize Park. These were all enrolled that evening as original members of the Rugby Football Union, and paid their entrance fees and first year's subscriptions on the spot, thus saving the treasurer the trouble of writing dunning letters, and setting an example which, unfortunately for his successors in office, has not been too generally followed. The main points of difference between the original bye-laws and those now in force were the following:—The entrance fee and annual subscription were 5s. each; the officers comprised a president, honorary secretary and treasurer, and a committee of thirteen; there was but one general meeting in each year—in October; and each club was permitted to send two representatives to a general meeting. The greater part of the credit for the bye-laws and the businesslike manner in which the Union was founded attached to E. H. Ash, than whom it would be very difficult to find a man better qualified to set going a society in connection with any of our national games; he was the principal mover in getting up the meeting under notice, and its success was mainly due to his efforts.

The following are the names of the Union officers for 1871, to whom was entrusted the drafting of the laws of the game:—President, Algernon Rutter (Richmond); hon. secretary and treasurer, Edwin H. Ash (Richmond). Committee: R. H. Birkett (Clapham Rovers), F. I. Currey (Marlborough Nomads), W. F. Eaton (Ravenscourt Park), A. J. English (Wellington College), J. H. Ewart (Guy's Hospital), A. G. Guillemard (West Kent), F. Hartley (Flamingoes), E. C. Holmes (Richmond), R. Leigh (Law), F. Luscombe (Gipsies), L. J. Maton (Wimbledon Hornets), E. Rutter (Richmond), and F. Stokes (Blackheath). Leaving these gentlemen busily engaged

F. STOKES.
(From a Photograph by Debenham and Gould, Bournemouth.)
President, 1874-75.

L. J. MATON.
(From a Photograph by Debenham & Co., Southsea.)
President, 1875-76.

A. BUTTER.
(From a Photograph by H. J. Godbold, Hastings.)
President, 1871-74.

C. D. HEATLEY.
(From a Photograph by Mr. Owen, Salisbury.)
President, 1876-78.

A. G. GUILLEMARD.
(From a Photograph by Joh. v. d. Fehr, Bergen.)
President, 1878-82.

with the Rugby School laws, let us glance at the position occupied by Rugby football amongst English games at this time, and the causes which operated towards the amalgamation of its interests in a parent body.

To commence with, it may be stated at once that as the rise, growth, and present status of the leading Rugby clubs round London and in the North of England are dealt with in other parts of this volume, the notes in this chapter must be of a general character and treat of the management of the Union and its laws rather than of the features of the play and the prowess of players. But, nevertheless, it is necessary here to devote a little space to a slight sketch of Rugby football as it was played between twenty and thirty years ago. When the writer left Rugby School in 1864 there were certainly not more than twenty clubs round London playing Rugby rules, including the R.M.A., Woolwich, and several "cramming" establishments, of which latter High House, Charlton, furnished the strongest team. Blackheath was the oldest club in point of foundation, and I can well remember watching the matches played by the Blackheath School Old Boys in 1857 and 1858, when they used short flag-posts for goals and had a goalkeeper in rear of the full-backs—a big, fleshy man, who always played in a felt hat, like Tom Hayward at cricket. His surname I never heard, but he was well-known by the *sobriquet* of "Soup-plates," probably derived from the shape of his hat. E. H. Ash was practically the founder of the Richmond Club early in "the 'sixties," and, enlisting the services of a large number of Old Rugbeians, they at once proved very formidable rivals to Blackheath. Indeed, during one season—1865, I think—when thirteen Old Rugbeians and two Old Marlburians formed the Richmond team week after week, and again in 1867 and 1869, the club did not suffer a single defeat. In those days the Blackheath v. Richmond matches were veritable battles of giants, and the largest crowds of the season attended on Blackheath and Richmond Green— where the club grounds then were—for the form shown was always of the best class, feeling ran high, and the British public—and particularly the unwashed portion of it—enjoyed the sight of a little hacking, which was then not forbidden. The two winters of 1866-67 and 1867-68 found these two clubs more evenly matched than ever; in the former season the two first matches were drawn, and Richmond won the rubber by a goal dropped by C. S. Dakyns, of whom more anon; in the latter the first match was drawn, and the return won for Richmond by E. Rutter, whose long left-foot drops were as useful to his club for many seasons as was his left-hand bowling to the Middlesex County Eleven. It is noteworthy that of the twenty-three players who represented the winners in the match last mentioned, as many as seventeen were Old Rugbeians, Blackheath mustering six from the same school.

E. M. ASH.
(From a Photograph by J. Middlebrooks, Kimberley.)

The crowds on these unenclosed grounds were a great nuisance, for they invariably declined—the ladies, especially at Blackheath, always excepted—to keep in touch, and the clear field of play was often not more than some thirty yards broad. Then did the wily half-back see his opportunity, and dive into the thick of the shouting throng so soon as the ball was in his hands. No woodcock flushed in cover is more wary to keep a tree between itself and the gun than was the said half-back to dodge amongst the flying spectators in such a way as to have one or more of them between himself and his would-be tacklers. The post of a full-back who could see nothing but the occasional flash of a coloured jersey nearing him at hundred yards' speed was no enviable one, and so persistently did some of the least civilised of the crowd stand between the full-backs and the ball that on one occasion at Blackheath my colleague, whose zeal sometimes outran his discretion, after vainly expostulating with a burly blacksmith, "dashed out his left" and knocked him several yards in the direction of the touch-line, behind which the injured one was careful to remain for the rest of the afternoon, nursing his jaw and venting threats of slaughter. In the matter of keeping the field of play clear things have improved wonderfully during the past twenty years, as nearly all clubs play in enclosed grounds where ropes and stakes can be utilised, but in old days the Metropolitan Board of Works forbade the use of them on the heaths and commons under their management.

In the provinces in "the 'sixties" there was very little Rugby football, except, of course, at Rugby, and also at the two universities, and at Marlborough, Tonbridge, Haileybury, Clifton, and Wellington; but in the North of England, and especially in Lancashire and Yorkshire, there were signs that the game was developing popularity, and by the end of the decade there were strong clubs at Manchester and Liverpool, which furnished a powerful contingent on the occasion of the first International match in 1871.

The earliest established clubs in nearly all cases laboured under no slight difficulties, for the majority of their members had not acquired a practical knowledge of the principles of the game in early years, and had no mentor to explain to them this rule and that. Blackheath and Richmond, thanks to their large drafts of old public-school boys, were specially favoured in this respect, and their colours shone pre-eminent, for their members not only knew the Rugby School rules thoroughly but had been trained to play a scientific game. It was not one of these, by-the-bye, who, penned within his own lines, and too proud to touch down, took a drop at the back of his own goal, and was surprised to see the ball descend into the hands of an opponent, who quietly grounded it between the posts.

This want of a practical knowledge of the rudiments of the game led to numerous divergences from the original code, the chief of which may be here briefly alluded to. The majority of the clubs round London, including Blackheath, Woolwich, and Sandhurst, allowed picking up the ball in the open so long as it was in motion, but Richmond and a few others adhered to the Rugby School law, which ran:—"It is not lawful to take up the ball when rolling as distinguished from bounding." The majority prevailed in the end, it being evident that this course would conduce to a material diminution in the number of disputes, there being no umpires in those days.

With regard to the return of the ball into play from

touch, previous to 1864 the law at Rugby was that it should be thrown in from a point on a level with the spot where it was touched down. But on one notable occasion, when the play was wavering round the Three Trees, a half-back dropped a tearing shooter when close to the touch-line, fifty yards from his opponents' goal, the result of which was that the ball rolled all that distance out of play till it went into touch-in-goal before any one could stop it. The absurdity of this led to a prompt alteration, and thenceforward the ball had to be thrown in from a point in a straight line from the spot where it first hit the ground in touch. Thus it was permitted to a good arrow-like drop to gain a considerable distance. Most of the London clubs, however, early adopted the plan of throwing the ball in from the spot where it crossed the line. Again, many clubs declined to allow a player having the ball in touch to bound it in the field of play and then play it himself.

The Rugby method of bringing the ball out for a try at goal after a run-in was considered too intricate, and failed to find favour outside the limits of the School Close. It need not, therefore, be described, but I may remark that it was really simple enough to anyone who had seen it once put into practice, and as it was a piece of play requiring a little skill, and as also it gave the defending side a chance of retrieving their position, it was not a little prized by Rugbeians. The method generally adopted was to bring the ball out in a straight line from where it was touched down, but if it had been touched down between the posts, then in a straight line from either of the posts. In dropping out it was allowable to drop into touch, and thus gain a considerable distance before the ball could be played by the opposite side.

As to the off-side laws, they were either not understood or flagrantly contravened by a large majority of the minor clubs in "the 'sixties." The Blackheath School boys were terrible offenders in this respect, and it was quite common to see the forwards charging down the ground as an advance guard to ward off opponents from the back who was in full run with the ball behind them. Law 18 of the Rugby code, obliging a player to have the ball down immediately when tackled outside the twenty-five yards' line at either end, was also similarly disregarded, and one often saw as vigorous a maul in midfield as if the ball were in goal. On one memorable occasion a maul of this kind was timed as lasting for ten minutes, the only object of the struggle being the privilege of putting the ball on the ground in the centre of the scrummage. Many spectators of the rougher class considered, judging from their excited shouting, that this

THE KICK-OFF—AFTER THE KICK.
(*From an instantaneous Photograph by E. Airey, Bradford.*)

feature of the game was more attractive than the most brilliant of runs, the cleverest dribbling, or the prettiest drop at goal.

From the above notes it will be gathered, as was the case, that before the commencement of any match it was absolutely necessary for the captains of the two sides to meet and exchange views on various points, it being usual to recognise the idiosyncrasies of the club upon whose ground the meeting was to take place. And as season followed season and clubs grew and multiplied, the want of a code revised under the authority of a parent body and accepted by all players became more and more urgent. Yet, great as was the urgency, the existence of this want was not the originating cause of the foundation of the Rugby Football Union. The real cause was twofold—firstly, an inaccurate and intemperate letter written by "A Surgeon" to the *Times;* and secondly, the fact that the Football Association arranged a match at the Oval under a title which was a misnomer. "A Surgeon" cited some half-a-dozen accidents at Rugby School, and alleged that they were one and all to be traced to the practice of hacking. He was silenced very promptly by direct contradictions from several members of the school and the medical officer; but the correspondence furnished matter for criticism in the daily papers, and a number of articles were published stigmatising the game as brutal and unmanly, and one calling for instant reformation, if not total abolition. *Punch* was very severe, but inasmuch as he stated that it was allowable to hack a player when lying on the ground, his arguments failed to carry conviction. In another journal the game was styled "a mixture of hacking, scragging, gouging, and biting," and regret was expressed that, however humanised, it could never "take rank as a drawing-room pastime." Scragging being tabooed and gouging and biting unheard of in connection with the Rugby game, it appeared evident that this correspondent had never witnessed a match which could be said to be played under that code; but, nevertheless, some of the mud which was so plentifully thrown was bound to stick, and though the leading clubs were not seriously alarmed by one writer's threat that Parliament should be moved to abolish the game, it was felt incumbent on them to place it on a recognised footing and under authoritative control.

The second cause leading to this end was the playing of a so-called "England *v.* Scotland" match, under the auspices of the Football Association, at the Oval on the 19th November, 1870. Only one of the side representing Scotland hailed from a Scottish club, and the connection of several of the others with the far North was said to be very problematical. It was stated, however, that one had been across the Border to shoot grouse, and this was considered a sufficient qualification; but it was seriously debated whether another, who was said to base his claim upon a liking for Scotch whiskey, should have been allowed to play. However, be that as it may, Scottish football players very promptly disclaimed recognition of the match as an international meeting, pointing out that the Association code had barely taken root north of the Tweed, and that nearly all Scottish clubs played the Rugby game. They followed this up by issuing a challenge for a *bonâ fide* international match between the Rugby players of the two countries, and this being accepted forthwith, the need of a governing body in England became the more imperative.

Before proceeding to comment on the revised laws of the game, a somewhat too prominent feature of the play in " the 'sixties," namely, hacking, which formed the chief count in the indictment in the daily papers, calls for passing notice. Hacking in the scrummage doubtless came into vogue at Rugby School from the large number of players—from 60 to 150—taking part in Bigside matches. Without energetic foot-work the ball could never be extricated from the forest of legs, for in those days a scrummage was a compact mass, the two sets of forwards forming up into a solid circle, with the players in the centre standing bolt upright instead of crouching down, as is generally the case now, much in the attitude of a bicyclist. And, as the ball could not be seen and only occasionally felt, it was necessary for a forward to kick where he considered it to be, and if it was not there but an opponent's shin instead, a hack was the result. "Hacking over," *i.e.*, hacking a player when running, probably grew out of tripping: lady spectators used to say that hacking over "looked terrible," but, judging from my experience as a player, which extended over fourteen seasons at Rugby and round London, its results belied its looks, for I cannot remember having seen any accident worse than a cut knee, and this was caused by the player hacked over falling across the touch-line on to a gravel path. It was in the scrummage that the worst hacks were received, and I am quite ready to admit that sometimes in Bigside, and still more often in house matches, there was very vicious play with the "navvies," as football boots were termed at Rugby. Tradition points to a notable match for the honours of Cock House some thirty years ago, when the losing twenty were so severely punished forward that their house master actually sat down on the grass in touch and cried like a child. The hacking was certainly very severe on that occasion, but the extent of it is not to be gauged from the tears, for I frequently saw the same master similarly affected when construing for his form's benefit a touching passage from some Greek play. The present Bishop of London, when head-master, set his face sternly against vicious hacking, and on one occasion, noticing a much-dreaded "hack" hewing his way through a Bigside scrummage with unnecessary violence, threatened to make him take off his navvies and play in slippers for the rest of the afternoon. Round London the Woolwich Academy team were considered to boast the fiercest set of forwards, and I well remember seeing the crack "hack" of one season, after coming through the scrummage, finish off his triumphal march by place-kicking the half-back in front of me clean off his legs. For six or seven years previous to the foundation of the Union the "Shop" always turned out a team very difficult to beat, for, added to their vigour forward, they had a splendid set of men behind the scrummage, of whom W. H. Sykes, H. T. S. Yates, H. S. Ferguson, H. B. Rich, H. W. Renny Tailyour, P. C. Walker, R. P. Maitland, F. Campbell, and E. M. T. Boddam were some of the most conspicuous. Amongst the minor clubs mauling and hacking were for a long time cherished as the principal features of the game, and it was unfortunately not uncommon to see a couple of players vigorously engaged in kicking each other's shins long after the scrummage had broken up. This it was that prompted the Richmond Club to issue a circular recommending the suppression of all unnecessary hacking, and, this view meeting with very general support, it was left to the newly-formed Union to go a step farther and declare all hacking and tripping illegal.

The principal features of the play of the leading clubs both round London and in the North during the years to which my remarks have been directed were the following:—Long and sure dropping by the backs, brilliant running by the half-backs, and dogged hard shoving, hacking, and following-up by the forwards. It was not until after hacking had been abolished that the scrummages degenerated into shoving matches, for, as soon as the ball had been put down, the solid mass of forwards was loosened by the play of the feet in the centre, and the ball quickly emerged. Indeed, in all matches where the players observed the Rugby School laws and discouraged mauling, the scrummages were never tedious, though, owing partly to the solidity of the formation of a scrummage in those days, and partly to the number of heavy weights, the forwards did not free themselves very quickly. A half-back, therefore, if the ball were kicked fairly to him, and he were a quick starter, had a grand chance, as frequently he had only the two half-backs and three full-backs of the opposite side to account with, and very exciting was the running in consequence. The tackling, however, was surer then than it is now, and there was the chance of a hack over as well. Passing in those days was mainly confined to the forwards, and a half-back who had got well under way kept his eye on his opponents and did his level best to run-in or get within dropping range of goal by his own unaided exertions, for his start as a rule precluded the possibility of anyone but his colleague getting sufficiently near to relieve him of the ball if tackled. As to the backs, of whom the centre player during the latter part of the period alluded to was generally brought forward as three-quarter-back, their duties were mainly dropping and tackling. Punting was practically unknown, and, when practised, generally elicited a howl from the crowd in touch.

E. BUTTER.
(From a Photograph by Barraud & Jerrard, Gloucester Place, W.)

It must not be thought that because a heavy forward was considered good value in those days, the forward play was generally slow, though the abolition of hacking certainly did much to render it so after 1871. There were many very fast forwards, even in the heavy division, adepts at piloting the ball through the opposing ranks, keeping it just in front of them, regardless of hacks, and dribbling it past the half-backs by a well-combined rush, travelling at top speed the while. Amongst the best of these were C. A. Crompton and C. W. Sherrard, of the

R.M.A.; F. Stokes, A. B. Colville, and H. Rawson, of Blackheath; R. Oliver, of West Kent; F. Luscombe and J. A. Body, of the Gipsies; and M. Davies, G. Hamilton, and E. C. Holmes, of Richmond. The last-named trio were specially good at passing from one to another; so that if one of them got a chance of a run, the other two generally managed to transact some important business with the ball before it was brought to rest. As a rule, perhaps, of all the forwards round London, the wearers of the red and black jerseys of Blackheath followed-up the hardest.

First and foremost of all half-backs, whether of this or any other period, was C. S. Dakyns, who, from 1861 to 1868, accomplished such marvellous achievements on Old Bigside at Rugby and in the ranks of the Richmond Club, as could hardly be credited by those who never saw him at his prime. About five feet eight inches in height, and squarely built, he appeared to be a mass of sinew; his dodging powers were wonderful, and he could run as fast, twisting and turning amongst a crowd of opposing forwards, as most players could when progressing in a bee-line over a clear expanse of turf. He caught and fielded a ball unerringly, and his science and knowledge of the intricacies of the game were as unequalled as the skill with which he turned them to the best advantage in a difficulty. His dropping powers with either foot were admirable, and many a time have I seen him drop a goal from a distance of fifty or sixty yards when an opponent has had firm hold of one of his arms but failed to get possession of the ball, which, held by the string, Dakyns would let fall from his unencumbered hand in front of an unerring foot. In the three principal matches of one Rugby season, Dakyns dropped two goals for the Sixth v. the School, one for Old Rugbeians v. Present, and a poster for the School v.

C. S. DAKYNS.
(From a Photograph by H. Webster, Bayswater.)

the two Cock Houses; when it is remembered that not less than 120 players were engaged in each match, some idea may be formed of the magnitude of this series of feats. His tackling was as deadly as his dropping at goal, and general was the regret when an accident to his knee obliged him to give up playing. I have no hesitation in stating my opinion—which, I should add, is shared by many players who have watched the Rugby game carefully for two or three decades—that the famous "Pup" Dakyns was the best all-round football player who ever donned a jersey.

Of the other half-backs of that period, C. S. Fryer, well-known as one of the best sprinters of the London Athletic Club, was very useful to Blackheath by reason of his pace and the trickiness of his spurts; as was R. Philpotts, who got over the ground by a series of jumps, and was very difficult to tackle. H. M. Hamilton, of the Marlborough Nomads, and J. A. Bentley, of the Gipsies, were both very fast, and the latter was much helped by his weight and strength, which on one occasion at Chislehurst enabled him to run-in, carrying two of his opponents on his back as easily as if they were mere rag dolls. Of the R.M.A. cadets, P. C. Walker played a rough, hard game, and R. P. Maitland a pretty one, with much effect; and F. Campbell was invaluable on a wet ground, and, being built on a small scale, was said occasionally to make a long run between the legs of his opponents, a feat which, I believe, was rivalled by R. T. Finch in later years. Walter Slade, the champion mile runner, had a happy knack of dropping goals, and was very useful to West Kent; whilst Richmond had an excellent trio in R. Murray, a very neat dodging runner; E. C. Holmes, one of the most hard-working of men, and equally good in or behind the scrummage; and J. A. Boyle. The last-named, an old Marlburian, was one of the surest of place-kicks, and also an admirable drop. Curiously enough, when about to drop, he did not hold the ball in the usual way, but allowed it to rest on the extended palm of one hand, in precisely the same manner as the late Mr. T. C. Goodrich, the famous Free Foresters' slow underhand bowler, treated a cricket-ball before delivering it.

This review of the game at the time when the Rugby Football Union was founded, may give to players of more recent times some idea of the position; but the fact that the rise and progress of the leading clubs is dealt with in another chapter has necessitated my confining myself in the main to general remarks, and leaving the details to other contributors.

We will now return to the doings of the committee of 1871, whom we left hard at work drawing up the laws of the game. E. C. Holmes, captain of Richmond, kindly placed his chambers in Bedford Row at the disposal of the committee, and there amongst piles of papers and books relating to laws of a very different kind many a long evening between February and June, 1871, was spent in earnest deliberation. After three meetings, however, at which general principles were very fully discussed and many points of difficulty settled, the actual drafting of the code was entrusted to A. Rutter (the president), E. C. Holmes, and L. J. Maton, three old Rugbeians, who had all the intricacies of the school laws, as well as the variations affected by London clubs, at their fingers' ends, and were famous players to boot. Even then the work progressed very slowly, and it appeared doubtful whether the code would be got into shape for approval by the full committee, and subsequently by a general meeting, before the opening of the next season, until, most fortunately for the Union, though not for himself, Maton, the elected draftsman of the trio, broke a leg. Anxious for some employment whilst thus laid on the shelf, and accepting his colleagues' offer of a large supply of tobacco if he completed the work before he left his sofa—his just claim for this has, I hear, never been met, but is probably now statute-barred—the sturdy captain of the Wimbledon Hornets performed his arduous task so satisfactorily that by the 22nd June the new code had been approved by the committee, and on the 24th July was accepted in its entirety by a special general meeting. Inasmuch as in his carefully-written "Athletics and Football" (Badminton Library, 1889) Mr. Montague Shearman has been good enough to give expression to the view that E. H. Ash and I had the chief hand in drafting the code, I think it right on our joint behalf here to state our disclaimer. Maton and his two colleagues did the whole of the work.

A few words now on the original Union code. The

G

Rugby School laws consisted in 1871 of six definitions, followed by a lengthy introduction, which was practically a treatise on the game interlarded with numerous laws, and winding up with thirty-four rules, nine of which were merely of local import. Out of these three parts the Union legislators formed a set of fifty-nine laws, the chief points of difference from the School code being the following: Hacking, hacking over, and tripping up were abolished; a player being off-side was placed on-side by one of his own side having run in front of him either with the ball or having kicked it when behind him, and the off-side laws generally were more fully explained; in the case of a knock-on or throw-forward, if no fair catch had been made, a scrummage on the spot might be claimed; the ball was to be returned into play from the spot where it crossed the line of touch; the elaborate method of bringing the ball out for a try at goal was abandoned in favour of its being brought straight out from a mark made on the goal-line opposite to the spot where it was touched down; and the captains of the sides were to be the sole arbiters of all disputes. In other respects the Rugby School game was preserved in all its leading features, and except that punting-out has been abolished, the main principles which characterised the original Union code remain practically unchanged to the present day. The style of play has of course very materially altered, numerous penalties have been prescribed to meet cases of violation of certain laws, and a system of scoring by points introduced, but the old principles are still retained.

A. Rutter as president, E. H. Ash as hon. secretary and treasurer, and the original committee were re-elected for the season 1871-72, and no alteration was made in either the bye-laws or the laws of the game. The enrolled clubs numbered thirty-one, and it is worth remarking that, though Edinburgh University, the Glasgow Academicals, and the West of Scotland had joined, the clubs in the North of England stood aloof. This season saw the decision of the first international match that was played in England, and the gallant victory achieved by the English Twenty, who were on this occasion under Union auspices for the first time, increased not a little the public interest in the game.

The following season's general meeting passed off

without any alteration in the laws of the game, but Bye-law 2 was amended, two vice-presidents being created, and two members added to the committee, which thus numbered fifteen. A. Rutter was again re-elected president, and F. Stokes, then captain of the English Twenty and of the Blackheath Club, and E. C. Holmes, formerly captain of Richmond, filled the vice-chairs. The writer succeeded E. H. Ash as hon. secretary and treasurer; the retirement of the latter, owing to pressure of business, was a great loss, for he had done more than anyone else to establish the Union on a sound foundation and bring it up to the satisfactory position it occupied at that time. During this season the number of clubs belonging to the Union was nearly doubled, there being an addition of twenty-eight new members. The North of England sent a first instalment with Hull, Liverpool, Manchester, Rochdale, and Wigan; the Scottish contingent was swelled by the joining of the Edinburgh Academicals, Edinburgh Wanderers, and Royal High School; Trinity College, Dublin, posed as the first representative from Ireland; Oxford University threw in their lot, and Dulwich College, St. Paul's School, and Tonbridge School followed the excellent example set by Wellington College. The fact that the six leading Scottish clubs were members, although in the course of this season they formed a Union of their own, was a welcome proof of their appreciation of the work of the parent society. Indeed, this appreciation was expressed at a meeting of five of the English and five of the Scottish Committee held in Glasgow on the morning of the international match, when the Rugby Union game was discussed, the object of both parties being that the two Unions should go hand in hand.

The season of 1873-74 saw the addition to Bye-law 5, at the instance of F. I. Currey (Marlborough Nomads), of a second annual general meeting to be held in March for the consideration of the bye-laws and laws of the game. The fact that a goal had been claimed on the occasion of a ball bounding from the ground over the cross-bar led to a slight alteration in the laws, and it was also laid down that a player could not be off-side in his own goal. Attempts were made by F. Luscombe and E. C. Hill respectively, to allow the bringing out of the ball in a straight line from where it had been touched down, even if between the posts, and to provide the penalty of a free kick for off-side play; but the proposers failed to carry their points, though, as will be seen hereafter, this was simply because they anticipated events a little too much. A. Rutter was elected president for yet another year, and the two vice-presidents were also retained in office; but the writer, being about to make a tour round the world, was replaced as hon. secretary and treasurer by F. I. Currey, one of the winning English Twenty of the previous season, who, from the foundation of the Union to the present time, has proved himself one of the most hard-working, conscientious, and enthusiastic members of the Union Committee. A challenge was received from Ireland for an international match, but it was felt necessary to intimate that it could not be accepted until the following season. The winter under notice, however, was productive of a step in advance in the shape of the first meeting of teams representing the North and South of England. The match, which was played at Rugby on January 29th, 1874, between two Twenties, was drawn: it was not actually managed by the Union, as they then had so few northern adherents that it was felt that the northern clubs had better select their representatives; F. I. Currey, got up the southern team. In the course of this Union year the number of affiliated clubs rose to eighty-one, Cambridge University being the most conspicuous of the new members; whilst the northern contingent was swelled by the joining of four more clubs. Football was much increasing in popularity in Lancashire and Yorkshire, and four northern forwards won places in the English Twenty.

The following season saw the promotion of F. Stokes to the post of president; A. Rutter, who had done excellent work throughout the opening three and a half years of the Union, retiring to a seat amongst the committee. C. D. Heatley, captain of Richmond, and L. J. Maton were elected vice-presidents, and the writer of these pages returned to the office of hon. secretary and treasurer, the duties of which F. I. Currey, at considerable personal inconvenience and with signal success, had performed during his absence. It may be noted that all the four officers this season were Old Rugbeians. The accession of northern clubs led to the election of

E. Kewley (Liverpool), and James MacLaren (Manchester), as members of the committee. The North v. South match was placed on a permanent footing this season, to be played alternately in London and the North under Union control, the proposal being made by Roger Walker, of the Manchester Club. The first of the series of England v. Ireland matches was brought off successfully in London. The amount of the entrance fee and subscription was this year raised to £1 1s. in each case; the

BALL OUT OF SCRUMMAGE: PASSING FROM ONE HALF-BACK TO THE OTHER.
(*From an Instantaneous Photograph by E. Airey, Bradford.*)

auditing of the accounts and publication of a balance sheet were provided for; and Law 59 was amended so as to allow of the appointment of umpires, if desired. A system of scoring by points was mooted, but rejected, the proposal that three touches down should equal a try not meeting with approval. Forward play during this season was very unsatisfactory as a rule, shoving being apparently considered the main object, and good foot-work at a discount. The heavy-weights seemed afraid to use their feet in a scrummage, and ignorant how to do so when the ball was in the open. One hundred and thirteen—including twenty-one northern —clubs were on the Union list, in spite of the retirement of most of the Scottish and Irish subscribers, owing to their now having Unions of their own: the Calcutta Club and Marlborough College were perhaps the most notable accessions.

The season of 1875-76 saw the following officers at the head of Union affairs :—L. J. Maton, president; C. D. Heatley and Hon. H. A. Lawrence, who had captained the English Twenty the previous season, vice-presidents; A. G. Guillemard, hon. secretary; and W. Slade, treasurer. The outcome of a circular addressed to the Scottish and Irish Unions and the English clubs, was an amendment to Law 7, to the effect that a match should be decided by a majority of goals; but if no goal or an equal number of goals should be kicked, then by a majority of tries. This amendment, which was brought forward by A. Rutter and F. Stokes, became law at a special general meeting held in November, 1875. Other alterations made in the code at the March meeting provided for the change of goals at half-time, and forbade kicking the ball so as to pitch in touch after a kick-off. A proposal emanated from the Scottish Union that the numbers in the international matches should be reduced to fifteen a side, but the season was then too far advanced for the change to be accepted so as to apply to the forthcoming match. In the course of this season the staff and gentlemen cadets of the Royal Military Academy, Woolwich, generously offered a challenge cup of the value of £150 to be competed for by Union clubs. Although such competitions had never found favour with the Union, the offer was gratefully accepted, and a sub-committee drafted a set of rules to govern the tournament; eventually, however, it was found that the proposal did not commend itself to the Governor of the Royal Military Academy, and the offer was accordingly withdrawn. The deterioration in forward play may be gathered from the following extract from an article in *Bell's Life*:— "How much longer are we to see forwards chosen simply for weight and solidity, and not for knowledge of the game or skill in its practice? How much longer are we to be wearied by monotonous shoving matches instead of spirited scrummages, and disgusted at seeing a 14st. Hercules straining every muscle to move an opposing mountain of flesh a yard or two further from his goal-line, whilst he is all the time blissfully oblivious of the fact that the ball is lying undisturbed at his feet ? We do not for an instant fail to recognise the worth of a heavy forward if he knows the game and can use his feet, but if he can only shove—and not unfrequently off his side—and, when he finds the ball before him after the scrummage has broken up, must needs pick it up and sling it under his arm, imagining himself a half-back, instead of taking it on goalwards by dribbling it in the fore-front of a well-concerted rush of his fellow-forwards, we would sooner that he donned his ulster and hid his massive frame amongst the crowd of spectators in touch." The Union Committee drew special attention to the very indifferent form shown by forwards in a report issued at the close of the season.

The fact that there is no special feature to chronicle in connection with the winter of 1876-77 affords conclusive evidence that Union affairs proceeded smoothly. The officers were C. D. Heatley, president; Hon. H. A. Lawrence and A. G. Guillemard, vice-presidents; and H. J. Graham (Wimbledon), hon. sec. and treasurer. There was no alteration in the laws calling for remark, but the number of players in all matches under Union auspices was reduced to fifteen a-side ; Ireland proposed a twenty a-side match, but did not press the point, as the English Committee held strongly to the view that forward play would be improved by the lesser number. And this view seemed to be fairly borne out, for the heavy forwards in the leading matches were much quicker on their feet than they had been for several seasons. There was also some improvement in the play of the backs, who practised dropping rather more instead of running until they were tackled. Doubtless, not a few players took a leaf out of the book of L. Stokes, whose superb dropping in England v. Ireland at the Oval was the leading feature of the match. The Union finances were in a sufficiently satisfactory state this season to allow of the investment of £150 in Consols, forming the nucleus of a fund which by the time that the Union attained its majority in January, 1892, had swelled to very considerable proportions. The Southern Rugby Union of New South Wales, comprising sixteen clubs, had by this time adopted the Rugby Union laws, and there were also many adherents in New Zealand. This year the North had their first captain of the English team in E. Kewley (Liverpool), an excellent forward and very popular representative.

C. D. Heatley was again elected president for the season 1877-78, and his colleagues were A. G. Guillemard and F. Luscombe (Gipsies), the latter superseding Lawrence, whom pressure of business prevented from again accepting office; H. J. Graham remained at his post as hon. secretary and treasurer. Amendments were made in the bye-laws making past presidents *ex-officio* members of the committee, and providing for the striking off the Union roll of all clubs whose subscriptions, due in October, had not been paid by the following March. In the laws of the game a salutary amendment was made, providing that, on a player being tackled, the ball, if firmly held, must be put down at once. The object of this was to make the game faster: previously it had been the custom to hold the ball till the forwards had all come up. Some players, indeed, if on the ground with the ball under them, would rise with it; others would leave it on the ground but deny the right of anyone to kick it so long as the tackled player kept his fingers on it. Rugby Union football had by this time made great strides in the North, and the energetic administration and vigorous play of E. Kewley, A. N. Hornby, J. MacLaren, R. Walker, H. W. T. Garnett, G. Harrison and others had led to a considerable increase in the number of clubs, twenty-six of whom were members of the Union. Complaints, however, came from them that the off-side laws were in many cases persistently disregarded, and it was suggested that a penalty should be imposed to counteract the evil. Such a measure, however, failed to commend itself to the general meeting, and a sub-committee was appointed to consider the question during the recess. This was done very thoroughly, and a minute was presented to the October meeting, 1878, which was subsequently printed and sent to all Union clubs, thoroughly explaining the off-side laws and calling upon all players to observe them and play the game in the proper spirit, in which case the imposition of penalties—which were then considered undesirable—would be unnecessary. A very handsome silver cup of Indian workmanship was this season presented to the Rugby Union by the Calcutta Club to be played for annually by England and Scotland; G. A. J. Rothney, the hon. secretary, who, it is believed, was the prime mover in the matter, subsequently received the Union's thanks in person at an international match dinner at Manchester. With regard to the merits of players of this period it deserves mention that L. Stokes, captain of Blackheath, and one of the three-quarter-backs of the English team, ran in no fewer than thirty-two times in his club's matches during this and the preceding season; from this it will be judged how much Blackheath, then the premier club, owed to his efforts.

THE CALCUTTA CUP.
(From a Photograph by J. Moffat, Edinburgh.)

The season of 1878-79 was a fairly eventful one so far as the work of the Union was concerned, but a very severe winter materially reduced the number of matches played, some of the grounds in the North being under a thick covering of snow for ten or twelve consecutive weeks, and both North v. South and England v. Ireland had to be postponed. The officers for the year were: A. G. Guillemard, president; E. Kewley and F. I. Currey, vice-presidents; and W. Wallace (Richmond), hon. secretary and treasurer. It is noteworthy that the first five presidents were all Old Rugbeians. The spread of football in the North led to the election of six representatives to the committee. County matches had now become very popular, especially in the North, where a representative fifteen could more easily be commanded than in the South. The Union Committee took a step in the right direction when they issued a note defining the qualification for a county player, and County Committees were formed for the management of matches. No alterations of sufficient importance to call for comment in these pages were made in the laws, except that in the law regulating charging it was provided that no player should obstruct an opponent unless the latter were holding the ball or the player were himself running at the ball. But a revised code of laws, drafted by A. K. Butterworth, captain of the Marlborough Nomads, was submitted to the committee, and subsequently at the March general meeting proposed by A. Budd and G. R. Hill for general adoption; it failed, however, to obtain sufficient support. This code was cleverly drafted, the author, himself a capital half-back, being well-versed in the game; but he appeared to have somewhat sacrificed clearness of explanation to an absorbing desire to be terse. However, the promoters by a single vote carried a motion for a sub-committee to revise the laws, and F. R. Adams, J. V. Brewer, A. K. Butterworth, G. R. Hill, J. MacLaren, and L. Stokes, with the president, were accordingly appointed. The entire Union Code was carefully considered in the course of a series of meetings during the ensuing summer, and the result of the deliberations reported at the opening general meeting of the following season. There was some talk during this winter of a visit of a team of Rugby Union players to the Australasian Colonies; but the colonists were not prepared to guarantee expenses, and, as it was also considered that Rugby football had hardly made sufficient headway in the sunny south to ensure good matches, the project fell through.

The following winter, though a severe one, was fairly dry, and the Union enjoyed a most satisfactory season. The outgoing officers were all re-elected, except E. Kewley, who found it difficult to spare sufficient time for the post of a vice-president, and so retired in favour of J. MacLaren (Manchester), a very energetic and efficient administrator. The alterations in the code which were proposed by the Special Committee were considered at the opening general meeting, and passed *en bloc*. They were few in number, and the main points were the limiting of the size of the field of play; the option given to the opposite side to have the ball kicked off or dropped out (as the case might be) again, if it should pitch in touch; the preventing of any obstruction to a player within twenty-five yards of his own goal-line when about to drop out; and the providing for the ball being put down in a scrummage at the place where any breach of law not otherwise dealt with occurred, upon a claim to that effect being made by the opposite side. No change of any importance was made at the March meeting. The forward play during this season was fast and full of spirit, and showed decided improvement.

A TRY: THE PLACE KICK AT GOAL.
(From an instantaneous Photograph by E. Airey, Bradford.)

This was mainly due to the law that the ball, on its being held, must be put down immediately, for a high premium was consequently set upon pace and good dribbling and foot-work. Both players and spectators profited by the change, for the monotonous long-drawn-out scrummages disappeared as if by magic. This was the first season in which the travelling expenses of players in Union matches were defrayed out of the Union funds, a resolution to that effect having been carried *nem. con.* at a special general meeting held in January. The Union matches drew very large attendances this season, and the profits of that against Scotland at Manchester, after a liberal gift to local charities, exceeded £250, so that the Consols held by the trustees were increased to £600. A proposal was received from a gentleman in Sydney, New South Wales, to bring an Australian team to play a series of matches in England during the ensuing season, provided their expenses were guaranteed, but this being reported impracticable, the proposal was withdrawn.

The above notes will serve to show the administrative work of the Union during its first ten seasons, and I leave the record to be carried on by another pen in the following chapter. Wonderful indeed had been the spread of the Rugby game during the twenty years following the foundation of the Blackheath Club in 1860, and especially in the North, as may be judged from the fact that on one Saturday in March, 1880, no fewer than one hundred and six matches were fixed for decision in the counties of Lancashire, Yorkshire, and Cheshire alone. This large increase in the number of clubs resulted in the drafting into their fifteens of a large proportion of tyros, very keen and full of pluck, but ignorant not only of the laws, but of the leading principles of the game. And as, in addition to this, partisanship ran high, umpires had by no means a pleasant time of it, their decisions being freely disputed, and the Union Committee had plenty of work on their hands. However, as time went on and the laws became better understood by the players, matters improved in this respect. Match reports, too, as sent up to the sporting papers, grew more intelligible, and one read less frequently of "touch in Q" instead of touch-in-goal—Q was the reference letter in the plan of the field; of "rouges" and "dead balls" instead of touches down; of "packs" and "bullies" where scrummages were meant; of "collaring" instead of tackling, and the like. Indeed, football, the literature of which began with Mr. C. W. Alcock's carefully-edited "Football Annual" in 1868, developed various journals specially devoted to its interests before a dozen years were past. A great contrast this to the state of affairs fifteen or twenty years previously, when it was an unusual circumstance if *Bell's Life*, then the leading sporting paper, contained a column of match reports emanating from the public schools.

Players of the present day may well ask how the young men of thirty years ago passed their Saturday afternoons in the winter. The answer is not easy to find, but it must be remembered that in those days a half-holiday on Saturday was by no means the general custom, and a very large number of offices were not closed until four o'clock, so that outdoor exercise by daylight was possible to but a few. Hockey was but little played, and I am by way of thinking that, if there was no ice available for skating, most men adjourned to billiard-rooms or went straight home and smoked or slept until dinner-time. We live a more vigorous and healthy life now.

CHAPTER VIII.

PROGRESS OF THE RUGBY FOOTBALL UNION FROM SEASON 1880-81 TO THE PRESENT TIME.

By G. Rowland Hill, Hon. Sec.

DURING the season 1880-81 A. G. Guillemard was again president, and Messrs. F. I. Currey and J. MacLaren remained vice-presidents, and W. Wallace was again secretary. For the first time a challenge was accepted from Wales to play England. Welsh football was then, comparatively speaking, in its infancy, and the Welshmen proved to be no match for their opponents. Since that time Wales have made wonderful strides. It was mainly through the energy and perseverance of R. Mullock, who was hon. sec. of the Welsh Union then, and who has retained the post up to the present time, that England consented to play Wales, and by doing so set a good example to the other nationalities, and the credit is largely due to him for the present satisfactory position of Welsh football. At the March meeting an alteration in the laws emanating from a well-known Yorkshireman, B. Schofield, was proposed, giving a penalty of a "fair catch" for an infringement of the "off-side" laws: this proposition was not passed, but, considering the novelty of its character, it received considerable support. At that time penalties practically did not exist in the laws, and it is easy to understand that those who had not had the practical experience of the necessity for them should be opponents of the innovation. The opposition was led by such able authorities as Messrs. A. Budd and E. T. Gurdon, and it will be admitted that times have indeed changed when they, in common with all their colleagues, admit that a thorough system of penalties is needed if the

F. I. CURREY.
(From a Photograph by Herman Ernst,
St. John's Wood, N.W.)
President, 1884-86.

L. STOKES.
(From a Photograph by Lock & Whitfield
Regent Street, W.)
President, 1886-88.

J. MACLAREN.
(From a Photograph by the London and County Photographic Co.)
President, 1882-84.

A. BUDD.
President, 1888-89.

F. T. GURDON.
(From a Photograph by W. D. Downey,
Ebury Street, S.W.)
President, 1890-92.

game is to be played properly. At the same meeting a proposal to alter the scoring laws was made. Nothing was, however, then done in the matter. Reference to the changes which have since been effected in this respect are referred to in these pages.

The question of the desirability of instituting a Challenge Cup for the Union was again mooted; the suggestion met with but little approval, and though cups have multiplied under the management of bodies allied to the Union yet there has never been a serious effort made to institute a competition open to all clubs in membership of it.

G. ROWLAND HILL.
(From a Photograph by Morgan and Kidd, Greenwich, S.E.)

When I state that, on the whole, I consider that cups have been prejudicial to the game, I am aware that I lay myself open to the charge of want of consistency, as in my own county of Kent I supported the introduction of the system. The competition was introduced in Kent as a last resource, in the hope of stopping the game from dying out in certain parts of the county. Cup competitions have undoubtedly created a large amount of interest, and if, after they had given a genuine impetus to the game, they could have been dropped, good rather than evil might have resulted from them, but in some districts the system has been permitted to assume very large proportions, and it is responsible for many evils which have crept into the game, notably betting, which is an unmitigated curse to any branch of athletics which it contaminates.

For season 1881-2 the president and vice-president were the same as in the previous season. W. Wallace, whilst still retaining the post of treasurer, resigned the secretaryship, and the position was filled by the writer, who has had the privilege of holding it up to the present time.

At the suggestion of H. Vassall, who at the time was

captain of Oxford University, a new match was arranged between London and a combined team of the Universities of Oxford and Cambridge. The fixture has been continued ever since, and has been of the greatest assistance to the authorities in the selection of the South team. The London team of recent years has not only been selected from Metropolitan clubs, but also from Western and Midland clubs, so that the match is now the very best trial match for the South team. Trial matches have been tried to assist the Northern members in the selection of the North team, but have been found unnecessary owing to the keen interest in county fixtures, which supply the requisite opportunities properly to judge the merits of players.

Whilst touching on the question of selection of teams, it may be of interest to point out the mode of selecting players for the South and International matches. The Northern members of the Union Committee choose the North team, and the Southern members the South team. The International teams are chosen by a sub-committee of six, three of whom are Northerners and three are Southerners. The full committee have the power of altering the recommendations of the sub-committee.

In January, 1882, a Special General Meeting was called by Yorkshire representatives to consider proposals dealing with the place at which general meetings should be held, and the question was again raised of giving penalties for "off-side" play. A proposition to give power to the referee to order players off the field for wilful breaches of the law or foul play was also considered.

The general meetings had always been held in London, and the proposal to have the meetings alternately in the North and South met with little favour at the meeting. In the following March, at the usual general meeting, Bye-law 1 was altered so as to make it clear that they should always be held in London. An attempt to alter this bye-law has been made from time to time, but it has not met with the general approval of the football community, even though, at the meeting held in September, 1891, a majority voted in favour of the alternate system, but, as a two-thirds majority is required to carry an alteration in the bye-laws of the Union, and this not being obtained, the bye-law remains unchanged. It should be pointed out that the majority was almost entirely composed of Yorkshire representatives, which county, owing to a regulation which does not permit a club to enter the Yorkshire Cup Competition unless the club belongs to the Rugby Union, has by this means alone largely increased the numbers of its clubs in membership with the parent body.

I am accurate in stating that the majority of clubs in every other district in England are opposed to the change, so in view of the widespread and significant opposition to the proposal, it is to be hoped that it will not be pushed any further; that the change would be detrimental to the good government of the Union I have no shadow of doubt. London has been found to be convenient for representatives from all parts; the work done at the meetings has been the result of a general consensus of opinion, not affected specially by the views of the workers in any particular district. If a change is made, the meetings will lose their representative character; the body will be governed by sections; reprisals will inevitably arise: one district will be found when its opportunity comes endeavouring to upset the decisions of the other, and the continuity of policy which has produced such good effects would be at an end. Though at this meeting no penalty laws were passed, yet the committee showed that the necessity for their introduction was becoming more fully realised by promising that they would carefully consider the subject and report on it; the other proposals respecting wilful breaches of the laws and foul play obtained but little support; steps have, however, had to be taken since to deal with these matters. This is another instance of the general unwillingness for change which exists, unless practical experience shows the necessity, a perfectly sound doctrine so long as we do not allow our unwillingness to blind us to the signs which arise and which should be used to form our judgment. These proposals were literally scouted at the time: now sad experience has made converts of all the authorities.

As the result of the promise to consider the off-side question, at the March meeting the committee proposed penalties. They were not of a very stringent character, as, for instance, from the "free kick" awarded a goal could not be secured.

Time has proved that this penalty did not meet the requirements, reference to which will be made further on in these pages. The experiment of having neutral referees for International matches was tried this season, and gave general satisfaction: the system has now been thoroughly adopted in all matches.

For the season 1882-83 J. Maclaren was appointed president, and L. Stokes joined F. I. Currey as vice-president. J. Maclaren was the first Northerner to hold this position. He has rendered and still renders the most valuable services to the Union. It was at his suggestion that the first match was played between the North and the South, and he has laboured incessantly to create and cement a good feeling between players in both divisions of the country. No matters of special interest cropped up that season: peaceful progress alone reigned supreme.

In the season 1883-84 the officers were unchanged. At the October General Meeting several alterations in the laws were passed: the practice of "punting-out," which had almost grown into disuse, was done away with, and the practice of allowing a second try to be obtained after an ineffectual shot at goal was abolished. Both of these changes were great improvements. "Punting-out" had long lost its scientific points, as were exemplified in the old Rugby game, and of recent years had only been used to obtain a "tricky" second try. As regards the other point, the practice of the attacking side charging before the kick had become prevalent, and further in those cases in which a player who secured a second try had acted quite fairly, the score resulting was out of all proportion to the piece of play which obtained it.

The "maul in goal" question was also then considered: a proposal to abolish them altogether was made, and has since from time to time been repeated. Nevertheless, the "mauls in goal" have been able to maintain their miserable struggling existence even up to the present time, partly owing to their comparatively rare occurrence, and partly from the difficulty of finding a satisfactory solution of the question. Under the new laws "mauls" have been abolished.

This season will be noted for the unfortunate difficulty which occurred between the Rugby Union and the Scottish Union, arising out of the International match played at

Blackheath. To start with, I would point out that the
Scotch, Irish, and Welsh Unions played at that time
identically according to the laws of the Rugby Union,
and one of the most unfortunate outcomes of this dispute
was the breaking up of the practice by which players in all
parts of the globe played according to the same code of laws.

I will briefly give the facts which gave rise to the
dispute.

In the course of play, the ball was knocked back by
a Scotsman (ruled so by the referee, E. Scriven, a well-
known Irish player), one of the English team secured
it, and a try was obtained. The Scotch claimed that
"knocking back" was illegal: the English held that it
was not an illegal act, and even though it had been, the
act was done by a Scotsman, and as no Englishman
claimed for it (decided by the referee), the Scotch could
not claim for or profit by their own infringement.

The Scotch Union held that the point should be
adjudicated on by a neutral person: the Rugby Union
maintained that as it was a question of fact on which the
referee alone could decide, they could not agree to the
point being submitted to a neutral party, and they
claimed the match as a win for England. A long
correspondence took place, and as during the season of
1884-85 the Unions were unable to come to a satisfactory
agreement, the England *v.* Scotland match was not
played in 1885. No further steps were taken in the
matter until early in 1886, when a proposal was made by
H. G. Cook, then the hon. sec. of the Irish Union, that
representatives of the various Unions should meet to
talk over the matter. To this proposal England and
Scotland consented, and a meeting was accordingly held
in Dublin in February of that year: the result of that
meeting was that Scotland awarded the match to
England on the understanding that England joined an
International Board composed of equal representatives of
the four Unions, whose duties would be to decide any
dispute which might arise in future International
matches on questions of construction of points of law.
It was hoped that this arrangement would have put an
end to the international difficulties. Unfortunately this
was not to be. An alteration made in the scoring law by
the Rugby Union in October, 1886, brought the matter up again. Previous to this change being made,

the practice in vogue of consulting the other Unions before proposing alterations in the laws had been adopted; but none of them were prepared to give a decided opinion. However, when the change had been carried they jointly protested against its coming into operation in International matches, and England agreed to play during the season 1886-87 according to the old system, as the matches had been arranged with the other Unions prior to the date on which the scoring law had been altered.

LORD KINGSBURGH.
(From a Photograph by J. Horsburgh, Edinburgh.)

During the next season, 1887-88, the other nationalities did not play England. They desired to extend the powers of the International Board so that the laws guiding International matches should be made by that body. The Rugby Union held that the Board would inevitably become the law-makers of the game in general, and that therefore, in justice to the number of clubs they governed, they could not join on a basis of equal representation with the other Unions. Repeated efforts were made to come to an amicable settlement, but no step had a practical result until December, 1889, when the Rugby Union offered to submit the whole question to arbitration. The other Unions fell in with this proposal, and Lord Kingsburgh and Major Marindin, who kindly had in the meantime consented to act as arbitrators, met in April, 1890, and shortly after gave their award.

MAJOR MARINDIN.
(From a Photograph by Fradelle & Young, Regent Street, W.)

I give the portion of the award which defines the regulations of the Board.

1. International matches shall be played under one code of laws.
2. The laws presently existing of the Rugby Football Union, except such parts of Laws 25 and 30 as impose a penalty of a free kick if the ball be knocked on when thrown in from touch, shall be the first code of laws for International matches.
3. The International Rugby Football Board shall consist of twelve members, six of whom shall be elected to represent England, two to represent Scotland, two to represent Ireland, and two to represent Wales.
4. The International Board shall have power to settle all disputes arising at or in connection with International matches, by a majority of their number.
5. The International Board shall have power by a majority of not less than three-fourths of their number to amend, alter, or cancel any law in, and add new laws to, the International code.

The warm thanks of the football community are due to these gentlemen for their labours. I trust, as I know it to be their wish, that they have been the instruments in making a lasting settlement. I now go back to the season of 1883-84. On account of increasing interest in county football in that season it was felt that the necessity had arisen for defining the qualifications for county players, and at a meeting of representatives of counties, regulations were agreed to which have worked well. Year after year since that time county football has gone on prospering, and owing to a general demand in March, 1888, the Union Committee, much on the same lines as those previously agreed to, recommended regulations binding all the counties, and these were accepted at the general meeting.

At the commencement of season 1884-85 F. I. Currey was appointed president, and the late G. T. Thomson became a vice-president, and the treasurership was taken by H. Vassall. The new president was one of the original founders of the Union, and he has from its earliest days even up to the present moment faithfully served the Union. The late G. T. Thomson was the first Yorkshireman to hold the office of vice-president, and from the good services which he rendered to the game richly deserved the honour conferred upon him. In H. Vassall the Union secured as good a treasurer as an athletic body has ever had, and it is with great satisfaction we note that he still retains the post.

For the season of 1885-86 the same officers were appointed as for the previous season.

It had been felt for some time past that there was a necessity for clearly defining the duties of the referee and umpires, and the matter was considered during the summer of 1885 by the Union Committee. The result of their labours was brought before the October meeting of that year, and an excellent code of regulations was adopted. These regulations have well borne the test of time, and have merely been added to as the alterations in the laws giving increased powers to referees have required.

For the first time the introduction of the "whistle" and "flag" was tried, and the wonderful success which has attended its introduction must cause those who had the experience of umpiring or refereeing prior to this time, to reflect how it was possible that they were able to carry on their work at all: the difficulty of letting players know when an appeal was granted, and the uncertainty as to the decision of the referee caused endless stoppages and confusion. Few things have done more to improve the game than the whistle system. Players have absolute security in stopping when they hear it. This point has several times been before the Union Committee, and they have never deviated from deciding in accordance with this principle.

Whilst dealing with this question reference should be made to a further change which has been made in recent years, viz., allowing a side to claim to have touch judges instead of umpires. It is not pleasant to have to admit that this alteration was largely made owing to the fact that umpires in many cases had lost their sense of fairness in acting in matches in which their own clubs were engaged. It is a monstrous thing that a team in many cases should be a loser by having a fair umpire, but quite apart from this consideration the "referee and touch judge" system is vastly superior to the old one. The referee is able to give his decisions with much greater promptitude, and we believe with equal if not with greater accuracy. Under the old system his attention was diverted from the game by the necessity to watch the umpires, and in many cases from unfairness, incompetency, or slowness, they were a serious hindrance to him. I admit that some points do occur which a referee is unable to see, but I am strongly of opinion that in most of such cases he would not receive much assistance from an umpire. I think the majority of players like the change; I know that most of the referees whom we have met are delighted with it; some of the best in the country have mentioned that they would decline to act in cases where umpires are appointed.

A proposal emanating from the Football Association for the Union to join with them in a charity festival was cordially approved of by the committee. The result of the festival was that a substantial sum of money was devoted to charitable purposes. A similar understanding has several times since been carried out with marked success, and it is cordially to be hoped that such an excellent institution will not be permitted to die out: it gives players and spectators an opportunity to help the noble cause of charity. It is gratifying to know that in many districts those in authority have under this head recognised their duty.

During this season, 1886-87, His Royal Highness the Prince of Wales graciously consented to become Patron of the Union. Important changes were made in the officers. L. Stokes became president, and A. Budd one of the vice-presidents, the former in my opinion certainly the most scientific player that played in his own time. It is a very difficult matter to compare him with men of the present day, as the game has in the last few seasons altered so much; and my judgment may be at fault, however I feel that he possessed those qualities which would have enabled him, even at the present time, to be equal, if not superior, to any of our players. The new vice-president has been, and is, one of the most useful friends the game has ever had. He, in conjunction with H. Vassall, wrote for the *Football Annual* "Hints on Play," the ablest production on the game which has ever been given to the public. In all parts of the world where the game is played it has been reproduced, and has proved invaluable to players.

At the October General Meeting the committee of the Union brought forward a series of regulations dealing with the question of professionalism. There had been rumours abroad for some time past that players had been making money or improving their position in life by playing football. The aim of these regulations, broadly

speaking, was to prevent profit of any sort being made
out of the game. The proposals were unanimously
adopted, and met with the cordial approval of the leaders
of the Union in all parts of the country. They were of a
far-reaching and stringent character. By this action the
committee and the football public pledged themselves to
be the deadly opponents of professionalism. The committee have faithfully endeavoured to grapple with the
evil, and are at the time of writing as determined
opponents of it as ever. The professional has, however,
shown himself, and more in Yorkshire than in any other
county. The manner in which the Yorkshire Union
have grappled with the question is very much to the
credit of that energetic body. They have taken the
right course in fearlessly attacking leading clubs in
cases where suspicion has arisen, and they have in
numerous cases proved their point, and dealt out punishment to the offenders. I feel bound to give some
reasons for the consistent support that I have given
to the suppression of professionalism. Firstly, I hold
that it is injurious to the individual who becomes a professional. A man finds for a time that it is more re-
munerative to play football than to follow his regular
occupation. He is induced in many cases to give up his
work at an age the most important in his life for forming
habits of industry; he does not realise that a man cannot
play for many years in sufficiently good form to earn good
wages from the game. After a time his play falls off and
he has to go. He has got out of the way of work, and lost
valuable time in which he should have been learning a
trade. He then recognises that football has unfitted
him for other work, and finds it very difficult to get any
employment; and if he is able to get work it will probably
be at a much smaller rate of wage than he would have
received if he had from the first stuck steadily to work.
I am often met in discussing this question with the
statement that professionalism has not worked badly
in cricket; to this I give my assent, but I decline to
admit that cricket and football can be dealt with on
parallel lines. As stated above, a man can only play
football in good form for a few years, and then he has
nothing to fall back upon; whilst a cricketer can retain
his form for a long number of years, and when getting
on in years he can still be a ground bowler, a teacher of

the game, a ground man or an umpire, so that through cricket a man can get genuine occupation for a number of years.

I believe that professionalism would increase rough play. The necessity to win will be felt more by the paid player than by the amateur, the necessity to win will create a determination to win at all hazards; this will inevitably lead to rough play. These two points have much influenced me in forming my judgment.

I know that there are numerous other arguments

A FREE KICK: PLACING THE BALL.
(*From an instantaneous Photograph by E. Airey, Bradford.*)

against professionalism which will be given in this book by abler pens than mine. A. Budd has written a very vigorous article for this work on the subject, in which he deals exhaustively with the question in all its bearings, and I am quite content to leave this part of the subject to him. At the same time I would record my own opinion that the admission of professionalism would be injurious to the Rugby game.

At the same meeting the scoring laws were again on the *tapis*, and an alteration was agreed to. The matter had been prominently before the public for some time past, and the power of the "goal," to maintain which such struggles had been made, was now to be somewhat shorn of its glory. It was decided that three tries should equal a goal, a useful but cautious reform. The question, though partially settled, was not to be entirely closed. There were a large number of men who thought that three tries should be equal to more than a goal; and supporters of this view have persistently kept it forward, and a further change was made in September, 1891, by which three tries are superior to a goal.

The law as it now stands is as follows—

A match shall be decided by a majority of points; a try shall equal two points; a penalty goal shall equal three points; a goal from a try (the try not also to count) shall equal five points. Any other goal shall equal four points. If the number of points be equal, or no goal be kicked or try obtained, the match shall be drawn.

In coming to this arrangement a compromise was effected. This is a question on which a very wide divergence of opinion exists. In such cases unanimity of action can only be attained by a spirit of compromise being displayed.

This alteration received the approval of the other Unions. It is eminently satisfactory that this general approval has been obtained. It will be very unwise to do anything that may interfere with this unanimity unless the very strongest reasons arise for it.

During the season regulations dealing with the insurance of players from accident were passed. There is nothing in principle wrong in permitting clubs to insure their players; care must be taken that under the guise of insurance, players do not make a profit out of the accident fund.

For the season 1887-88 the officers remained as before. No International matches took place this season, owing to the deadlock to which reference has been made.

To make up for these matches a return North v. South match was for the first time played; this procedure met with general approval. A team under the management of Messrs. Shaw and Shrewsbury went over to New Zealand and Australia. This was the first undertaking of the kind, no other team having ever gone to our colonies. The Union Committee, while not interfering with the enterprise, were unable to give any encouragement to it. They regarded it as a money-making speculation, and further, as it was not under the management of any recognised body in the colonies, they refused to support it. Proposals of a like character had in the past been before the committee: in dealing with these matters they endeavour to act up to these two principles:—

First. That no one identified with the team, either as a manager or a player, shall make money out of such projects: and, secondly, that a team shall not go out to the colonies unless under the auspices of a recognised body out there.

The tour was a success. The team was a fairly strong one, and by playing together became formidable, and gave to our colonial friends a scientific exposition of the game. In playing according to the Australian code, which widely differs from the Union laws, they did as well as was expected of them.

For the season 1888-89 A. Budd became president, and the vice-presidents were H. W. T. Garnett and E. T. Gurdon.

During the summer of 1888 a sub-committee of the Union considered the question of further penalties for infringements of the laws, and, in consequence of their report at the October General Meeting, numerous alterations were made.

It was determined that a goal could be scored from a free kick penalty for off-side play, and numerous other free kick penalties were enacted, from all of which goals could be obtained, except that for a "knock-on out of touch," which has since been done away with. The changes have worked well. There are a small section of players who will act unfairly if they consider it pays their side to do so. To this class the penalties have acted as an excellent deterrent; they have had the effect largely of making a side a loser instead of a gainer by unfair play. The questions of rough play and the disputing of referees' decisions were also dealt with, and power was given to the referee to order a player off the field for rough play, and to report to the Union Committee cases in which his decisions were disputed. Since then power has also been given him to order players off the ground for such conduct. The effective dealing with these two questions vitally affects the game. With an iron hand rough play must be suppressed, or rough play will suppress the game. A sympathetic public, increasing from year to year in their interest for our game, watches with anxiety the efforts of those in authority to grapple with this question. Referees may be assured of the determined support of the Union and County Committees if they use the powers given them to stamp out the evil. The treatment of referees, much to be deplored, is becoming worse and worse—not, we mean, that players in many cases act so as to be able to be dealt with by the laws, but the growling and exhibition of discontent to which referees are subjected after a game is over is most painful. Continually one is told of a wrong decision given by such and such a referee. This grumbling and growling is a species of disease from which, we regret, all classes of players are suffering. No laws can meet this evil: good feeling and good sportsmanship can alone effect any good.

On this question I would give expression to feelings of the greatest anxiety. There is an increasing demand for referees who are qualified to act, but there is a decreasing desire on the part of such men to undertake the post. The task is a most difficult one under the most pleasing conditions, but it is an intolerable one if the referee is not treated properly. It will be a bad day for the game when those best qualified to act decline the post; but if the good feeling of players is not aroused, the danger is imminent.

During the season a New Zealand team, largely composed of Maoris, visited this country. They decided to come on their own responsibility, without receiving encouragement from the Union. However, that body felt bound to arrange matches for them, and an excellent programme was prepared. Matches were played with English, Irish, and Welsh clubs, and with the International teams of the respective countries. Their play, though unscientific at the start, showed great improvement before the tour was concluded. They made very good matches with several of the leading clubs. The tour was not, however, without some unpleasant incidents. I am of the opinion that the result will confirm the authorities in their decision to give no encouragement to a similar undertaking unless it comes under the auspices of some recognised body in the colonies.

This season several cases of professionalism were brought before the committee. It was found that it was quite impracticable for them to deal satisfactorily with them, consequently they decided to delegate to the County Committees power to deal with such cases, reserving to themselves the right to override the decisions of those bodies; at the same time they allowed, on a deposit of £50 (which deposit can be forfeited), an appeal to them from a club against a decision of a County Committee. These powers have been wisely used. There has only been one case of appeal, and on that occasion the deposit was forfeited.

Owing mainly to the International deadlock, it was decided, with the approval of all the County Committees, to institute a match between the Champion County and the Rest of England. This fixture has, however, been continued, even though the International difficulty is at an end, and has proved a decided success. Not only has it created a great amount of enthusiasm—more especially amongst the clubs in the Champion County—but it has also been of great service to the committee in choosing the teams against Scotland on the occasions in which it has been found practicable to play it before the Scotch match. Since the introduction of the match a well-defined code of regulations has been adopted for deciding the championship.

For the season 1889-90, H. W. T. Garnett was appointed president—the first Yorkshireman to hold this office—and W. Cail joined E. T. Gurdon as vice-president. Both the newly-appointed officers in their respective districts, as well as on the Union Committee, have rendered the game invaluable services. At the October General Meeting it was resolved to fix a "close time" for playing; it is now illegal for the game to be played (between May 1st and August 31st) on any ground where gate money is taken.

In the next season 1890-91, E. T. Gurdon became president, a position which, at the time of writing, he still occupies, and Roger Walker became a vice-president.

The former captained the English fifteen for several years, and was one of the best forwards of his day, and is an excellent and popular president. The new vice-president is an old Lancashire and International player; is a real good friend to the game. At the General Meeting in October, 1890, the "free-kick" penalty for "knock-on out of touch," to which reference has been made, was done away with. This was the only point on which the arbitrators decided that the International Board laws should differ from those of the Union; and in taking this earliest opportunity of making this alteration, the Union showed their desire to do everything in their power to again get established one universal code of laws by which all players should be bound.

To further this good object at this meeting, alterations were also made in the "maul in goal" and "offside" laws, in accordance with the Scottish laws. At the first meeting of the newly-constituted International Board, held in November, 1890, at Manchester, these changes were unanimously adopted, and the Rugby Union code became identical with that of the Board.

At the request of the March General Meeting, the Board having considered the scoring question, recommended the alteration to which reference has been made, and the change was adopted at the General Meeting, 1891.

At the time of writing the Board are engaged upon the task of recodifying the law; there is very good reason to hope that success will attend their efforts. The Union code of laws adopted at its formation in 1870, have, under the circumstances, worked extremely well. The game has very much changed, and the frequent and important alterations in the laws have made the code somewhat of a patchwork one. W. Cail has given a very clear head, and a very large amount of time to the work of recodification, and the Board are working on his draft. It is very much to be hoped that a code will be arrived at which will satisfy all the nationalities.

During the summer of 1891, a team got together by the Union Committee, captained by W. E. Maclagan, with Edwin Ash, the first hon. secretary of the Union, as manager, went out to the Cape. The team were the guests of the football authorities in South Africa; all expenses were guaranteed by them, but there was nothing of a money-making speculation in the undertaking. From a football as well as from a social point of view, the tour was a great success. The team did not lose a match, though they had some hard struggles. There are good grounds for concluding that their success has in no wise discouraged our colonial friends. They appreciated fully the scientific points of play of their opponents, and profited by their example. I have little doubt that in the future a representative South African team will be found well to hold its own with the best of British teams.

For the present season, 1891-92, the officers are the

THE KICK-OFF: READY FOR THE KICK.
(From an instantaneous Photograph by E. Airey, Bradford.)

same as last season. At the General Meeting at the commencement of the season the professional question was again to the front. Instances of the migration of players from one club to another had occurred under circumstances which, to say the least, were open to grave suspicion. It was felt that such practices were likely to lead to veiled professionalism, and that it was desirable to have some control over migratory players, so regulations dealing with the transfer of membership from one club to another, and from one county to another were adopted, as also were regulations dealing with the formation of leagues. An addition was also made to the bye-laws, by which it is enacted that only clubs entirely composed of amateurs are eligible for membership of the Union. We hope and feel that the action taken at this meeting more than ever binds our clubs and the committee not to alter their policy on the professional question.

In taking a general survey of the period about which we have been writing, we are amply justified in stating that during it the game has made wonderful strides in popularity, not only in Great Britain, but in the colonies; and in this development the Rugby Union has played an important part. This is illustrated by the large number of clubs which now subscribe to it. At the commencement of the season 1880-81, 130 clubs were on the books; at the present moment 388 are members. But this in no measure demonstrates the number of clubs which play according to its laws or are governed by its regulations. There is a large number of clubs which do not subscribe to the parent body, but which belong to county bodies; and Unions in the colonies, which are members of the Union; all of these are governed by the same laws and regulations. I cannot look back upon this period without being reminded that the hand of death has deprived the game of some of its best friends; I will make reference to those only who were officially connected with the Union. The earliest loss was that of W. Wallace, who was the secretary immediately before the writer took the office; he laboured long and faithfully for the game. The next to be taken away was H. Fox, the father of West of England football; his sad death was keenly felt by all who had the privilege of working with him. We then lost A. E. Hudson and G. T. Thomson, both of whom were Yorkshiremen, and had rendered invaluable services to the game. To this number must be added the names of J. D. Vans Agnew, and G. W. Burton, who for several years was one of the auditors of the Union. Both of these men were extremely popular, and left a host of friends behind them.

From the remarks that have been made, it will easily be gathered that the governing body of the Union have had their share of difficulties with which to contend. I may fairly say that they have wonderfully well surmounted them. This is owing to the generous confidence reposed in them by their clubs, as well as to the extremely good feeling which has existed amongst the members of the committee themselves. It has been a great pleasure to work with such a body of men. No miserable personal animosities have ever crept in to spoil the harmony of their work; they have been solely guided by a genuine affection for the game. I know there are difficulties at the present moment to be grappled with; but if the same spirit prevails as in the past, we may look forward with confidence to the future.

CHAPTER IX.

PAST DEVELOPMENT IN RUGBY FOOTBALL, AND THE FUTURE OF THE GAME.

By Arthur Budd.

NO one who watched a Rugby football match twenty years ago could have prophesied the wonderful changes the game has since undergone, or have foreseen that two decades would bring about an entire metamorphosis in the style of play.

When I played as a schoolboy at Clifton, where the Rugby School game—the progenitor of the Rugby Union game—was adopted in its entirety, the number of players was twenty a-side in an ordinary match, and, in the Sixth and School game, the latter were allowed forty to the twenty of their sturdier seniors. Old Boys who had gained their caps in bygone days were accorded the privilege of joining in all Bigside matches whenever they pleased, so that it was not at all an uncommon thing to see a dozen supernumeraries ranging themselves on one side or the other. Hacking over the first on-side was permissible, and tripping over a runner was quite as much practised as tackling. A player who could not take and give hacks was not considered worth his salt, and to put one's head down in a scrummage was regarded as an act of high treason. We were frequently boxed in a scrummage for three or four minutes together, only to discover that the half-back had by that time absconded with the ball to the other side of the ground.

The arrangement of the players behind was two half-backs, one three-quarter, and two whole backs.

Scrummaging was then the real article. It meant carrying the pack by superior weight and propelling power, and was not at all badly described by the definition which is still to be found in our present code, and which speaks of a scrummage as taking place when the ball is put down, and "all who have closed round on their respective sides *endeavour to push their opponents back, and by kicking the ball* to drive it in the direction of the opposite goal line." I cite this definition because it affords a graphic illustration of the magnitude of the change which has occurred since those days in the style of play. In 1870, the above definition presented a very fair picture of what a scrummage was; now (in 1892) it depicts exactly what a scrummage is not. Then, men pushed straight ahead might and main, while to heel out was regarded as unfair and discreditable: to-day, they never by any chance do the former, while they do not scruple to do the latter at their own sweet will.

An individual dribble was sometimes — though not very often — seen, but a concentrated dribble was an impossibility, owing to the extreme difficulty forwards experienced in extricating themselves from the scrummage *en masse*. Passing was an unearthed treasure bequeathed to the discovery and elaboration of more modern philosophers. Forwards, halves, and three-quarters played with a mutual irresponsibility, and without any notion of forming themselves into the links of the cleverly co-ordinated machine, which a high-class team of the present day can manufacture. In fact, the game might be summed up as one where the forwards pushed and plugged away, and gave and took punishment without stint or fear, where the halves ran and played for themselves, and the solitary three-quarter had to cover the entire field between the halves and two backs, who guarded the goal.

It is the conversion of these factors from isolation into machinery which has transformed the game from what it was to what it is.

And though this does not read like an attractive game, either to play or witness, such, I can assure the reader, was the case.

The fact is that the attractiveness of any game is, like everything else, in a great measure a question of habit and education. To the uninitiated, golf does not offer much fascination, yet its patrons — and they number amongst them some of our best athletes — assure you that there is no game like it; and I once heard the chairman of the Blackheath Golf Club, at a dinner of that venerable club, at which I had the honour to be present, describe it as "the king of sports, possessing all the glories of hunting without any of its dangers." This, I own, is not exactly the description I should, from what I have seen, have applied to it; but it serves to illustrate what I have said above, that you must understand and play a game before you are capable of pronouncing judgment on its merits. And so it was with the old Rugby game, which, notwithstanding its slowness and roughness, was a most enjoyable one, and demanded for success physical strength and pluck—both admirable qualities in a man.

I have often in old days heard spectators cheer vociferously over the prolonged equipoise of a well-balanced scrummage—just as you see the doubtful issue of a tug-of-war will provoke enthusiasm at an assault-at-arms. Your modern player and spectator would vote your trial-of-strength scrummage a bore, simply because hard-working, straightforward scrummaging has ceased to be a feature of the game, and has been supplanted by others which have proved more attractive. I once heard an old International three-quarter, on his return from the Cape, alluding in most uncomplimentary terms to the innovation of passing, and adjuring his team in Heaven's name to put a stop to "this infernal new passing game." *Tempora mutantur, nos et mutamur in illis.* Maybe posterity will smile at what we now regard with pride as our modern scientific game.

That the Rugby game in its infancy was a rough one no one could seriously dispute, and it is, I suppose, for the reason that the sins of the father are visited on the children, that this reputation, which the parent acquired, has stuck ever since like a leech to her progeny. To this day, despite the fact that the advance of science has removed the coarseness of the primeval game and reduced to a minimum the risks that attend it, the horrors of football still remain a favourite theme with journalists and correspondents; who, with a profound ignorance of what modern football is like, and without taking the trouble to go and see it played, burst forth into fiery philippics whenever an accident is recorded.

Hunting is the pastime of hundreds, football of

thousands; nevertheless, the percentage of accidents in the former is in excess of that of the latter. And yet, who, pray, ever yet read an article expatiating on the dangers of the hunting field, or suggesting the suppression of what has been dubbed the "King of Sports" on account of the perils which attend its pursuit? Skating, swimming, and rowing all contribute a larger percentage to the annual chapter of accidents, yet not one of these has been the subject of censure at the hands of petticoat penmen.

A LINE OUT: WAITING FOR THE BALL.
(From an instantaneous Photograph by E. Airy, Bradford.)

The real truth is that in every sport there is an element of danger. It would not be sport if there were not; and though it is, of course, possible to import brutality into football as into any other game, still, when it is properly played, the dangers of accident are as small as in any other department of sport; and the athlete who indulges in this healthy and manly exercise runs less risk of bodily harm than the bar-loafer who impairs his kidneys and liver with alcohol, or the billiard-saloon frequenter who loads his lungs with the carbonic-acid gas of a vitiated atmosphere.

And here, inasmuch as Inter-Public School matches have in the past been vetoed on the score of danger, I will digress to urge the advisability of their becoming a general institution under the present style of play. The experiment was years and years ago tried in a match between Clifton and Marlborough, but resulted in the expenditure of much blood and ill-feeling, and very wisely was not again repeated. Under the altered condition of things there is no fear of a repetition of such a fiasco, and the great number of Scottish Public School players who year by year gain their blues at the Universities is without doubt due to the institution of these matches in Scotland, which afford an admirable exchange and mart of style for the different schools. On two occasions, I have had the pleasure and privilege of umpiring when Wellington and Marlborough have met, and can testify to the game being played with an entire absence of roughness, and with the best of good feeling, and I confidently hope that the rest of our great public schools will hasten to follow in the footsteps of this most excellent example.

Such, then, was the game of the past, and from such materials at their disposal, time and science have evolved another of a totally different character. Indeed, I believe that the parent, if she could herself speak, would tell you that she had considerable difficulty in recognising her own offspring. The roughness of the Iron Age has yielded to the science of the Golden. The game is now as fast as it was slow, as open as it was confined. The new forward is not merely a robust propeller—indeed, it would be a misnomer to call many of our present forwards propellers at all—but fleet of foot, and versed in passing and concentrated dribbling. The half, who formerly played and ran for himself, is to-day essentially a conduit pipe between the forwards and three-quarters, and the latter, three and sometimes four instead of one in number, have constituted themselves into a machine for the transmission of the ball from one to the other.

The change from the old to the new, however, was not accomplished by a jump but by a gradual process, in which three departments of the game—forwards, halves, and three-quarters—have in turn played a separate part.

The first phase was a more open and a faster game by the forwards; the second, the introduction of passing amongst the forwards exclusively; the third, the passing by halves to the three-quarters; and the final, the passing of the three-quarters amongst themselves. The forward was the first subject to be infected by the epidemic, the centre three-quarter the last.

The reduction of the number of players from twenty to fifteen may be said to have marked the dawn of modern scientific football. At first, despite this reduction, the arrangement of the back players remained intact, but the forwards, no longer hampered by an overplus of numbers, found themselves able to take an active part in the open play. Fast following up, breaking away *en masse*, concentrated dribbling, and forward tackling henceforth became features of the game. In this departure the forwards were greatly assisted by the general recognition of the practice of scrummaging with heads down, which, instead of being regarded with disfavour as hitherto, had by degrees become one of the *sine qua non* qualifications of a good forward. This innovation was the landmark of scientific scrummaging. Henceforth players were able to watch with certainty the whereabouts of the ball, and try by skilful manipulation to control its destination, and, henceforth, for this very reason, which so much facilitated a means of exit for the ball, the breaking up of the scrummage became a comparatively easy matter. This fact the forwards were not slow to appreciate, and by breaking up the scrummage as quickly as possible placed this advantage to the scale of open play.

In breaking up the packs recourse has been had at different periods to three distinct methods: (1) "foiking"; (2) "heeling out"; (3) "screwing or wheeling."

"Foiking"—the definition of which would puzzle the ingenuity of a qualified referee who had weathered the exhaustive examination of a Yorkshire committee—was another name for a forward fishing at the side of the scrummage and extricating the ball with a sweep of the foot—it was, in fact, the correlative of screwing or wheeling, with a difference.

In "wheeling," the ball is first of all consigned to a back row of the scrummage, and there manipulated in the dark till a convenient opportunity for screwing the foe arrives; in "foiking," the extrication of the ball used to be laterally accomplished by a dexterous swing of the foot. In both cases the object in view was identical, viz., to get the ball out of the scrummage with forwards prepared to rush it onwards—a similarity of purpose with a variety of legerdemain, one trick being performed in the dark, the other in the light of day.

As in all fishing, so here, success very much depended on the skill of the angler. At one time, given an adept at the art, and forwards who thoroughly understood the little game, the method met with considerable success; but it may now be regarded as obsolete, and has been superseded by wheeling, an evolution which has the very obvious advantage of being carried out behind the screen of a row of forwards, and, moreover, is not dependent for success on the dexterity of a single individual. Wheeling and heeling-out I shall have occasion to refer to later on.

At a juncture when the forward game had made considerable strides in the direction of open foot-work, there stepped most opportunely on the stage a most important personage, the Genius of "passing," who was destined to play the leading rôle in the coming transformation scenes. It is not too much to say that his presence entirely revolutionised the game and succeeded in time in consolidating into a uniform machine the component parts of a football fifteen.

For a time, passing was confined to the forwards exclusively, and was what is termed "short" passing. The wonderful successes of the Blackheath Club in 1878-9, whose very fast and clever forwards may fairly claim the credit of being the first illustrators of the method, soon drew public attention to the innovation. The season's record was 54 goals, 30 tries, with 15 victories in 16 matches, a score they, to a large extent, compiled through the instrumentality of their forwards, who, in addition to possessing great pace, had thoroughly mastered the essence of the theory, which consisted in backing each other up broadcast and passing to the open side of the carrier. Forthwith the epidemic spread far and wide, and every southern club went in for the new school of play, though in their exaggerated efforts to imitate the inventors, many of them reduced the system to a burlesque. For some reason or other, which I am unable to fathom, the North for a long time did not catch on, and had to pay the penalty for their abstinence in a succession of defeats at the hands of the South.

When, then, the forwards, by their adoption of hand and foot play in the loose, had become formidable aggressors in the open, it was found that one three-quarter was no longer able single-handed to cover the field between the half and full-backs, and it became necessary to bring up one of the latter to reinforce him.

For some years this arrangement was adhered to. The first occasion on which the South played three three-quarters against the North was in 1882, when the South team was mainly composed of Vassall's Oxford team. The innovation came about in a somewhat curious way. P. Newton, who had been selected to play forward for the South, was unable to take his place, and H. Vassall had formed such a high opinion of the capabilities of Wade—an opinion more than confirmed by his subsequent career—that he wrote to the Selecting Committee strongly advocating his inclusion in the team. After much deliberation and some misgivings—for these were the good old days, when forwards really worked in a scrummage—the committee resolved to hazard the experiment. The success it met with practically settled the question, and for the future three three-quarters were universally adopted.

It was not long before the contagion of passing, which had attacked the forwards, spread to the half-backs. Hitherto they had played an individual game, but with three men behind them, who they knew must not be left idle in the cold, and with the means of transmission handy in the mechanism of passing, they were bound to consider their own play as subservient to providing the three-quarters with favourable opportunities. What half first set the example of "feeding" I am unable to say. Rowland Hill tells me that the first time he ever saw a pass by a half to a three-quarter was in the North and South match in 1881, when J. Payne slung the ball out to Bartram, who gained a try. There can be no doubt, however, that the man who reduced the art to a science, and thereby revolutionised half-back play, was A. Rotherham, of Oxford and Richmond—the equal of whom we have never, in my opinion, since seen.

This player, though coming from Uppingham School, where they do not, I believe, play the Rugby game proper, originated at Oxford a totally different half-back game from what we had hitherto been accustomed to see. He was the first to clearly demonstrate that a half-back ought not to run and play for himself, but ought essentially to be the connecting link between the forwards and three-quarters, and he showed how this ought to be done, not merely by stationary but by what I may term "opportune" passing, i.e., running himself and not passing till he had got his three-quarters on their legs, and till he had fogged his opponents as to whether they ought to go for him or the three-quarters he was intent on feeding. And he not only showed how and when to pass, but how and when not to pass, and how a half ought to run on himself when, by a feint, he had decoyed his tacklers to the three-quarter and left an open field for himself.

A. ROTHERHAM.
(From a Photograph by Hills and Saunders, Oxford.)

"Rotherham's game," as it was popularly called, created the type of an ideal half, and he still to this day remains the standard by which the qualities of players are measured, and the example which every half still strives to imitate.

And as a single individual was responsible for the change in half-back play, so are we indebted to another for the evolution of a centre three-quarter. What Rotherham did for the halves, Rawson Robertshaw, of Bradford, did for the three-quarters. Till he came on the scene and demonstrated that a centre ought not to play for himself but for his wings, a centre such as we look for nowadays was never before typified. His game might be described as a reproduction at three-quarter of Rotherham's at half, the idea of playing for his wings rather than himself, and feeding them by what I have previously termed "opportune" passing, being the main axioms which lay at the root of his theory. And thus he became the last existent link, though the future may add others—in the machinery which has brought about the co-operation of forwards, halves, and three-quarters.

Before I leave the past development of the game, I will revert to two devices in scrummaging to which I have previously alluded, viz., wheeling or screwing, and heeling-out.

The former is unquestionably at present the most fashionable method of scrummaging; and though it is a process which requires great skill in its execution, and has been the means of shortening the scrummages, still its introduction cannot, in my opinion, be considered an unmixed blessing. For, as I have previously mentioned, in order to screw successfully it is necessary that your side should first obtain possession of the ball. Having obtained it, the practice is to deposit it behind the first or second row of forwards, where it lies safe from the interference of your opponents, and to there manipulate it till you screw your adversaries off it and rush on with it yourself. All this has led to a most objectionable practice. What one now sees in every match, no matter where one goes, is that the moment the ball is put down in the centre of the scrummage both sides try to be the first to pull it back, and you will behold a forest of legs scraping for its possession. This *modus operandi* is extremely unfair, and entirely opposed to the spirit of the off-side laws, seeing that the bulk of the scrummagers are in front of the ball. It has, however, by general consent been admitted as legitimate, and it is, I am afraid, too late to protest against its continuance. I will therefore content myself with saying that this practice of scraping, and the practice of heeling-out, have done more than anything else to destroy honest scrummage work, the want of which is the greatest flaw in our present English style, and was undoubtedly the cause of our humiliating defeat last year at the hands of the Scotsmen. You cannot serve God and Mammon, and you cannot balance yourself on one leg and scrape for the ball with the other, and at the same time apply your weight instantaneously *so as to get the first momentum on a scrummage*—the latter a good old crusted axiom which has borne the brunt of time, and holds water to-day quite as well as it did twenty years ago. It is not wheeling in itself that I am objecting to, but the *modus operandi* employed, which is an unfair one, and has been the chief agent in inducing the now ever-growing inclination to shirk scrummage work. I should very much like to see a team such as the South team of 1882, which included such men as the two Gurdons, C. Wooldridge, and forwards who worked as well as played in the open,

LOOSE PLAY.
(From an instantaneous Photograph by E. Airey, Bradford.)

scrummage the scraping brigade. You would find, I think, that they would sweep the scrapers before them.

The other canker-worm of work is heeling-out. You can bet your bottom dollar that a team who habitually heel-out are no pushers. Their sole anxiety is to get the ball to their halves, and the same miserable scraping goes on as in wheeling. And here, again, I ask you, Is it possible for a man to be kicking backwards and pushing forward simultaneously? Of course not. Since football began it has been, and till football ends it will be, an enormous advantage to carry the scrummage. Do this, and you can swamp the best halves that ever put jerseys on. If, on the contrary, two sides are going to lean against one another and heel, it becomes a mere matter of chance which side gets it, and the very obvious advantage of routing your opponents—and this it is that wins games—is thrown away. You can depend upon it, that however much these devices may pay against teams who do not work, they are bound to break down against an honest scrummaging team, who, by their quick rush, will not allow you the requisite time for manœuvring, but will rout you pell-mell and submerge your play behind the pack. The real honest scrummager is a *rara avis* in England, and I very much fear that unless we foster the breed most carefully, he will soon be as extinct as the dodo.

But, in addition to this very serious mischief, heeling-out has been the originator of another of a still graver character. I allude to the now prevalent practice of half-backs on defence standing on their opponents' side of the scrummage. I can imagine nothing more directly opposed to the spirit of the game than this anomaly. If it is, as I fear it is, too late to stop heeling-out (and if we had foreseen what it was going to lead to we should have nipped it in the bud years ago), it is not, I hope, too late to put a stop to this latest creation of off-side play, which may, if admitted, entirely spoil the half-back's game of the future. I submit that the half-back so behaving is, clearly, an obstructionist under Law 40, and renders himself liable to the penalty of a free kick. For if it is not in order to spoil the play of his *vis-à-vis*, tell me, in the name of goodness, with what earthly object in view is he to be found out of his position, on the wrong side of the scrummage? The Yorkshire wing forward, who played a precisely similar game—*i.e.*, the spoiling of the half-back game—is severely dealt with by our code, but he is quite a mild creature as compared with this most recent form of pestilence.

To the best of my power, in the foregoing pages, I have endeavoured to trace the footsteps of development; and before I turn from the past to the future, I propose to briefly consider what we have gained and what we have lost by these changes.

That the game has been vastly improved from a

spectator's point of view, and that it is more open and faster at present than ever it was, there cannot be the shadow of a doubt. Nevertheless, in proportion as the whole tendency of modern play has been to weld a football team into a machine, so individual excellence has had, to some extent, to suffer. To illustrate what I mean, I will take the three-quarters. When the centre began to feed his wings, an enormous premium was put on pace, and it is a fact that at the present time a great number of the most successful try-getters are not football players at all, but sprinters pure and simple. I do not believe that there is a three-quarter back playing, who, if we could transplant him to the past, could cover the entire field as Lennard Stokes used to. In those days a three-quarter had not his chances made for him —he had to make them for himself. He was dependent entirely on his own resources, and had mainly to rely on his fielding, drop-kicking, and tackling powers. The pure sprinter would have been a fiasco; the position needed something more—a football player. To the premium thus placed on pace is, no doubt, due the deterioration in the drop-kicking of English back players. When the art was practised, in the days of one or two three-quarters, as it had to be a great deal more than it is now, it was neater and more accurate, and you could, in most cases, rely on the ball going into touch. At the present time, Lockwood is the only English player who can show us the old style of timely and accurate kicking.

I hope in making these remarks I shall not be considered a *laudator temporis acti*. As a machine, I confess that the game has improved, but whether or not the component parts of the machine are as good as they used to be some five years ago, I think is open to considerable doubt.

So much for the past, and so prolific has it been in changes that he would be a rash man who would dare prophesy what the future has in store. There is no reason, however, to suppose that the tendency will be other than it has been, viz., towards open play, and it follows as a corollary to this hypothesis that the faster the game the shorter will be the scrummages, and the shorter the scrummages the less the scrummage work.

The supposition, then, that the game will grow more and more open, and that forwards will henceforth rely on *finesse* rather than scrummage work, brings us face to face with *the* question of the hour: Is it advisable to play four three-quarter-backs?

Some years ago, in an article of mine on the game which, though scarcely up to date, still appears in the "Annual," I wrote very strongly against the system of four three-quarters. I did so on the ground that it is essential that your forwards should not be routed, and that, *cæteris paribus*, nine forwards ought to rout eight. This opinion was written before the introduction of wheeling and wholesale heeling-out, when forwards really carried the scrummages by weight and pushing; and if the forwards of that era were to appear *redivivi*, I would unhesitatingly reiterate that view. But things have altered, and it is now unanimously agreed upon by all who are qualified to judge, that, as far at all events as English play is concerned, scrummage work has reached a minimum. The Southern Selecting Committee, in choosing their team last season, decided to sacrifice brilliancy to work, and were confident that their forwards, whom they believed to be pushers, would carry the packs against the North, whom they knew to be exceedingly fast, but not gluttons for work. The event proved that their hopes were misplaced. The scrummages were very evenly balanced, and neither side can be said to have had the best of them. Again, it was regarded as a certain fact that the nine best English forwards were bound to over-run eight of Wales, yet no one who saw that match could say that we had any advantage whatever in the scrummage, though in the open we were undoubtedly superior. I am told by William Cail that eight forwards of Northumberland more than held their own against Durham, who had forsaken their former successful practice of four three-quarters; and I am told by the same authority that in their county match, eight Durham forwards had the better in the scrummage of nine Yorkshire forwards—reputedly the best county team in England.

With such data before me, which I could multiply if necessary, I am entitled to ask—Where does the advantage of your ninth forward come in? In the open he may, but in the pack he decidedly does not,

under the style in which we play in England to-day.
And I am also entitled to ask what other deduction
you can draw from these statistics, except that the
method of scrummaging no longer consists in getting
on the first momentum and carrying the scrummage
before you by pushing, but that it has resolved itself
into a game of *finesse*, in which the most skilful
manœuvres gain the day.

It then becomes a question, if you admit these
premises, in which position is the player, who makes
no material difference in scrummaging, best utilised—as
a forward, who, I own, strengthens the forward open
play, or as a fourth three-quarter?

In my opinion, which I submit with great deference,
for I know that the balance of expert judgment is
against me, I think there is no question about it.

In which position is the man most advantageously
placed, both from an offensive and a defensive point of
view? In considering the latter does it not stand to
reason that your defence at three-quarter is immensely
strengthened? Is it not a very much more difficult
job to get through four men than three? If not, then
one three-quarter is as good for defence as two, two as
three, and three as four. This reads like a self-evident
proposition, but as a great authority, for whose opinion
I hold the highest respect, is opposed to this view, I am
pleased to be able to confront him with mathematical
logic.

The same problem meets us when we come to
offence. Are not two men better than one? And assuming that you have skilful players who can pass with
machine-like rapidity I cannot for the life of me see
how one three-quarter can possibly check two who are
as good as himself.

The objection generally advanced against the system
is that the ground is not broad enough to afford room
for four. Those who advance this argument have surely
forgotten this most important fact, that it is not merely
the latitude at touch-line which a three-quarter has to
manœuvre in, but that the whole of the field can be
again retraversed.

For instance, the third three-quarter either (1) passes
to the fourth, or (2) feints to do so and runs on himself.
In either case the last three-quarter of the three-system

J

is at the disadvantage of two to one. Supposing, then, the third three-quarter has passed to the fourth, his wing opponent is bound to make for the latter, and if the fourth is wedged in on the touch-line it surely is a very simple thing for him to repass to the third, the third to the centre, and so on, so that one might imagine the ball, by rapid exchanges, travelling to and fro across the field *ad infinitum*. Your third three-quarter has to stop two of the four-system—he must go for one of

A TIGHT SCRUMMAGE.
(*From an instantaneous Photograph by E. Airey, Bradford.*)

them. If he makes for the wing the latter can repass, if for the third the latter can pass to the fourth. It is simply a question of stratagem, in which, believe me, two are bound to outmanœuvre one, if they are skilful players.

Again, by the four-system we are able to bring in short passing, which is both quicker and more precise than long passing, and, therefore, a far better thing.

The most inexplicable proceeding on the part of a great number of the opponents to the scheme is that when they meet four they play four themselves. I asked W. P. Carpmael why, when Blackheath meet Cardiff, they adopt the system, and his answer was that though he does not believe in the game he thinks it pays against four. But surely, if the three is the superior game, ought it not to pay better than four against four? I will leave Carpmael to solve this conundrum, and wait patiently but confidently for time to show me whether I am right or wrong in my opinion.

On this vexed question of four three-quarters there are some who suggest that the extra man should be employed as a flying man between the halves and three-quarters without any fixed position, but whom you could move as circumstances required—*i.e.* if on offence, to a position most favourable to give an opportunity to the three-quarters; if on defence, to a position where he could best stop his adversaries. The Maoris, when over here, tried this experiment, and, I believe, with some degree of success. It, however, does not to my mind possess the facilities for perfect mechanism which the four three-quarter system undoubtedly does.

Another eventuality which time may have in store is the reduction in the number of forwards. To such a change I should myself be very strongly opposed, for the reason that the game is quite fast enough at present, and by the innovation you would be putting a premium on pace and discounting qualities which we have hitherto considered as essential to a good Rugby forward. To my mind it is not desirable to reduce the game to a pure matter of speed. If you did, you would shut out many who are at present considered our best forwards. You would to a large extent exclude physique and strength, both admirable qualities in an athlete, and a great deal more Rugby in character than mere fleetness of foot. You would never again see such men as C. and E. T. Gurdon, Charles Reid or Gissy Graham—who, in my eyes, typify ideal forward play—I advert to this, not because there is any danger of an immediate movement in this direction, but because I often hear the question discussed, and I happen to know that several good judges are in favour of the innovation.

Apart, however, from the changes which may occur in the future from the alterations in the number or arrangement of the players and the advance of science, the question which will most materially affect the destiny of the Rugby game is that of professionalism. Since the working man has become so prominent an element in our game, there are many who advocate the introduction of professionalism *in toto*, and others, the moderate party, who are in favour of compensation for loss of time. And though both these schools may be honest and sincere in their opinions, I venture to think that they hold these views because they are enthusiasts in the welfare and success of clubs entirely or almost entirely composed of the working man, and have not thought out the problem of what would happen if he were allowed to get his living at Rugby football, or to be recompensed for his absence from labour. To begin with, if one were asked to define "sport," it ought to be described as a recreation pursued for love of itself, and devoid of emolument. To go a step further, you may accept it as a *lex non scripta* that into whatever branch of athletics an entrance has been opened for profit without amateur supervision, at the same door hand in hand there has stepped in also the element of corruptibility. Secondly, is it not an incontrovertible axiom that a man who gives his whole time and energies to a game is bound to outstrip another who only devotes his leisure moments to its pursuit? And thirdly, what professional sport is there which has thriven permanently under its own administration in this country, or which has not under the test of time sooner or later fallen a victim to corruptibility, disrepute, and sometimes absolute decay? The case of cricket may, *primâ facie*, seem to contradict these axioms, but on analysis will be found to confirm them. Our best amateur cricketers devote quite as much time to it as the professionals. As a consequence, while they are able to maintain an equality of play, they are at the same time able to retain a monopoly of government. But if W. G. Grace, A. N. Hornby, A. E. Stoddart, and others could not, by their constant devotion to the game, keep pace with the professionals as competitors, the power of governing would leave them with their inferiority of play. The answer, then, to those who urge that the working man ought to be compensated for the "loss of time" incurred by his recreation is that, if he cannot afford the leisure to play a game, he must do without it. How many splendid athletes are never heard of again when they leave their universities and schools, because they have to follow avocations which will not allow them to play football matches, which necessitate one, two, or three days' desertion of their profession?

If A. B. of the Stock Exchange were to ask for compensation for loss of time for a two-days' football tour, such compensation to be fixed on a scale commensurate with his earnings, the football community would denounce it as a scandal. A. B., the stockbroker, has therefore to stop at home at his desk because he cannot afford to play, but C. D., the working man, is to be allowed his outing and compensation for leaving his work, which under any other circumstances he could not afford to abandon. If, to come to my second point, a man who gives his whole time to a game is bound to best the amateur, who devotes only his leisure to it, the inevitable law of the survival of the fittest must intervene, and it simply becomes a question as to how long the amateur can survive. If ever a vivid illustration of the gradual process of amateur extinction were afforded to us, the Rugby Unionists, as though by Providence, it has been by the history of the Association game from the day that this body legitimised professionalism. I am correct, I believe, in saying that in the whole of the North of England and the Midlands there is not a single amateur football eleven. What does this mean? Why that the amateurs in those districts have been out-classed, and been submerged by professionals, and have now to seek other modes of recreation than Association football for their leisure. But a few years ago such clubs as the Old Etonians and the Old Carthusians were competitors in the final tie of the Association cup; this year every Southern amateur team was beaten in the first round of the ties. It comes then, to this, that where amateurs are not sufficiently numerous and powerful to form clubs amongst themselves, and play against each other, you get a professional absorption of districts; and while you allow a man to play for money, you prevent another playing for love of the game without emolument. Is this sport?

And, again, what does this professionalism lead to? Does it encourage native or residential talent, which, mark you, should be the first and only object of every football club? On the contrary, it leads to the wholesale importation of players of repute from other districts or, it may be, countries, to the exclusion of indigenous ability. Is this sport? I say, certainly not. It is nothing more nor less than handing over success in the game to the best capitalised club. If you could give me the wealth of the Duke of Westminster and professionalism in Rugby football to boot, I would in a very short time produce the most formidable fifteen in the United Kingdom. They should be called the "Charing Cross Crusaders," though, probably, on their arrival from the North the majority would have to make inquiries as to the whereabouts of that metropolitan centre. If the hiring of these aliens constitutes sportmanship, then Sir Augustus Harris, who, at great outlay, brings to Drury Lane the best pantomimists of the day, has earned this distinction equally as well as the controllers and financiers of our Association professional football teams. One can understand people becoming enthusiastic over a bona-fide club —that is, a club composed of players who have been born or reside in the district—but it is past my comprehension to understand how eleven men, transported from various points of the compass, can inflame with partisanship the natives whom they are actually excluding from the team which they ought themselves to be representing. The *summum bonum* of football and every other game consists in the encouragement and development of local ability, and not in the transportation of peripatetic exhibitioners. What further happens in this game of barter is this. As long as a team can win their matches they draw great gates, and with the money rolling in the extradition goes on, and the supply of recruits is maintained. But when a club loses its games it loses all its powers of attraction. The gates fall off, the coffers are depleted, and the once famous club gradually fades into insignificance. The financiers are no longer able to pay the professional his salary, and the latter packs up his trunk and departs either to his native soil or to some more prosperous "sporting" community, and the native talent which has been swamped cannot rise to the surface to fill the breach.

To sum up, the system of migration, which is a necessary concomitant of professionalism, must inevitably lead to (1) the extinction of the amateur, (2) the exclusion of native talent, and (3) the seduction by pecuniary inducement of players from (*a*) club to club, (*b*) county to county, or even (*c*) country to country. Is this sport? I should call it the prostitution of it. Games won, and great gates, read well in the newspapers, and I doubt not pander to the vanity of those people who can deceive themselves with the hallucination that renown accrues to Birmingham, Nottingham, or Preston by victories earned through the prowess of imported Scotsmen who have as much to do with either of those cities as I have with Jerusalem, forgetting the while that the whole credit of success attaches to Scotland, who bred and exported the materials of war, and not to themselves who have merely hired them. Scores and gates are not, thank goodness, the Alpha and Omega of our game; and the great game of football of either code was never invented by the schoolboy, who was the *fons et origo* of both, to provide a livelihood for professionals and exclude amateurs, or to become a medium of speculation for gate-money financiers. These, if we legitimise professionalism, are the dangers which face us, and the crisis is consummated in my last axiom, that no professional sport under its own government, and independently of amateur supervision, has ever yet permanently prospered in this country; and, though at the present time the Football Association, an amateur society, are nominally the governors of the game, there is no blinking the fact that with such an organisation as the League behind them the professionals could at any moment cast off the fetters of management of the head and elect to govern themselves. In illustration of my last contention take a retrospect of the past, compare the performances of the English professional and amateur, and tell me why it is that while the latter still remains in most branches of athletics invincible, and in all branches can still hold his own against the best competitors the two hemispheres can produce, there is not a single sport, save cricket, at which Australians, Americans, and Canadians have not soundly thrashed our professionals.

Take, as an instance, any English professional sport where there is not amateur intervention.

English professional rowers were once the best in the world. Where are they now? They have become absolute nonentities; and you cannot name an oarsman for whom a soul would put down his money for a match against an Australian or American, a Canadian, or a French-Canadian. The famous pair and four-oars of the

Thames and Tyne are a thing of the past, and a few
matches between third-raters, and Doggett's Coat and
Badge Race represent the melancholy ruins of a sport
which has first been degraded and has then decayed.
Mr. Innes, the greatest patron of English professional
rowers, found out to his cost the utter rottenness of English
professional rowing, and refused any longer to allow
his pocket to be made a raffle of by competitors. On
the other side of the picture you have our amateurs, *who
always have been and still are* the finest amateur oarsmen
in the world, and remain, as yet, invincible.

LOOSE GAME: FORWARDS FOLLOWING UP.
(*From an instantaneous Photograph by H. J. Whitlock, Jun., Birmingham.*)

Again, if it were not for the Sheffield Handicaps,
which are popular as a vehicle for betting, professional
running would be dead as mutton. The Cummings and
George, and the Hutchens and Gent matches are the
only ones of recent years which have excited public
interest, and yet never was amateur running so flourishing
or so ardently supported by popular enthusiasm as
at present.

And again, take the English professional boxer and
compare him with his ancestor—Sayers. In default of
anything like champion form—though, if it were not for
the low repute into which the sport has fallen, there are
heaps of champions to be found in this country—we have
to find purses for colonials to fight for.

And once more, and lastly, though one could multiply

examples, we know that the Cumberland and Westmorland Wrestling Society discontinued their annual Good Friday meeting because they found that the wrestlers from the North split up the prizes between them before they left for town.

Here is a catalogue of corruptibility and decay in branches where our professionals were once without rivals in other parts of the world, and in which our amateurs still remain so.

History repeats itself, and there is no reason to suppose that a Rugby football professional would be a more moral person than his fellow in any other branch, and spurn the temptations which fall across his path. On the contrary, the presumption is the other way, viz., that inasmuch as these temptations would be before him Saturday after Saturday, he would be more likely in time to yield to their influence upon him.

Moreover, it is not a game like cricket, which affords sufficient occupation to justify the devotion of a man's entire time to it. Three days a week are as much as anybody can play, and then only for an hour and a half at a stretch. This brings the total of the week's play to four and a half hours. Allowing for training and practising in addition to this, the greater part of a man's time would still remain unutilised. The profession of football, then, means a life of idleness while it lasts. But it is also a game at which a man cannot play for many years, and after his career is finished it leads to absolutely nothing; so that the superannuated professor, when his short day of activity is over, finds himself stranded without resources, and has to begin life again to get his bread.

If, with the lesson before them, which facts such as these so cogently supply, if with the warning of "breakers ahead," blind enthusiasts of working men's clubs insist on introducing professionalism, there can be but one result—disunion. The amateur must refuse to submit himself to the process of slow extinction which has been going on in the sister game, and say at once that henceforth he will play and compete with his own class alone, and let professionals for the future look amongst themselves for opponents. And if this black day comes, which I hope never will, it will be the duty of the Rugby Union to see that the division of classes dates from the dawn of professionalism, and not to wait, before seeking to apply a remedy as the short-sighted Associationists have done, to see the whole of the North and part of the South denuded of amateurs and given up to subsidised players. To them the charge of a game of great traditions has been committed, and, if they would be willing to consign the future of these to the baneful influence of professionalism, they would assuredly be betraying the trust reposed in them, and live regretfully to see the game of to-day depraved, degraded, and decayed.

CHAPTER X.

INTERNATIONAL MATCHES AND PLAYERS.
1871 TO 1880.

By Arthur G. Guillemard.

INASMUCH as the series of International matches played under the auspices of the Rugby Football Union has extended over a period of twenty years, and the annual meetings of the picked players of the four countries which, I hope, may long continue to form the United Kingdom, are the leading features in each recurring season, there is no occasion here to dilate upon their interest and value. A few words, however, are required by way of introduction to the records which follow.

It is not too much to say that in the year 1870 there were but very few English players who were aware that Rugby football had taken any hold upon the affections of Scotsmen; a twelvemonth later all knew it only too well. As stated in a preceding chapter, certain of the leading Scottish clubs—Edinburgh Academy, Edinburgh Academicals, Merchistonians, St. Andrews, and West of Scotland—declining to recognise a so-called England *v.* Scotland match under Association rules at the Oval as an International meeting, the dribbling game being almost unknown north of the Tweed, published a challenge in *Bell's Life* to play a picked twenty of England under Rugby School laws, during the winter of 1870-71. The challenge saw the light a few weeks before the Rugby Football Union was founded, and there was a little doubt as to who should pick up the Scottish glove. However, F. Luscombe, the energetic captain of the Gipsies, who was "spoiling for a fight," suggested to F. Stokes, then captain of Blackheath, that his club, as the oldest in point of foundation, ought to take the lead, and accordingly B. H. Burns, the Blackheath secretary, promptly wrote accepting the challenge. The principal clubs in London, Liverpool, and Manchester were communicated with, and a committee formed to select the players, choose a uniform, and make the necessary arrangements. The task was a difficult one, but the co-operation of the chief Northern clubs was enlisted, and a strong detachment of their best men joined forces with the Southern division. Unfortunately it was impossible to obtain the services of any member of the Woolwich Academy team, and of only one of Richmond, as also to arrange any trial matches; and thus the twenty suffered materially in the matter of individual players, and also of combination, for the first match between North and South was not played until three years after this.

Subsequently it became the custom to institute a series of trial matches, which were managed by a sub-committee, who selected the International team subject to confirmation by the full committee. For several years the Northern clubs were not represented by reason of there being no organisation or society capable of sifting the wheat from the chaff, and reporting to the Union Committee. But when J. MacLaren, R. Walker, and E. Kewley joined the committee, the selection of Northern players was placed in their hands, and the annual matches between North and South made the task of getting together a thoroughly representative team comparatively easy. And nowadays, with a plethora of county matches and club tours, the good and bad points of every leading player are well known to all the members of the English Selection Committee, who are carefully chosen according to their knowledge of the game, and have to attend all the Union matches. And it is satisfactory to note that it has never yet been asserted that a place in the English team has been gained by favouritism.

March 27th, 1871, Edinburgh.
Scotland beat England by a goal and a try to a try.

The first International match between England and Scotland was played at the Academy Ground in Raeburn Place, Edinburgh, on the 27th March, 1871. The weather was magnificent and the turf in excellent order, and an attendance of some 4,000 spectators showed that Rugby football had already attained considerable popularity north of the Tweed. The ground measured some 120 yards in length by 55 in breadth, and its narrowness compared with English grounds materially handicapped the excellent running of the English half-backs.

It was arranged before kick-off that the match should be played for two periods of fifty minutes each, that no hacking-over or tripping-up should be allowed, and that the ball should not be taken up for a run unless absolutely bounding, as opposed to rolling. There were other points, too, upon which the Scottish fashion of playing the Rugby game had to be followed. The match was very evenly contested until half-time, after which the combination of the Scotsmen, who knew each other's play thoroughly, and their superior training began to tell a tale, and after a maul just outside the English goal-line the umpires ordered the ball to be put down in a scrummage five yards outside the line. It was taken out accordingly, but, instead of putting it down, the Scottish forwards drove the entire scrummage into goal, and then grounded the ball and claimed a try. This, though illegal according to English laws, was allowed by the umpires, and a goal was kicked by Cross. England then penned their opponents for some time, and ultimately R. H. Birkett ran in close to touch, but the captain's place-kick, a long and difficult one across the wind, failed. Scotland gained another try just before "no side," Cross touching the ball down after an unintentional knock-on by one of his own side. His place-kick, however, was unsuccessful. The English twenty in this match averaged 12st. 3lb. per man, and the Scotch probably about the same. J. F. Green and F. Tobin for England and M. Cross for Scotland played splendidly behind the scrummage. The Scotch forwards were distinctly quicker on their feet, and in better training than their opponents.

In this match an extraordinary charge was made by Osborne. Finlay had got well away with the ball, and was sprinting towards the English goal at hundred yards' speed, when Osborne, folding his arms across his chest, ran full tilt at him, after the fashion of a bull charging a gate. Both were very big, heavy men, and the crash of the collision was tremendous, each reeling

ENGLISH TEAM V. SCOTLAND: EDINBURGH, MARCH, 1871.
(SCOTLAND—1 GOAL, 1 TRY. ENGLAND—1 TRY.)

J. E. Bentley, A. E. Gibson, F. Tobin, D. L. P. Turner, F. Stokes, J. H. Clayton, R. R. Osborne, J. H. Luscombe, A. St. G. Hamersley, W. McLaren, C. W. Sherrard, H. J. C. Turner, R. H. Birkett, J. F. Green, C. A. Crompton, A. Davenport, A. G. Guillemard, J. M. Dugdale, A. Lyon, B. H. Burns.

some yards, and finally falling on his back. For a few seconds players and spectators alike held their breath, fearing terrible results, but the two giants promptly resumed their places, apparently none the worse. Burns played as substitute for F. W. Isherwood, one of the best English forwards, who was unable, owing to an accident, to fulfil his promise to play.

A few words on the leading English players. F. Stokes, who learnt his football at Rugby, was a most excellent and popular captain of the English twenty for this and the two succeeding years, combining a thorough knowledge of the game with admirable tact and good temper, and being gifted with power of infusing spirit and enthusiasm into his team similar to that possessed by A. N. Hornby on the cricket field. As a player, he was one of the very best examples of a heavy forward, always on the ball, and first-rate either in the thick of a scrummage or in a loose rally, a good dribbler, very successful in getting the ball when thrown

J. F. GREEN.
(*From a Photograph by J. Weston & Sons Folkestone.*)

out of touch, a very long drop and a particularly safe tackle. For his club he often played half-back with success as, though not one of the fastest runners, his powers of "shoving-off" were very great. He was also one of the very longest and best of place-kicks. J. F. Green for several years was one of the most brilliant of half-backs, being an excellent field, and when once under way as speedy a runner as was ever seen with a ball under his arm, his stride being magnificent. Unfortunately an accident to his right knee obliged him to give up playing when he was quite at the top of the tree. F. Tobin was also a grand player, not quite so fast a runner as Green, but more dodgy. Of Bentley and his weight-carrying powers I have written in another chapter. R. H. Birkett, who played in four International matches, was very useful both forward and behind the scrummage, and had plenty of pace. A. St. G. Hamersley was a very tall, powerful forward, working most resolutely in the scrummage, and first-rate at getting the ball on its being thrown out from touch; his departure for New Zealand, where he did much towards improving the colonists' game, was a great loss to England. D. P. Turner, who played against Scotland in five successive matches, was a desperately hardworking forward, always keen and untiring, and as regardless of risk or danger as an Irishman. No fewer than ten of the English twenty—F. Stokes, A. G. Guillemard, A. Lyon, J. F. Green, F. Tobin, J. H. Clayton, A. Davenport, J. M. Dugdale, C. W. Sherrard, and D. P. Turner—were Old Rugbeians.

ENGLAND.—F. Stokes (Blackheath), captain; A. G. Guillemard (West Kent), A. Lyon (Liverpool), R. R. Osborne (Manchester), backs; W. MacLaren (Manchester), three-quarter back; J. E. Bentley (Gipsies), F. Tobin (Liverpool), J. F. Green (West Kent), half-backs; R. H. Birkett (Clapham Rovers), B. H. Burns (Blackheath), J. H. Clayton (Liverpool), C. A. Crompton (Blackheath), A. Davenport (Ravenscourt Park), J. M. Dugdale (Ravenscourt Park), A. S. Gibson (Manchester), A. St. G. Hamersley (Marlborough Nomads), J. H. Luscombe (Gipsies), C. W. Sherrard (Blackheath), D. P. Turner (Richmond), and H. J. C. Turner (Manchester), forwards.

SCOTLAND.—F. Moncrieff (Edinburgh Academicals), captain; W. D. Brown, and T. Chalmers (Glasgow Academicals), B. Ross (St. Andrew's University), backs; J. W. Arthur (Glasgow Academicals), F. Cross (Merchistonians), T. R. Marshall (Edinburgh Academicals), half-backs; A. Buchanan (Edinburgh University), A. B. Colville (Merchistonians), A. Drew (Glasgow Academicals), R. Forsyth (Edinburgh University), F. Finlay, R. Irvine, W. Lyall, and H. Mein (Edinburgh Academicals), J. W. McFarlane (Edinburgh University), D. Munro (St. Andrew's University), T. Ritchie (Merchistonians), F. Robertson (West of Scotland), and W. Thomson (St. Andrew's University), forwards.

FEBRUARY 5TH, 1872, THE OVAL.
England beat Scotland by 2 goals and 2 tries to 1 goal.

The second meeting of the two countries took place at the Oval, Kennington, on the 5th February, 1872, in presence of some 4,000 spectators, and under favourable circumstances of weather and ground. The English twenty averaged on this occasion 12 st. 8 lb. per man, whilst the Scotch but little exceeded 12 st., but were an extremely athletic and wiry lot. The ground set apart for play at the northern end of the Oval measured 120 yards by 70, and as a consequence of this additional breadth the running was far more brilliant than at Edinburgh the previous year. Matters opened auspiciously

for Scotland, for C. Cathcart, getting the ball out of
a loose scrummage, dropped a neat goal for Scotland
after some ten minutes' play. This caused the English
forwards, who, as usual, began rather slowly, to wake up,
and, led by the captain, F. W. Isherwood, A. St. G.
Hamersley, and D. P. Turner, they gradually forced
their opponents back into goal, where Hamersley
touched the ball down after a short maul. From this
Isherwood kicked a goal. The second half of the match
was principally remarkable for the grand forward play
on the English side, and for
a magnificent left foot drop
by Freeman, which obtained
a second goal for England.
D'Aguilar and Finney also
got in, but Isherwood's place-
kicks failed. England's victory was mainly due to their
excellent forward play, and
their extra weight and
strength told an unmistakable tale on the Scottish side
of the scrummage. They
were, possibly, one of the
fastest sets of forwards, considering their weight, that
have ever taken part in an
International match. R. P.

F. LUSCOMBE.
(From a Photograph by Messrs. Nics.)

Maitland (half-back) played very brilliantly for Scotland,
and Finney (half-back), and Freeman (three-quarters
back) faultlessly for England.

On this occasion several notable players made their
first appearance in an International match. Harold
Freeman, who played in three successive matches against
Scotland, dropped a goal in the first and third, and a
poster in the second. He was a very dashing three-
quarter back, a grand drop with either foot, a very sure
tackle, and possessed of great judgment and coolness in
a dilemma. S. Finney, who learnt the game at Clifton
College, was the crack half-back of this era; very quick
at picking up the ball and starting, and a brilliant runner;
especially good in a desperate rush through a crowd of
opponents when close to goal; towards the close of a
hard match he generally wore the appearance of having

been engaged in a prize-fight, but the more wounds he received the better he seemed to play. He was a deadly tackle, but possessed no dropping powers. F. Luscombe, an old Tonbridgian, who played four years against Scotland, was one of the very keenest of forwards, following up splendidly, and never sparing himself; very quick on his feet, a good dribbler, and a capital tackle. J. A. Body—a pocket Hercules—who hailed from the same school, was equally energetic and always on the ball. J. A. Bush, the well-known Gloucestershire wicket-keeper, was the giant of the team, and conspicuous in the centre of every scrummage; he played four times against Scotland. F. W. Isherwood was a grand forward—perhaps the best playing on this occasion—and very fast for his weight; also an excellent place-kick. Seven Old Rugbeians and four Old Marlburians played for England, who had six of the previous year's team, whilst Scotland mustered eleven. F. Stokes again proved himself an excellent general.

The following were the players:

ENGLAND.—F. Stokes (Blackheath), captain; A. G. Guillemard (West Kent), F. W. Mills (Marlborough Nomads), W. O. Moberly (Ravenscourt Park), backs; H. Freeman (Marlborough Nomads), three-quarter back; J. F. Bentley (Gipsies), S. Finney (I. C. E. College), P. Wilkinson (Law Club), half-backs; T. Batson (Blackheath), J. A. Body (Gipsies), J. A. Bush (Clifton), F. I. Currey (Marlborough Nomads), F. B. G. D'Aguilar (Royal Engineers), A. St. G. Hamersley (Marlborough Nomads), F. W. Isherwood (Ravenscourt Park), F. Luscombe (Gipsies), J. E. H. Mackinlay (St. George's Hospital), W. W. Pinching (Guy's Hospital), C. W. Sherrard, R.E. (West Kent), D. P. Turner (Richmond), forwards.

SCOTLAND.—F. Moncrieff (Edinburgh Academicals), captain, half-back; L. Balfour (Edinburgh Academicals), W. D. Brown, and T. Chalmers (Glasgow Academicals), backs; T. R. Marshall (Edinburgh Academicals), R. P. Maitland (Royal Artillery), three-quarter backs; J. W. Arthur (Glasgow Academicals), W. Cross (Merchistonians), half-backs; J. Anderson (West of Scotland), W. Bannerman (Edinburgh Academicals), C. Cathcart (Loretto), A. G. Colville (Merchistonians), J. Finlay, R. Irvine, W. Marshall (Edinburgh Academicals), J. H. L. McFarlane (Edinburgh University), J. H. M'Clure (West of Scotland), T. H. Maxwell (Royal Engineers), W. Mein (Edinburgh Academicals), and H. W. Renny-Tailyour (Royal Engineers), forwards.

MARCH 13TH, 1873, GLASGOW.
England v. Scotland. A drawn match.

The third match took place at the West of Scotland ground, Partick, Glasgow, on the 13th of March, 1873, and was drawn, England making their opponents touch the ball down on five occasions. When the English twenty arrived in Glasgow they found the country under snow, but this quickly thawed under a hot sun, and was followed by a downpour of rain which continued throughout the day. The turf was consequently spongy and slippery at the top, and the running of the backs was seriously affected. The ground measured 130 yards by 70, and was surrounded by some 5,000 spectators in spite of the miserable weather. The English twenty averaged 12st. 6lb. per man, and their opponents 12st. 1lb., but England's fourteen forwards (as compared with Scotland's thirteen) were at a slight disadvantage in point of weight. The forward play was very fairly even; behind the scrummage McFarlane made some very brilliant runs, whilst the half-back play of Finney and Boyle was beyond all praise, and the former on several occasions was within a foot or two of getting in. A magnificent drop by Freeman from a fair catch some 50 yards from the Scottish goal resulted in a poster, and thus no definite point was gained by either side.

M. W. MARSHALL.
(From a Photograph by Owen, Salisbury.)

In connection with this match a singular incident occurred. The greasy nature of the ground caused the English captain to direct his men to have bars of leather affixed to the soles of their boots. Freeman and Boyle, who with Finney were considered the most dangerous men on the side, reported, when the cobbler had done his work, that they were each minus a boot. Several of the team proceeded to ransack the cobbler's shop, but without success, and it was not until after the match—in which Boyle played with a dress boot on his left foot—that the canny tradesman produced the missing articles. Boyle, unfortunately, represented England on this occasion only; he came from Clifton College, and was Oxford's fast bowler this same year, but must not be confounded with C. E. Boyle, the Old Carthusian, who was in the Oxford eleven eight years before. He was a fine runner, and excellent tackle. S. Morse played three years in the English team, and was a dashing runner and good drop with either foot. Hon. H. A. Lawrence was a very keen, hard-working and indefatigable forward, and followed up brilliantly. M. W. Marshall, hailing, like Lawrence, from Wellington College, played in no fewer than ten International matches—six v. Scotland, and four v. Ireland—and was in every respect one of the best forwards England ever turned out. Possessed of great height and strength, he was invaluable in a scrummage, used his feet well when the ball got loose, and was a very clever tackle.

The public schools were well represented this year, the team including five Old Rugbeians, five Old Marlburians, three Old Cliftonians, three Old Wellingtonians, and two Old Tonbridgians.

Scottish hospitality ran high at Glasgow, and this perhaps is accountable for the fact that a certain gallant English forward was found by some of his colleagues shortly after midnight, driving one of Her Majesty's mail carts to the railway station. They fortunately succeeded in persuading him that he had done quite enough work already, or he might have found out to his discomfort that the verb "to run in" could be used by a policeman in the active sense as effectually as by a football player in the neuter.

The following were the players :—

ENGLAND.—F. Stokes (Blackheath), captain ; F. W. Mills (Marlborough Nomads), S. Morse (Law Club), C. H. R. Vanderspar (Richmond), backs ; H. Freeman (Marlborough Nomads), three-quarter back ; C. W. Boyle (Oxford University), S. Finney (I.C.E. College), half-backs ; J. A. Body (Gipsies), J. A. Bush (Clifton), E. C. Cheston (Law Club), W. R. B. Fletcher and A. St. G. Hamersley (Marlborough Nomads), Hon. H. A. Lawrence (Richmond), F. Luscombe (Gipsies), J. E. H. Mackinlay (St. George's Hospital), H. Marsh (I.C.E. College), M. W. Marshall (Blackheath), G. A. Rickards (Gipsies), E. R. Still (Ravenscourt Park), and D. P. Turner (Richmond), forwards.

SCOTLAND.—F. Moncrieff (Edinburgh Academicals), captain ; W. D. Brown and T. Chalmers (Glasgow Academicals), J. L. P. Sanderson (Edinburgh Academicals), backs ; G. B. M'Clure (West of Scotland), J. L. McFarlane (Edinburgh University), three-quarter backs ; W. St. Clair Grant (Craigmount), T. R. Marshall (Edinburgh Academicals), half-backs ; H. W. Allen (Glasgow Academicals), A. Anton (St. Andrew's University), E. M. Bannerman (Edinburgh Academicals), C. C. Bryce (Glasgow Academicals), C. W. Cathcart (Edinburgh University), T. P. Davidson (I.C.E. College), R. W. Irvine and T. Mein (Edinburgh Academicals), A. G. Petrie (Royal High School), T. Whittington (Merchistonians), R. Wilson (West of Scotland), and A. Wood (Royal High School), forwards.

FEBRUARY, 23RD, 1874, THE OVAL.
England beat Scotland by a goal to a try.

On this occasion the Scotsmen had a slight advantage in point of weight, but the English forwards held their own throughout. As in the previous year, rain fell heavily throughout the match, and the ground was in an exceedingly bad state. As usual, the pace of the Scottish forwards caused their opponents to be much penned at the beginning of the match, but when the teams got their second wind the tables were turned. Twice the Scottish goal was endangered by drops by Morse and Milton, and ultimately just before "no side" Freeman, as in 1872, with a magnificent left-foot drop effected its downfall. The try for Scotland was obtained by J. Finlay. The twenties both in and behind the scrummage were very evenly matched.

Of the English twenty this year M. Brooks will be identified as the famous high jumper. W. E. Collins, who played in five International matches, was an admirable and extremely plucky half-

W. E. COLLINS.
(*From a Photograph by Netherelle Briggs, London.*)

back, very quick on his feet, dodging well, and a capital drop with either foot; like Hamersley he left for New Zealand when still at his best. C. W. Crosse was one of the very best of forwards that ever came from Rugby, but a commission in the 6th Dragoons demanded his services in another sphere of action. The North had had no representatives playing for England since 1871, but on this occasion four obtained places. E. Kewley, who took part in this and the following four matches *v.* Scotland, and in two *v.* Ireland, was throughout his career a most excellent forward, and a keen, determined and plucky player, always on the ball, a most brilliant dribbler, and a sure tackle. Roger Walker played five times for England, and proved himself a sterling useful forward, bringing his weight and strength well into play in the scrummages.

The following were the players—

ENGLAND.—A. St. G. Hamersley (Marlborough Nomads), captain; J. M. Batten (Cambridge University), M. Brooks (Oxford University), backs; H. Freeman, three-quarter back; W. E. Collins (Old Cheltonians), W. H. Milton and S. Morse (Marlborough Nomads), half-backs; T. Batson (Blackheath), H. A. Bryden (Clapham Rovers), E. C. Cheston (Richmond), C. W. Crosse (Oxford University), F. Cunliffe (Royal Military Academy), E. Genth (Manchester), E. Kewley (Liverpool), Hon. H. A. Lawrence and M. W. Marshall (Blackheath), Hon. S. Parker (Liverpool), W. H. Stafford (Royal Engineers), D. P. Turner (Richmond), and R. Walker (Manchester), forwards.

SCOTLAND.—W. D. Brown (Glasgow Academicals), captain, and T. Chalmers (Glasgow Academicals), backs; H. M. Hamilton and W. H. Kidston (West of Scotland) and T. R. Marshall (Edinburgh Academicals), three-quarter backs; W. St. Clair Grant (Craigmount), A. K. Stewart (Edinburgh University), half-backs; C. C. Bryce (Glasgow Academicals), T. P. Davidson (I. C. E. College), J. Finlay (Edinburgh Academicals), G. Heron (Glasgow Academicals), R. W. Irvine and J. Mein (Edinburgh Academicals), W. Neilson (West of Scotland), A. G. Petrie (Royal High School), J. Reid (Wanderers), J. K. Todd (Glasgow Academicals), R. Wilson (West of Scotland), A. Wood (Royal High School), and A. Young (Edinburgh Academicals), forwards.

FEBRUARY 19TH, 1875, THE OVAL.
England beat Ireland by 2 goals and a try.

This, the first meeting, of the two countries, was not favoured by the weather, heavy rain during the previous night quite ruining the turf, which presented the appearance of an extensive quagmire, no less than four matches having being played on the same ground during the previous week. This was something like asking the Gentlemen to meet the Players at cricket on a wicket which had done duty for a county match during the three preceding days. The ground measured 130 yards by 75, and the spectators were some 3,000 in number. England penned their adversaries almost throughout the game, and obtained 2 goals, one from a good drop by Nash, the other from a place-kick by Pearson, after a run in by Cheston. Michell also made a fine run-in, but Fraser's place-kick failed. On the winning side Nash was conspicuous for the way in which he got through the mud. The Irish team showed great want of practice, both in play and dropping, and their backs were badly placed, but tackled well. Cronyn was conspicuous on their side. The forwards played a good and plucky game.

Lennard Stokes, a younger brother of F. Stokes, who was captain of the first three English twenties, donned an International cap and jersey for the first time in this match. He played in six successive matches *v.* Scotland, five times *v.* Ireland, and also in the first match *v.* Wales. He played full-back in his opening match, but nearly always afterwards three-quarter back, and it is not too much to say that at this post his equal, either in science or play, has never been seen from the date of the foundation of the Union. Six feet in height, and of sinewy frame, he was the very model of an athlete, and his great pace made him the champion sprinter at the sports of the United Hospitals. He was a faultless catch and field, and a very quick starter, and with his speed of foot, wonderful dodging powers, and clever " shoving-off," was an extremely difficult man to tackle. An excellent place-kick, he was also for several seasons the longest drop in the three kingdoms. Some of his drops at goal from difficult positions when hemmed in by opponents were simply marvellous. His feats in International matches are referred to in the following pages, but it may be recorded here that in a match between Kent and Surrey he dropped three goals in an hour. His tackling was not quite up to the standard of the rest of his play, as he frequently aimed too high, but his great speed often enabled him to rectify an error by a second attempt. His knowledge of the game and *finesse* were quite on a par with his play. He enjoyed a wonderful hold of his men, and worked them in a most determined manner. Admirable play and a great reputation naturally made him the idol of the ring, and during his career he undoubtedly won more matches for his side than any other player.

Two other good players behind the scrimmage who made their *début* in this match were A. W. Pearson, of Guy's Hospital and Blackheath, who played in six International matches, and was a very steady back, a good tackle, and excellent drop and place-kick; and A. T. Michell, of Oxford University, an admirable half-back, very unselfish, and a capital drop and sure tackle. Forward, F. R. Adams, of Richmond, who played in seven International matches, proved himself well worthy of his place, being very keen and energetic, and a valuable player by reason of his weight, strength, and vigorous following-up. Like two other sterling forwards, Murray Marshall and Lawrence, he learnt his football at Wellington College.

The following were the players:—

ENGLAND.—Hon. H. A. Lawrence (Richmond), captain; A. W. Pearson (Guy's Hospital), L. Stokes (Blackheath), backs; W. H. Milton (Marlborough Nomads), three-quarter back; W. E. Collins (St. George's Hospital), A. T. Michell, and E. H. Nash (Oxford University), half-backs; F. R. Adams (Richmond), T. Batson (Blackheath), E. C. Cheston (Richmond), C. W. Crosse, and E. C. Fraser (Oxford University), H. J. Graham (Wimbledon Hornets), W. H. Hutchinson (Hull), F. Luscombe (Gipsies), J. E. H. Mackinlay (St. George's Hospital), M. W. Marshall (Blackheath), E. S. Perrott (Old Cheltonians), D. P. Turner (Richmond), and R. Walker (Manchester), forwards.

IRELAND.—G. Stack (Dublin University), captain; J. Cox (Dublin University), R. Walkington (North of Ireland), backs; R. Bell, junior (North of Ireland), A. Cronyn (Dublin University), three-quarter backs; R. Galbraith and J. Myles (Dublin University), E. McIlwaine (North of Ireland), half-backs; J. Allen (Wanderers), G. Andrews and W. Ash (North of Ireland), M. Barlow (Wanderers), B. N. Casement (Dublin University), A. Combe (North of Ireland), W. Gaffikin (Windsor), E. Galbraith (Dublin University), H. Hewson (Wanderers), F. McDonald (Methodist College), J. Magennis (Dublin University), and H. D. Walsh (Dublin University), forwards.

MARCH 8TH, 1875, EDINBURGH.
England v. Scotland. A drawn match.

Edinburgh was the scene of the fifth England and Scotland match, the ground selected being that on which the first contest had taken place. The field, however, was considerably larger, measuring 130 yards long by 85 wide, and the game was very fast. On this occasion the arrangement of the English backs behind the scrummage was as follows: two half-backs, one three-quarter back, and three backs, and it answered well. The ground and weather were all that could be desired, and the spectators were some 7,000 in number. The result was almost a counterpart of that recorded at Glasgow two years previously, the only advantage gained being that England obliged their opponents to touch-down on six occasions. The dropping of both sides in this match formed a very brilliant feature of the play, and on some half-dozen occasions a foot or so in point of direction would have caused the downfall of one goal or the other. In this respect A. T. Michell and M. W. Marshall were conspicuous for England, and T. Chalmers and N. Finlay for Scotland.

This was L. H. Birkett's first International match. A brother of R. H. Birkett, who played in the first English twenty, he was a capital full-back and first-rate drop. W. A. D. Evanson also made his *debut* on this occasion; he was a very strong and dashing runner, dodging well, and quicker on his feet than most men of his weight.

The following were the players:—

ENGLAND.—Hon. H. A. Lawrence (Richmond), captain; L. H. Birkett (Clapham Rovers) and A. W. Pearson (Guy's Hospital), backs; S. Morse (Marlborough Nomads), three-quarter back; W. E. Collins (Old Cheltonians), W. A. D. Evanson (Civil Service), and A. T. Michell (Oxford University), half-backs; F. R. Adams (Richmond), R. H. Birkett (Clapham Rovers), J. A. Bush (Clifton), E. C. Cheston (Richmond), W. R. B. Fletcher (Marlborough Nomads), H. Genth (Manchester), H. J. Graham (Wimbledon Hornets), E. Kewley (Liverpool), F. Luscombe (Gipsies), M. W. Marshall (Blackheath), Hon. S. Parker (Liverpool), J. E. Paul (I. C. E. College), and D. P. Turner (Richmond), forwards.

SCOTLAND.—W. D. Brown (Glasgow Academicals) captain, and T. Chalmers (Glasgow Academicals), backs; M. Cross (Merchistonians), Ninian Finlay (Edinburgh Academy), and H. M. Hamilton (West of Scotland), three-quarter backs; J. R. Hay-Gordon (Edinburgh Academicals) and J. K. Todd (Glasgow Academicals), half-backs; A. Arthur (Glasgow Academicals), J. Dunlop (West of Scotland), A. Finlay and J. Finlay (Edinburgh Academicals), G. R. Fleming and G. Heron (Glasgow Academicals), R. W. Irvine, A. Marshall, and R. Mein (Edinburgh Academicals), A. G. Petrie (Royal High School), J. Reid (Wanderers), and A. Wood (Royal High School), forwards.

DECEMBER 13TH, 1875, DUBLIN.
England beat Ireland by a goal and a try.

A hard frost had prevailed in Ireland for ten days preceding the departure of the English team, who, however, declined to be put off in spite of numerous telegrams, and were finally rewarded by the news of a "mighty thaw." Clark and Kewley each ran in for England, and Pearson kicked a splendid goal from a difficult position. The forward play was very even, and the dropping of the Irish backs showed great improvement. The piece of play which evoked most enthusiasm was a dribble by Kewley and Bulteel almost the entire length of the ground.

The following were the players:—

ENGLAND.—F. Luscombe (Gipsies), captain, S. H. Login (Royal Naval College), and A. W. Pearson (Blackheath), backs; C. R. Gunner (Marlborough Nomads) and A. T. Michell (Oxford University), three-quarter backs; C. W. H. Clark (Liverpool) and W. E. Collins (St. George's Hospital), half-backs; J. Brewer (Gipsies), C. C. Bryden (Clapham Rovers), A. J. Bulteel (Manchester), J. A. Bush (Clifton), H. J. Graham and J. D. Graham (Wimbledon), W. Greg (Manchester), W. H. Hutchinson (Hull), E. Kewley (Liverpool), E. E. Marriott (Manchester), M. W. Marshall (Blackheath), E. B. Turner (St. George's Hospital), and C. L. Verelst (Liverpool), forwards.

IRELAND.—R. Bell, jun. (North of Ireland), captain, and A. Cronyn (Dublin University), half-backs; H. Moore (Windsor) and R. Walkington

(North of Ireland), backs; B. N. Casement (Wanderers) and J. Hobson (University), three-quarter backs; G. Andrews (North of Ireland), D. T. Arnott (Lansdowne), W. H. Ash (North of Ireland), H. Cox (Lansdowne), W. Cusenden (Bray), W. Finlay (Windsor), R. Galbraith (Dublin University), R. Greer (Kingstown), J. Ireland (Windsor), J. Macdonald (Methodists College), J. Magennis (Dublin University), E. N. M'Ilwaine (North of Ireland), H. D. Walsh and J. Westby, (Dublin University), forwards.

MARCH 6TH, 1876, THE OVAL.
England beat Scotland by a goal and a try.

This was the sixth match of the series. The turf of the field of play, 120 yards by 80, not having been played on during the previous fortnight, was in very fair order. England as usual had the heavier team, averaging 12st. 4lb. to Scotland's 11st. 13lb. Up to the call of half-time the play was wonderfully even, but shortly after the ball had been again started, Collins obtained it, and after a short but brilliant run passed it to Hutchinson, who made the run of the match. Passing the half-backs by sheer pace, shaking himself free from the grasp of the three-quarter backs, and traversing nearly the entire length of the ground, he was not brought to bay until within twenty yards of the Scottish goal. Here Lee, well known at Oxford for his brilliant following up, found the ball "going about," and completed the best piece of play in the whole Rugby season, by passing the last back and running in behind the posts amidst such a roar of cheers as the Oval could but seldom have heard. From this try Stokes easily kicked a goal. Collins also made a brilliant run-in, but the place-kick was unsuccessful. The Scottish team were better together forward than the winners, but their inferiority in weight was not compensated for by any special superiority in point of pace. Cross was brilliant as usual behind the scrummage, but otherwise the backs were distinctly inferior to those of England.

W. C. Hutchinson, who made a very brilliant first appearance in this match, was a first-rate half-back, a quick starter, with a very fair amount of pace, an unselfish player, and good tackle. He took part in two matches only, and died in India early in life. F. H. Lee, an Old Marlburian, was a sterling forward, full of energy, a good stayer, and always on the ball. W. H. Hunt was a very powerful and useful man in a scrummage.

ENGLAND.—F. Luscombe (Gipsies), captain; A. H. Heath (Oxford University), A. W. Pearson (Blackheath), backs; R. H. Birkett (Clapham Rovers), L. Stokes (Blackheath), J. S. Tetley (Bradford), three-quarter backs; W. E. Collins (St. George's Hospital), W. C. Hutchinson (R.I.E. College), half-backs; F. R. Adams (Richmond), J. A. Bush (Clifton), E. C. Cheston (Richmond), H. J. Graham (Wimbledon), W. Greg (Manchester), W. H. Hunt (Preston), E. Kewley (Liverpool), F. H. Lee (Oxford University), M. W. Marshall and W. C. Rawlinson (Blackheath), G. R. Turner (St. George's Hospital), and R. Walker (Manchester), forwards.

SCOTLAND.—R. W. Irvine (Edinburgh Academicals), captain; J. S. Carrick and T. Chalmers (Glasgow Academicals), backs; M. Cross (Glasgow Academicals), N. J. Finlay (Edinburgh Academicals), D. H. Watson (Glasgow Academicals), three-quarter backs; G. Q. Paterson (Edinburgh Academicals), A. K. Stewart (Edinburgh University), half-backs; A. Arthur (Glasgow Academicals), W. H. Bolton (West of Scotland), N. T. Brewis (Institution), C. W. Cathcart (Edinburgh University), D. Drew and G. R. Fleming (Glasgow Academicals), J. H. S. Grahame (Edinburgh Academicals), J. E. Junor (Glasgow Academicals), D. Lang (Paisley), A. G. Petrie (Royal High School), J. Reid, and C. Villar (Wanderers), forwards.

FEBRUARY 5TH, 1877, THE OVAL.
England beat Ireland by 2 goals and a try.

This was the first International match played by teams of fifteen a side, and from first to last the play was fast and brilliant. Though the Irish team were second best throughout, the match was never so one-sided as to be uninteresting. Hutchinson made a brilliant run-in, and Stokes kicked a goal eight minutes after the commencement of play. Hornby subsequently made a very pretty run-in, but the place-kick was unsuccessful. Hutchinson, however, ran in again just before "no side," and Stokes kicked a second goal. The English forwards were not only heavier but also quicker on their feet than their opponents, and the winners, as was to be expected, knew more of the science of the game.

This was A. N. Hornby's first International match. He played nine times for England, and it may safely be said that no player has achieved greater distinction both at cricket and football. Educated at Harrow, he did not take up Rugby football until many years after he had left school; indeed, his International cap was not donned until within a week of his attaining his thirty-first year. But the spirit of the Rugby game was quite to his liking, and his activity, energy, and pluck were all in his favour. He soon mastered the laws, but the science of back play, only to be gained by experience, took him longer to learn, though he was often clever enough at extricating himself from a difficulty. He was a brilliant, dashing runner, with a quick dodge which baffled many an opponent, never famous as a drop but punted capitally, a splendid catch and field, and one of the surest tackles ever seen. A regular die-hard, he instilled much of his spirit and energy into his fifteen, with whom, as also with his opponents, he was very popular. G. Harrison played thrice each against Ireland and Scotland, and once against Wales. He was a most useful, hard-working forward, and used his feet well, both in the scrummage and when the ball got loose, being a fine dribbler.

ENGLAND.—E. Kewley (Liverpool), captain; L. Birkett (Clapham Rovers), L. Stokes (Blackheath), backs; R. H. Birkett (Clapham Rovers), A. N. Hornby (Preston), three-quarter backs; W. C. Hutchinson, and P. L. Price (I.C.E. College), half-backs: F. R. Adams (Richmond), R. H. Fowler (Leeds), G. Harrison (Hull), W. H. Hunt (Preston), F. H. Lee (Oxford University), M. W. Marshall (Blackheath), C. J. C. Touzell (Cambridge University), and E. B. Turner (St. George's Hospital), forwards.

IRELAND.—R. Galbraith (Dublin University), captain; R. B. Walkington (North of Ireland), backs; H. Brown (Windsor), F. W. Kidd (Lansdowne), three-quarter backs; T. G. Gordon (North of Ireland), A. Whitestone (Dublin University), half-backs; T. Brown (Windsor), H. L. Cox and H. G. Edwards (Dublin University), W. Finlay (North of Ireland), W. J. Hamilton (Dublin University), I. Ireland (Windsor), H. W. Jackson (Dublin University), H. C. Kelly (North of Ireland), and W. H. Wilson (Dublin University), forwards.

MARCH 5TH, 1877, EDINBURGH.
Scotland beat England by a goal.

The seventh England v. Scotland match was played at Raeburn Place, Edinburgh, on the 5th March, 1877, when, to the delight of the majority of some 5,000 spectators, Scotland won their second victory. This was the first meeting of the two countries with teams of fifteen a side, and the play was remarkably even up to half-time. Subsequently the English team were rather penned, but the good runs and tackling of A. N. Hornby and L. Stokes at three-quarter back kept their opponents at bay until the last ten minutes, when Malcolm Cross obtained a goal for Scotland by a capital drop.

SCOTLAND.—R. W. Irvine, captain ; J. S. Carrick (Glasgow Academicals), H. H. Johnston (Edinburgh Collegiate), backs; M. Cross and R. C. McKenzie (Glasgow Academicals), three-quarter backs; J. R. Hay Gordon (Edinburgh Academicals), E. J. Pocock (Edinburgh Wanderers), half-backs; J. H. S. Graham (Edinburgh Academicals), J. E. Junor (Glasgow Academicals), H. M. Napier (West of Scotland), A. G. Petrie (Royal High School), T. R. Reid (Edinburgh Wanderers), T. J. Torrie

(Edinburgh Academicals), C. Villar (Edinburgh Wanderers), D. H. Watson (Glasgow Academicals), forwards.

ENGLAND.—E. Kewley (Liverpool), captain; L. Birkett (Clapham Rovers), A. W. Pearson (Blackheath), backs; A. N. Hornby (Preston), L. Stokes (Blackheath), three-quarter backs; W. A. D. Evanson (Richmond), P. L. Price (I.C.E. College), half-backs; C. C. Bryden (Clapham Rovers), H. W. T. Garnett (Bradford), G. Harrison (Hull), W. H. Hunt (Preston), A. F. Law (Richmond), M. W. Marshall (Blackheath), R. Todd (Manchester), and C. J. C. Touzell (Cambridge University), forwards.

MARCH 4TH, 1878, THE OVAL.
England v. Scotland. A drawn match.

The eighth meeting of England and Scotland was favoured by brilliant weather, and, after a very hard-fought struggle, left drawn, neither fifteen being able to boast any tangible advantage, though Scotland had perhaps a trifle the best of the penning. The attendance—about 4,000—was disappointing, and led to a change of *venue* in 1880. The Scottish forwards, as usual, showed rather superior pace and activity, but behind the scrummage England had the whip hand, and Hornby and Stokes each narrowly missed dropping a goal. Adams made a good run-in for England, but it was given up, as the Scots were taken at a disadvantage owing to a misconception of one of the laws. Kewley and Marshall played grandly forward.

This was E. T. Gurdon's first appearance for England: he played no fewer than seven times against Scotland, five times against Ireland, and four times against Wales: this record of sixteen matches has never been equalled by any English player, and evidences his sterling worth. Educated at Haileybury and Cambridge, he was in the front rank of Rugby players, both at school and the University, and on coming up to London joined the Richmond Club, of which later on he was captain for several seasons. In every respect he was one of the best forwards that ever represented England; though not built on so large a scale as his younger brother, who made his *début* two years later, he was very muscular, and used his weight and strength to the best advantage, and was usually to be found in the very heart of the scrummage. His use of his feet amidst a crowd of forwards was admirable, but better still was his dribbling when he had got the ball before him in the open, and many a time has the ring been wrought up to a pitch of frenzy watching the two Gurdons steering the ball past half-backs and three-quarter backs straight for the enemy's quarters. A grand example was that set by the brothers of resolutely keeping the ball on the ground when they had taken it through a scrummage, knowing how much more difficult it is for a half-back to stop a combined rush of two or three good dribblers than a single man with the ball under his arm. E. T. Gurdon was also a deadly tackle, and followed up hard and unflaggingly from kick-off to "no side." An excellent knowledge of the game and thorough unselfishness

PUTTING THE BALL INTO A SCRUMMAGE.
(*From an instantaneous Photograph by E. Airey, Bradford*).

helped to make him an admirable and popular captain (the Bradford team will well remember his excellent generalship when, with a strong forward, but weak back team compared with the brilliant back combination of the Northern Club, he compelled the Yorkshireman to play a purely forward game throughout the match), and he is invaluable in the councils of the Union, of which he is now president for the second year. G. Thomson also played his first match for England on this occasion, and took part in eight subsequent matches. He was a very useful and energetic forward, running strongly and playing a dashing and plucky game; he was for several years on the Union Committee, and little did his colleagues think that he was destined to fall a victim to consumption. Another first appearance was that of the Old Rugbeian, G. F. Vernon, perhaps still better known as a cricketer. He played five times for England, and was an excellent forward, working very hard in the scrummage, and being a most difficult man to stop when he got a chance of a run. Another good feature of his play was his cleverness in getting the ball when thrown out of touch, and he was certainly one of the very best forwards of his time.

ENGLAND.—E. Kewley (Liverpool), captain; H. E. Kayll (Sunderland), and A. W. Pearson (Blackheath), backs; A. N. Hornby (Preston), and L. Stokes (Blackheath), three-quarter backs; W. A. D. Evanson (Richmond), and P. L. Price (I. C. E. College), half-backs; F. R. Adams (Richmond), J. M. Biggs (University College Hospital), H. Fowler (Oxford University), F. D. Fowler (I. C. E. College), E. T. Gurdon (Old Haileyburians), M. W. Marshall (Blackheath), G. Thomson (Halifax), and G. F. Vernon (Blackheath), forwards.

SCOTLAND.—R. W. Irvine (Edinburgh Academicals), captain; W. E. M'Lagan (Edinburgh Academicals), back; M. Cross (Glasgow Academicals), and N. J. Finlay (Edinburgh Academicals), three-quarter backs; J. Campbell (Merchistonians), and J. Neilson (Glasgow Academicals), half-backs; L. C. Auldjo (Abertay), N. T. Brewis (Institution), J. H. S. Graham, D. R. Irvine, and G. M'Leod (Glasgow Academicals), H. M. Napier (West of Scotland), and A. G. Petrie (Royal High School), forwards.

MARCH 11TH, 1878, DUBLIN.

England beat Ireland by 2 goals and a try.

This was the fourth meeting, and, though not represented by their full strength, England secured an easy victory. The first try was obtained by Gardner owing to a bad piece of play by the Irish back, and the second was obtained in exactly the same manner by Penny. The goals were splendidly kicked by Pearson, though the try in each case was obtained close to touch-in-goal. The third try was obtained by E. B. Turner. The Irish forwards played up pluckily, as usual, and penned their opponents during the second half of the match, though without being able to obtain any definite advantage. Kelly played very finely for Ireland.

A. Budd, who played twice each v. Scotland and Ireland, and once v. Wales, made his first appearance in this match. His football education was gained at Clifton College, Cambridge University, and in the ranks of the Blackheath Club, and for several years he was one of the fastest and most useful forwards—a very determined runner, not averse to a collision with an opponent, a plucky charger, and excellent tackle. He played on the verge of the scrummage as a rule, and, if occasionally he robbed a half-back of a chance, was in the habit of getting well off and making a dashing run. A veritable enthusiast, he is as well up in the science of the game as any man in the kingdom, has done excellent work in many special committees, and is invaluable on a point of law. In conjunction with H. Vassall he may be said to have been mainly instrumental in developing amongst forward players the theory of "passing," as to which I am inclined to think that he joins with not a few of the older school of players in considering it to be somewhat over-developed nowadays.

ENGLAND.—M. W. Marshall (Blackheath), captain; A. W. Pearson (Blackheath), and W. J. Penny (King's College), backs; H. J. Enthoven (Richmond), and A. N. Hornby (Preston), three-quarter backs; J. L. Bell (Durham), and A. H. Jackson (Guy's Hospital), half-backs; T. Blatherwick (Manchester), A. Budd (Blackheath), F. Dawson (I. C. E. College), H. P. Gardner (Richmond), W. Hunt (Manchester), E. B. Turner (St. George's Hospital), C. L. Verelst (Liverpool), and G. F. Vernon (Blackheath), forwards.

IRELAND.—R. B. Walkington (North of Ireland), captain, back; F. W. Kidd (Lansdowne), R. Matier (North of Ireland), three-quarter backs; F. Hagan (Kingstown School), T. G. Gordon (North of Ireland), half-backs; E. Croker (Limerick), H. G. Edwards (Dublin University), W. Finlay (North of Ireland), W. Griffiths (Limerick), R. Hughes (Windsor), H. C. Kelly (North of Ireland), J. McDonald (Windsor), W. Moore (Windsor), H. W. Murray (Dublin University), and F. Schutt (Wanderers), forwards.

MARCH 10TH, 1879, EDINBURGH.
England v. Scotland. A drawn match.

England and Scotland played their ninth match at Raeburn Place, Edinburgh, on the 10th March, 1879, and again a draw was the result. Both fifteens were thoroughly representative, and England, playing with the wind at the outset, gave Scotland plenty of work to do, Evanson's running being very brilliant. Burton at length ran in, and Stokes kicked a goal. In the second half a good drop by Finlay made the score equal. No further advantage was gained, though a fine drop by Stokes almost obtained a second goal for England, the ball hitting one of the posts. His dropping and the running of the English backs and the excellent defensive play of Maclagan for Scotland were very noticeable.

This was H. C. Rowley's first match for England, and

he played in eight other International matches. He was
built as a runner, and was an excellent player either
forward, half-back, or three-quarter back. He had
plenty of strength and pace, was a fine drop and a very
sure tackle, and always one of the keenest men on his
side. H. H. Taylor, who hailed from Merchant Taylors'
School, played in five International matches; in the sixth
(1881) he lost the night mail to Scotland. Except that
he possessed no dropping powers, he was a first-rate half-
back, wonderfully quick on the ball and at utilising an
opening in his adversaries' defence. He ran low, and
very strongly, though not very fast, and used his arms
with great effect; his tactics in point of attack were his
best points, and he did excellent service for England.
G. W. Burton, whose recent death was much regretted by
a large circle of football players, took part in six International matches, and was a very fast and brilliant player
when the ball was in the open; like his old friend Budd,
he did but little work in the scrummage itself, but in
their own particular style both did good service for
Blackheath and England. He was a fine dribbler, having
been educated at Winchester, and a sure tackle, and had
a happy knack of running in. S. Neame, who played
for England in four matches, learnt the game at Cheltenham, and was a useful and occasionally brilliant forward,
working well in the scrummage, and a dangerous man
when the ball was loose.

ENGLAND.—F. R. Adams (Richmond), captain; H. Huth (Hudders-
field), W. J. Penny (United Hospitals), backs; L. Stokes (Blackheath),
three-quarter back; W. A. D. Evanson (Richmond), H. H. Taylor (St.
George's Hospital), half-backs; A. Budd and G. W. Burton (Blackheath),
F. D. Fowler (Manchester), G. Harrison (Hull), N. F. McLeod (I. C. E.
College), S. Neame (Old Cheltonians), H. C. Rowley (Manchester), H.
Springmann (Liverpool), and R. Walker (Manchester), forwards.

SCOTLAND.—N. W. Irvine (Edinburgh Academicals), captain; W. E.
Maclagan (Edinburgh Academicals), back; M. Cross (Glasgow Academi-
cals), N. J. Finlay (Edinburgh Academicals), three-quarter backs;
J. Neilson and J. A. Campbell (Glasgow Academicals), half-backs; R.
Ainslie and N. T. Brewis (Edinburgh Institution), J. B. Brown and
E. Ewart (Glasgow Academicals), J. H. S. Graham and D. R. Irvine
(Edinburgh Academicals), J. E. Junor (Glasgow Academicals), H. M.
Napier (West of Scotland), and A. G. Petrie (Royal High School),
forwards.

MARCH 30TH, 1879, THE OVAL.
England beat Ireland by 3 goals.

The fifth match against Ireland, originally fixed for
the 3rd February, but postponed owing to frost, was

played at Kennington Oval on the 24th March, 1879. Unfortunately, Ireland was very indifferently represented, and, though the forwards showed up fairly well, the fifteen were quite over-matched, only once forcing the ball over the English goal-line. England obtained 3 goals, one brilliantly dropped by Stokes, and the other two kicked by him from runs-in by Rowley and Twynam. The English team was not quite so strong as that which played against Scotland.

H. T. TWYNAM.
(From a Photograph by Elliott & Fry, London.)

It is somewhat singular that H. T. Twynam, who played five times for England v. Ireland, and twice v. Wales, should have only taken part in one match v. Scotland, and that in his last year, 1884, when he certainly played in finer form than on any previous occasion, and was invaluable from first to last. He was a brilliant half-back, a fine runner with a very difficult dodge, but was a trifle uncertain, and had no powers of dropping. Better at attack than defence, he always played a hard, resolute game, and was full of energy and pluck.

ENGLAND.—F. R. Adams (Richmond), captain; W. J. Penny (United Hospitals), back; W. A. D. Evanson (Richmond), L. Stokes (Blackheath), three-quarter backs; W. E. Openshaw (Manchester) and H. T. Twynam (Richmond), half-backs; H. D. Bateson (Liverpool), J. M. Biggs (United Hospitals), A. Budd and G. W. Burton (Blackheath), F. T. Gurdon (Richmond), G. Harrison (Hull), N. F. M'Leod (I.C.E. College), S. Neame (Old Cheltonians), and H. C. Rowley (Manchester), forwards.

IRELAND.—W. C. Neville (Dublin University), captain; W. Pike (Kingstown), back; J. Bagot (Dublin University), W. J. Willis (Landsdowne), three-quarter backs; J. Heron (North of Ireland), A. M. Whitestone (Dublin University), half-backs; J. D. Bristow (North of Ireland), B. Casement and J. L. Cuppaidge (Dublin University), W. Finlay (North of Ireland), J. J. Keon (Limerick), H. W. Murray (Dublin University), Purdon (North of Ireland), F. Schute (Wanderers), and G. Scriven (Dublin University), forwards.

JANUARY 30TH, 1880, DUBLIN.
England beat Ireland by a goal and a try to a try.

The seventh match of the series, and a seventh victory for the Rose. The weather and ground were favourable, and the spectators numbered some three thousand. The English Committee were unable to get together their best team, and the match was a very hard-fought one. This was L. Stokes's first appearance as captain, and he was obliged to work his team very hard to score a win. Ireland, playing with the wind behind them for the first half of the match, showed to great advantage, their forwards—always their strongest department—working very hard. At last Cuppaidge ran in—this was the first try ever gained by Ireland in these matches—but Walkington's place-kick was a failure. After half-time England got the upper hand: Markendale got in, but Hunt missed the shot at goal. Ellis shortly afterwards ran in, and Stokes kicked a goal. The losers showed much better form than any Irish team in the six previous matches.

The record of this match brings to notice the performances of C. Gurdon, to whom reference has already been made in reviewing his brother's play. He, too, was educated at Haileybury and Cambridge, and on coming up to London joined the Richmond Club. Taller, and built on a larger scale than his brother, with enormous strength in his thighs and shoulders, he was one of the most massive and muscular forwards that ever stripped, and averaged about 13st. 7lb. when in hard training. Great advantage, however, as his side derived from his weight and strength,—for in his day a scrummage was worthy of its name,—they derived still more from his admirable play. A very zealous worker in the scrum-mage, he devoted all his attention to the ball, and was very careful not to overrun it whilst steering it through the ranks of his opponents. When he had got it free he dribbled fast and with unusual skill and success, and half- and three-quarter backs dreaded his rush more than that of any other player. He was also one of the surest

CHARLES GURDON.
(*From a Photograph by Window & Grove, Baker Street, W.*)

ENGLISH TEAM v. SCOTLAND: MANCHESTER, FEBRUARY 28, 1880.

ENGLAND, 2 GOALS 3 TRIES; SCOTLAND, 1 GOAL.

H. PHILLIPS. C. M. SAWYER. C. H. COATES. R. WALKER. G. F. VERNON. E. T. GURDON. H. H. TAYLOR. G. HARRISON.
S. H. NEAME. L. STOKES (*Captain*). C. GURDON. H. C. ROWLEY.
T. FRY. H. T. FINCH. G. W. BURTON.

(*From a Photograph by Mr. F. Jones jr., B. Ann's Square, Manchester; and 12, Old Bond Street, W.*)

of tackles, and always in the front rank in following up.
His record of International matches shows six against
Scotland, five against Ireland, and three against Wales,
and but for an accident to one of his knees he would be
able to boast of a still longer list. T. Fry played thrice
for England ; he was a first-rate full-back, being a deadly
tackle, a very strong runner and excellent drop, but
might have had a rather safer pair of hands as a catch
and field. As a full-back he enjoys the—I believe, unique
—distinction of having run-in against Scotland.

ENGLAND.—L. Stokes (Blackheath), captain, and R. Hunt (Manchester), three-quarter backs; A. H. Jackson (Blackheath) and H. T. Twynam (Richmond), half-backs; T. Fry (Queen's House) and A. N. Hornby (Manchester), backs; S. Ellis (Queen's House), C. Gurdon (Richmond), B. Kilner (Wakefield Trinity), E. T. Markendale (Manchester Rangers), S. Neame (Old Cheltonians), H. C. Rowley (Manchester), J. Schofield (Manchester Rangers), G. F. Vernon (Blackheath), and C. Woodhead (Huddersfield), forwards.

IRELAND.—H. C. Kelly (North of Ireland), captain; R. B. Walkington (North of Ireland), back; J. L. Bagot (Dublin University) and A. Whitestone, three-quarter backs; W. T. Heron (North of Ireland) and M. Johnston (Dublin University), half-backs; J. L. Cuppaidge, A. J. Forrest (Wanderers), R. W. Hughes (Queen's College), F. Kennedy and J. A. Macdonald (Wanderers), A. Millar (Kingstown), H. Purdon (North of Ireland), G. Scriven (Dublin University), and J. Taylor, forwards.

FEBRUARY 28TH, 1880, MANCHESTER.

England beat Scotland by 2 goals and 3 tries to a goal.

In this, the tenth match of the series, England was
represented by probably the very strongest of all the
teams that, to the date of writing, have done battle for
the Rose. Scotland, however, owing to a very easy
victory over Ireland, were favourites and particularly
confident. They were led by the veteran Irvine, who
had played in all the previous matches. L. Stokes was
captain of England, and worked his fifteen admirably.
The ground was in fair order, but a trifle slippery at the
top ; a strong breeze blew from the upper end, of which
the visitors, winning the toss, had the advantage at the
outset. Recognising the necessity for a great effort, the
English forwards—usually slow at the start—got to work
in most vigorous style, and within some eight minutes
of kick-off Taylor made a short but brilliant run-in.
The captain's place-kick across the wind failed, and for
the ensuing half-hour the play was very even. Then
Taylor again ran-in very cleverly, but Stokes's shot was
again unsuccessful. After half-time the struggle was

still more desperate, but Fry made a fine run-in and Stokes kicked a good goal. Sorley Brown then ran-in cleverly for Scotland, and Cross scored a goal by a capital kick. The last twenty minutes showed clearly that England held the last trump, and two more tries were obtained from runs-in by E. T. Gurdon and Burton, from the latter of which Stokes kicked another goal. The forwards were very fairly matched, but England had a decided advantage behind the scrummage, where Finch, the smallest player in the two fifteens, played with great pluck. The match was productive of as good a display of football as has ever been seen either before or since, and was very evenly contested, despite the aspect of the score.

C. HUTTON COATES.
(From a Photograph by Hoggard, Redcar.)

ENGLAND.—L. Stokes (Blackheath), captain, and C. M. Sawyer (Broughton), three-quarter backs; T. Fry (Queen's House), back; R. T. Finch (Cambridge University) and H. H. Taylor (St. George's Hospital), half-backs; G. W. Burton (Blackheath), C. H. Coates (Cambridge University), C. Gurdon and E. T. Gurdon (Richmond), G. Harrison (Leeds), S. Neame (Old Cheltonians), C. Phillips (Oxford University), H. C. Rowley (Manchester), G. F. Vernon (Blackheath), and R. Walker (Manchester), forwards.

SCOTLAND.—R. W. Irvine (Edinburgh Academicals), captain; W. E. Maclagan (Edinburgh Academicals), back; M. Cross (Glasgow Academicals), and N. J. Finlay (Edinburgh Academicals), three-quarter backs; W. Sorley Brown and W. H. Masters (Edinburgh Institution), half-backs; R. Ainslie and N. T. Brewis (Edinburgh Institution), J. B. Brown (Glasgow Academicals), D. Y. Cassels (West of Scotland), E. N. Ewart (Glasgow Academicals), J. H. S. Graham (Edinburgh Academicals), D. M'Cowan (West of Scotland), A. G. Petrie (Royal High School), and C. Stewart (West of Scotland), forwards. Umpires, J. MacLaren (Manchester) and A. R. Stewart (Edinburgh Wanderers). Referee, A. G. Guillemard (President R. F. U.).

C. H. Coates, a fine powerful forward, and a splendid man in the scrummage, made his *début* in this match, and also played the two following years against Scotland.

Thus ended the first decade of International matches. Of the ten contests with Scotland, four had been won, two lost, and four drawn: of the six with Ireland, all had resulted in victories for the Rose.

CHAPTER XI.

INTERNATIONAL MATCHES AND PLAYERS.
1881-1892.

By A. Budd.

MARCH 19TH, 1881, EDINBURGH.

England v. Scotland. Drawn. England, 1 goal 1 try ; Scotland, 1 goal 1 try.

THE season 1880-81 will be memorable for the amount of interruption to the game by frost and snow, but the match England v. Scotland at Raeburn Place was played under the most favourable conditions of ground and weather. England was handicapped by the loss of two of the best men behind the scrummage, H. H. Taylor missing the train from London, and C. M. Sawyer being unable to play owing to business engagements. Taylor's place was taken by F. T. Wright, of Manchester, then a student at Edinburgh University, who for his age and strength played pluckily and well, but proved unequal to the task of facing such experienced halves as Campbell and Wauchope, and so throughout the match the English team had a comparatively weak spot in both defence and attack. Campbell Rowley, the other half-back, played magnificently, and drew attention away from the weaker side as much as possible. Scotland were the first to score by the aid of a clever run on the part of R. Ainslie, and Begbie almost kicked a goal, the ball rebounding from one of the posts. This was all the score at half-time. The game was fast and open, the fine combined action of the English forwards telling sorely against the lighter Scotsmen, whose backs, however, repeatedly regained the ground lost by the forwards. Then L. Stokes, catching the ball from a kick-out, obtained a goal by one of the grandest drop-kicks ever seen, the ball travelling fully 80 yards from kick to pitch. Roused by this success, the English forwards played up brilliantly, and Campbell Rowley obtained a try, which Stokes failed to improve. Defeat for Scotland now seemed certain, when within three minutes of time J. Brown grounded the ball beneath the bar, no English player attempting to tackle him, the general impression being that he was offside. Begbie succeeded in kicking a goal, and thus ended a most sensational International match in a draw with a score of a goal and a try for each side. R. Ainslie and J. Brown were most prominent amongst the Scotch forwards, and J. A. Campbell the most noticeable among the backs. A. R. Don Wauchope was outplayed by Campbell Rowley, and had few opportunities of showing his dodging powers. C. Reid, of the Edinburgh Academicals, made his first appearance against England. This player through his magnificent physique and clever play may fairly claim the title of "champion forward" of Scotland. At the line-out and in the scrummage he has had no equal, whilst his tackling was a terror to his opponents. Few will deny his claim to be considered the finest forward that ever played for Scotland. His only rival in England has been C. Gurdon.

TEAMS.

ENGLAND.—A. N. Hornby (Manchester), back; R. Hunt (Manchester), L. Stokes (Blackheath), captain, three-quarter backs; F. T. Wright (Manchester), H. C. Rowley (Manchester), half-backs; G. W. Burton (Blackheath), C. H. Coates (Leeds), C. W. L. Fernandes (Leeds), H. Fowler (Walthamstow), C. Gurdon (Richmond), E. T. Gurdon (Richmond), W. Hewitt (Queen's House), A. Budd (Blackheath), C. Phillips (Birkenhead Park), H. Vassall (Oxford University), forwards.

SCOTLAND.—F. A. Begbie (Edinburgh Wanderers), back; W. E. M'Lagan (Edinburgh Academicals), N. J. Finlay (Edinburgh Academicals), R. C. Mackenzie (Glasgow Academicals), three-quarter backs; J. A. Campbell (Glasgow Academicals), A. R. Don Wauchope (Edinburgh Wanderers), half-backs; J. S. Graham, captain (Edinburgh Academicals), C. Reid (Edinburgh Academicals), D. Y. Cassels (West of Scotland), D. M'Gowan (West of Scotland), J. Maitland (Edinburgh Institution), J. B. Brown (Glasgow Academicals), R. Ainslie (Edinburgh Institution), T. Ainslie (Edinburgh Institution), W. A. Peterkin (Edinburgh University), forwards.

FEBRUARY 5TH, 1881, MANCHESTER.

England 2 goals 2 tries ; Ireland, nil.

This match was deprived of much interest through differences in the Irish Council, which caused the Irishmen to play a team not quite representative of the full strength of that country. Notwithstanding defections the Irish forwards worked well in the scrummages, but, as usual, the Englishmen outmatched them behind. The English team could hardly have been improved upon, and played splendidly, though at the outset the forwards played a sluggish game. The Englishmen won by 2 goals and 2 tries to nothing. Taylor played magnificently, scoring twice, whilst Hornby, the full-back, and Sawyer, both Lancastrians, delighted the local crowd by each scoring a try.

TEAMS.

ENGLAND.—A. N. Hornby (Manchester), back; L. Stokes (Blackheath), captain, and C. M. Sawyer (Broughton), three-quarter backs; H. H. Taylor (Blackheath) and W. R. Richardson (Manchester), half-backs; E. T. Gurdon (Richmond), C. Phillips (Birkenhead Park), C. W. L. Fernandes (Leeds), W. Hewitt (Queen's House), H. C. Rowley (Manchester), G. F. Vernon (Blackheath), C. Gurdon (Richmond), J. Ravenscroft (Birkenhead), J. I. Ward (Richmond), G. W. Burton (Blackheath), forwards.

IRELAND.—T. Harrison (Cork), back; W. Pierce (Cork), W. W. Pike (Kingstown), three-quarter backs; M. Johnstone (Dublin University), F. H. Spunner (Tipperary), half-backs; H. Morell (Dublin University), H. Purdon (North of Ireland), A. J. Forrest, captain (Dublin University), A. W. Wallace, (Dublin University), G. Scriven (Dublin University), A. R. M'Mullen (Cork), D. Browing (Dublin Wanderers), J. C. L. Burkett (Cork), H. P. Cummins (Cork), F. Kennedy (Dublin Wanderers), forwards.

FEBRUARY 19TH, BLACKHEATH.

England beat Wales by 8 goals and 6 tries to nothing.

This was the first International match with Wales, who were thoroughly overmatched. Stokes kicked 6 goals, Hunt 1, and also dropped 1. The tries were obtained by Burton (4), Vassall (3), and Budd, Hunt, Fernandes, Rowley, Taylor, and Twynam, 1 each.

TEAMS.

ENGLAND.—T. Fry (Queen's House), back; L. Stokes, captain (Blackheath), R. Hunt (Manchester), three-quarter backs; H. H. Taylor (Blackheath), H. T. Twynam (Richmond), half-backs; A. P. James (Blackheath), G. W. Burton (Blackheath), C. W. L. Fernandes (Leeds), H. Fowler (Walthamstow), E. T. Gurdon (Richmond), C. Gurdon (Richmond), W. Hewitt (Queen's House), H. Vassall (Oxford University), H. C. Rowley (Manchester), C. P. Wilson (Cambridge University), forwards.

WALES.—C. H. Newman (Newport), R. H. B. Summers (Haverfordwest), backs; E. Peake (Chepstow), J. A. Bevan, captain (Grosmont), three-quarter backs; E. J. Lewis (Llandovery), J. Watkins (Llandaff), half-backs; E. J. Purdon (Newport), G. F. Harding, T. A. Rees (Llandovery), B. E. Gorling (Cardiff), B. B. Mann (Cardiff), W. D. Phillips (Cardiff), E. Trehearne (Pontypridd), G. Darbyshire (Bangor), R. D. G. Williams (Newport and Brecon), forwards.

MARCH 4TH, 1882, MANCHESTER.
Scotland beat England by 2 tries to nothing.

In 1882 the match was played at Manchester. L. Stokes had retired from the game, and E. Beswick, of Swinton, and W. N. Bolton, Blackheath, filled the important posts of three-quarter backs, and neither of them particularly distinguished himself. Beswick obtained his place through his excellent play in the North v. South match, whilst Bolton had shown extraordinary form for Blackheath. He subsequently did yeoman service for England. Tall and powerful, a magnificent runner, handing-off most powerfully, and being very difficult to stop, he was the type of a wing three-quarter to meet the strong tactics of a Scotch team; and with G. C. Wade for companion on the opposite wing, England was perhaps never more strongly represented in attack and defence at three-quarters. A. N. Hornby was again at back, and was captain of the team, furnishing the first instance of a player who has combined the two offices of captain of the leading cricket and football teams of England. Experts were by no means sanguine as to the prospects of the Englishmen's success, and the issue of the match bore out their evil forebodings. But the circumstances were altogether unfavourable for an exhibition of good football. The ground was heavy, wet, and greasy, and the heavy English forwards were at a disadvantage. They exhibited fair individual form, but displayed very little combination, whereas the Scotch forwards played like one man. There was an enormous crowd of spectators, and the management utterly failed to cope with the numbers, who climbed over the barriers and invaded the field of play. It was a marvel how the game was continued at all. It went all in Scotland's favour, who won by 2 tries to *nil*. The only point in England's favour was a good run by Payne, who

W. N. BOLTON.
(From a Photograph by J. Hawke, Plymouth.)

but for the spectators might have crossed the line. With that exception the Englishmen were fairly penned, and playing two three-quarters as against three, Hornby proved unequal to the task of keeping the Scotsmen out. His tackling was good, but in fielding the ball and in punting he was far removed from his best form. Sorley Brown was a thorn in the sides of the Englishmen, and was undoubtedly the most prominent player of the match.

This was the first of the matches between Scotland and England in which either side had been victorious away from their own country. It was also the first match in which a neutral referee officiated, so altogether the match of 1882 was memorable in precedents and records.

TEAMS.

ENGLAND.—A. N. Hornby (Manchester), back; E. Beswick (Swinton), W. N. Bolton (Blackheath), three-quarter backs; H. H. Taylor (Blackheath), J. H. Payne (Broughton), half-backs; C. H. Coates (Yorkshire Wanderers), H. G. Fuller (Cambridge University), E. T. Gurdon (Richmond), C. Gurdon (Richmond), J. T. Hunt (Manchester), P. A. Newton (Cambridge University), H. C. Rowley (Manchester), H. Tatham (Oxford University), G. T. Thomson (Halifax), H. Vassall (Oxford University), forwards.

SCOTLAND.—J. P. Veitch (Royal High School), back; W. E. Maclagan (Edinburgh Academicals), A. Phillips (Institution F.P.), three-quarter backs; A. R. Don Wauchope (Fettes Lorettonians), W. Sorley Brown (Institution F. P.), half-backs; R. Ainslie (Institution F. P.), F. Ainslie (Institution F. P.), J. B. Brown (Glasgow Academicals), D. Y. Cassels, captain (West of Scotland), R. Maitland (Institution F. P.), D. McCowan (West of Scotland), C. Reid (Edinburgh Academicals), A. Walker (West of Scotland), J. G. Walker (Fettes-Lorettonians), W. A. Walls (Glasgow Academicals), forwards.

FEBRUARY 6TH, DUBLIN.

England v. Ireland. Drawn, each side scoring 2 tries.

A very evenly contested game, in which the Irishmen more than held their own, playing a very sound game. Pike at three-quarters displayed brilliant style. Individually the Englishmen were superior, but they lacked combination, and manifestly exhibited want of condition. To these two causes may be attributed the failure of England to win an International match this season.

TEAMS.

IRELAND.—R. B. Walkington (North of Ireland), back; W. W. Pike (Kingstown), R. E. M'Lean (Dublin University), E. J. Wolfe (North of Ireland and Armagh), three-quarter backs; G. C. Bent (Dublin University), M. Johnstone (Dublin University), half-backs; J. W. Taylor (North of

Ireland, Queen's College, Belfast), A. J. Forrest (Wanderers), M. B. Henry (Dublin University), C. Stokes (Cork Bankers), W. A. Cummins (Cork), J. A. Macdonald (Queen's College, Belfast), R. Nelson (Queen's College, Belfast), R. W. Hughes (Ulster), T. R. Johnstone-Smyth (Lansdowne), forwards.

ENGLAND.—A. N. Hornby (Manchester), back ; E. Beswick (Swinton), R. Hunt (Manchester), W. N. Bolton (Blackheath), half-backs ; H. C. Rowley (Manchester), H. T. Twynam (Richmond), quarter-backs ; C. Gurdon (Richmond), captain, G. T. Thomson (Halifax), H. G. Fuller (Cambridge University), H. Vassall (Oxford University), W. Hewitt (Queen's House), B. B. Middleton (Birkenhead), J. T. Hunt (Manchester), J. I. Ward (Richmond), A. Spurling (Blackheath), forwards.

JANUARY 14TH, NEWPORT.
North of England beat Wales by a goal to a try.

In consequence of the crushing defeat experienced by Wales in 1881, it was decided to put a North of England team against them. The North only won by a goal to a try, and the good form shown by the Welshmen, added to their victory over Ireland, gained for them a place in the International fixtures of the future.

MARCH 3RD, EDINBURGH, 1883.
England beat Scotland by two tries to a try.

In the thirteenth match England retaliated on Scotland by winning at Edinburgh, for the first time on Scottish soil. The Scotch team was mainly the same as that which took part in the great victory at Manchester in 1882, though A. R. Don Wauchope and J. G. Walker were unable to play through injuries. Wauchope's place was taken by P. W. Smeaton, of the Edinburgh Academicals. The English team was largely composed of new men, who all played in fine form, and in every instance laid the foundation of special fame as International players. H. B. Tristram, as back, played as substitute for A. S. Taylor, incapacitated by an accident to his knee, and demonstrated that he was the best man who had ever officiated in that position. W. N. Bolton, A. M. Evanson, and G. C. Wade were the three-quarters, and a finer trio never wore the English jersey. Allan Rotherham, the half-back of the decade, made his first appearance. Among the forwards the Gurdons, Fuller, Thomson, and Tatham were as good as ever; whilst of the young players, E. J. Moore, R. M. Pattison, and C. S. Wooldridge, quite justified their selection. The English team played a distinctive style, the Oxford passing, inaugurated by that prince of captains, H. Vassall, was

understood by the whole team, and as practically the
same men took part in all three matches of the year,
they worked together in perfect unison. In the previous
year England had played five backs in opposition to six.
This year the numbers were reversed, Scotland playing five
backs and England six. The result of the match was
also reversed, for whereas England with five backs in
1882 lost the match, Scotland with five backs in 1883
lost the match in their turn. The game is noteworthy
as being the last occasion on which two three-quarter

A FORWARD RUSH.
(*From an Instantaneous Photograph by E. Airey, Bradford.*)

backs were played in an International Match, and the
policy of the Scotsmen in adopting that system is
questionable, when it was well known that the play of
the three "three-quarters" was the strong point in the
English game. Possibly the selectors of the Scotch
team relied upon the strength of their ten forwards to
rush the English nine and thus spoil the back play.
But the Englishmen, led by C. Gurdon, who displayed
wonderful form, worked hard and frustrated these tactics,
and so the forwards were fairly evenly matched. Now
and then England slacked; Scotland never did, and by
their unfailing energy considerably interfered with the
"passing" game; but when the Englishmen did get a
chance they illustrated the efficacy of the system. The

Scotch forwards, prominent amongst whom was C. Reid, played their characteristic strong game, but their back play was weak and disappointing. Reid obtained the try for Scotland ; Rotherham and Bolton scored for England, the latter's try being the result of a brilliant run ; but though he landed the ball between the posts the kick at goal was a failure. The match throughout was well contested, and was practically a struggle between determined forward play and scientific combination amongst the back players.

TEAMS.

ENGLAND.—H. B. Tristram (Oxford University), back ; W. N. Bolton (Blackheath and R.M. College Sandhurst), A. M. Evanson (Oxford University), G. C. Wade (Oxford University), three-quarter backs ; A. Rotherham (Oxford University), J. H. Payne (Broughton), half-backs ; E. T. Gurdon (Richmond), captain, C. Gurdon (Richmond), H. G. Fuller (Cambridge University), R. M. Pattison (Cambridge University), W. M. Tatham (Oxford University and Marlborough Nomads), C. S. Wooldridge (Oxford University), G. T. Thomson (Halifax), E. G. Moore (Oxford University), R. S. F. Henderson (Blackheath), forwards.

SCOTLAND.—D. W. Kidston (Glasgow Academicals), back ; W. E. Maclagan (London Scottish), M. F. Reid (Loretto), three-quarter backs ; P. W. Smeaton (Edinburgh Academicals), W. Sorley Brown (Edinburgh Institution), half-backs ; D. Y. Cassels, captain, A. Walker (West of Scotland), D. M'Cowan (West of Scotland), J. Jameson (West of Scotland), J. B. Brown (Glasgow Academicals), W. A. Walls (Glasgow Academicals), J. G. Mowat (Glasgow Academicals), C. Reid (Edinburgh Academicals), D. Somerville (Edinburgh Institution), T. Ainslie (Edinburgh Institution), forwards.

FEBRUARY 5TH, MANCHESTER.

England beat Ireland by a goal and 3 tries to a try.

The English team again showed a want of "lasting power," for whilst scoring a goal and 2 tries before half-time, they were able to score only a try to a try during the second half. The Irishmen played in a wonderfully plucky manner in an uphill game, and, as usual, exhibited honest work in the scrummage. Their dribbling was excellent, A. J. Forrest being particularly prominent. England won by a goal (placed by Evanson from a try by Tatham) and 3 tries (Wade, Bolton, and Twynam) to a try (Forrest). The play of the winners was disappointing ; at times brilliant, and at other times slack, the scrummage work being very poor. Several changes were made in selecting the team to meet Scotland.

TEAMS.

ENGLAND.—A. S. Taylor (Blackheath), back ; A. M. Evanson (Oxford University), W. N. Bolton (Blackheath), G. C. Wade (Oxford University), three-quarter backs: H. T. Twynam (Richmond), J. H. Payne (Broughton), half-backs: E. T. Gurdon, captain (Richmond), C. S. Wooldridge (Oxford University), W. M. Tatham (Marlborough Nomads and Oxford University), B. B. Middleton (Birkenhead Park), G. T. Thomson (Halifax), H. G. Fuller (Cambridge University), G. Standing (Blackheath), R. M. Pattison (Cambridge University), E. G. Moore (Oxford University), forwards.

IRELAND.—R. Morrow (Queen's College, Belfast), back; R. E. M'Lean (North of Ireland), T. Scovell (Kingstown), three-quarter backs; W. W. Fletcher (Kingstown), J. P. Warren (Kingstown), half-backs; Dr. Scriven, captain (Dublin University), T. Taylor (Queen's College, Belfast), A. J. Forrest (Wanderers), H. King (Dublin University), F. Henston (Kingstown), A. Miller (Kingstown), D. F. Moore (Wanderers), S. Bruce (North of Ireland), R. W. Hughes (North of Ireland), J. S. M'Donald (Queen's College, Belfast), forwards.

DECEMBER 15TH, 1882, SWANSEA.
England beat Wales by 2 goals and 4 tries to nothing.

In this, the second match between these countries, England was very strongly represented, and the back combination was far too strong for Wales. The great feature of the match was the powerful and dodgy running of G. C. Wade, who obtained 3 tries; the other tries were scored by Thomson and Henderson. Though the score was large, the match was not a "runaway affair," for the Welshmen pressed their opponents on several occasions, their forwards working most honestly, whilst the Englishmen occasionally slackened in the scrummage work.

R. S. F. HENDERSON.
(*From a Photograph by J. Moffat, Edinburgh.*)

TEAMS.

ENGLAND.—A. S. Taylor (Blackheath), back; W. N. Bolton (Royal Military College, Sandhurst), A. M. Evanson (Oxford University), G. C. Wade (Oxford University), three-quarter backs; A. Rotherham (Oxford University), J. H. Payne (Broughton), half-backs; E. T. Gurdon, captain (Richmond), H. G. Fuller (Cambridge University), H. Vassall (Oxford University), W. M. Tatham (Oxford University), R. S. F. Henderson (Blackheath), C. S. Wooldridge (Oxford University), R. S. Kindersley (Exeter), G. Standing (Blackheath), G. T. Thomson (Halifax), forwards.

WALES.—C. P. Lewis (Llandovery), J. Bowen (Llanelly), backs; W. B. Norton (Cardiff), J. Clare (Cardiff), D. Gwynn (Swansea), three-quarter backs; C. H. Newman (Newport), E. Treharne (Pontypridd), half-backs; G. F. Harding (Newport), R. Gould (Newport), G. L. Morris

(Swansea), A. Cattell (Llanelly), T. B. Jones (Newport), J. H. Judson (Llanelly), T. J. S. Clapp (Nantyglo), F. W. Purdon (Swansea), forwards.

MARCH 1ST, 1884, BLACKHEATH.
England beat Scotland by a goal to a try.

The year 1884 was memorable for the famous dispute as to the validity of the try gained by England, a dispute which caused the abandonment of the England v. Scotland match in 1885, and was also the unavowed reason of the great embroglio of 1888 and 1889. Blackheath was the venue of the match, and an even game was anticipated. The only guide to the merits of the respective teams was the result of the English and Scotch matches with Wales, inasmuch as though Ireland had been soundly beaten by Scotland, whilst playing England a tight game, no line could be drawn from the matches with that country, since England with a weak team had met Ireland with its best, whilst the Irishmen had been poorly represented when meeting Scotland with its best team. The match bore out the anticipations of a keen contest, but, strangely enough, where England was expected to be strong they were weak, whilst Scotland shone at their weak point. Generally, England has been superior to Scotland in the open, and the passing has been more scientific and well-timed, whilst the Scotch teams have shone in the tight scrummages, but have generally failed in the open. In this match the open play of England was not brilliant, though at times the players exhibited their proper form, notably during the concluding minutes of the match. Scotland, though beaten, had slightly the better of the match, and had not the English forwards done good scrummage-work, the Thistle would have triumphed over the Rose. C. Reid, as usual, was the bulwark of the Scotch forwards, and scored for his country. Grant Asher and Don Wauchope were the Scotch halves, and rarely have two more brilliant players appeared on the same side as the rival cracks of Oxford and Cambridge Universities. They were most equally matched by Rotherham and Twynam, and as a consequence brilliant play was conspicuous by its absence, the several halves frustrating the open tactics of the respective *vis-à-vis*. The English three-quarters were expected to be superior to their opponents, but in actual play they showed to no advantage compared with the Scotch trio.

ENGLISH TEAM v. SCOTLAND: BLACKHEATH, MARCH 1st, 1884.

(England, 1 Goal; Scotland, 1 Try.)

(From a Photograph by Hills & Saunders, Oxford.)

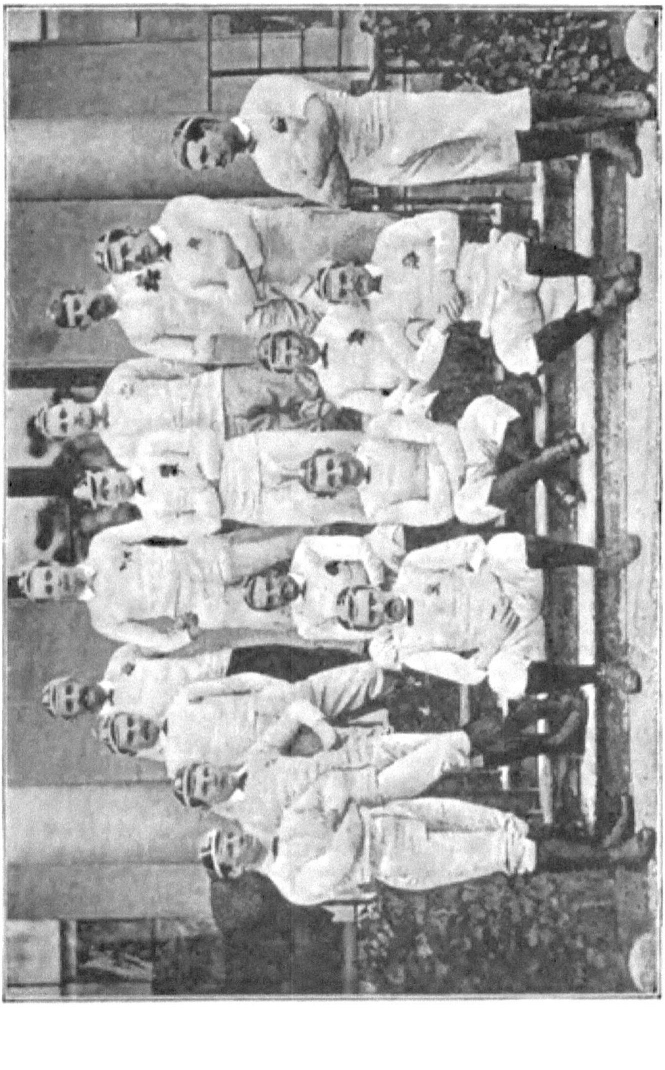

C. Gurdon. R. S. Kindersley. A. Rotherham. G. T. Thomson.
E. L. Strong. A. M. Evanson. C. S. Wooldridge.
W. M. Tatham. H. T. Twynam. H. B. Tristram.
G. C. Wade. R. S. F. Henderson. E. T. Gurdon. C. J. B. Marriott. W. N. Bolton.

The disputed point was a try gained by Kindersley, from which a goal was scored. The facts of the dispute were simple, and admitted by both sides. A Scotch player knocked the ball back, and an Englishman secured it and Kindersley obtained a try. The contention of England was (1) "that it was lawful to knock back"; (2) "that even if it was illegal to do so the Scotsmen could claim no advantage from an illegal act committed by one of their side"; (3) "that as no Englishman appealed, the subsequent play was legal"; (4) "that the referee decided that a try was obtained, and based his decision on a point of fact, the point put before him being whether an Englishman had appealed or not." The Scotsmen contended that "the point in dispute was the interpretation of the law dealing with knocking the ball, and denied the right of the Rugby Union to be sole interpreters of the laws of the game." The Rugby Union, for the sake of argument, conceded the Scotch interpretation of the law, viz., "that knocking back was illegal," but firmly refused to allow the decision of the referee on a point of fact to be submitted to any arbitration. To quote from a statement sent by G. R. Hill, the secretary of the Rugby Union, to the clubs belonging to the Union:—

"The committee hold that the referee's decision upon the only point on which the issue of the match turns is plain, and it is this decision that my committee have urged Scotland to accept. Their refusal to do so has resulted in the abandonment of the annual match between the two countries this year (1885). My committee much regret this result, but they are firmly convinced that the abandonment of the match is a matter far less important than the upholding the principle that a referee's decision is unimpeachable. Whilst expressing their willingness to consider any proposal that Scotland might bring forward for the settlement of disputed points in future International matches in connection with the construction of the laws, they have felt it their plain duty to decline all overtures for the discussion of the referee's ruling. The establishment of a precedent of this nature would be a fatal blow to the interests of Rugby Union football; the spirit in which the game should be played will be entirely lost if the decisions of the officials appointed for the purpose of seeing fair play are to be discussed and set aside. In holding this view my committee are convinced that they have the loyal support of every club in the Rugby Football Union."

The Scotch Union were correct in their contention that the Rugby Union could not claim the right to interpret the laws of the game as governing International matches, but they were wrong in endeavouring to argue that this was the point at issue as regards the match in question. It was the referee's decision on a point of fact that was assailed, and the Rugby Union evinced clearness of judgment in keeping the real issue before them, and performed true and lasting service to the best interests of the game by declining to consent to any arrangement which should arraign the decision of the referee on a point of fact. Out of the dispute good ensued, and on the Scotsmen agreeing to admit the victory of England, the Rugby Union consented to the formation of an International Board to settle future disputes in International matches. The functions of this Board were further developed in 1890, and it finally acquired the power of making and interpreting the laws governing International matches. This occurred after a dispute between the Rugby Union and the Unions of the other countries lasting two years, during which period, though Scotland, Ireland, and Wales played International matches, England had no fixture with any of the other countries.

TEAMS.

ENGLAND.—H. B. Tristram (Oxford University and Durham), back; A. M. Evanson (Oxford University and Richmond), G. C. Wade (Oxford University), W. N. Bolton (Blackheath), three-quarter backs; A. Rotherham (Oxford University), H. T. Twynam (Richmond), half-backs; E. T. Gurdon (Richmond), captain, C. Gurdon (Richmond), R. S. F. Henderson (Blackheath), W. M. Tatham (Oxford University and Marlborough Nomads), E. L. Strong (Oxford University and Somerset), C. J. B. Marriott (Cambridge University), C. S. Wooldridge (Hampshire, late Oxford), R. S. Kindersley (Devonshire and Oxford), G. T. Thomson (Halifax), forwards.

SCOTLAND.—J. P. Veitch (Royal High School), back; D. J. Macfarlan (London Scottish), E. L. Roland (Edinburgh Wanderers), W. E. Maclagan (London Scottish), three-quarter backs; A. G. Grant Asher (Fettes-Loretto), A. R. Don Wauchope (Fettes-Loretto), half-backs; C. Reid (Edinburgh Academicals), J. B. Brown (Glasgow Academicals), W. Walls (Glasgow Academicals), T. Ainslie (Edinburgh Institution), W. A. Peterkin (Edinburgh University), C. W. Berry (Fettes-Loretto), D. McCowan (West of Scotland), J. Jamieson (West of Scotland), J. Tod (Watsonians), forwards.

FEBRUARY 4TH, DUBLIN.
England defeated Ireland by a goal to nothing.

Against Ireland this year England played a very weak team, and barely escaped defeat. The forwards played a sound though not brilliant game. Had the Irish backs been scorers instead of defensive players the Irishmen would probably have won the match. Bolton was in his best form, and obtained a try, and Evanson kicked the goal.

TEAMS.

ENGLAND.—C. H. Sample (Cambridge University and Northumberland), back; W. N. Bolton (Blackheath), H. Wigglesworth (Thornes), H. Fallas (Wakefield Trinity), three-quarter backs; J. H. Payne (Broughton), H. T. Twynam (Richmond), half-backs; E. T. Gurdon (Richmond), captain, W. M. Tatham (Oxford University and Marlborough Nomads), E. L. Strong (Oxford University and Somerset), C. J. B. Marriott (Cambridge University), C. S. Wooldridge (Hampshire County, late Oxford University), A. Wood (Halifax), G. T. Thomson (Halifax), A. Teggin (Broughton Rangers), H. Bell (New Brighton), forwards.

IRELAND.—R. W. Morrow (Belfast Albion), back; D. Ross (Belfast Albion), R. H. Scovell (Dublin University), R. E. McLean (North of Ireland), three-quarter backs; M. Johnston (Dublin University), W. Higgin (North of Ireland), half-backs; J. A. Macdonald (Queen's College, Belfast), captain, S. Bruce (North of Ireland), R. W. Hughes (North of Ireland), O. Stokes (Cork), F. Lewis (Cork), W. G. Rutherford (Tipperary), J. B. Buchanan (Dublin University), J. A. Brabazon (Dublin University), D. F. Moore (Wanderers), forwards.

JANUARY 5TH, LEEDS.

England defeated Wales by a goal and 2 tries to a goal.

The ground was very heavy, but the Welshmen seemed to like the wet, and fairly put the Englishmen on their mettle. The tries for England were gained by Rotherham, Wade, and Twynam, Bolton kicking the goal. Allen obtained the try for Wales, and Lewis kicked the goal. The English backs, who had very few chances, were very difficult to hold when once they got fairly off. W. H. Gwynn played a very clever game at half-back for Wales, and Taylor nearly succeeded in lowering the English goal by a drop-kick. The Welshmen were delighted at the good fight they made.

TEAMS.

ENGLAND.—H. B. Tristram (Oxford University and Durham), back; G. C. Wade (Oxford University), C. E. Chapman (Southampton Trojans and Cambridge University), W. N. Bolton (Blackheath), three-quarter backs; A. Rotherham (Oxford University), H. T. Twynam (Richmond), half-backs; E. T. Gurdon (Richmond), captain, C. Gurdon (Richmond), R. S. F. Henderson (Blackheath), W. M. Tatham (Oxford University), E. L. Strong (Oxford University), H. G. Fuller (Cambridge University), C. J. B. Marriott (Cambridge University), C. S. Wooldridge (Hampshire County, late Oxford University), J. T. Hunt (Manchester), forwards.

WALES.—C. P. Lewis (Llandovery), back; C. P. Allen (Beaumaris), W. B. Norton (Cardiff), C. G. Taylor (Wrexham), three-quarter backs; C. H. Newman (Newport), W. H. Gwynn (Swansea), half-backs; T. J. S. Clapp (Newport), W. D. Phillips (Cardiff), J. S. Smith (Cardiff), R. Gould (Newport), H. S. Lyne (Newport), H. J. Simpson (Cardiff), G. L. Morris (Swansea), F. Margrave (Llanelly), F. G. Andrews (Swansea), forwards.

FEBRUARY 7TH, 1885, MANCHESTER.

England beat Ireland by 2 tries to 1 try.

In February England met and defeated Ireland at Manchester by 2 tries to 1. Sample filled Tristram's place at back; Bolton, Wade's at three-quarter, and C. Gurdon, Horley, and Wooldridge replaced Court, Kindersley, and Teggin. The form was nothing approaching the brilliancy of the Welsh match. The English forwards were palpably worsted by the Irishmen in the scrummage, and it was only the great superiority of the back players which won the game.

TEAMS.

ENGLAND.—C. H. Sample (Northumberland and Cambridge University), back; A. E. Stoddart (Blackheath), J. J. Hawcridge (Bradford), W. N. Bolton (Blackheath), three-quarter backs; J. H. Payne (Broughton), A. Rotherham (Oxford University), half-backs; E. T. Gurdon (Richmond), captain, C. Gurdon (Richmond), C. S. Wooldridge (Hampshire and Blackheath), C. H. Horley (Swinton), A. T. Kemble (Liverpool), F. Moss (Broughton), G. T. Thomson (Halifax), G. Harrison (Hull), J. Ryalls (Cheshire County), forwards.

IRELAND.—G. Wheeler (Queen's College, Belfast), back; R. E. M'Lean (North of Ireland), J. P. Ross (Lansdowne), E. H. Greene (Dublin University), three-quarter backs; E. C. Crawford (Dublin University), R. G. Warren (Lansdowne), half-backs; W. Rutherford (Tipperary), captain, R. W. Hughes (North of Ireland), T. Allen (North of Ireland), F. Moore (Dublin Wanderers), T. R. Lyle (Dublin University), T. Hobbes (Dublin University), R. M. Bradshaw (Dublin Wanderers), J. Shanahan (Lansdowne), H. J. Neill (North of Ireland), forwards.

JANUARY 3RD, 1885, SWANSEA.

England beat Wales by 1 goal and 4 tries to 1 goal and 1 try.

Owing to the dispute which arose on the occasion of the last match the game between England and Scotland unfortunately did not take place. That against Wales was played in the first week in January, on the ground of the Swansea Club; and though the Englishmen were not over-confident as to the result, they won handsomely by 1 goal and 4 tries to 1 goal and 1 try. The game was the fastest that we ever recollect seeing in an International match, and adapted to a nicety to the pace of the English fifteen, who with Stoddart, Hawcridge, and Wade at three-quarter, and J. Payne and Rotherham at half, were irresistible as scorers. Wade never played so well in his life, and the Welshmen could make nothing of him. He ran and dodged just as he liked, and veteran Welshmen from that day's experience still hold the opinion that he is the finest three-quarter England ever sent against them. The halves, both masters of the art of feeding, played in their most finished style, and kept their three-quarters continually at work. Forward the teams were evenly matched in the scrummage, but in the open the Welshmen were outpaced and outclassed. A. J. Gould and C. G. Taylor performed creditably for Wales, and Jordan sprinted hard for his two tries when he got an open field.

TEAMS.

ENGLAND.—H. B. Tristram (Oxford University and Durham), back; J. J. Haweridge (Bradford), A. E. Stoddart (Blackheath), G. C. Wade (Oxford University), three-quarter backs; A. Rotherham (Oxford University), J. H. Payne (Broughton), half-backs; E. T. Gurdon (Richmond), captain, R. S. Kindersley (Oxford University), E. D. Court (Blackheath), H. J. Ryalls (New Brighton), F. Moss (Broughton), A. T. Kemble (Liverpool), G. Harrison (Hull), A. Teggin (Broughton Rangers), R. S. F. Henderson (Blackheath), forwards.

WALES.—A. J. Gould (Newport), back; H. M. Jordan (Newport), C. G. Taylor (Cardiff), F. E. Hancock (Cardiff), three-quarter backs; W. H. Gwynn (Swansea), C. H. Newman (Cambridge University), half-backs; R. Gould (Newport), T. J. S. Clapp (Newport), H. S. Lyne (Newport), T. B. Jones (Newport), L. C. Thomas (Cardiff), S. Goldsworthy (Swansea), R. D. Richards (Swansea), J. S. Smith (Cardiff), M. Rowland (Lampeter), forwards.

MARCH 13TH, 1886, EDINBURGH.
England drew with Scotland, neither side scoring.

England and Scotland once more met, and a very stubborn game ended without points to either. The match cannot be described as a brilliant exposition of football, but from the toughness of the struggle and the always doubtful issue, it was intensely exciting. For two-thirds of the game England had to act on the defence, but just when she appeared beaten, she took the whip hand, and very nearly won in the last quarter of an hour. Bonsor hurt his knee badly in the first ten minutes, and was a cripple throughout the game, so that not only could he not feed his three-quarters, but he could not keep Asher in check, and the latter did pretty much as he liked. Rotherham and Robertshaw of our back players alone did themselves justice. Stoddart was indisposed, and Brutton, painfully nervous, allowed his *vis-à-vis* Morrison to show him a clean pair of heels in every sprint. Robertshaw played a masterly game on this occasion. He was the first to show in an English and Scotch match how a typical centre three-quarter ought to play not for himself but for his wings. To him,

Rotherham, and the forwards—amongst whom especial mention should be made of C. Gurdon, N. Spurling, Inglis, and Wilkinson—the credit of the draw belongs. On the Scotch side Wilson and Morrison played well, Holms was nervous, and A. R. Don Wauchope never got off.

Several players appeared for the first time in this contest, notably Rawson Robertshaw, of Bradford, the centre three-quarter *par excellence* of his day; and A. E. Stoddart, without doubt the most agile and finished wing three-quarter who has done service for England. This athlete, by his performances in the cricket field, and as a Rugby Union player, has earned for himself a fame that has fallen to the lot of no other man, and his deeds have equalled even those of the renowned A. N. Hornby. Of great speed, and possessed of wonderful dodging powers, Stoddart has left behind him a unique record of achievements on the football field. These qualities, combined with great powers both as a drop and place-kicker, have caused him to be regarded as one of the best men who has filled the position of wing three-quarter. Unfortunately for him absence from England, and the discontinuance of International matches in 1888 and 1889 as far as England was concerned, prevented him displaying his unrivalled powers in the great matches as often as he would have liked; and thus his record of appearances in the classic fixtures has suffered in comparison with others whose playing days fell in more propitious times. But by general consensus

A. E. STODDART.
(*From a Photograph by Walery, Regent Street, W.*)

Stoddart is regarded as *the* wing three-quarter during the middle and latter part of the decade now under description.

TEAMS.

ENGLAND.—C. H. Sample (Northumberland), back; A. E. Stoddart (Blackheath), R. Robertshaw (Bradford), E. B. Brutton (Cambridge University), three-quarter backs; A. Rotherham (Richmond), F. Bonsor (Bradford), half-backs; E. T. Gurdon (Richmond), captain, C. Gurdon (Richmond), W. G. Clibborn (Richmond), C. J. B. Marriott (Blackheath). N. Spurling (Blackheath), R. E. Inglis (Blackheath), G. L. Jeffery (Cambridge University), E. Wilkinson (Bradford), A. Teggin (Broughton Rangers), forwards.

SCOTLAND.—J. P. Veitch (Royal High School), back; R. H. Morrison (Edinburgh University), J. Wilson (Royal High School), W. F. Holms (Cooper Hill College), three-quarter backs; A. G. Asher (Fettesian-Lorettonians), A. R. Don Wauchope (Fettesian-Lorettonians), half-backs; J. B. Brown (Glasgow Academicals), W. A. Wallis (Glasgow Academicals), C. Reid (Edinburgh Academicals), T. W. Irvine (Edinburgh Academicals), A. T. Clay (Edinburgh Academicals), M. M. Evans (Edinburgh Academicals), Dr. Tod (Watsonians), C. J. B. Milne (West of Scotland), D. A. McLeod (Glasgow University), forwards.

FEBRUARY 6TH, 1886, DUBLIN.

England beat Ireland by 1 try to nothing.

England met Ireland in Dublin on February 6th, and won by 1 try to nothing. The score does not represent the play, which was greatly in favour of the English team, who beat the Irishmen forward, where they expected to excel, while behind they quite out-classed them. A. S. Taylor played back, Wade three-quarters, and P. F. Hancock forward, *vice* Sample, Brutton, and E. T. Gurdon. The other players' names appear in the team *v.* Scotland.

TEAMS.

ENGLAND.—A. S. Taylor (Blackheath), back; A. E. Stoddart, R. Robertshaw (Bradford), G. C. Wade (Oxford University and Richmond), three-quarter backs; A. Rotherham (Richmond), F. Bonsor (Bradford), half-backs; C. Gurdon (Richmond), W. G. Clibborn (Richmond), C. J. B. Marriott (Blackheath), captain, P. F. Hancock (Somersetshire), N. Spurling (Blackheath), E. Wilkinson (Bradford), A. Teggin (Broughton Rangers), forwards.

IRELAND.—R. W. Morrow (Lisburn), back; J. P. Ross (North of Ireland), D. J. Ross (Albion), E. H. Greene (Dublin Wanderers), three-quarter backs; R. G. Warren (Lansdowne), M. Johnston (Dublin Wanderers), captain, half-backs; R. H. Mossey-Westropp (Limerick and Monkstown), R. W. Hughes (North of Ireland), T. Shanahan (Lansdowne), J. Johnstone (Albion), H. Brabazon (Dublin University), W. C. Rutherford (Clanwilliam), T. R. Lyle (Dublin University), J. Chambers (Dublin University), V. C. Le Fanu (Cambridge University and Lansdowne), forwards.

JANUARY 2ND, 1886, BLACKHEATH.
England beat Wales by 1 goal 2 tries to 1 goal.

England played Wales at Blackheath, on January 2nd, and won by 1 goal (placed by Stoddart from a free catch) and 2 tries (Wade and Wilkinson) to 1 goal placed from a try by Stadden. The performance was not a great one. The forwards never showed any dash, and after a quarter of an hour slacked away to nothing. Elliot and Moss were in the forwards in this match, but did not play against Scotland. The English goal was

FORMING THE SCRUMMAGE.
(*From an instantaneous Photograph by E. Airey, Bradford.*)

obtained from a foolish piece of play on the part of Elliot, which luckily proved the winning point. That player, catching the ball from a miss-kick of the Welsh back, had a clear-run in, but, to the astonishment of his fellow-players, made his mark, from which Stoddart placed a goal.

TEAMS.

ENGLAND.—A. S. Taylor (Blackheath), back; G. C. Wade (Richmond), A. E. Stoddart (Blackheath), R. Robertshaw (Bradford), three-quarter backs; A. Rotherham (Richmond), F. Bonsor (Bradford), half-backs; C. Gurdon (Richmond), W. G. Clibborn (Richmond), C. J. B. Marriott (Blackheath), captain, G. L. Jeffery (Cambridge University and Blackheath), R. E. Inglis (Blackheath), P. F. Hancock (Somersetshire), E. Wilkinson (Bradford), F. Moss (Broughton Rangers), C. Elliot (Sunderland), forwards.

WALES.—D. Bowen (Llanelly), back; C. G. Taylor (Blackheath and Rusbon), W. M. Douglas (Cardiff), A. J. Gould (Newport), three-quarter backs; C. H. Newman (Newport), captain, W. Stadden (Cardiff), half-backs; A. F. Hill (Cardiff), D. Morgan (Swansea), E. P. Alexander (Cambridge University), J. W. R. Gould (Newport), W. H. Thomas (Llandovery), E. Roberts (Llanelly), W. Bowen (Swansea), D. H. Lewis (Cardiff), G. A. Young (Cardiff), forwards.

MARCH 5TH, 1887, MANCHESTER.
England drew with Scotland, each side scoring 1 try.

England met Scotland at Manchester, and once more the teams left the field with honours easy. The match was played in so thick a fog that it was impossible to see across the field of play. Scotland were supposed to have an easy job on hand, but the English team played in the most determined fashion, and at half-time led by a try. In the succeeding half the Scotch equalised matters. Jeffery, who gained the try, was decidedly the man of the day, and gave as finished and skilful exhibition of modern forward play as could be wished for. W. N. Bolton once more, after only a few weeks' practice, took his place at three-quarter, and played a remarkably fine robust game. Tristram at full-back was magnificent, and his tackling of Maclagan in full stride on the goal-line was a performance which nobody who witnessed it will ever forget. On account of their form against Ireland and Wales, the English team which met Scotland, and which was a very different one from the two who played in the other International matches, was undoubtedly a greatly underrated one, as will be gathered from the names of the fifteen. Behind they were decidedly superior to Scotland, and on the day's play certainly their equals forward. Jeffery, Hickson, Clibborn, Cleveland, Dewhirst, and Wilkinson were all great players; the names of the back division speak for themselves; and the team as a whole, though estimated lightly, was probably one of the best that ever represented England. On the Scotch side C. Reid once more showed himself to be the finest forward of this or any other time, and had able supporters in M'Ewan and MacMillan, both of whom played in characteristic Scotch style. The halves, Orr and P. R. Don Wauchope, were by no means a match for Rotherham and Bonsor. Maclagan was as sound as ever, but Lindsay played nervously, and Woodrow was not up to International class.

TEAMS.

ENGLAND.—H. B. Tristram (Richmond), back; W. N. Bolton (Blackheath), R. Robertshaw (Bradford), R. E. Lockwood (Dewsbury), three-quarter backs; A. Rotherham (Richmond), captain, F. Bonsor (Bradford), half-backs; J. H. Dewhirst (Cambridge University), H. Springman (Liverpool), W. G. Clibborn (Richmond), G. L. Jeffery (Blackheath), C. R. Cleveland (Oxford University), J. L. Hickson (Bradford), E. Wilkinson (Bradford), R. Seddon (Broughton Rangers), A. Teggin (Broughton Rangers), forwards.

SCOTLAND.—W. F. Holms (London Scottish), back; W. E. Maclagan (London Scottish), G. C. Lindsay (London Scottish), A. N. Woodrow (Glasgow Academicals), three-quarter backs; C. Orr (West of Scotland), P. H. Don Wauchope (Edinburgh Wanderers), half-backs; C. Reid (Edinburgh Academicals), T. W. Irvine (Edinburgh Academicals), M. C. M'Ewan (Edinburgh Academicals), A. T. Clay (Edinburgh Academicals), H. Kerr (Glasgow Academicals), J. French (Glasgow Academicals), C. W. Berry (Edinburgh Wanderers), J. G. MacMillan (West of Scotland), D. Morton (West of Scotland), forwards.

FEBRUARY 5TH, 1887, DUBLIN.

Ireland beat England by 2 goals to nil.

The English and Irish match on the 5th of February at Dublin resulted in the first victory for Ireland by 2 goals (from tries by Montgomery and Tillie) to *nil*.

The cause of England's defeat must be attributed to the mediocre display of her forwards, who allowed themselves to be hustled all over the field by their opponents, and never gave their players behind a ghost of a chance. To make matters worse, Fagan, who started with a sprained ankle, and never ought to have played, broke down shortly after the start. The Irishmen played in the most resolute style, and it was their determination and cohesion which enabled them to beat England, who were unquestionably their superiors behind the scrummage. The English team was largely remodelled before they met Scotland, Roberts (back), M. T. Scott (half), C. J. Marriott, Seddon, and Pease being supplanted by players whose names appear in the team *v*. Scotland.

TEAMS.

ENGLAND.—S. Roberts (Swinton), back; E. Lockwood (Dewsbury), W. N. Bolton (Blackheath), A. Fagan (United Hospitals), three-quarter backs; M. T. Scott (Cambridge University), A. Rotherham (Richmond), captain, half-backs; W. G. Clibborn (Richmond), G. L. Jeffery (Blackheath), C. J. B. Marriott (Blackheath), J. H. Dewhirst (Cambridge University), R. Seddon (Broughton Rangers), A. T. Kemble (Liverpool), A. Teggin (Broughton Rangers), J. L. Hickson (Bradford), F. Pease (Durham), forwards.

IRELAND.—D. B. Walkington (North of Ireland and Dublin University), back; C. R. Tillie (Dublin University), D. F. Rambaut (Dublin University), R. Montgomery (Queen's College, Belfast), three-quarter backs;

R. G. Warren (Lansdowne), captain, J. M'Laughlin (Derry), half-backs; T. R. Lyle (Dublin University), J. Chambers (Dublin University), V. C. Le Fanu (Lansdowne and Cambridge University), H. J. Neill (North of Ireland), E. J. Walsh (Lansdowne), J. Dick (Queen's College, Cork), J. Johnstone (Albion), R. Stevenson (Lisburn), J. M'Cauley (Limerick), forwards.

JANUARY 8TH, 1887, LLANELLY.

England drew with Wales, neither side scoring.

England met Wales at Llanelly on the 8th of January, when a drawn game resulted. The ground was not in a fit state for football, a morning's thaw supervening on a severe frost. Till the last moment it was in doubt whether the match could be played, and it was only carried out under the greatest difficulties. Not a player on the field could keep his legs on the skating rink, and both sides funked the hard frost-bound ground with a slippery top. Scientific football was out of the question, and the game, which consisted of slipping and sliding, demands no serious comment.

TEAMS.

ENGLAND.—S. Roberts (Swinton), back; R. Robertshaw (Bradford), J. Le Fleming (Cambridge University), R. E. Lockwood (Dewsbury), three-quarter backs; F. Bonsor (Bradford), A. Rotherham (Richmond), captain, half-backs; W. G. Clibborn (Richmond), N. Spurling (Blackheath), G. L. Jeffery (Blackheath), C. R. Cleveland (Oxford University), J. H. Dewhirst (Cambridge University), H. C. Baker (Gloucestershire), F. Wilkinson (Bradford), J. L. Hickson (Bradford), R. Seddon (Broughton Rangers), forwards.

WALES.—D. H. Bowen (Llanelly), back; C. G. Taylor (Ruabon and London Welsh), A. J. Gould (Newport and London Welsh), T. Douglas (Cardiff), three-quarter backs; C. H. Newman (Newport and Durham), O. J. Evans (Cardiff), half-backs; E. P. Alexander (Cambridge and London Welsh), W. H. Thomas (Cambridge and London Welsh), D. Morgan (Swansea), W. Bowen (Swansea), A. J. Hybart (Cardiff), A. F. Bland (Cardiff), W. S. Capp (Newport), R. Gould (Newport), T. W. Lockwood (Newport), forwards.

1887-88.—England played no International matches this season, declining to recognise an International tribunal constituted on the basis of an International numerical equality. A team was, however, chosen, and caps presented to its members.

TEAM.

A. Fagan (Richmond), back; J. Valentine (Swinton), P. Robertshaw (Bradford), C. G. Hubbard (Blackheath), three-quarter backs; F. Bonsor (Bradford), F. H. Fox (Somerset), half-backs; G. L. Jeffery (Blackheath), N. Spurling (Blackheath), W. G. Clibborn (Richmond), J. H. Dewhirst (Richmond), A. Robinson (Cambridge University), P. F. Hancock (Somerset), H. Eagles (Salford), J. L. Hickson (Bradford), C. Anderton (Manchester Free Wanderers), forwards.

FEBRUARY 16TH, 1889, BLACKHEATH.

England beat the Maoris by 1 goal 4 tries to nothing.

The only International match in which England engaged this season was that against the Maoris on the 16th of February at Blackheath. As was expected would be the case, the visitors were completely outclassed and defeated by a goal and 4 tries to nothing. Bedford got in twice, Evershed, Stoddart, and Sutcliffe once.

The match will be remembered for the rough play and extraordinary conduct of the Maoris, who during their visit to this country displayed a remarkable aptitude for disputing the decisions of the officials. The English umpire and the referee were anathematised and threatened, and at one period of the game five of the Maori team left the field, but were induced to return by their manager. The English team was an exceedingly strong one, and it was a great pity that they had no opportunity of showing their prowess to the other countries.

TEAM.

A. Royle (Broughton Rangers), back; R. E. Lockwood (Dewsbury), A. E. Stoddart (Blackheath), J. W. Sutcliffe (Heckmondwike), three-quarter backs; F. Bonsor (Bradford), W. M. Scott (Cambridge University), half-backs; C. Anderton (Manchester Free Wanderers), H. Bedford (Morley), J. W. Cave (Cambridge University), F. Evershed (Burton), D. Jowett (Heckmondwike), F. W. Lowrie (Batley), A. Robinson (Blackheath), H. Wilkinson (Halifax), W. Yiend (Hartlepool Rovers), forwards.

MARCH 1ST, 1890, EDINBURGH.

England beat Scotland by 1 goal and 1 try to nothing.

This year will ever be memorable by reason of the satisfactory settlement of the International difficulty, and the resumption of International matches. England and Scotland recommenced their battles at Edinburgh on the 1st March, when the former proved victorious by a goal and a try (the scorers being Evershed and Dyson) to *nil*. As may be supposed, the game after the suspension of hostilities for a couple of years excited the greatest interest. England thoroughly deserved her victory, and showed superior play at every point of the game. The play was open and attractive, and the English forwards, five of whom were Yorkshiremen, for once in the way worked together with the combination of a club team, and were much too fast for the Scots in the open.

ENGLISH TEAM v. SCOTLAND: EDINBURGH, MARCH 1st, 1890.

(ENGLAND, 1 GOAL 1 TRY; SCOTLAND, NIL.)

B. JOWITT, M. T. SCOTT, W. G. MITCHELL, H. BRYDONE, J. DYSON, R. L. ASTON, A. ROBINSON,
S. M. J. WOODS, P. H. MORRISON, J. TOOTHILL, E. HOLMES, J. L. HICKSON,
J. H. ROGERS, F. H. FOX (capt.), F. EVERSHED.

Evershed, Woods, Toothill, and Bedford were brilliant. Aston, the English three-quarter, played as fine a centre game as has ever been shown in an International match, and the way he fed his wings was a revelation to Scotch football. He practically got the try for Dyson by a most skilful piece of passing. The Scotch forwards were not seen at their best, and did not work in the scrummage in their traditional style. For the first time in his career Maclagan, who had done such sterling work for Scotland in her past International matches, failed, and clearly showed the signs of wear. M'Ewan and MacMillan were the best of their forwards. Stevenson is not a centre three-quarter, and though he is undoubtedly a clever player, being a very skilful kick in particular, he plays his own game and not the game of his wings.

TEAMS.

ENGLAND.—W. G. Mitchell (Richmond), back; P. H. Morrison (Cambridge University), R. L. Aston (Cambridge University), J. Dyson (Huddersfield), three-quarter backs; F. H. Fox (Somerset), captain, M. T. Scott (Northumberland), half-backs; J. L. Hickson (Bradford), J. Toothill (Bradford), E. Holmes (Manningham), D. Jowett (Heckmondwike), H. Bedford (Morley), S. M. J. Woods (Cambridge University), F. Evershed (Burton), J. H. Rogers (Moseley), A. Robinson (Blackheath), forwards.

SCOTLAND.—G. MacGregor (Cambridge University), back; W. E. Maclagan (London Scottish), H. J. Stevenson (Edinburgh Academicals), G. R. Wilson (Royal High School), three-quarter backs; C. E. Orr (West of Scotland), D. G. Anderson (London Scottish), half-backs; M. C. M'Ewan (Edinburgh Academicals), J. D. Boswell (West of Scotland), J. E. Orr (West of Scotland), D. Morton (West of Scotland), R. G. MacMillan (West of Scotland), A. Dalgleish (Gala), F. W. J. Goodhue (London Scottish), I. M'Intyre (Edinburgh Wanderers), H. T. Ker (Glasgow Academicals), forwards.

MARCH 15TH, 1890, BLACKHEATH.

England beat Ireland by 3 tries to nothing.

England met and defeated Ireland by 3 tries to nothing at Blackheath on the 15th of March. The points were scored by Stoddart (who played *vice* Dyson), Rogers, and Morrison. After playing well in the first half the English team slacked off, and the Irishmen were several times near scoring towards the end of the game. The English form was nothing like so good as against Scotland.

TEAMS.

ENGLAND.—W. G. Mitchell (Richmond), back; P. H. Morrison (Cambridge University), R. L. Aston (Cambridge University), A. E. Stoddart (Blackheath), captain, three-quarter backs; F. W. Spence

(Birkenhead Park), Mason T. Scott (Northumberland), half-backs; J. L. Hickson (Bradford), J. Toothill (Bradford), E. Holmes (Manningham), D. Jowett (Heckmondwike), H. Bedford (Morley), S. M. J. Woods (Cambridge University), F. Evershed (Burton), J. H. Rogers (Moseley), A. Robinson (Blackheath), forwards.

IRELAND.—D. B. Walkington (Dublin University), back; R. Dunlop (Dublin University), R. W. Johnstone (Dublin University), T. Edwards (Lansdowne), three-quarter backs; R. G. Warren (Lansdowne), captain, B. Tuke (Bective Rangers), half-backs; J. H. O'Connor (Bective Rangers), J. Waites (Bective Rangers), V. C. Le Fanu (Lansdowne), E. Forrest (Wanderers), J. Roche (Wanderers), R. Stevenson (Dungannon), W. Davis (Bective Rangers), J. N. Nash (Queen's College, Cork), J. Lyttle (North of Ireland), forwards.

FEBRUARY 15TH, 1890, DEWSBURY.
Wales beat England by a try to nothing.

Wales gained her first victory over England by a try to nothing. A sleeting snow-storm, which continued throughout the game, rendered the ground a veritable quagmire. Indeed, we never recollect seeing a football ground in such a condition. The English forwards, a very heavy lot, were quite unable to keep their feet or show anything like approaching their proper form. The English fifteen were remodelled before meeting Scotland. The Welsh try was cleverly gained by Stadden, who tricked the opposing half by bouncing the ball out of touch. The Welsh passing by the four three-quarters was very fine, considering the state of the ground.

TEAMS.

ENGLAND.—W. G. Mitchell (Richmond), back; P. H. Morrison (Cambridge University), A. E. Stoddart (Blackheath), J. Valentine (Swinton), three-quarter backs; F. H. Fox (Somersetshire), J. Wright (Bradford), half-backs; A. Robinson (Blackheath), P. F. Hancock (Somersetshire), J. H. Dewhirst (Richmond), S. M. J. Woods (Cambridge University), R. D. Budworth (Oxford University), F. Evershed (Burton-on-Trent), J. H. Rogers (Moseley), J. L. Hickson (Bradford), F. W. Lowrie (Batley), forwards.

WALES.—W. J. Bancroft (Swansea), back; D. Gwynn (Swansea), Percy Lloyd (Llanelly), R. Garrett (Penarth), A. J. Gould (Newport), three-quarter backs; W. Stadden (Cardiff), C. Thomas (Newport), half-backs; W. O. Williams (Cardiff), D. W. Evans (Cardiff), A. E. Bland (Cardiff), J. Hannen (Newport), W. H. Thomas (London Welsh), S. Thomas (Llanelly), W. Bowen (Swansea), J. Meredith (Swansea), forwards.

MARCH 7TH, 1891, RICHMOND.
Scotland beat England by 3 goals to 1 goal.

The English fifteen which met Scotland at Richmond on the 7th March were certainly the most disappointing that ever represented this country, and gave an exhibition entirely unworthy of the reputation of the players who composed it. They carried with them the confidence of the public, who expected to see a repetition of the Edinburgh performances in the previous season. Not only, however, were they beaten, but badly beaten, by 3 goals to 1. Tries were got by J. E. Orr and W. Neilson, and a goal dropped by P. R. Clauss. Chiefly to blame for this were the forwards and halves. The former were hustled and routed, and there was not an ounce of scrummage work amongst the nine of them, while it is not the slightest exaggeration to say that in the second half they literally chucked it. Berry, who had shown good form at half in the previous International matches, cut up most indifferently, and probably realised at the end of the game that it is advisable to train for an International match, especially to meet the determined play indulged in by Scotsmen. The game clearly demonstrated that Berry's forte was trickiness in attack, and that his defence was deplorably weak. Behind beaten forwards he was useless. Leake was not strong enough to withstand the rushes of the Scotch forwards, and Christopherson at three-quarter was far below his proper form. Of the backs Alderson, Lockwood, and Mitchell, alone played up to their true form, the first especially kicking and defending with great coolness and judgment under the most trying circumstances. The clever goal dropped by Clauss in the first ten minutes may have helped to demoralise the Englishmen, but certainly cannot be advanced as a complete excuse for the very worst display which any English team ever gave. The Scotsmen played with great dash. McGregor made a most excellent centre, and Clauss's dropped goal was the thing of the match. Anderson at half was far too strong for his opponents.

TEAMS.

ENGLAND.—W. G. Mitchell (Richmond), back; P. Christopherson (Blackheath), F. H. R. Alderson (Durham), R. E. Lockwood (Yorkshire), three-quarter backs; J. Berry (Lancashire), W. R. M. Leake (Harlequins), half-backs; R. D. Budworth (Blackheath), E. Bonham-Carter (Oxford University), S. M. J. Woods (Cambridge University), J. H. Rogers (Moseley), E. H. G. North (Oxford University), J. Richards (Yorkshire), R. P. Wilson (Lancashire), T. Kent (Lancashire), D. Jowett (Yorkshire), forwards.

SCOTLAND.—H. J. Stevenson (Edinburgh Academicals), back; P. R. Clauss (Oxford University), G. McGregor (Cambridge University), W. Neilson (Merchiston), three-quarter backs; C. E. Orr (West of Scotland),

D. G. Anderson (London Scottish), half-backs; M. C. M'Ewan (Edinburgh Academicals), J. D. Boswell (West of Scotland), J. E. Orr (West of Scotland), G. T. Neilson (West of Scotland), F. W. J. Goodhue (London Scottish), J. G. Macmillan (London Scottish), Ian M'Intyre (Edinburgh Academicals), H. T. O. Leggatt (Watsonians), J. Gibson (Royal High School), forwards.

FEBRUARY 7TH, 1891, DUBLIN.

England beat Ireland by 2 goals and 3 tries to nothing.

At Dublin, on the 7th of February, England gained a very easy victory over Ireland by no less than 2 goals and 3 tries to nothing.

Two tries were obtained by Lockwood, and one each by Wilson, Jowett, and Toothill. The Irishmen were never in the hunt, and a very high estimate was made of the abilities of the English team, an estimate which the Scotch match most effectually disproved.

TEAMS.

ENGLAND.—W. G. Mitchell (Richmond), back; P. H. Morrison (Cambridge University), F. H. R. Alderson, captain (Durham), R. E. Lockwood (Yorkshire), three-quarter backs; J. Berry (Lancashire), W. R. M. Leake (Harlequins), half-backs; E. H. G. North (Oxford University), T. Kent (Lancashire), L. J. Percival (Oxford University), R. P. Wilson (Lancashire), J. Toothill (Yorkshire), W. E. Bromet (Yorkshire), S. M. J. Woods (Cambridge University), D. Jowett (Yorkshire), J. Richards (Yorkshire), forwards.

IRELAND.—D. B. Walkington (North of Ireland), back; R. G. Dunlop (North of Ireland and Dublin University), S. Lee (North of Ireland), R. Montgomery (North of Ireland and Cambridge University), halfbacks; B. Tuke (Bective Rangers), A. C. M'Donnell (Dublin University and Richmond), quarter-backs; J. Roche (Wanderers), J. H. O'Connor (Bective Rangers), V. C. Le Fanu (Lansdowne), W. Davis (Bessbrook), E. Forrest (Wanderers), J. Lyttle (North of England), L. Nash (Queen's College, Cork), T. Rook (Dublin University), J. Waites (Bective Rangers), forwards.

JANUARY 3RD, 1891, NEWPORT.

England beat Wales by 2 goals and 1 try to a goal.

The Welsh match was played at Newport on the 3rd of January, when England took her revenge for the previous season's defeat, scoring 2 goals and a try (Christopherson 2 tries and Budworth 1) to a goal from a try by Pearson.

TEAMS.

ENGLAND.—W. G. Mitchell (Richmond), back; R. E. Lockwood (Yorkshire), F. R. Alderson (Durham), captain, P. Christopherson (Blackheath), three-quarter backs; J. Berry (Lancaster), W. R. M. Leake (Harlequins), half-backs; W. E. Bromet (Yorkshire), J. Toothill (Yorkshire), T. Kent (Lancashire), R. D. Budworth (Blackheath), D. Jowett (Yorkshire), R. P. Wilson (Lancashire), J. Richards (Yorkshire), E. H. G. North (Oxford University), S. M. J. Woods (Cambridge University), forwards.

WALES.—W. J. Bancroft (Swansea), back; C. S. Arthur (Cardiff), T. P. Pearson (Cardiff), P. Lloyd (Llanelly), D. Gwynn (Swansea), three-quarter backs; H. M. Ingledew (Cardiff), C. J. Thomas (Newport), half-backs; W. Bowen (Swansea), captain, J. Hannen (Newport), P. Bennett (Cardiff Harlequins), W. Rice-Evans (Swansea), E. V. Pegge (Neath), D. W. Evans (Cardiff), R. L. Thomas (London Welsh), H. Parker (Newport), forwards.

MARCH 5TH, 1892, EDINBURGH.
England beat Scotland by a goal to nothing.

This year will be memorable from the fact that England won all her matches without a point being scored against her, a performance she had hitherto never accomplished. The Scotch match was played at Edinburgh on the 5th of March. Both sides were confident as to the issue, and speculation was rife as to whether England would be able to retrieve the crushing defeat of the previous season. No fewer than eight places were filled by Yorkshiremen. The game, though a close one, was disappointing in the extreme, and very much more resembled a cup-tie than an International match. It was

PERCY CHRISTOPHERSON.
(From a Photograph by Gillman & Co., Oxford.)

slow, uninteresting, and devoid of incident or polish. Activity and skill were at a discount, and very rough play was indulged in by both sides, the brandy bottle having frequently to be requisitioned for the knocked-out ones. In adopting this method of warfare one side was as much to blame as the other, but we hope it will be the last occasion when the slow-coach game, which we thought was buried years ago, will be adopted in an International match. The style was not adapted to the English team, who possessed great pace forward, as they showed on the very few occasions when there was any open play. They wanted to play an open game, but as they were unable to make it a fast one, they have only to blame their own inability to do so. There can be no doubt, however, that the present style of English forward play is very ill-suited to the tight game, which is practically extinct on this side of the border.

England gained the winning point (Bromet scoring) just before half-time. On the day's play, such as it was, there was nothing to choose between the teams. As there was not the smallest scope for brilliancy, it is impossible to individualise excellence. Neither of the English halves were up to International form, and the halves on both sides indulged in off-side tactics. Indignant Scotsmen have written to the papers complaining of the play of Briggs and Varley in this respect, but if they had the many opportunities which Londoners have of seeing Anderson play, they would realise that at this game he is very difficult to beat. Alderson and Lockwood, the latter of whom is a long way the finest three-quarter in the three kingdoms, played with sound judgment, though on account of the character of the game the little Yorkshireman never had an opportunity of showing his wonderfully brilliant powers. Coop, the back, kicked cleverly, but did not play a safe game. Anderson worked hard, but had a very rough time of it; and Campbell played excellently at three-quarter.

Teams.

ENGLAND.—J. Coop (Leigh), back; R. E. Lockwood (Heckmondwike), F. H. R. Alderson (Hartlepool), J. Dyson (Huddersfield), three-quarter backs; A. Briggs (Bradford), H. Varley (Liversedge), half-backs; J. Toothill (Bradford), W. Nichol (Brighouse), W. E. Bromet (Tadcaster), H. Bradshaw (Bramley), F. Evershed (Blackheath), E. Bullough (Wigan), W. Yiend (Hartlepool), T. Kent (Salford), S. M. J. Woods (Somerset), forwards.

SCOTLAND.—H. J. Stevenson (Edinburgh Academicals), back; P. R. Clauss (Oxford University), W. Neilson (Cambridge University), G. T. Campbell (London Scottish), three-quarter backs; D. G. Anderson (London Scottish), C. E. Orr (West of Scotland), half-backs; M. C. McEwen (Edinburgh Academicals), R. G. McMillan (London Scottish), F. W. J. Goodhue (London Scottish), J. E. Orr (West of Scotland), J. D. Boswell (West of Scotland), J. N. Millar (West of Scotland), G. T. Neilson (West of Scotland), W. A. Macdonald (Glasgow University), W. R. Gibson (Royal High School), forwards.

FEBRUARY 6TH, MANCHESTER.
England beat Ireland by a goal and a try to nothing.

A closely contested match in which the Irish forwards thoroughly routed the Englishmen in the early part of the game. Towards the finish condition told, and when once the packs were held, the superior speed of the Englishmen told, and Evershed scored a brilliant try;

later on he again broke away, and getting close to the line transferred to Percival, who scored. The English team was strengthened by the inclusion of some Yorkshire scrummagers.

TEAMS.

ENGLAND.—S. Houghton (Cheshire), back: R. E. Lockwood (Heckmondwike), J. H. Marsh (Swinton), G. C. Hubbard (Blackheath), three-quarter backs; E. W. Taylor (Rockliffe), A. Briggs, half-backs: S. M. J. Woods, captain, W. E. Bromet (Tadcaster), A. Ashworth (Oldham), J. Toothill (Bradford), L. J. Percival (Oxford University), E. Bullough (Wigan), T. Kent (Salford), F. Evershed (Burton and Blackheath), W. Yiend (Hartlepool Rovers), forwards.

IRELAND.—T. Peel (Limerick), back: R. Dunlop (Dublin University), S. Lee (North of Ireland), T. Gardiner (North of Ireland), three-quarter backs; T. Thornhill (Wanderers), B. Tuke (Bective), half-backs; V. C. Le Fanu (Lansdowne), E. J. Walsh (Lansdowne), J. E. Jameson (Lansdowne), A. Wallis (Wanderers), C. Rooke (Dublin University), W. Davis (Bessbrook), T. Johnstone (Queen's College, Belfast), J. O'Connor (Bective Rangers), forwards.

JANUARY 2ND, BLACKHEATH.
England beat Wales by 3 goals and a try to nil.

The score does not indicate the state of the game. The Welsh eight forwards outplayed the English nine, and had their half-backs fed the three-quarters the game must have been won by Wales, who had all the worst of the luck. The brothers James were unable to play for Wales. The Welsh passing was erratic and often forward. Bancroft played superbly at back. The tries for England were scored by Nichol, Hubbard, Alderson, and Evershed. Lockwood was the shining light amongst the England players.

TEAMS.

ENGLAND.—W. B. Thomson (Blackheath), back: R. E. Lockwood (Heckmondwike), F. H. R. Alderson (Hartlepool), captain, G. C. Hubbard (Blackheath), three-quarter backs: C. Emmott (Bradford), A. Briggs (Bradford), half-backs: A. Allport (Blackheath), W. Yiend (Hartlepool), W. Nichol (Brighouse), W. E. Bromet (Tadcaster), J. Toothill (Bradford), T. Kent (Salford), E. Bullough (St. Helen's), J. Pyke (St. Helen's), F. Evershed (Burton-on-Trent and Blackheath), forwards.

WALES.—W. J. Bancroft (Swansea), back; R. Garrett (Penarth), A. J. Gould (Newport), captain, T. W. Pearson (Cardiff), W. McCutcheon (Oldham and Swansea), three-quarter backs: P. Phillips (Newport), G. Bowles (Penarth), half-backs; T. C. Graham (Newport), A. W. Bouchier (Newport), W. Watts (Newport), J. Hannen (Newport), C. B. Nicholl (Cambridge and Llanelly), J. Deacon (Swansea), R. L. Thomas (Llanelly), F. Mills (Swansea), forwards.

CHAPTER XII.

INTERNATIONAL FOOTBALL: SCOTLAND.

By R. W. Irvine.

WHILE the Scotch maintain, and no doubt with truth, that football is a national game, and has existed in Scotland in some form or other since the time when the Caledonian savages first took to wearing boots, nevertheless Rugby football as at present played is, it cannot be denied, a game adopted from across the border. Its very name implies this, and when he considers how important a part the great English school, Rugby, played in developing and fostering the game, in establishing the present laws of the game, and in popularising it throughout the country, no Scotsman, however patriotic, will grudge that the name Rugby should be for ever associated with the game, even though he may be the last to admit that either Rugby or the country in which it lies has any present pre-eminence over his own country in that sport. Football seems to be a game peculiarly congenial to the "*perfervidum ingenium Scotorum.*" Not only is it played well and enthusiastically in the schools, but it is also astonishing how kindly grown men who never saw a Rugby ball till nearly twenty, and to whom, when they begin, the meaning of " off-side " is one of the mysteries, take to the sport, and how soon they become, at least in the scrummage, first-rate players.

Scotch Rugby football may be said to have sprung up from boyhood into robust manhood with the first International match in 1871. In saying this there is no disparagement to the earlier players. Far from it. "*Vixerunt fortes ante Agamemnona multi.*" Many of us can recall to mind Rugby players, heroes of our boyhood, who flourished before International matches were

dreamed of, and the idea of a football Union had not
yet taken shape, players who would have made many of
our cracks of the present day look small. The Rugby
game was played, and played well, by school and club
thirty years ago and more; but in those days inter-
scholastic matches were very local and comparatively
few, while inter-club matches were even fewer. Except in
Edinburgh and Glasgow there were very few properly
organised Rugby clubs in Scotland. There was one, and
a good one—St. Andrews—a club whose prowess was
known far and wide, and
which made up for the
paucity of its matches by the
fervour with which it entered
into those it did play. Provincial Rugby football hardly
existed. There is no evidence
of any provincial Rugby club
out of Edinburgh (and district), Glasgow (and district),
St. Andrews, and Aberdeen
University, playing regularly
as a club, before 1870. For
some years prior to that,
however, signs of greater
activity and enterprise were
becoming visible in the
Scotch Rugby world. Edin-

R. W. IRVINE.

burgh and Glasgow clubs were playing more matches
among themselves, and journeying more frequently
to each other. But what gave the great impetus to
the game had to do with our neighbours across the
border. For some years previous to 1871 an annual
match had been played in London—an International
match it was called—it was played according to the laws
of the dribbling game. England usually won, but the
Scotch made a good fight always. This match at first
attracted only a sort of curiosity in Scotland, and a
languid sort of interest. But in course of time, as the
Scotch were beaten time after time, and it was quite an
accepted truth that Scotland was in football, as in
cricket, wonderfully good for its opportunities, but far
behind England, the souls of certain Scotch past and
present players stirred within them. The idea dawned

upon them, "If there is to be an International match, let it be a real one, and don't let the relative merits of England and Scotland in football matters be decided purely by Association football, let us ask them to send a Rugby team north and play us on our native heath." The Scotch leaders felt that they could not be so very far behind their opponents, and at all events, better to know the truth than to be set down as inferior, as it were, by proxy. At last, after much consultation, and in some trepidation, but not at all in despair, the missive was despatched. Scotland did not undertake to play only Scotsmen residing in Scotland. She reserved to herself the right to get them from wherever she found them, and it was to be a really representative team: and she would admit that if it was beaten. There was no Scottish Rugby Union then, except the rough-and-ready Union, in connection with which Scottish Rugby players should always hold in venerable remembrance F. Moncrieff the first Scotch captain, H. H. Almond, J. W. Arthur, Dr. Chiene, B. Hall Blythe, and Angus Buchanan. A team was selected without wrangle and without jealousy, and invitations were sent to the team to play in a great match, and responded to with alacrity.

The first Scotch team was selected from Edinburgh Academicals, Edinburgh University, Royal High School F.P. (which was supposed to mean former pupils), St. Andrews, Merchistonians, Glasgow Academicals, and West of Scotland. The men were requested to get into training, and did it. It was twenty a-side, and the Scotch forwards were heavy and fast. We were ignorant what team England would bring, of what sort of players they had, and of how they would play: and though assured by Colville, a London Merchistonian—and a rare good forward, too—that we would find their size, strength, and weight not very materially different from our own, many of us entered that match with a sort of vague fear that some entirely new kind of play would be shown by our opponents, and that they would out-manœuvre us entirely. The day of the match soon settled that uncertainty. The English twenty were big and heavy—probably bigger and heavier than ours, but not overpoweringly so. Before we had played ten minutes we were on good terms with each other. Each side had made a discovery—we that our opponents were flesh

SCOTTISH TEAM v. ENGLAND, EDINBURGH, MARCH 27, 1871.
(SCOTLAND—1 GOAL, 1 TRY.   ENGLAND—1 TRY.)

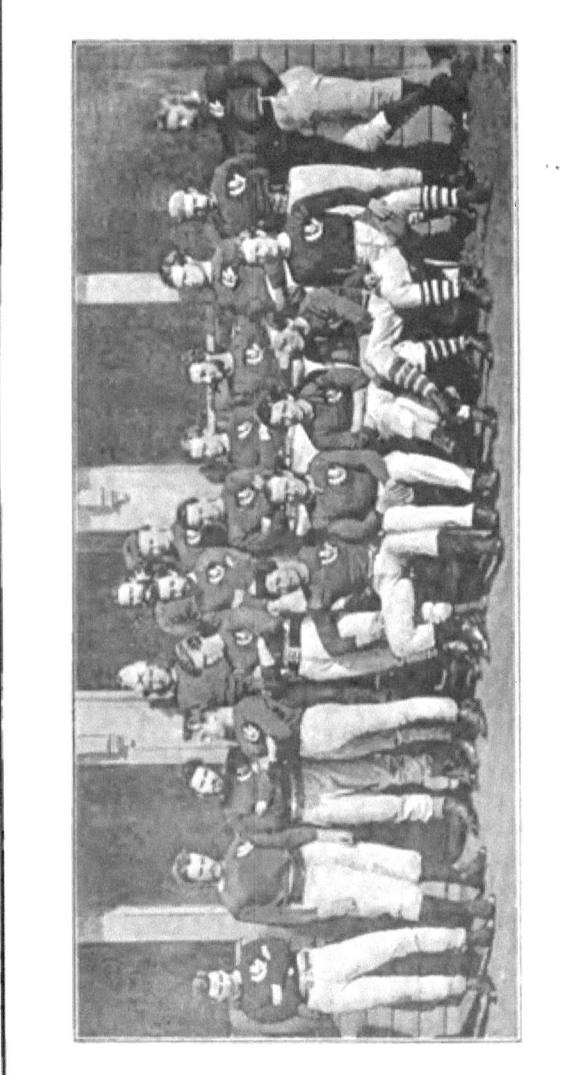

A. BUCHANAN. J. COLVILLE. W. FORSYTH. J. MEIN. R. W. IRVINE. J. W. ARTHUR. W. D. BROWN. D. DREW. W. CROSS. J. FINLAY. HON. F. J. MONCRIEFF (CAPT.) G. RITCHIE.
A. C. ROSS.   W. LYALL.   T. R. MARSHALL.   J. W. MACFARLANE.   J. ROBERTSON.
J. MUNRO.   J. THOMPSON.   T. CHALMERS.

and blood like ourselves, and could be mauled back and tackled and knocked about just like other men: they that in this far north land Rugby players existed who could maul, tackle, and play-up with the best of them. There was one critical time during the match. Feeling was pretty highly strung. It was among the first no-hacking matches for many of the players on both sides. Now, hacking becomes an instinctive action to one trained to it: you hack at a man running past out of reach as surely as you blink when a man puts his finger in your eye. There were a good many hacks-over going on, and, as blood got up, it began to be muttered, "Hang it! why not have hacking allowed?" "It can't be prevented—far better have it." The question hung in the balance. The teams seemed nothing loth. The captains (Moncrieff and F. Stokes) both looked as if they ought to say "no" and would rather like to say "yes," and were irresolute, when Almond, who was umpire, vowed he would throw up his job if it were agreed on, so it was forbidden, and hackers were ordered to be more cautious. The match was won by Scotland by a goal and a try to a try—the Scotch goal placed by Cross (not Malcolm, but his big brother) from a very difficult kick—and though many matches have been played since then between the countries, there has not been one better fought or more exciting than this, the first one. The Scotsmen were exultant, and the winning ball hung for many a day in the shop of Johnnie Bowton, at the Stock Bridge, adorned with ribbons like the tail of a Clydesdale stallion at a horse show. With this match and victory the life of Rugby football as a national institution fairly commenced. It was the end of the season, and the last match played; but by the beginning of another year enthusiasm was fairly taking possession of the Scotch Rugbeians. The winter of 1871-72 saw an activity in Rugby football that it had never known before. Not merely was this so in Scotland, England, too, was waking up and girding up her loins. Her defeat had nettled her. The Rugby Union was formed—the "Rugball Footby Union," as it was once styled by a hilarious and bibulous Scotch forward. The leading Scotch clubs joined it, and in 1873 the Scotch Football Union was formed, the original clubs forming it being the same that had originated the International match—

viz., the Universities of Edinburgh, St. Andrews, and Glasgow, the Academicals of Edinburgh and Glasgow, the Royal High School, the West of Scotland, and the Merchistonians, with power to add to their number. The original object of the Union was stated in three propositions, which still hold good:—(1) To encourage football in Scotland; (2) to co-operate with the Rugby Union; (3) to select the International teams.

The spring of that year saw the second International match played at Kennington Oval. Much deliberation was bestowed on the selection of the Scottish team. Trial matches were played; London was appealed to to supply some good Scots, and on February 5th, 1872, the Scottish twenty turned out full of hope on Kennington Oval. The match was peculiar. Almost immediately after kick-off the Scotch forwards carried a scrummage, followed up well, and in a trice Cathcart had dropped a goal. England looked dubious. One of them remarked, " We have no chance against your pace." The result showed how far off his reckoning he was. The rest of the match was one continual penning of the Scotsmen, the only flash of luck they had being when Chalmers once made his mark near the centre of the field, and L. M. Balfour, an Academy boy of sixteen, very nearly placed a goal from it. Scotland was beaten by two goals and two tries to a goal. The English team was a grand one; forward it was the heaviest football twenty that ever played together. Back, very little was required, but Freeman and Finney could have done all that was required behind by themselves. The licking did Scotland good. Their previous victory had made them very cocky. They thought that because they had beaten England in 1871, that, therefore, they had nothing to learn from them. They now saw that in the proper arrangement of their men, and in the proper selection of

L. M. BALFOUR.
(From a Photograph by Marshall Wane, Edinburgh.)

men for the back places, they were a century behind England. They also found out that touch is something more than merely the boundary of the field of play, and that half the game of backs is played across the touch-line. They also found that light fast forwards were no good against heavy fast forwards in a twenty a-side match. Like wise men they took the lesson to heart. They formed their own Union in the next year, and they instituted the inter-city matches between Edinburgh and Glasgow.

The inauguration of the inter-city match was a great hit. It has become between Edinburgh and Glasgow what the International is between England and Scotland, and has given the same impetus to the game in the respective cities. Edinburgh won both matches, a team was chosen, and the third International match was played in Glasgow at Partick. The ground was a quagmire, and the match ended in a draw, after a game which while stubbornly fought out by the players, must have been monotonous to a degree to the onlookers, and must have had a great deal to do with depopularising the Rugby game in Glasgow. It was one succession of weary mauls, broken by an occasional rush, but at this interval of time the impression left was that of a muddy, wet, struggling 100 minutes of steamy mauls, and standing out in bold relief, Freeman, the English three-quarter back, making his mark, and having such an appalling drop at goal as one seldom sees in a football lifetime.

The next season saw the International played in London, and won by England by a goal (dropped by the demon Freeman) to a try and a disputed try. In this match Scotland had, admittedly on all hands, the pull all through. She was superior for the first time behind the scrummage. Kidston, St. Clair-Grant, and A. K. Stewart, shone brilliantly, and the forwards had rather the pull of their opponents. Still the luck was against Scotia, and she had to pocket another defeat. How lucky the Southerners thought themselves was well seen in the fervour with which their skipper, in a speech at the dinner of the match, thanked God that Jupiter Pluvius had come to the rescue, and made the ground so slimy as to take the heels from the fleet Scotch backs.

1875-76 saw much the same state of matters. The

inter-city matches continued to be toughly and grimly fought, but the metropolis always kept the whip-hand. The International of 1875 was played in Edinburgh, and was a draw—as usual, Scotland fully holding its own forward, but being lamentably weak behind. The number of shaves the Scotch goal had from the dropping of Pearson and Mitchell that day no Scotsman playing will ever forget. Another draw in favour of England.

1876 saw the fight again removed to London; and on the Oval, for the third time in succession, the Thistle was nowhere. Scotland had the pull forward, but behind were far inferior. She had one half-back who weighed somewhere about nine stone, and the other dislocated his thumb early in the game, and R. Birkett and Collins ran over them as they pleased, while Hutchinson had a run for England, which will live in football history, nearly the whole length of the ground, and the try was consummated by Lee. England had a goal and a try to the good, and two matches to the good on the whole.

1877 saw a change. An agreement had at last been come to regarding the fifteen a-side, and it was to be tried this time. Scotland had previously routed Ireland in a match remarkable for the number of goals gained—six goals to *nil*—played at Belfast. In this match Ireland showed much good material, but it was raw. Much good Hibernian breath was expended in shouting which would have done more good to the distressed country if spent in shoving. "Oireland, Oireland, get behind yourselves," a despairing son of Erin was heard to cry, as the Scotch forwards were wedging through the Irish with the ball before them, and the Irish did not seem to know where it was, and were not coming round. But if Scotland had the best of it on the field, the vanquished were the victors at the social board, and if Ireland was raw at the game that day, Scotland was certainly boiled next morning. Flushed with this victory, Scotland met England full of confidence a fortnight after in Edinburgh. The teams were well matched. Scotland was in good form behind and fully held its own; the match was fast and furious to a degree never before seen in an International, and when within five minutes of "No side," Grahame got the ball and chucked to Malcolm Cross, and Cross, quick as lightning, dropped at goal, the excitement beggared description. The match was won by Scotland by this dropped goal—and we felt that our long struggle for fifteen a-side had not been in vain. The verdict of players and public was hearty and unanimous, and the twenty a-side International was from that date a thing of the past. In that year, too, the first attempt was made to have a more true trial match for the selection of the team than had hitherto been accomplished—and the East v. West match was the remedy proposed and adopted. Whether it has been a success or not is a question, but it has ever since been the substitute of the second Inter-city, and now there is an Inter-city before New-Year in one city, and the East v. West after New-Year in the other.

J. H. S. GRAHAME.
(From a Photograph by Moffat, Edinburgh.)

1878 saw Scotland's fifteen again on the Oval; again saw a splendid fast match, and at last saw the spell of Scotch ill-luck on the Oval broken, for not only was she not beaten, she very nearly won—in fact, many of the team thought she had won—but it was only a draw; no score either side. The Scotch had there probably the best forward, and indeed, all-round team, they ever put on a field. Their backs, too, were good—had much improved on their three years' before form—but had not yet acquired anything like the finish and easy certainty in catching and dropping the ball that we saw in Stokes and Pearson and used to see in Freeman. They could drop as far, and Finlay, probably, was the longest drop in Britain, Stokes not excepted. They could tackle—I would rather fall into the hands of any back in the three kingdoms than into those of W. E. Maclagan when roused. They could utilise touch—none neater at taking a little punt or drop at a nice angle into touch at a critical moment than Malcolm Cross. But with all that they wanted the freedom, dash, and style altogether which characterised the play of the English. Their play, compared with that of the Englishmen, was like the play of clever ponies, or big active Clydesdales, to that of thoroughbred racehorses. Ireland didn't raise a team to come across to play us.

1879 came round. Things still went on well. The Union flourished. New clubs were joining. A team was sent across to Ireland and again defeated its opponents, but this time by half the former score, and the Irish forward play had improved in a way that promised to give Scotland and England some trouble to hold their own at no distant date. The English International of 1879 was played at Edinburgh. A tough and splendid match resulted in a goal placed by Stokes from a run by Burton being equalised by a most cleverly dropped goal by Ninian Finlay, and the result was a draw in favour of nobody.

In 1880 the Scotch Union prospered, the funds prospered, new clubs joined. There were now 24 clubs composing it, whereas in 1879 there were 21, and in the first year, 1873, there were 8. Ireland came over to Glasgow, and, while showing good mettle, was well beaten in all points of the game, but the Irish had left their souls in the Irish Channel the night before. England had previously been over in Dublin and just escaped being beaten by Ireland. Scotland was thus the favourite—she had never such a good team. The English team was too old and the men stale. Never was a greater mistake made. The Scotch as usual were fully as good as the others forward, but the backs might, half of them anyhow, have just as well been left in Scotland. Once an English back was past the Scotch forwards the backs seemed suddenly seized with paralysis, pawed him like old women, as if to encourage his onward career, and England won by 2 goals and 3 tries to 1 goal placed by Cross from a try by Sorley Brown.

W. E. MACLAGAN.
(From a Photograph by Negretti & Zambra, Crystal Palace, Sydenham.)

This was the biggest beating Scotland had yet had on paper, and certainly the sorest disappointment. It was also the least easily explained. England certainly had a magnificent team, admittedly on all hands, but Scotland had also a first-rate team. The men had been doing wonders all the season. Certainly the ground was simply not fit for football, hardly fit for mudpies, and a gale of wind blowing, but that was the same for both sides. It was just what happens sometimes in a man and in a team—they were not in form and not in luck. They seemed to play with the funk on them, and never played to win, and didn't win. This match is noticeable as the first English International played out of London. It was played at Whalley Range, Manchester, and the crowds that witnessed it surpassed anything hitherto seen at any football match in the three kingdoms.

W. A. PETERKIN.
(From a Photograph by W. Crook, Edinburgh.)

The match with England in 1881 was splendidly contested. Scotland were the first to score, by R. Ainslie making a good run from the 25-yard line, but Begbie's kick failed, the ball grazing the post. This was all the score in the first half, the play being so equal that it was impossible to award the preference to either side. The Scotch backs now played a defensive game, but Stokes getting the ball chucked to him lowered the Scotch goal by perhaps the most magnificent drop-kick ever seen in the International matches. Immediately afterwards Campbell Rowley romped over the line. The place-kick was a failure. With England a goal in advance, the Scotsmen had little hope of saving the match. Three minutes from time the match seemed a certain victory for England, when J. Brown securing the ball eluded Hornby and grounded the ball between the posts, and Begbie kicked a goal. Thus ended the most sensational International match, the result being a draw, a goal and a try for each side.

The match with Ireland ended in a great surprise. There was a schism in the Scotch Union, and some clubs considering themselves hardly dealt with because so few of their men were selected in the team, resorted to the unpatriotic course of withdrawing those who had been chosen. Thus Scotland appeared at Belfast without her best team, and Ireland won by a goal to a try.

SCOTTISH INTERNATIONAL FOOTBALL FROM 1881 TO THE PRESENT TIME.

In dealing with Scottish football in its relationship with England for the past ten years, we may not have as bright a tale to tell as we might have wished for, and we may find that we have been subjected to one or two rather unpleasant castigations; but at the same time the record for the period is quite presentable, and it contains at least two achievements which outshine any performances in the whole history of the game north of the Tweed. In March, 1882, our team at Manchester gained a victory which set the whole country into an ecstasy of delight. Ten years later our men went up to London to meet what was styled one of the finest teams England ever produced, and, to our huge satisfaction, Scotland won by the largest score she had ever compiled in one of these matches. These are the particular bright spots on the roll, but on the other side of the account we have to swallow an unpalatable defeat in 1883, when for the first time we were beaten on our own ground, followed in 1890 and 1892 by two more humiliating downfalls on our native heath. These defeats were more than rebuffs, and they were doubly unpleasant from the fact that we had been waiting since 1877 to see Scotland win at home—and we are waiting still. Old players have a way of marking off years on their fingers' ends, and they will tell you such and such a team was much better than England's, although it lost, while another fifteen which won ought never to have had the slightest chance with their opponents. Such a process is too intricate to follow, besides being apt to lead to people "begging to differ," and for the sake of lucidity we shall here treat of the teams as the balance of the account in goals and tries stands favourably or unfavourably to them. To get at the condition of Scottish football in any given year we must examine the positions and performances of the leading clubs. In 1882 Edinburgh Institution football players were at their zenith. The Edinburgh Academicals were at low ebb, and Raeburn Place had lost its monopoly. In Glasgow the Academicals were still a strong team, but they were slowly giving way before the West of Scotland. Naturally, these influences affected our national selection, and it is not surprising to find a strong "'Stution" element in the fifteen. Among the forwards we had the brothers Ainslie and R. Maitland, and behind Sorley Brown partnered A. R. Don Wauchope at half-back, with A. Philp and W. E. Maclagan at three-quarter. Our full-back was the sturdy High School man, J. P. Veitch, and among the other forwards were C. Reid, not yet quite at his best, rough-and-ready W. A. Walls, J. B. Brown, and D. Y. Cassells as captain of the team. Our two tries' victory gave unbounded satisfaction in Scotland, and none who saw the game will forget how our forwards cut out the work that afternoon. The Scotsmen seemed to have stones the worst of it on weight, but they had all the best of the pushing, and there was only one team in it in the loose. R. Ainslie added greatly to his reputation by his fine tackling and play in the open. To W. N. Bolton he was most attentive, and the big Blackheath man did not get much time to consider his movements. It is generally acknowledged that R. Ainslie stands out as one of the very best forwards ever we had. His weight was not great, but he used every ounce, and we have never had a forward who came through on to the opposing backs more quickly. One of his strongest points was his tackling, which was always safe and low, and his great speed often brought him within reach of a man who seemed clear of the forwards.

R. T. AINSLIE.
From a Photograph by George Shaw, Edinburgh.

When at his best he left Edinburgh for the South of Scotland, and gave up football when he still seemed to have a long career before him. T. Ainslie had most of his brother's points, but not so well developed, and although he played for a much longer period, and was in more Internationals, he was not the same brilliant forward. Still he was a fine all-round player, and belonged to the true type of Scotch scrummagers.

That year we had not a single weak spot in our back team, which included two men who belong to a very limited class of players standing on a platform quite by themselves. No stronger defence than W. E. Maclagan's has ever been seen in Scotland, and we never had a man to make the same electrifying run as A. R. Don Wauchope. N. J. Finlay made great runs in his day, and probably scored as often as Wauchope did, but he was never so difficult to follow, and his movements did not produce the same fever of excitement on a crowd that Wauchope's raised. Although defence was undoubtedly Maclagan's strong point, if he got the ball within a dozen yards of the line he was a most dangerous man in more ways than one, and an ordinary player might well be excused if he took second thoughts about standing up before him when he was bent upon scoring. Roughness has often been imputed to him, and there is no doubt in his younger days he now and again gave exhibitions of his strength which were not good for the subject. More than once he has tossed a man, full pitch as the bowlers would say, on to the little paling at Raeburn Place and made the timber crack. He was one of the most powerful players we ever had, and no man on the football field could put his strength to more use than Maclagan when he cared to, or as Dr. Irvine says, "when he was roused."

From a splendid victory of 1882 we have to pass to a more than unusually unpleasant defeat. Our troubles in 1883 began with our team, which behind the maul was of a most patchy description, and it is safe to say we were never more poorly represented behind than we were that year. Our team before the match did not inspire confidence, and in the actual play some of the men cut up badly, and as a climax we were beaten for the first time at Raeburn Place. A comparison of the opposing rear divisions will almost tell the tale of our disaster. England was represented by—Full-back, H. B. Tristram; three-quarters, W. N. Bolton, H. M. Evanson, and G. C. Wade; half-backs, J. H. Payne and A. Rotherham. Scotland.—Full back, W. D. Kidston; three-quarters W. E. Maclagan and M. F. Reid; half-backs, P. W. Smeaton and W. S. Brown. This we should certainly say was the finest back team England played during the decade under notice, and when we consider that Maclagan, far from well, had practically all the work behind our halves to do, and England had three three-quarters playing against our two, the marvel is that we escaped with a two tries to one try beating. But our forwards as usual did splendid work, and if they did not win the match they saved us from heavy defeat. This was decidedly Bolton's year, and he left an impression which was not soon forgotten. Evanson we had heard much about, but he did not sustain his reputation. Tristram did, however, and many present thought it a little rough on Scotland that she should have reared for England the best full-back she ever had.

Our half-backs in this match did quite their share of the work. P. W. Smeaton's selection had been taken exception to in some quarters, but he proved one of the most useful men on our side, and frequently his punt, which he got in from all sorts of awkward positions, gained us ground when we most wanted it. He had never much speed, but he was always a most tenacious tackler, and nobody ever saw him shirk his work. Probably to this day he is of opinion that he scored a try in this match which would at least have made it a draw. At the beginning of the game an incident happened which may have put into Wade's head a perverted idea of Scottish football, and perhaps influenced his play, for he did very little after it. Getting the ball in good position, the Anglo-Australian was making off, and had just got up a good turn of speed when T. Ainslie came in his way. The Institution representative finding he could not reach his man, deliberately shot out his foot and knocked the Oxonian's legs right from under him. Wade rose looking as if he had been hurt—inwardly, and no doubt he made mental comparisons of football as practised in England and Scotland.

During the season 1883-84 a great many changes took place at home. The two three-quarters system, which had received almost its deathblow at Raeburn Place, had not been entirely discarded by the clubs, but in all the Union teams three were chosen. A. R. Don Wauchope, who had been off for a year in consequence of an injury to his knee, returned to active participation in the game.

In club football the Institution had sunk from their high position, and their place was taken by the West of Scotland, who were now the champion team. The Wat-

A FREE KICK: TAKING A PUNT.
(From an instantaneous Photograph by E. Airey, Bradford.)

sonians under J. Tod had sprung into prominence. Edinburgh University were strong, and C. Reid, with M. C. McEwen and J. W. Irvine as young players, was building up for the Edinburgh Academicals a fine team which a couple of years later swept all before it. We had never been better off for players, and after defeating Wales and Ireland we had great hopes of the fifteen that went up to London. Everybody knows that the match gave rise to the "unfortunate dispute," and that Scotland, after holding out for a long time, gave up her claim, and allowed England the game rather than be without the match. England's back team on that occasion was exactly that which represented her the year previous at Raeburn Place, while Scotland had—back, J. P. Veitch; three-quarters, D.J. Macfarlane, W. E. Maclagan, and E. Roland; half-backs, A. R. Don Wauchope and A. G. G. Asher; forward, J. B. Brown, W. A. Walls, and T. Ainslie remained of the old brigade. J. Jamieson, a West of Scotland man, over whose selection there had been newspaper debates, made his second appearance. J. Tod got his place for the first time, and another new player, C. W. Berry, was introduced. Jamieson may not have been all that his friends claimed for him, but he was a smart, clever player and an exceptionally fine dribbler. Berry was one of the best place kicks ever we had, though in English matches it was always a doubtful qualification to urge on a man's behalf that he was "worth his place for his place-kicking alone." Berry, however, was a sterling forward of the heavy class, and was always of great service in the tight work. In this match Wauchope and Asher played together against England for the first time, and continuing to represent us several seasons, they without doubt constituted the best pair we have had in this decade. Asher was a very fine player, who seldom showed poor form, and if he did not shine with the same brilliancy as Wauchope, he was always of immense service to his side. His running was his weak point, and he was never counted a dangerous scorer. When a man does not shine as a runner, and is strong in other points, his friends at once put in a claim on his behalf as an "all-round" player. All-round in this sense is misapplied, and if a man be no runner and scorer he is not entitled to have the term bestowed upon him. Wauchope, in the strictest sense of the word, was an all-round player, as he could not only run, but his kicking, tackling, and general defence were very strong when he

J. GORDON MITCHELL.
(From a Photograph by J. H. Millar, Hamilton.)

saw occasion to exert them. Asher's running was poor, and he therefore cannot justly be considered an all-round man. At the same time he was one of our most successful half-backs. He and Wauchope did splendid service for us in this game.

In 1885 we were without our English fixture, but through a freak of the weather, which interrupted our game with Ireland at Belfast, we unexpectedly had the Irishmen at Raeburn Place on the English date. This match we won by a goal and two tries, and it is memorable for Wauchope's running and Green's play on behalf of Ireland. Among our clubs the Edinburgh Academicals broke the West of Scotland's record, beat the Glasgow Academicals in the return by the largest score made in an Inter-Academical match for ten years, and finally established their claim to be considered the best team in the country by defeating the Watsonians by three goals and a try.

After the lapse of two years we renewed hostilities, and at Raeburn Place had a great game with England, which resulted in a scoreless draw. This, in our opinion, was one of the best matches in the series, and we very narrowly missed winning it. Veitch reappeared for us at full-back, and our three-quarters were R. H. Morrison, G. Wilson, and W. F. Holms, while opposed to these were C. H. Sample, back, A. E. Stoddart, A. Robertshaw, E. B. Brutton, halves, with A. Rotherham and F. Bonsor, at quarter. In our forward team were J. B. Brown, W. A. Walls, T. W. Irvine, A. T. Clay, C. Reid, M. C. McEwen, and J. Tod.

C. REID.
(From Photograph by Stillard & Co., Oxford.)

England's forwards were strong, and we had heard a deal about C. Gurdon's "hooking" process, which was said to be most deadly on the line. No English team ever came with such a reputation as this one, and it was said the passing of the backs would bewilder us. In fact they were over advertised, and if we were not conversant with their strong points, it was not because the southern papers had failed to impress them upon us. As often happens in these cases, the strong points proved weak, and we were very little troubled by the English running and passing. Somehow or other we in Scotland could never come to look upon Stoddart as a great player, and while he was highly esteemed in England, we calculated that we had not much to fear from him—and we were not disappointed. Robertshaw we thought more of, and we never liked his wide accurate passing; but G. Wilson that day did his duty admirably as regards Robertshaw, and frequently the Bradford man, when he was looking for a pass from his half-backs, received Wilson and the ball at the same moment. Early in the game our centre three-quarter got behind, but there is no question about his having "knocked on" when he was gathering the ball. We missed a grand opportunity of winning the match in the second half, when C. Reid broke away and ran up to Sample, close on the line. Many people believe that had Reid gone on he would never have been held, but seeing Irvine following hard at his side, he no doubt thought to make more sure of it by passing. The throw was a bad one, hard and low, and pitched at Irvine's feet. It was not taken and the chance was lost. Towards the close we were having rather an anxious time, but were much relieved when the hardy little John Tod emerged from the thick of it with the ball tucked under his arm, and resolutely pushed his way to the centre. Tod was always as hard as a bullet, a powerful, tightly knit little player, with no end of stamina, and playing with as much vigour at the end as the beginning of the game. Two men on the English side impressed us that year, C. H. Sample by his fine play at back, and C. Gurdon by his obnoxious "hook." This latter feat hardly seemed to come under the category of fair football, and on one occasion when Gurdon was at work, a handling he received from C. Reid was keenly relished by a section on one of the stands, where by the way, one old International man exhausted more of his breath on behalf of Scotland than ever he did on the actual field of play. As with H. B. Tristram, we half grudged having given to England such a good man as Sample. At Edinburgh Academy he played in the same fifteen with Frank Wright, who on another occasion rendered great service to England. Sample at school was a fine drop and a good tackler, but heavy and slow in his movements. When he appeared at Raeburn Place his Cambridge training appeared to have fined him down greatly, and while he still retained his drop, and had the real Scotch schoolboy tackle, he was much smarter in his general movements, and his judgment had greatly matured. It is doubtful if C. Reid ever played a better game than he did on this occasion; and if we consider him not as a great individual player, but as a power in any team, it can be realised what Reid at his best meant to Scotland. He was the forward of his time. There was no man to compare with him in England, Scotland, Ireland, or Wales. Neither was there before nor has there been since. Besides the physical qualities which rendered him a dangerous adversary, his football at all points was perfect, and we had no specialist in our team of whom it could be said that in his own particular game he was superior to Reid. His speed was much above that of the average forward, and in many matches he made as big runs as the backs. In fact, in the International under notice, his run in the second half was the best performance of its kind of the day. Roughness has been imputed to him, but the charge is almost groundless, and if on occasion he did use his strength, it must be remembered in extenuation that he had to put up with all manner of annoying attentions, often from aspiring individuals who would have preferred the distinction of having knocked down C. Reid to the honour of half a dozen International caps. We have seen a shaved-headed Yorkshireman in the line-out fix on to Reid like a limpet long before the ball was thrown out from touch, and hang on till he had to be forcibly shaken off. G. Wilson was one of the central figures in this match, and from his play all parties declared him to have a great career before him. As his subsequent performances testify, he failed to fulfil expectations, and it cannot be said that he did not get the opportunity, for no man ever lived longer on one game than Wilson did. He was always a dodgy runner, and often very difficult to hold, but his football was faulty, and he was addicted to mistakes, which were liable at any time to endanger the prospects of his side.

1887 was the year of the foggy International at

SCOTTISH TEAM V. ENGLAND: RICHMOND, MARCH 7th, 1891
Scotland, 3 Goals; England, 1 Goal.
(From a Photograph by R. T. Watson, Hull.)

Manchester, which, from the performances of our team against Ireland and Wales, and the large selection of good men at our command, we had hoped to win. The draw, therefore, was not at all satisfactory, and it was all the more tantalising from the fact that the old story of players, brilliant against other countries, curling up when they came to meet England, had to be repeated. It was this ever recurring failure that prejudiced the national mind against scoring men, and accounts for the estimation in which many of England's backs were held on this side of the Border. Had some of our players shown a semblance of their form we should have won the match. At one period we thought we had won it, but for once Maclagan's rush at the line was unsuccessful. We had abundance of first-rate men in the country that year, and our final choice fell on W. F. Holms, back; G. C. Lindsay, W. E. Maclagan, and A. N. Woodrow, three-quarter-backs; C. E. Orr and P. H. Don Wauchope, half-backs; with C. Reid (capt.), T. W. Irvine, M. C. McEwen, A. T. Clay Berry, H. Kerr, French, McMillan, and Morton among the forwards. We had beaten Ireland and given Wales a hiding by the tall score of 4 goals and 8 tries. The Welsh match was at Raeburn Place, and G. C. Lindsay spent the greater part of the time running behind. W. A. Cameron, the Watsonian full-back, gained his only International cap upon this occasion, and he certainly has not been overloaded with honours, for he was always a reliable back, who had the correct style in all his actions. H. J. Stevenson was at this time beginning to make for himself a reputation as a three-quarter, and J. Marsh was playing in the Institution. P. H. Don Wauchope, who succeeded his brother as one of our national halves, had much the same style, but was not so effective. He did not possess the same weight and strength, but he was probably as fast, and although not such an inimitable dodger as the elder member of the family, he was a very clever runner, and must have scored a great number of tries during his career. Kerr and French were two of a type of Glasgow forwards who seemed peculiarly calculated to raise the gall of the Edinburgh people. Oceans of ink were spilled over them, and it was needless waste, for French was well worth his place, and Kerr was, at the lowest estimate, the fourth best forward in the country.

During 1888 and 1889 the "unfortunate dispute" in another phase cropped up again, and robbed us of our great match. In 1888 our pride was much hurt by Wales beating us at Newport. On that occasion we played three centre three-quarters, H. J. Stevenson, M. M. Duncan and W. E. Maclagan with C. E. Orr and C. P. Fraser as our halves. The latter division were blamed for our defeat, but no section of the team played above itself.

In 1889 we had a great game with Ireland, which almost compensated for the loss of the English fixture. We won by a try, but as the *Scotsman* said at the time, it was "one of the most exciting and hotly contested games ever seen in connection with an International match." LeFanu and M'Laughlin left great impressions behind them. LeFanu, as one of the best forwards that has played against us, and M'Laughlin as a most extraordinary worker for a quarter.

The English International of 1890 was a very bad one for us. A great surprise was sprung upon the country in the selection of W. E. Maclagan, and in giving G. Wilson a place the Union made anything but a popular choice. Our half-backs were again blamed for losing the match by not feeding their halves, but it would have been very hard for them to feed without the ball. Where we really lost the game was in the scrummage, where the English took possession of the ball, and held our forwards while Fox and his companion nipped it back to their halves. The match taught us this species of attack most impressively, and when our team went to London in 1891 and scored our greatest victory, the English press complained that we had learned it too well. Our forwards undoubtedly won us this match, and our backs, as they very well might, were seen to great advantage. Our three-quarters, W. Neilson, G. Macgregor, and P. Clauss, were scoring men and behind winning forwards were all that was wanted. Had our Union fully realised in 1892 that we should require backs who were able to cut out the work for themselves, we should never have lost the game that year. G. T. Campbell, W. Neilson, and P. Clauss made a very poor show, and our half-backs were disappointing.

H. J. Stevenson, M. C. McEwen, C. E. Orr, and R. G. McMillan are the prominent men of the last three years. Orr, in the true sense of the word, is one of our best all-round quarters, McEwen is one of our great forwards, a powerful player, strong in all points of the game. Of Stevenson it has to be said we never had a more versatile player. His defence at three-quarters in 1890 materially kept down the score, and when the Union saw fit to place him at full back in 1891 and 1892 he filled the position as adequately as any man ever we had. Centre three-quarters, however, is his true place, and in it he has never been known to play a poor game, a fitting testimony to the merit of one of the most remarkable players the country has produced, and a back who will be remembered along with N. J. Finlay, W. E. Maclagan, and A. R. Don Wauchope.

CHAPTER XIII.

INTERNATIONAL FOOTBALL: IRELAND.

By J. J. MacCarthy.

FOOTBALL in Ireland may be said to consist of three parts—Rugbeian, Associationist, and Gaelic. The rule of play in these organisations has been defined as follows:—In Rugby, you kick the ball; in Association, you kick the man if you cannot kick the ball; and in Gaelic, you kick the ball if you cannot kick the man. This puts the present procedure and position of the rival devotees into a nutshell. The Associationists are mainly confined to Belfast, where they form a body which it would be as difficult to convict of professionalism as it would be for them to prove that they are amateurs. The Gaels are a free and festive community, who have their headquarters at Clonturk Park, Drumcondra, co. Dublin. This park is conveniently situated between Glasnevin graveyard and the Mater Misercordia Hospital. A man has been known to pass from the football field direct to the hospital, and from the hospital to the cemetery; another match being then got up to raise funds for the benefit of the next-of-kin, thus running the risk of killing a few more for the benefit of the deceased! Gaelic football, which is almost exclusively played on Sunday, flourishes enormously all over the country, and its most important rule is that no man who has played Rugby shall be permitted to participate until he has purged himself by two years' abstention from the pseudo-Saxon game.

With these and the Associationists, however, this work has little or nothing to do, the object of the present undertaking being simply to record the establishment, development, and present position of the Rugby game in

Ireland. It has been a very uphill pursuit all along, the principal obstacle, until very recently, being the scarcity of cash. Indeed, no one who belongs to the present ranks of wealthy and pampered ease in the way of football, can conceive the struggles, obstacles, and sacrifices which have confronted the founders and pioneers of our game. It must be acknowledged that what money we had at times was not always expended on the necessities of football life: an escapade in a Waxworks, after a certain International match, costing us about fifty pounds, while a ceremony known as "Highland honours," viz., smashing champagne glasses and bottles against the wall of the dining-room, which was covered with mirrors, cost us over eighty pounds. These debts lay like logs round our necks for a long time, so much so that Rowland Hill, on behalf of the English Football Union, offered us a very considerable sum, but this was declined by our then honorary secretary, H. G. Cook, who, in conjunction with E. McAllister and J. Redmond Blood, eventually managed to work our finances into their present satisfactory condition.

H. G. COOK.

There is no necessity to go back to the actual mythology of the game. Suffice it to say that it was played after a very primitive fashion by the peasantry of the west and south over a hundred years ago, and at times matches between rival parishes remained

E. McALLISTER.

undecided until the representatives of one were able to carry the ball home by force. Any method to prevent this capture was permissible—sticks, sods, and stones being freely used, and many serious injuries were sustained on both sides. It was in about 1868 that the game began to assume some civilised shape: but the clubs were very few—Dublin University, North of Ireland, Catholic University, Rathmines School, Belvedere College, Clongowes College, and Tullabeg College being almost the only organisations which recognised any discipline in their play. The two last-named colleges had methods of their own, which mainly consisted of dribbling—an art which they brought to a pitch of perfection never excelled in an Association International match. They used to play on gravel, and the ball, which was made by the college shoemaker, was about double the size of an orange. Three or four of these would be used in the course of a match, which usually lasted for two hours or more. Tullabeg College was disbanded three or four years ago, the students of it going over to Clongowes, where the Rugby code was adopted during the year after, and there is a very smart team in Clongowes now. Several subsequently celebrated men played under the old rules at Clongowes, such as John Naish, Lord Chancellor of Ireland; the Rev. Robert Curtis, Fellow of the Royal University; Rev. V. Naish, Professor of Stonyhurst College, etc.

In 1871, a club was raised at Scott's Military Academy, which comprised amongst its members Darley, who was afterwards killed when leading his men at Abu Klea; C. Higginson, who was killed in some other battle; and Crookshank, who has now a vast sugar estate in South America. This Scott's Academy team was almost as good as any in Ireland. Bray had a good fifteen, as also had Kingstown School and Kingstown Football Club. North of Ireland Football Club, Windsor and Methodist College represented almost the full strength of Belfast. There were two clubs in the County Limerick, but there is no record of any organisation in Cork.

Then came an event which had an important effect in the development of football in Ireland, and this was the establishment of the Dublin Wanderers Football Club in 1872. This was mainly accomplished by

R. M. Peter, who is justly entitled to be considered the "Father of Irish football." Peter had just come back from Blackheath School, and seeing a lot of youngsters, including myself, playing in a field off Morehampton Road, proposed to them the construction of a club, in which both "young 'uns" and "old 'uns" subsequently had equal representation on the committee. Their first club-house was a mud cabin, but later on they moved down to a stable at the rear of the houses in Clyde Road; and this was really the nursery of our present game. Many of the University fellows joined, with the proviso that none of them should play against the College First Fifteen, and amongst these were A. P. Cronyn, B. Casement, Wallace-Beatty, etc.; while the Brothers Barlow, Walter Higginson, J. Ross-Todd, Allen, the Darleys, Frank Collier, C. C. Byrne, T. and H. F. Spunner, Kernaghan, etc., were of the distinctly home division. It was a rule then that to be entitled to play Trinity First Fifteen a club should have previously

R. M. PETER.
(*From a Photograph by Robinson, Dublin.*)

beaten their "Second," the "First,"—who had "Bram" Stoker of Henry Irving fame, Arnold Graves, Ivor M'Ivor of rowing repute, and Henry Hacket—chiefly contenting themselves with playing the Engineering School, the Medical School, and other internecine contests when foreign opposition was not forthcoming. For a long time the Wanderers had to put up with playing the Second Fifteen, and even this they could not defeat, as in the absence of any registered or well-defined "First," it was very easy to strengthen the "Second," according to taste or necessity. "Spud" Murphy came along, also Ralph Benson, Harry Robinson, and his brother J. J.—a splendid dribbler—"Darkey" Smith Malet; and at last the spell was broken by big Jack Myles casting traditional restrictions to the winds, and scoring the first try for the Wanderers, who had previously

P

beaten the "Second," against Dublin University First Fifteen.

In 1873 we had our first visit from an English team —the Dingle Football Club, I think, of Liverpool. They wore green jerseys, and had a very even match with Dublin University in the College Park. It was now thought that the formation of some governing body was necessary. After practices or matches in Trinity, George Stack used to invite Peter, the Barlows, the Galbraiths, Walsh, Wilson, etc., up to his rooms, and thus many a time was the question discussed over a pleasant tumbler of punch. Poor Stack, who did so much for us, afterwards accidentally poisoned himself with an overdose of chloral. The following is a list of the founders and officers of the Irish Football Union with the date of November, 1874:—

President—His Grace the Lord Lieutenant. *Vice-Presidents*—The Right Hon. the Lord Mayor, the Hon. David Plunket, M.P., Sir Arthur Guinness, Bart., M.P., Edward Gibson, Q.C., M.P., Rev. J. Leslie, F.T.C.D. *Hon. Secretary*—H. D. Walsh, Esq., B.C.E., 14, Merrion Square, South Dublin. *Hon. Treasurer*—R. M. Peter, Esq., 24, Upper Merrion Street, Dublin. *Executive Committee*—G. H. Stack, Esq., B.A., M. Barlow, Esq., R. Galbraith, Esq., B.A., A. P. Cronyn, Esq., E. Galbraith, Esq. Clubs at present in the Union, with names of representatives on the Central Committee: Dublin University—G. H. Stack, Esq. (captain), R. Galbraith, Esq. Engineers—H. D. Walsh, Esq., D. Neill, Esq. Wanderers (Dublin)—R. M. Peter, Esq., M. Barlow, Esq. Bray (Co. Wicklow)—W. H. Wilson, Esq., H. Adams, Esq. Lansdowne Road (Co. Dublin)—J. D. Ogilby, Esq., G. Burke, Esq. Rathkeale (Co. Limerick)—Captain Bowyer, T. B. Bolton, Esq. Portora (Co. Fermanagh)—C. Murphy, Esq., E. Galbraith, Esq. Dungannon (Co. Tyrone)—W. Smyth, Esq., W. Beatty, Esq. Kingstown (Co. Dublin)—R. Greene, Esq., — Abbot, Esq. Monaghan (Co. Monaghan)—A. P. Cronyn, Esq., J. Cronyn, Esq. Rathmines (Dublin)—A. E. Jacob. Esq., D. Stokes, Esq. Arlington (Queen's Co.)—J. Shannon, Esq., W. Carson, Esq. Scott's Military Academy (Dublin)—R. Crookshank, Esq., G. Heenan, Esq.

Nearly all these were Trinity or Wanderers' men, although representing such places as Monaghan, Dungannon, etc. which had no clubs, but still their subscriptions were paid. We got £35 in public subscriptions, and of this some £23 were devoted towards the expenses of our team for the first International match with England. Before this engagement, however, in the words of "Enniscorthy," a "dreadful row arose," and in this way: The first Inter-Provincial meeting between Dublin Wanderers and North of Ireland F. C. took place at Ormeau on a terribly wet day in November, and the natives won very easily. None of us Dubliners knew the necessity of bars on our boots. Under these circumstances the victory should not have carried much solid significance, but it served more than its intrinsic purpose. The "North," of course, "dined" us, and after dinner the health of the Queen had been barely honoured, when the "hooley" began. How dared we Dubliners? What right had we to establish a so-called Irish Football Union without first consulting Belfast? They had shown us that day that they were better players, they had more money, more enthusiasm, etc. We did all that we could in the endeavour to pacify them, urging that they were specifically invited to join, in the preliminary prospectus; but our pacific overtures were rejected, and they formed an opposition Union under the title of the "North of Ireland Union." John Heron was president; "Dickey" Bell, an old International College boy, hon. sec.; and R. B. Walkington, hon. treasurer.

A compromise was arranged between the two Unions to the effect that each should nominate ten of the Irish twenty, which was to play England in London on the 15th of February, 1875. Such an enterprise, and such a twenty! They had never previously seen each other; the twenty a-side game was absolutely unknown in Ireland, and some of the team did not turn up at all. H. L. Robinson and the celebrated "Darkey" Smith, the two best backs in Dublin University, were absentees, although their names were on the cards sold about the Oval. Backs were put to play forward and *vice versa*, and the whole lot were immaculately innocent of training. Almost every one of the North men wore beards, and Ashe was like Falstaff—"a mountain of mummy." On the other hand, England had been playing Scotland since 1871, and her team was thoroughly disciplined and trained. We did not arrive in London until midday Sunday, Valentine's Day, and it rained mercilessly all the afternoon. Monday morning was equally discouraging, but by one o'clock a strong sun had set in, and although the ground was soft and sloppy, the weather overhead and around was delightful. George Stack won the toss and kicked off towards the gasometer goal; and Milton returning, Ireland almost immediately touched down. The drop out by Walkington distinctly demonstrated the difference between

IRELAND V. ENGLAND; THE OVAL, FEB. 19, 1875.
(ENGLAND—2 GOALS, 1 TRY. IRELAND—NIL.)

E. GALBRAITH, W. ASHE, R. GALBRAITH, J. MYLES, R. CASEMENT, W. GUFFINS, M. BARLOW, H. L. COX, W. S. ALLEN, ANDREWS.
E. McILWAINE, H. D. WALSH, A. P. CRONYN, M. GUINNESS, G. STACK, F. McDONALD, H. D. WALKINGTON, H. HEWSON, A. COMBE, R. BELL.

the teams. There was not a man on the Irish side who could drop twenty-five yards, and they never dreamed of punting, which Roger Walker introduced into Ireland a few years later. In the tight scrummages they could do what they liked, often shoving the Saxons the length of a cricket crease; but when the ball got loose, they were too blown to follow up. Then Stokes or Milton would coolly pick up, and, uncharged, would drop about fifty yards back. Mitchel got a try close to touch halfway through the first period; but this would not have won the match, as we only counted goals then. In the second period, however, Nash dropped a goal and Pearson placed a goal off a try by Cheston, so that England won by two goals and a try to *nil*. This by no means adequately indicated the superiority of the English team, who won at all points as they liked, except in solid scrummaging. Some of our men were simply unfit for any fourth or fifth rate team. And the late football editor of the *Field*, H. O. Moore, asserted that

A. P. CRONYN.
From a Photograph by Lafayette, Dublin.

he could whip up twenty Irishmen, then resident in London, who would make hares of this pseudo-Irish twenty. The quarter-backs were the only redeeming features, and of these Cronyn was distinctly superior. He was a strong, heavy, little fellow, as hard as nails, with tremendous pace; in fact, he was champion of Ireland for 440 yards. He tackled well, and although in cold blood he could not drop across the Strand, he frequently got in a very long kick into touch at the end of a run. He joined the army a few years later, and he is at home alive and well spending the Christmas in Dublin, where his mother and brother reside. He was the best half-back of the old school that the whole United Kingdom ever produced. Poor "Dickey" Bell, a universal favourite, on the other hand, had lots of hard luck, and died of dropsy in 1885.

It was feared for a long time that we would have no match in 1876, fully a fortnight's frost interfering with it, but at last a thaw setting in the Englishmen travelled on one day's telegraphed notice. The match was played for the only time on the Leinster Cricket Ground, Rathmines, on the 13th of December. The Irishmen had discarded their stout woollen green-and-white jerseys of the previous season for wretched thin cotton vests, but even these possessed an advantage. Cronyn, in being tackled, was denuded to the waist, and before he could get another jersey the ball came to him again. Away he went from his own twenty-five through almost the whole English team, for no one could get a grip on his slippery skin. He dodged Clarke and Collins, handed off Mitchel and Gunner, Login dropped at his knees, but he jumped over him amidst terrible excitement, but, slipping on landing, Pearson pounced on him at the very verge of the goal line. This was probably the finest run ever made in an International match, and in the connection it should be recollected that there were twenty men to be passed.

Although England won by a goal, which Pearson kicked from Kewley's try in the second half, and a try by Clarke in the first, the Irishmen showed much improvement, the backs being able to drop fairly. They were also complimented on their tackling; but this was not an unmixed blessing, because they collared their own men as often as the enemy, the jerseys being the same, and the Irishmen were no better acquainted with each other than with their visitors. It is noteworthy that Richard Galbraith, one of our most pronounced backs, who played "half" in the first match, was amongst the forwards on the present occasion. This will convey an idea of the helpless ignorance which characterised our councils; and it was not for want of forwards, for they had J. J. Robinson, one of the best that Ireland ever produced, at their command. He and his brother, H. L. Robinson—as also were R. M. Peter and several others—were trained at Blackheath School, which was then the home and headquarters of hacking. The match, however, gave a tremendous impetus to the game and clubs commenced to sprout up all over the country. A cup was given for competition amongst the northern schools, and was won by Armagh Royal, a

D. F. MOORE.
(From a Photograph by Robinson & Sons, Dublin.)

F. W. MOORE.
(From a Photograph by Robinson & Sons, Dublin.)

MALCOLM MOORE.

THE BROTHERS MOORE.

school which has produced more first-rate players than all the others put together. Rambaut, M. Johnson, A. C. McDonnell, A. M. Whitestone, Malcolm Moore, etc., are all Armachains. Ulster had all the best of it with regard to foreign matches, being so near to Scotland, and thus the Caledonian clubs crossed over very often.

Several subsequently celebrated men cropped up now simultaneously, viz., J. Heron, H. C. Kelly, T. Gisborne-Gordon, F. Kidd, W. J. Hamilton, A. M. Whitestone, H. Spunner, all of whom worthily wore the shamrock later on. A club called the Phœnix was started in the Phœnix Park, and it quickly became one of the strongest in the country. The famous brothers Fred, Frank, and Malcolm Moore, all of whom afterwards gained their International caps, were members of it, as also were A. C. Rodger, G. L. Fagan (brother of A. Fagan, the English International), W. J. McBlain, and these found their way to the Irish fifteen. The triumvirate, Joseph, Daniel, and John Ross, are the only other three brothers who got green caps. We travelled to Limerick to give the game a lift there, all those mentioned above, except Malcolm Moore, playing, and although we won very easily, our visit did a deal of good. We were only once beaten (having changed our name to Kingsbridge), and that was by Kingstown School, which we may remark, *en passant*, is the oldest regular club in Ireland. The score was a dropped goal by G. L. Fagan; and there was something almost uncanny about his dropped goals. It did not matter where he was or what the angle or distance inside of fifty yards, he always dropped a goal. The only one he ever did miss was against England, when the ball was going straight for the bar, but H. C. Rowley put up his hands and touched it. Fagan also introduced the tactics of the half-back following round the scrummage and pouncing on the opposing half-back the very instant that he would bend for the ball.

There were great changes in 1877. The number of players was reduced from twenty to fifteen, and as is well known this did not conduce to the benefit of the weaker side. Walsh resigned the secretaryship and was succeeded by W. H. Wilson, whom we subsequently elected to a place in the Irish fifteen *because he could place goals*. This was most Hibernian, considering the little chance we had of scoring a try and thus affording him the opportunity of having a shot at goal. R. Galbraith, who captained us, was put full back this time and nearly dropped a goal, but we were beaten by two goals, both kicked by Lennard Stokes off tries by Hutchinson, and a try (Hornby) to *nil*. Neither Cronyn nor Bell donned the jersey at the Oval, their places on this occasion being taken by T. Gisborne-Gordon and A. M. Whitestone. It would be weary work wading through the minutiæ of the next three years. In March, 1878, the Irish venue was changed to Lansdowne Road, and here England beat us by two goals and a try to *nil*, but it was a very even match notwithstanding. W. C. Neville had succeeded W. H. Wilson as hon. secretary this year, and after him came the renowned R. M. Peter. Civilisation succeeded, and football throve apace all over the land. Despite this, however, we got a dreadful beating at the Oval in 1879. The match had been postponed owing to frost from February 3rd to March 24th, and then we could get no one to travel. W. W. Pike, who played so brilliantly at three-quarter-back a few years later, was full-back on this occasion, and made as many mistakes as possible. Willis, another young schoolboy from Portarlington, was also a disastrous failure, and J. Heron missed two or three easy tries. Stokes dropped a goal and placed two others off tries by Rowley and Twynam; Adams and Openshaw also gained tries.

1880 may be termed the "turning year," when A. J. Forrest, McEwan, Crawford, and other subsequent celebrities, left Cheltenham College of which Forrest was captain, and his advent to Ireland created a great revolution in the forward play. Forrest was not a very hard pusher, but he went fast; was a tricky dribbler, and when he laid his hand on a man, well, that man was his. He went straight on to the Irish fifteen, and had no companion men of his own type, only pushers as well, including R. W. Hughes, who has played in more International matches than any other Irishman. Scriven, Cuppaidge, Hugh Kelly, McDonald, and J. W. Taylor, were all forwards of this same team. No better six men ever entered a scrummage on the same side. Hugh Kelly, who is now Sheriff of the County Down, was a magnificent man, six feet six or so, and built in proportion. He was a splendid scrummager, but the softest hearted and gentlest creature alive. To sum up shortly, the Irish forwards fairly ran over their opponents, with the result that Cuppaidge gained the first try that Ireland ever scored, right under the bar; but Walkington, who trembled from head to toe, missed it badly. Then Forrest gained another try; but McLaren and Neville disagreeing, Nugent disallowed it. Then in the second half Mackendale gained a try for England which R. Hunt missed, so that we were equal; but later on Ellis crossed the line for England, and Stokes taking the kick, landed an easy goal. Just before call of no side, Stokes made the finest shot at goal I ever saw. The ball was hopping into touch at half-way when he grabbed with his left hand, passed it round behind his back to the right, and dropped within a foot or two of the bar.

Let a veil be drawn over our English engagement of 1881, although as a counterpoise we achieved our first International victory over Scotland, to which allusion is made elsewhere. Owing to disputes, misadventures, and jealousies, more than half the originally chosen team cried off, and we were very happy to find that we had a full team of fifteen men of any sort on our arrival at Manchester. They did fairly well for the first few minutes, but afterwards they went all to smash, and H. H. Taylor (2), Sawyer, and Hornby, gained tries off which Stokes placed two goals. This was one of the very best teams that ever represented England; while on the other hand, ours was the very worst that ever played for Ireland.

FOUNDATION OF THE IRISH RUGBY FOOTBALL UNION.

We must not forget to note that before the commencement of this season, R. M. Peter at last succeeded in reconciling the antagonistic elements which were distracting our game; and Leinster, Ulster, and Munster, joining hands cordially, buried the various Irish Football Unions, and established the Irish Rugby Football Union in their place. The officers elected were:—W. C. Neville, M.B. (Leinster), president; R. Bell (Ulster) and W. J. Goulding (Munster), vice-presidents; hon. secretary, R. M. Peter (Leinster); hon. treasurer, Edwin Hughes (Ulster); committee—Leinster: W. C. Neville, R. M.

Peter, F. Kennedy, G. P. Nugent, G. Scriven, F. Schute. Ulster: R. Bell, J. A. Macdonald, R. W. Hughes, W. T. Heron, H. C. Kelly, and G. Shaw. Munster: W. J. Goulding, Walter Kelly, T. Harrison, J. J. Keen, with two vacancies, until Munster should defeat either Leinster or Ulster, or even play a draw with them. The victory she accomplished very soon, as Leinster sent a wretched team down to Cork and got well beaten. The hon. secretaries of the branches were: Leinster, F. Kennedy; Ulster, W. T. Heron: Munster, A. McMullen. Later on was organised the province of Connaught, which was allowed a representation of three, viz., Richard Biggs, LL.D., Rev. George Baile, and J. J. MacCarthy. Ever since the establishment of this Irish Rugby Football Union everything has been peaceful and pleasant; but the most marvellous performances in connection with it were unquestionably those of E. McAllister and J. Redmond Blood. When Peter resigned the hon. secretaryship, and Kennedy and Buchanan had held it like a hot coal, McAllister succeeded to the office in 1886.

Reverting to the progress of the game as regards International matches between Ireland and England, the year of 1882 will be long remembered as phenomenal in the football history of Ireland. The match was played at Lansdowne Road, and, without any possibility of contradiction, Ireland won by a goal and a try to two tries, but the official result was a draw. This was the famous Pike *cum* Nugent match, Pike, the player, winning it, while Nugent, the umpire, lost it. McLean kicked a goal for Ireland off a try by Taylor, but Dr. Nugent decided that it was no goal. The actual score was two tries each, Stokes scoring for Ireland almost immediately after the kick-off, but Walkington missed the kick; then Hunt got in for England, Rowley missing. W. N. Bolton (an Irishman, by the way), whose first appearance it was in an International match, then scored for England, and finally M. Johnston got a try, which was virtually gained by Taylor. Off this McLean kicked the goal above referred to, and which was disallowed by Dr. Nugent amidst universal dismay. In addition to this Morrell gained another try for Ireland, but, as neither umpire nor referee could see it, the claim was waived, and thus the match resulted in a draw altogether in favour of Ireland.

In 1883 the match was played at Manchester on the 3rd of February. As usual, being without money, we could get no travelling expenses allowed us, and, to make matters worse, the cross-Channel journey was something frightful. Hughes was so sick that we had to carry him to his hotel, and after ten minutes' play he was obliged to retire, so that we were playing fourteen against fifteen. Ireland started, against a blinding sun, and, in consequence, Morrow, the phenomenal full-back, was in this match a most undisguisable failure. Forrest gained a very clever try for Ireland through fast following up, but then Tatham (a good man), Bolton, Wade, and Twynam, got in for England. Evanson placed a goal off Tatham's try.

In the succeeding season Ireland got the worst beating that she ever sustained—on the merits of the match—from England at Lansdowne Road, although the score was only one very fluky try to *nil*. The three-quarter-back combination of England was Wade, Robertshaw, and Stoddart, and never did three men play better together. Stoddart and Wade, not to mention free kicks, had unmolested darts at Morrow who brought them down time after time after a fashion that stamped him as the full-back of an age. Morrow was like a man baling out a row boat for his life, so often did he repel the assaults. In the end Bolton was awarded a try. 1885 in Manchester was only a repetition of 1883 in the same place. Most of our men were seasick, despite which Greene gained a try for Ireland uphill in the first few minutes. Shanahan, following a run of Ross's, missed another badly, mainly through Ross's fault. Haweridge and Bolton ultimately got in for England, the latter country thus winning a match by two tries to one. Wheeler, of the Queen's College, Belfast, who never played full-back until this match, was a great failure, and Sample, of Cambridge, was given a good deal of credit in the opposite position which he did not deserve. This brings us on to our first victory over England. Never was a team so determined to win as the Irish one was on this occasion, and in the connection, as an illustration of this determination, a funny fact may be mentioned. Macaulay, of Limerick, was chosen for a place amongst the Irish forwards, and as he had already had his holidays, he could only devise the expedient of getting married in order to obtain the necessary leave of absence. This was heroic, and his wife fully endorsed the enthusiasm. We beat England "all ends up" fore and aft, but there are secrets about this match which must remain for the instruction of a future generation. Everything was arranged "ready cut and dry," even to the very ball which was played with. There was not a weak point in the team as a winning one, and this was the game they went out to play. McLaughlin, of Derry, a big, strong man, was told off to charge everything, while Warren, captain, as co-half-back, remained as a scorer, with Stevenson to save him. These tactics worked admirably, although the Irish forwards were not as good as was expected, and the result was that Ireland won by two goals, placed by Rambaut, off tries by Tillie and Montgomery. The last-named was the hero of the match, and his barely unsuccessful free kick from half-way fairly paralysed the visitors. Lockwood got stunned in the last ten

J. W. TAYLOR.
From a Photograph by R. Seggon, Belfast.

minutes; but, as a matter of fact, they (the Englishmen) never had a look in.

After this came the International deadlock.

If J. W. Taylor had been able to play on the 1886 team (instead of Dick) it would have been as strong as Ireland could possibly produce, for it is unquestionable that he was the finest forward in the country. Many people, including J. B. Browne and Malcolm Cross, of the Scottish fifteen, have frequently declared in public that Taylor was the best forward they had ever seen. He was even bigger than Hugh Kelly, stronger, and much faster, and could play back just as well as forward. His entrance into the football arena was quite an accident. Queen's College, Belfast, Football Club were short one day, and putting a jersey over Taylor's waistcoat, they put him *nolens volens* into the

IRISH TEAM V. ENGLAND: DUBLIN, FEBRUARY 5TH, 1887.

(IRELAND—2 GOALS. ENGLAND—NIL.)

scrummage, where he quickly proved himself to be the best forward on the ground. He has now retired from the game, and has an extensive medical practice in Belfast.

As the International difficulty which caused a suspension of active hostilities between Ireland and England will receive treatment from other hands, it may be passed over. However, while our backs were improving, our forwards were getting worse every day, and, what is more, they were becoming generally smaller in stature as the season progressed. Any big men that we now had—with very rare exceptions—were our worst; and the almost universal adoption of the detestable wing game left us without a centre to our scrummage. When peace was restored, England put a magnificent team on the Rectory grounds, with the strongest, heaviest, and fleetest forwards that I ever saw wearing the Rose. Our team was not a bad one, although very new, and, really, we were extremely unlucky in being beaten by three tries to *nil*. To start with, the fact that a blunder had been made in the arrangement of our hotel, which kept us walking about the streets for half a night, placed us at a terrible disadvantage; then, again, we had at least two tries disappointingly allowed. Dunlop, who had been stripped of his jersey, walked off the ground to get another one when we were within a yard of the English line, and there were several other misadventures. Stoddart, Rogers, and Morrison, got the tries—that by the last-named being unopposed. Last year's business at Lansdowne Road, must be fresh in the minds of everybody. We were beaten by two goals and three tries to *nil*; Lockwood got the first try, which was missed by Alderson; R. P. Wilson the second, missed by Jowett; Wilson also got the third, which was all wrong. Lockwood scored in the second half.

IRELAND AND SCOTLAND.

To relate our experience with the Thistle would be to tell one continuous tale of woe; but the superiority of Scotland is solely attributable to the tremendous strength of her forwards. They are also very rough, and there is scarcely an Ireland *v.* Scotland match on record in which two or three Irishmen have not been carried off the field hurt. In 1883 this actually happened to no less than four men—viz., Morrow, concussion of the brain; Wallis, broken ankle; Whitestone and Macdonald, wrenched knees. Our first match was played in Belfast, during the height of the dispute between Leinster and Ulster, with the result that Ulster had thirteen men on the team, and the two that Leinster sent up might have been much better at home in bed. Sorley-Brown and Hay-Gordon were running in every instant, and the final verdict was six goals and two tries to *nil*. The list of results given elsewhere will show how the other games went; but we may dwell a little upon a description of our only victory. It was at Belfast, in 1881, when by some as yet unexplained miracle, the amphibious inhabitants of the northern Athens were favoured with a fairly fine day, and the Ormeau grounds were packed with the largest assemblage of spectators that ever passed the gates. They commenced fiercely, but when Spunner and "big" Jock Graham had gotten black eyes, and a certain hot Scotsman had come second-best out of an independent boxing match with David Browning, milder methods were adopted. No tangible score was gained in the first half, but in the second, M'Mullen, of Cork, making a miss-catch at a long kick, placed the whole Scottish team on side; and Graham, who was leaning against the Irish goal-post, rubbing his shin after a recent hack, leisurely limped over and touched the ball dead. Nothing could be more galling or tantalising than this; but some slight relief was forthcoming when Begbie missed the kick, which was as easy as possible. Only five minutes remained. Could we win? Surely we deserved it, as we had been on the Scottish goal line all day, and thrice compelled them to touch a defence with very narrow escapes. The spectators became simply hysterical, and never ceased shouting from this to the very end. J. W. Taylor got possession immediately after the drop out, and, with all his team attending him, ran and worried his way, amidst frantic exhortations, up to the Scottish twenty-five, where he passed to "Merry" Johnston, who returned him the leather on the very verge of the Scottish line. Here it was heeled out from the scrummage to Johnston, who amidst vociferous profanity missed his pick up, and Campbell, darting through, shot the ball into touch—ten yards down. "Barney" Hughes, however, rapidly realised the situation, and threw it out to Taylor before the Scotsmen could line up, and Taylor transferred to Johnston, who, quicker than you could think or write, tossed to Bagot, who dropped it over the Caledonian goal. Such frantic excitement as these lightningly executed, triumphant movements, evoked, was never seen; and men, women, and children embraced each other indiscriminately. The spell of sorrow was broken, and we returned to Dublin by the five o'clock train, supremely happy.

Several of the other matches were very close, and, strange to say, the really worst beating that we ever got on the merits of the game was in 1889, when the score was only a goal—flukily dropped by Stevenson. We had by a long way the best of the match at Edinburgh in 1888.

Some Prominent Players.

Amongst Irish full-backs four stand out with remarkable prominence. These are R. B. Walkington, North of Ireland Football Club; T. Harrison, Cork Football Club; R. Morrow, Belfast; and D. B. Walkington, North of Ireland Football Club. These appeared in the above order. Strange to say, it will thus be seen Dublin never produced a custodian of more than average merit, although a man named Macready (who only played once, and that for the Wanderers when they won the Leinster Cup) showed astonishing excellence on this occasion. R. B. Walkington always affected a coolness which he never really felt, and often in endeavouring to demonstrate his confidence allowed himself to be charged down. He was also greatly inclined to run too much, but during his time he was unquestionably the best full-back we had. His failure to convert Cuppaidge's try—the first gained by Ireland—through over-confidence will never be forgotten, nor forgiven either. Almost contemporaneously, though slightly later, came T. Harrison, of Cork, and of him it may be truly said that he never got a fair chance. He was isolated away from everybody in Cork, which is 200 miles from Dublin and 300 from Belfast. These were the only centres of football in Ireland during his time. No one ever knew how good he was, and through all his trials, especially against

Scotland, he came out with flying colours. He was a marvellous drop; I never saw him miss a man, but, strange to say, he took little or no interest in football, and it was very difficult to persuade him to play. It was not only possible, but highly probable, that he may have been the very best that the world has produced, if all was known.

J. C. BAGOT.

R. W. Morrow, like H. B. Tristram, was of the "Single Speech Hamilton" type. The best full-back performance in Ireland was that of Morrow against England at Dublin in 1884. Morrow, if he did nothing but stop Wade, Stoddart, and Robertshaw as often as he did unaided, achieved a reputation which must last for all football time. He never received the slightest assistance from his three-quarter backs, nor did his forwards run back to goal; but still he brought down each of these three (who were the most dangerous triumvirate of the time) over and over again. Morrow was somewhat short in his kicking, and, moreover, spoiled himself by his desire to play three-quarter back, which he did whenever he could persuade his captain to permit him. He never properly recovered from the concussion of the brain which he sustained against Scotland, and few people could ever divine how it was that he lost his wonderful form when he went to Edinburgh. D. B.

R. D. WALKINGTON.
(From a Photograph by Magill, Belfast.)

Walkington, younger brother of R. B., is as good as can be on a bright day, but in the dark his delicate sight tells terribly against him. He looks to be about eleven stone weight, but he is really over thirteen, and many a man who tried to push him over has been very much "sold." He is a magnificent kick into touch, and very often drops goals, as he did from full-back against Wales last year. G. Wheeler, Pike, and others, who have played full-back for Ireland, were three-quarter backs, who never occupied the post of full-back except in International matches.

Looking down the list of three-quarter-backs from the very first, I do not think that there can be mentioned anyone who could be considered as fairly first-rate. We never produced a Lennard Stokes, a Stoddart, a Bolton, a Haweridge, a Malcolm Cross, or a Ninian Finlay. Perhaps intrinsically our best production (W. N. Bolton is an Irishman) was A. M. Whitestone, who was chivied about between forward, three-quarter, and half-back, but he was always neat, quick, and clever. He could run like a hare, was an inevitable tackler, and a perfect beauty for a straight drop. The majority will swear by J. C. Bagot and W. W. Pike, but really neither of this pair was soundly good. Both were plucky and lucky at times; but when they were out of form, their presence would be much more felt to the disadvantage of their side than their absence. Pike played a phenomenal game in our drawn match with England; but he never again approached this form, not even in school matches. He was a dasher of the most pronounced type, but if his dashes failed early, he did not try any more. Bagot was a most extraordinary man; he used to stop stock-still in the middle of the ground, and the whole opposition would *ricochet* off him, although he was very light and fragile, but then he would go on again. This attribute, supplemented by really excellent dropping and punting powers, enabled him to gain a great deal of ground when it was least expected and most wanted. The present R. Dunlop, of Dublin University, is by far the soundest and most brilliant three-quarter back that Ireland ever produced. He is very strong, a fine kick, has great pace, is a certain tackler, never knows when he is beaten, and above all has the grand attribute of always being in the exact spot where he is required. He gets behind a full-back when the latter is in danger very quickly. R. S. Montgomery was a tremendous scorer. He does everything like a flash of lightning, and no one ever stopped him when he once got fairly moving after his well-known "limp" dodge; but if he got roughly handled in the first fifteen minutes, he never could do anything afterwards; besides, he was always an irresolute tackler. E. H. Greene was exactly of the same class, with the addition of being a deadly drop at goal. C. R. Tillie, who was partner (wing-three-quarter) with Montgomery, was dreadfully nervous; but he was a better tackler, and almost as good a scorer. With D. F. Rambaut in the centre of this pair, the Irish attack was as good as any that ever was seen, excepting Stoddart, Robertshaw, and Wade. Another fine centre-three-quarter was A. Walpole, who was well known in London, where he played for the Royal Engineers, but he spoiled most of his work by passing forward. R. E. McLean was a somewhat uncertain and surely an unambitious wing-three-quarter, but a sound defence man as a rule. The brothers Ross were most harebrained, being either phenomenally brilliant or frightful failures. Scovell was a child, and Fletcher the same. F. W. Kidd was a great big strong man, but, like most of this type, trusted too much to his strength. J. Atkinson was very slow, but a wonderful drop at goal. There would not be the least use in criticising the very early Irish three-quarter-backs, because they had not the slightest idea of the game at all. H. L. Robinson, "Darky" Smith, and Malet ran with wonderful pace, dash, and dodging powers, but this was all that they could do; and the play of the later ones not here specified is well known wherever it ought to be.

R. G. WARREN.

Unquestionably R. G. Warren would be named as our best half-back, were it not for the fact that he could never play up against a score. If nothing had been gained against his side he was grand, but one try against him completely broke his heart. He was faster than most people thought, but he often stopped when past the full-back to look for someone to pass to, when he might have run in. Otherwise he displayed a most profound knowledge of the game, and neither his club (Lansdowne) nor his country has done any good since he retired. He had a wonderful knack of keeping his men together, and was a resolute charger and tackler, but he usually bargained for a wing forward to protect him. He was a fat, strong little fellow like Rambaut, and few have shown so much solid service for the shamrock. Of the old style, A. P. Cronyn was a long way the best in Ireland. He has been described elsewhere. A. C. Rodger was the link between the past and present, with marvellous pace and dodging powers, and had he not been hurt just as his merit was being recognised, he must have made a great name for himself. Meredith Johnston played in several International matches, including the drawn one against England, and was of the slow and sure order. He never let his *vis-à-vis* away, and very often covered a whole lot of ground in galloping fashion. McLaughlin, who virtually won the English match of 1888, was a pure "bruiser," being a deadly tackler and dribbler; and the same remark applies to H. F. Spunner, who knocked the Scotsmen out of time when we beat them. W. T. Heron, brother of the other International half-back, James Heron (now of Manchester) promised to be a wonder, having great pace and dash, but he unfortunately died very young. He was about the same size as, and in many other ways resembled, Hay-Masters, who was a much underrated Scottish half-back. Great hopes were also confidently entertained about Tuke and Cameron, the famous Beetive Rangers' combination of later days; but neither could play without the other, and never getting on a worthy International together, they were comparative failures. They played the same game as the now celebrated Brothers James, of Wales, Tuke being much more like the Jameses. There was a young fellow named Collier, who played in the Ulster fifteen and for Ireland against Scotland, who was a great man on a wet day, and played a sort of cross between the P. W. Smeaton (Scotland) and W. Openshaw (England) game. He spoiled as well as did Smeaton, and dribbled as well as Openshaw, but dribbling was his forte. E. C. Crawford was essentially like Rotherham; and Ernest Greene, when half-back, was exactly the same as A. R. Don Wauchope, standing on his mark like a sprinter for the whole day, but when he did get a run he finished it with a try. The last game, however, that "the Don" played for Scotland against Ireland at Edinburgh was very different, for he did more tackling than any two men on his side. A. C. Macdonald, now of Richmond, imitates Grant Asher, but he has not so much dash, especially at present.

R. W. HUGHES.
(From a Photograph by Robt. Neggons, Belfast.)

When we approach the forward ranks it is very sad, and the reverse of reassuring, to recognise that the Irish scrummagers are not what they used to be when Ireland was the premier forward nation of the four. The like of the following does not exist at present, viz., J. W. Taylor, J. L. Cuppaidge, J. A. Macdonald, R. W. Hughes, G. Scriven, Oliver Stokes, H. C. Kelly, W. J. Hamilton, T. R. Lyle, or E. J. Walsh. Walsh plays occasionally, but very seldom. These were the best forwards we ever produced, and, considering that the first six played together, the present deterioration is more accentuated. These were all of the "thorough" forward type, i.e., who went doggedly and determinedly right through the scrummage, forcing their way through the opposing forwards by sheer strength, weight, and determination. This is what any of the above always did; and the world never produced a forward like J. W. Taylor. He was heavy, he was big, he was fast, he was a good kick, he never missed a tackle, and he never tired nor loafed. Cuppaidge was a good understudy to him, and Macdonald would have been as good, only that he was so small and light. He was a rigid disciplinarian, and led the life of an anchorite. The same remark applies to J. Roche, our present premier forward. R. W. Hughes was too unselfish, and never counted himself for his worth. He was heavy and strong, but silent

and apparently unenthusiastic, but still he did the
work. Hugh Kelly was a great, grand, big fellow,
whom only the goal line—and not the guarder of it—
could stop; but he had a generous, gentlemanly, and
soft heart, which cost him much merit and his side
more than one important match. W. J. Hamilton was
an old-time player—gaunt, with all-spreading legs—an
earnest shover and perfect dribbler, but he played too
early for the present game. Lyle was a converted
Associationist, and a splendid shover and dribbler.
Walsh was our champion high jumper and hurdle
racer. He would have been a champion back
—being a phenomenal kick and tackler—but for his
sight, so by compulsion played forward, and was really
a champion player in that position. V. C. Le Fanu
merits a high place, but the demon of wingism overcame him. J. H. O'Connor is as good as they are
made for pace, strength, tackling, and staying powers,
but he has no idea of clever dribbling. James Moffat
was A 1 until he took to Micawberism, and the same
fault overcame the Forrests, Shanahan, Finlay, Rutherford, Brabazon, J. Johnston, and, indeed, a great many
others who could not be excelled when they used to
make their own work. T. H. Hobbes, H. Niell, T. Allen,
were men who had not quite the strength to do all that
their energy and honesty suggested. H. King, who
had a chest and much the same build as Toothill,
was an honest wonder for hard work, and S.
Bruce, who got his leg smashed by Hickson, in

O. SCRIVEN.
From a Photograph by Lafayette, Dublin.

addition to being a grand forward, was the longest drop
of his time—1877-8. Nor must we omit Oliver
Stokes of the Cork Bankers, who, considering his opportunities, achieved the unimpeachable character of being
not only a sincere shover, but a certain scorer. He
scored in almost every match that he played in, even

including the English International. H. Morell, of Dublin University Football Club, did great service to that club as captain, making his men play and work whether they liked it or not. About his time—1882—they had a little Welshman named Edwards, who subsequently played for both Ireland and the Principality, and it is said that he never figured in a losing team. W. A. Wallis was the first Irish forward that ever frightened a Scotsman, and he did it "considerably." W. Hogg, of Dublin University, 1884, was seldom seen, but he was always felt. If an opponent got past the full-back, Hogg was always sure to be in the way, for the purpose of obstruction if not absolute arrest, after he had shoved as hard as the best of them in the mauls. Of course there were many other men of much merit, and few achieved their places in any Irish fifteen without admirable attributes.

CHAPTER XIV.

INTERNATIONAL FOOTBALL: WALES.

THE youngest but the most energetic of the four Unions, Wales, has every reason to be satisfied with the progress of the game in the southern parts of the Principality. Though the Welsh International matches date six years after the first fixture between England and Ireland, the Welsh record against the mighty Scots and the Englishmen is as good as that recorded for Ireland, whilst the "Taffies" have defeated the "Paddies" four times as against thrice.

In no Rugby circle is the game pursued with such energy, assiduity, and invention as in South Wales. It would not be quite correct to say that there are only four clubs in Wales, for such assertion would be at once combated by such clubs as Penarth, Neath, Pen-y-Craig, and others. But the game is played in four district circles, of which Swansea, Llanelly, Cardiff, and Newport are the centres, and the clubs of those four towns generally play four matches each amongst themselves in the season. The geographical position of South Wales prevents matches being systematically arranged with English clubs, save those situated in the neighbouring counties of Gloucester and Somerset, though the country is a favourite touring ground of many Yorkshire and Lancashire clubs, such as Halifax, Dewsbury, Huddersfield, Swinton, Salford, Oldham, and the like; and not unfrequently Blackheath, and other prominent London clubs, arrange fixtures with one or other of the crack Welsh teams.

Yet, when all is said and done, Rugby football is confined practically to the southern counties of Wales, and the four great clubs have been the developers of home-made talent by continually playing and replaying amongst themselves. This concentration of strength in a comparatively small area, and with a few leading clubs, has given Welsh football a style of its own. Naturally, in so limited a district, the number of first-class players has been comparatively few, and therefore the choice open to the Union has been more select than varied. The Welshmen have made up for their paucity in numbers by their science in play; and it is no flattering tale which records that in many a match in which the Welshmen have been defeated they have succumbed to superior weight, strength, and speed, which have broken down the system carefully planned and practised by the wily, ingenious "Taffs."

R. MULLOCK.

Richard Mullock, the father of Welsh football, was the main agent in the formation of the Welsh Union, and in arranging International matches. The ground was prepared for him by the South Wales club and the South Wales Football Union. The origin of the Welsh Rugby Union was the South Wales Club. This club was formed to encourage Rugby football, and to get some good matches played. Individual players joined, and were not debarred from playing with other clubs; but were eligible to play for the South Wales club in the better matches which that club was able to arrange. In

C. H. NEWMAN.

the year 1877, and under the auspices of the South Wales Football Club, a challenge was instituted for competition among South Wales clubs. In 1878 the South Wales Football Club was dissolved, and in its place the South Wales Football Union was established, thus providing for clubs to join the Union in place of individuals joining a club as heretofore.

In March, 1880, a meeting was held at Swansea, when the South Wales Football Union was dissolved, and the Welsh Football Union was formed. The change was more in name than in membership, and was made with the object of securing International matches with the English, Scotch, and Irish Unions.

W. D. PHILLIPS.
(From a Photograph by A. Freke, Cardiff.)

The first match was played against England, February 19th, 1881. No one expected to win or to make even a close fight, but the Welsh leaders were anxious to impart the feeling of patriotism into the game, which was then struggling in its infancy. But this first effort was not attended with any very encouraging result: that 8 goals 6 tries defeat at Blackheath was a rude awakening, and showed that Wales had a lot to learn before her football education could be considered complete. Amongst the first team were C. H. Newman and W. D. Phillips. C. H. Newman came from Monmouth Grammar School, which has proved a great nursery for the Newport Club, having furnished such players as G. F.

D. GWYNN.
(From a Photograph by Battersby, Manchester.)

Harding, T. Harding, George Rosser, T. B. Jones, T. L. Nicholas, and others. Newman's football honours were varied. He obtained his "blue" at Cambridge in 1882. He went to Durham in 1883 and played half-back for that county. He played continually for Wales up to 1887, and captained the team for three years, from 1884-7. He was thick-set, short in stature, but powerful, and for tricky play he has only been excelled by Arthur Gould. He was the first man in South Wales to introduce the passing game. W. D. Phillips was the founder and captain of the Cardiff Wanderers in 1872, which office he held till the amalgamation of that club with the "Glamorgan," the level town club at that time. Up to the season 1884-85, the termination of his football career, he was either captain or vice-captain of the Cardiff Club, holding the former office in the years 1879, 1880, and 1882. He represented Wales in 1881, and played in all the International matches in 1882 and 1884. He is now a vice-president of the Welsh Union, to which office he was elected in 1885. An enthusiastic follower of the game, Phillips has done good service in the field, and his counsel has been valued in debate.

JOHN HENRY BOWEN.
(From a Photograph by Lucas & Co., Llanelly.)

In 1882 there was no match with England, but a North of England team was sent to Newport. The good fight made by the Welshmen gave encouragement to the game, and caused England to favour them with another fixture. The match with Ireland at Dublin ended in a win for Wales, and the new Union had now won its spurs, and established its right to admission to matches with the other Unions.

In 1883, David Gwynn, of Swansea, played against England for the first time. From 1879 to April, 1890, he played regularly as centre or wing-three-quarters for the Swansea first fifteen, generally heading the scoring list. He first represented Wales in 1882, and his last match for his country was at Newport, in 1891. Altogether he took part in about a dozen International matches. He removed to Oldham in 1890, and was captain of that team in 1890, 1891, and 1892, playing centre three-quarter for Lancashire when they won the County championship in 1890-91. He fields the ball cleanly, dodges smartly, receives and passes cleverly, and kicks splendidly in any position.

Harry Bowen, of Llanelly, then a lad of seventeen, played at full-back against England, and shares with D. Gwynn the honour of being the only member of the 1883 Welsh teams still taking active part in football. Bowen played thrice for Wales, viz., v. England in 1883, v. Scotland in 1886, and again v. England in 1887, where the match was drawn. His forte is powerful punting in little room.

Three famous players came to the front in 1884 : C. G. Taylor of Ruabon, W. H. Gwynn of Swansea, and H. S. Lyne of Newport. C. G. Taylor was one of the cleverest men in the kingdom with his feet. He was originally an Association player of some note. His first Rugby experience was with the Royal Naval Engineering College, at Portsmouth. H. S. Lyne happened to hear of his ability in the year 1882 through a brother of his who was at Portsmouth College. Taylor was asked to play for a scratch Welsh team against the 'Varsity at Oxford. He played a clinking game, and scored the only two tries obtained against the then redoubtable Oxford team. He was immediately after chosen for Wales, and played in most of the International matches. He was one of the most extraordinary players that ever played, as he retained much of his old Association style of play; indeed, he was one of the very few really good players that went in for flying kicks, and hardly ever failed to bring them off—a style of play then, as now, much deprecated. He was very fast and a good kick.

W. H. Gwynn was probably the most scientific half-back that has ever played for Wales. He played for two seasons, viz., 1884 and 1885, and his best performance was against England at Leeds, in his first appearance in International matches. He is now vice-president of the Union, and a representative of Wales on the International Board.

Horace S. Lyne has served Wales well both as a

player and legislator. He played for Wales as a forward for three seasons, 1882-83, 1883-84, 1884-85. On his marriage in 1885, he retired from actual participation in the game, but has taken active interest in legislation, having been for many years a vice-president of the Welsh Union, and a member of the Match Committee for the past three years. He has also been one of the representatives for Wales on the International Board since its formation.

H. S. LYNE.
From a Photograph by *Villiers & Son, Newport.*

In 1885, Wales succeeded in making a draw with Scotland. Four changes were made from the forward team that had played against England, and the team playing against Scotland was about the best that had represented Wales so far. The forwards were a grand lot, heavy and fast, and every man a scrummager. They had secured a couple of brilliant recruits in D. Morgans and W. H. Thomas. Morgans proved to be a gem of the first water, and when in his prime was the best forward in Wales. Thomas was a youngster at Llandovery College, that nursery for Welsh Internationals, where his merits were noticed by the Swansea Club, and his services enlisted in order to assist them against Llanelly in the cup ties. This brought him under the notice of the Welsh Union, and although only a stripling he was awarded a cap. A. F. Hill, the Cardiffian, and E. P. Alexander, of Brecon, also a famous member of the Cambridge team, were another

A. J. GOULD.

pair of forwards who in after seasons did yeoman service in the scarlet jerseys. But the season will be memorable for the introduction of two players who have had more influence on Welsh football than any other men. They were Arthur J. Gould and Frank E. Hancock. Arthur Gould made his *début* for Wales at full-back, but is unquestionably the best centre three-quarter that Wales has ever produced. He played for Wales in 1884, and with the exception of the season 1890-91, when he was absent from England, has been selected on every subsequent occasion, and thus holds the record amongst Welsh International players. He is exceedingly fast, a good tackler, and fine kicker, using both feet with ease. He has a peculiar knack of dropping goals. His remarkable agility has earned him the *sobriquet* of "monkey." His forte lies in taking passes and intercepting those of his opponents at top speed.

C. S. THOMAS
(From a Photograph by J. T. Daniels & Sons, Newport, Mon.)

In the Scotch match of 1886 the four three-quarter system was given a trial for the first time in an International match. The result was hardly successful. The Welsh forwards were rather below the usual standard, and quite failed to hold up the scrummage against the sturdy Northern forwards. With the forwards so badly beaten the backs never had a chance, and in order to make the best of a bad bargain, Harry Bowen was sent forward, and Gould took up his old position as back. This was not very encouraging to the supporters of the new system, and the Welsh Union did not muster up sufficient courage to repeat the experiment till four seasons later.

Passing over 1887, the season 1887-88 is notable for the victory over Scotland at Newport. There was no match with England owing to the regrettable misunderstanding with that country. The Welsh team had been thoroughly overhauled, and several of the veterans had made room for younger players. C. G. Taylor, C. H. Newman, E. P. Alexander, after doing gallant service, retired. They will ever be remembered as pioneers in the long march which Wales had made in her efforts to get a position among the nations. The new men exceeded the most sanguine expectations. The three-quarters proved themselves to be without exception the best two that had ever represented Wales. Gould was

DAVID AND EVAN JAMES.
(From a Photograph by J. H. Goldie, Swansea.)

then at his best, and showed himself more than a match for Stevenson ; Price Jenkins, who obtained the winning try, enjoyed the reputation of being one of the best three-quarter backs in London, while Bowen as a defensive player was perfection, tackling superbly, it being almost impossible to get by him.

In 1888-89 the four three-quarter system was adopted permanently by the Welsh Union, and again the season was attended with disastrous results, mainly through the selection of three-quarter players, good in themselves, but the dissimilarity of whose style of play prevented anything like combination. C. J. Thomas, of Newport, though gaining his cap in the previous season, made his mark this year. A versatile player, he has appeared for Wales in three positions, viz., half, wing-three-quarter,

and centre three-quarter. In either position he is clever
—short, sharp, dodgy runs being his forte. He also
tackles very surely.

In 1889-90 matches were renewed with England, the
International dispute having been brought to a satisfactory termination. For the first time Wales played four
three-quarters against England, and though the ground
at Dewsbury was all against the system, the Welshmen
played magnificently, and won by a try to nothing. The
tall English forwards were helpless in the mud, and the
sturdy, thick-set Welshmen
thoroughly outplayed them.
At three-quarters the long
English passing was frus-
trated by the greasy state of
the ball, whereas the Welshmen, by short sharp passing,
kept the ball going from
hand to hand and repeatedly
gained ground. In this
match Bancroft, only a mere
lad, was tried at back. He
had been discovered by the
Swansea Club, and met with
such marked success that he
has occupied the position of
back ever since. He is a good
kicker, punting and dropping

C. B. NICHOLL.
(From a Photo by Messrs. Stern, Cambridge.)

with both feet, and with a splendid length. He was a
little weak in tackling in his first season, but he improved
later on.

In 1890-91, the brothers James, of Swansea, played,
in conjunction, at half-back for the first time in an International match, and C. B. Nicholl, of Cambridge, who
had been playing occasionally for Llanelly, made his
début. He promises to be one of the finest forwards
ever turned out from Wales, and adds another name
to the long list of Llandovery boys who have made a
reputation for themselves. David and Evan James
are undoubtedly the finest pair of half-backs in Wales
that play regularly together. They have a style peculiar to themselves which is wonderfully effective. Considering their size, they are recklessly daring in defensive
tactics, tackling with great resolution and effect. David

R

generally works the scrums, picking up smartly and passing with low and rapid transfers to Evan, who handles brilliantly. Both dodge and feint cleverly, David particularly being very clever near the line. They run strongly, and, as they dodge in very little space, and pass and repass with great rapidity, they are remarkably difficult to stop when clear of the forwards. They are skilful dribblers, but rarely resort to kicking.

1891-92 was the most disastrous season, as regards International matches, that Wales has had in recent years, all three matches being lost. Wales thus earned the "wooden spoon" of International football for this season, a fate that has fallen to her lot only once before, viz., in 1888-89. In 1887-88 Wales was actually champion country, defeating both Scotland and Ireland, and there being no match with England. As regards the four three-quarter system a good judge remarks: "The system can be perfected only by constant practice and unison of style. In a club fifteen the practice can be had, and a player out of harmony with the rest can either be broken into the style or rejected altogether, whereas, in an International match, players who are unfortunately only too often selected for individual brilliancy fail to combine with one another or to keep their proper position." The writer has closely observed Club and International games for many seasons, and as the result of his observations emphatically declares that until Wales systematically practises the four selected three-quarters for some time previous to the match, she can never hope to show other countries what the system is capable of effecting. When her clubs play English teams they invariably either outplay the Englishmen behind, or compel them to bring out a man as an extra three-quarter. The cause is obvious: the club mates are combined and in their right places. The following account of the system by W. H. Gwynn, of Swansea, the International half-back, will emphasise and illustrate the above reflections.

THE FOUR THREE-QUARTER SYSTEM:

HOW IT SHOULD BE PLAYED.

By W. H. Gwynn.

Its Evolution.—As far back as 1878 many of the Welsh clubs played eight forwards and seven backs, the latter arranged into three halves—the centre one known as "flying-man"—two three-quarters, and two backs. The "flying-man" was entrusted with a roving commission, and, after a few seasons, settled down into a centre three-quarter. In the International match between England and Wales, at Swansea, in 1883, the Home fifteen had two halves, three three-quarters, and two backs. It soon became apparent that one of the backs could be better employed elsewhere, and, while most of the clubs drafted him into the forwards, a few, notably Cardiff, favouring the elaborate passing tactics then in vogue, added him to the three-quarters, and, as the experiment was phenomenally successful, this plan of marshalling the forces spread rapidly, and was speedily adopted by all the Welsh clubs.

W. H. GWYNN.
(From a Photograph by J. H. Goldie, Swansea.)

Its Characteristics.—The vitality and success of the four three-quarter system depend upon open play and scientific combination. For the attainment of these essentials it is absolutely indispensable (1) that the forwards and halves be content to work the play so that the attacking resources of the quartette be utilised to the fullest extent ; (2) that the passing be low and rapid, *with both hands on the ball*, and so delivered that the receiver is enabled to take when on the move ; (3) that the three-quarters stand not more than seven yards apart and fairly well behind one another.

Forwards.—The forwards should endeavour either by wheeling or heeling-out to make the game as loose as possible.

The wheeling should generally be towards the open, and the heeling-out should be promptly and cleanly executed, so that by smart passing the ball can be among the three-quarters before the opposing forwards have time to spread.

Half-backs.—The halves, one working the scrums, and the other about four or five yards away and clear of the pack, must pass *from* the ground with *low* and *swift* transfers. If well marked, the feet can be used in sending the ball across to the three-quarters.

Three-quarters.—I. THEIR POSITIONS.—It is of vital importance that the proper and relative distances among the three-quarters be carefully maintained.

The three-quarters on the open side of the pack should stand about six yards wide from each other, and from five to six yards behind. The near centre should be not less than seven yards wide of the pack and about seven yards behind. The wing on the near side should be not less than ten yards behind the scrummage ready to support the centres in defence, to block the rush along the touch side, and should gain ground mainly by kicking into touch. Posted at the above relative distances the quartette are best situated both for attack and defence.

II. ESSENTIAL QUALIFICATIONS.—All the three-quarters require to be able to kick *readily* in any position; the centres should be able to field cleanly, and to dodge well, in order to create openings for the wings, who ought to possess plenty of pace, and be able to handle well, and to take the ball when sprinting.

III. THEIR METHODS OF PLAY.—1. The first or near centre having obtained the ball on the run from a low pass by one of the halves, may either (*a*) sprint round the opposing centre, and thus afford a grand opportunity for his outside pair; or (*b*) dodge through, and as the opponents close in pass to sides; or (*c*) pass low and sharp to second centre; or (*d*) pass over centre to wing; or (*e*) kick into touch, if centre is well watched or hampered; or (*f*) punt high to drop between opposing three-quarters and back, for centre and wing to secure by following up; or (*g*) drop at goal.

2. The second centre on receiving the ball when on

the move down the field may either (*a*) race round opponent and make an opening for his wing ; or (*b*) dodge through, and when pressed pass to first centre or wing ; or (*c*) pass immediately to wing if he is favourably placed ; or (*d*) kick into touch if wing is badly situated ; or (*e*) *punt high*, for others to back up ; or (*f*) repass smartly to centre, if clear ; or (*g*) drop at goal.

3. The outside wing receiving ball from centres may either (*a*) sprint round opponents, and when pressed by opposing back repass to centres ; or (*b*) double back into play and dodge through, or pass out to centre, who by this time has moved outside ; or (*c*) repass to centre if well watched and centre favourably placed ; or (*d*) kick into touch ; or (*e*) drop at goal ; or (*f*) screw right across into play for forwards and other wing to secure ; this manœuvre is very effective when the ball has been carried into the corner.

SEQUENCES OF EFFECTIVE PASSES, which, when attempted under certain circumstances, are extremely difficult to check.

1. From halves to near centre, to second centre, back to first centre, right out over second centre to wing.

2. From halves to first centre, right out to wing, back to second centre, back to wing.

The Swansea Football Club.—This club was started in 1870. Mr. C. C. Chambers, as secretary and captain, took a prominent part in its formation and early career. Some three or four matches were yearly played on the Brynymor and Primrose fields.

In 1875 the cricket club completed the task of converting some sand-hills near the coast into the magnificent eight-acre enclosure now known as the St. Helen's field, which henceforth became the head-quarters of the football club. From 1880, when the Welsh Challenge Cup was won, to 1885, when the first tour was undertaken—Wakefield Trinity (won), Halifax (lost)—the game gradually acquired immense popularity, the visits of the English Fifteen in 1883 and 1885 creating great interest. The results of 1887—20 matches won and 3 lost — when they again won the Challenge Cup, brought Swansea into great prominence, placing them at the head of the first-class clubs. During the last three seasons,

WELSH TEAM V. ENGLAND: DEWSBURY, FEBRUARY 15TH, 1890.

WALES—1 TRY: ENGLAND—NIL.

(From a Photograph by R. T. Wotson, Anlaby Road, Hull.)

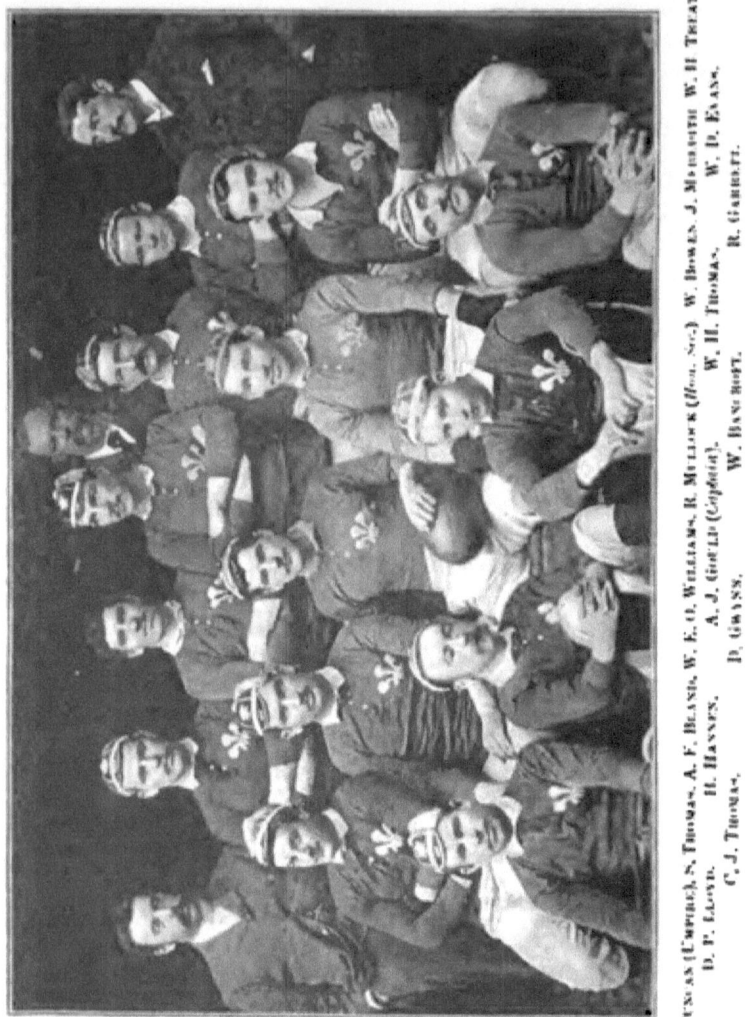

A. DUNCAN (Umpire), S. THOMAS, A. F. BLAND, W. E. O. WILLIAMS, R. MULLOCK (Hon. Sec.) W. BOWEN, J. MEREDITH, W. H. TREATT, D. P. LLOYD, H. HANNYS, A. J. GOULD (Captain), W. H. THOMAS, W. D. EVANS, C. J. THOMAS, D. GRASS, W. BANCROFT, R. GARRETT.

1889 to 1892, under the captaincy of W. Bowen, they have been marvellously successful, claiming the grand aggregate of 69 wins to 10 losses.

The Llanelly Club originated in 1872 in the desire of some gentlemen, among whom may be mentioned W. Y. Nevile, Ingram, Dr. Samuel, Colliver, Bewan, and J. C. Howell, to form a team to play against Swansea, then a strong combination. The first meeting took place in Matheas's photographic studio. This may be regarded as the foundation of the Llanelly Football Club. For a few years very little progress was made, and it was only when Buchanan became captain and Ingram secretary that the club was held "responsible for its actions." From then to the present day the club advanced by leaps and bounds, and now holds the position of being one of the four chief clubs in South Wales.

The following gentlemen have in turn watched over the clerical arrangements:—Ingram, John Brown, W. Wilkins, Harry Bowen, C. S. Antony, Gavin Henry. As mentioned above, Buchanan first captained the team. It seems but yesterday that the news of his death by a stray shot flew through the town. He was succeeded by Margrave, one of the best and most gentlemanly halfbacks that ever played. On his retirement the office fell to Harry Bowen, who held it for several years. Subsequently D. R. Williams, J. Jones, Wilson, A. C. Davies, and Percy Lloyd have captained the team. Among other prominent members may be mentioned Howell, Walkeys, Powell, Roderich, Lewis, Pyle, Sykes, Sails, Samuel, and Trubshaw.

The South Wales Challenge Cup has been twice won by Llanelly, Newport being the vanquished team each time in the final, while the final stage has been reached several times.

The Newport Football Club, or rather that section of the Newport Cricket, Athletic, Football, and Tennis Club, took its origin in the autumn of the year 1874, when C. H. Newman, W. Phillips, J. Leonard, W. Clifford Phillips, and a few others called a meeting of men likely to play football, and formed a committee, consisting of the above-named. The Association rules were adopted and played during that season, and the club wound up with a match against Cardiff, played at Cardiff under Rugby rules. The match was drawn as the rules then stood. The ground used by the club was "The Marshes," and continued to be used till the season 1878-79, when the club acquired the present athletic ground at Rodney Parade. J. Leonard was the first captain, and during the season 1875-6 various matches were played with Cardiff, Swansea, Lampeter, Hereford, and other neighbouring teams, and they were *all won*. Phillips became captain in 1876-7, and again the team was successful in every match, the list of fixtures including Cardiff, Swansea, Llanelly. In 1877-8 the club was drafted into the N. C. A. F. and T. Club, with R. Mullock and S. Bellerby as hon. secs. In this year the South Wales Cup was established, and was won by Newport; the team again were successful in every match. W. Phillips was still captain in the season of 1878-9, in which 17 matches were played, and all were won. These matches included the Cup Competition, in which Newport were again successful. At the end of the season 1879-80 the Blackheath Club came to Newport and inflicted a severe defeat on the club, the first defeat since the foundation of the club in 1874, *i.e.*, the team had gone through *four* successive seasons without losing a match, a feat without precedent in the history of any football club. In the first round for the cup, which was played against Swansea, at Bridgend, the club were beaten, and so lost the cup, which, on being won the third year in succession, would have become their property. These successes in the early days of the club, when it was not until the fifth year that defeat was known, are paralleled by the late season of 1891-92. In this season 33 matches were played, of which 29 were won and 4 drawn. One of the best judges in England of football described the fifteen as "the best club team of the season."

The Cardiff Club was founded in 1876 by an amalgamation of the Glamorgan and the Cardiff Wanderers, the two clubs then existing in the town. T. S. Donaldson Selby, the captain of the former, was elected the first captain of the new club, and W. D. Phillips, the captain of the Wanderers, to the vice-captaincy. The club has always taken a leading place in the game, but it came more prominently before the English public in the season 1884-5, by very successfully introducing the four three-quarter system, the game now adopted by all Welsh teams, and by a considerable number of clubs in the West of England. The captains of the Cardiff Club have been:— T. S. Donaldson Selby, E. C. Fry, R. H. Fox, W. D. Phillips (for three seasons), B. E. Girling, H. J. Simpson, F. E. Hancock, W. M. Douglas, G. A. Young, A. F. Hill, C. S. Arthur, W. E. O. Williams, and D. W. Evans.

THE WELSH CUP.

1878 ... Newport beat Swansea by 1 goal to *nil*.
1879 ... Newport beat Cardiff by 1 goal and 1 try to *nil*.
1880 ... Swansea beat Lampeter College by 1 goal and 1 try to *nil*.
1881 ... Cardiff beat Llanelly by 1 try to *nil*.
1882 ... Llanelly beat Newport by 1 goal to *nil*.
1883 ... Newport beat Llanelly by 1 goal to 1 try.
1884 ... Newport beat Swansea by 1 goal 2 tries to 1 goal 1 try.
1885 ... Newport beat Neath by 1 goal to *nil*.
1886 ... Llanelly beat Newport by 3 goals 1 try to *nil*.
1887 ... Swansea beat Llanelly by 1 goal to *nil*.

CHAPTER XV.

RUGBY FOOTBALL AT OXFORD.

By H. Vassall,
Late Captain of the Oxford University Football Club.

THE Oxford Rugby Football Club was started at a meeting of Old Rugbeians held in Balliol College on Nov. 2, 1869. Previous to this date there had been no organised football at Oxford. A few enthusiastic old boys of such schools as Eton, Harrow, Winchester and Rugby used occasionally to get up games to be played under the rules of their old schools, but the idea that football was only a schoolboys' game was then universal, and every freshman was expected to go down regularly to the river to be "tubbed" for his college torpids. It was not till quite ten years later that football was recognised as in any sense a genuine substitute for the river, and even then a man must have had a great reputation as a player at school to be able to escape the river altogether.

Some of the rules passed when the club was formed look curious when viewed in the light of the subsequent history of the game at Oxford; but they are interesting as evidence that in the early days of the club very few except Rugbeians and Marlburians took any part in the game.

The first rule was that the captain, the secretary, and one of the three committeemen, must always be Rugbeians.

As a matter of fact, this rule held good for the surprisingly long period of seven years, the captains during that time being A. Davenport, W. O. Moberly (two years), E. R. Still (two years), A. T. Michell, and W. H. Bolton: then came the Marlburian, F. H. Lee, and then another Rugbeian, H. D. Bateson, since whose time there have been only two Rugbeian captains—the International, C. Phillips, in the latter half of the season 1879-80, and P. Coles in 1886.

Another of the original rules of a like kind was that a subscription of half-a-crown be levied on all Rugbeian and Marlburian members of the club, but that it be optional to members of other schools.

If such a rule were in force now, there would be a notable diminution in the funds of the club.

The original committee consisted of the three Rugbeians—Devenport, who played for England v. Scotland in 1871, Oldham and Cook, and the two outsiders, E. F. S. Tylecote of Clifton, and H. Freeman of Marlborough, the former of whom is the famous Dark Blue cricketer, and the latter the hero of an England v. Scotland match, in which he dropped a wonderful goal.

It is amusing to note that the only games played by the club for the first two years were our old school-day friends, Sixth v. School, Dissyllables v. the Rest, etc., and that they used to play each match out for two days, with any number of players on each side. Sometimes over twenty a-side turned up, and sometimes only ten, and the numbers on each side were by no means always equal. Teams of Old Boys went down annually to Rugby and Wellington, but otherwise there was nothing of the nature of a foreign match.

We have now said enough to show that the game in its infancy at Oxford was merely a replica of the game as played on the Big Sides of the Rugby football schools of the time; and such it continued until the beginning of 1872, when it was decided to play a match with Cambridge. In preparation for this event a great trial match was played at Oxford between twenty Rugbeians and twenty of all other schools. The Rugbeians won easily by a goal and four tries to a try—possibly by two goals and three tries, as there is a delightful sentence in the account which runs as follows: "The last try, if not a goal, was very nearly one, but there were no umpires appointed." The days of referees and their whistles were yet a long way off.

The first Oxford team to do battle against Cambridge was picked after the game, and naturally contained a large proportion of Rugbeians, no less than fifteen out of the twenty hailing from that ancient home of football.

OXFORD UNIVERSITY RUGBY UNION FIFTEEN, 1882.

C. S. Wooldridge. H. B. Tristram. A. Rotheram. H. W. Cave. W. R. Richardson. F. J. Moore. E. D. Court. G. C. Wade. W. M. Tatham. A. G. Grant Asher. E. L. Strong. A. G. M. McKenzie.
A. M. Evanson. J. G. Walker. H. Vassall (Captain). A. R. Patterson.

As we have never seen any record of this match in print, we give the teams of both sides, as played on February 10, 1872.

Oxford:—Moberly (captain), Pearson, Michell (backs); Francis, Fletcher, Deacon (half-backs); Botfield, Brierley, Bulpett, Carlyon, Cholmondeley, Edgell, Fletcher, Gardner, Isherwood, Macgregor, Peake, Sayer, Still, and Weston (forwards).

Cambridge:—Lambert (captain), Riley, Lyon (half-backs); Batten, Hamilton, Luscombe (backs); Agnew, Back, Baxter, Collin, Deakin, Dudgeon, Hull, Macdonald, Margerison, Morse, Napier, Sisson, Sprot, and Winthrop (forwards).

Oxford won by a goal from a try by Isherwood to *nil*. Fletcher also kicked a flying-kick goal for Oxford, but as it was alleged that it had touched one of the Cambridge men on the way, it was not counted—another touching instance of the way the game was played before the referee had become a necessary institution. The Cambridge captain, Lambert, was the mainstay of his side, but the Oxford forwards proved too good for their heavier opponents.

It should be noted that the famous three-quarter back, H. Freeman, was unable to play for Oxford in this match, but he played in the same year for England v. Scotland, as did the Oxford captain, W. O. Moberly, following the example of his predecessor, A. Davenport.

R. W. Isherwood also got a place in that year's English team, and three more of this Oxford team, W. R. B. Fletcher, E. R. Still, and A. T. Michell, got their International caps later on. Still and Michell were afterwards captains of Oxford, and so the tradition was set going that the Oxford captain should always get his International cap—a tradition which has been kept up with remarkably few exceptions right down to the present day.

Freeman and Fletcher were members of their old school club, the then famous Marlborough Nomads, but all the others belonged, as most Rugbeians of that day did, to the Ravenscourt Park Club, and it was therefore natural that the first foreign match played at Oxford should be against the latter club. It was played a fortnight after the Cambridge match, and H. Freeman was once more able to play for Oxford. He scored 2 tries out of 3, but as no goal was kicked, the match counted as a draw in those days.

In October, 1872, Moberly resigned the captaincy in favour of E. R. Still, who secured his International cap at the same time as that huge forward, W. R. B. Fletcher and the Oxford fast-bowler C. W. Boyle. Moberly still continued to render invaluable aid to the club as secretary, and no small share of the credit for putting the club on a thoroughly firm footing is due to him for his services both on the field and off it—services which he has since repeated both in cricket and football for Clifton College, where he is still a master. Another member of the Committee of that year was R. Leach, who ran for Oxford in the quarter at Lillie Bridge, and was the eldest of the cricketing family of that name, hailing from Rochdale.

There is no record of any foreign matches being played in 1872, but in 1873 eight matches were played, of which four—those against Rugby School, Blackheath, Marlborough Nomads, Cooper's Hill (return)—were won outright. Three more—those against Cooper's Hill, Ravenscourt Park and Richmond—were then counted as draws, but would nowadays count as wins, whilst the match against Cambridge, played at the Oval on December 3rd, ended in a pretty even draw of one try each, though the Oxford men claim to have had the best of the "penning."

This was by no means a bad record for the season for a young club, for in those days Ravenscourt Park, Marlborough Nomads, and Cooper's Hill, were about on a par with Blackheath and Richmond.

The 1873 team were:—

M. Brooks, H. Field, W. O. Moberly (backs), W. H. Game (three-quarters), A. T. Michell, G. C. Vecqueray (half-backs), E. R. Still (captain), W. R. B. Fletcher, E. C. Fraser, C. W. Crosse, W. H. Bolton, H. Bourdillon, R. M. Edgell, R. W. Sheffield, J. Harrison, H. Russell, R. F. Brunskill, F. G. Cholmondeley, B. Powell, W. F. Gooding.

Three Oxonians played for England against Scotland in 1873-4, H. Freeman, C. W. Crosse and M. Brooks. Brooks afterwards gave up football, and devoted himself to jumping, for which he still holds the record at the 'Varsity sports, with his marvellous jump of 6 ft. 2½ in. H. Russell also was an athletic blue as a three-miler. It should be noted that the first appearance in the team of the famous cricketer W. H. Game coincides with the last appearance of W. O. Moberly, of whom it has been said that he is a long way the best cricketer who never got his blue.

The Oxford half-back, A. T. Michell, was a brother of the Cambridge full-back, W. G. Michell, now a master at Rugby School, and though each of them represented his University for four years, this was the only occasion on which they actually appeared on the field as opponents.

In the next season, 1874, the match list was enlarged by the addition of new matches with the Gypsies, Old Cheltonians, United Hospitals, Wasps, Woolwich and Clifton Club—names which inspired much more terror at that date than they do now—but Oxford managed to get through the season undefeated, and in it began to play fifteen a-side against any clubs which would consent to do so. This naturally developed a distaste for tight scrummages, and by the time of the 'Varsity match they had begun to fancy themselves for their play in the loose, and tried hard to persuade Cambridge to agree to fifteen a-side, but, as Cambridge had a good set of heavy forwards and were not nearly so strong behind as Oxford, they held out for the more orthodox number of twenty, with the result that the match was tight and uninteresting, ending in a draw in favour of Oxford by 2 tries to nil.

The Oxford team were:—

A. T. Michell (captain), E. H. Nash, R. W. Rücker (half-backs), E. H. Champneys, W. H. Game, D. B. Wilson (backs), W. H. Bolton, W. R. B. Fletcher, E. C. Fraser, C. W. Crosse, F. H. Lee, C. F. Harrison, H. Bourdillon, R. W. Sheffield, H. Merivale, H. D. Bateson, F. H. Bainbrigge, J. E. Lloyd, H. Russell, R. F. Brunskill (forwards).

This was the last twenty that played for Oxford, and the best match of the season was a fifteen a-side game with Blackheath, which ended in a draw, thanks to the magnificent play of L. Stokes.

The Oxonians who played against Scotland in this year were the captain A. T. Michell, and W. R. B. Fletcher; and besides Michell, C. W. Crosse, E. C. Fraser, and E. H. Nash also played in the Irish match, which was instituted in this season.

In 1875-6 W. H. Bolton was elected captain, and the committee consisted of Lee Forman, Fraser, and Game. A programme similar to that of the previous year was carried through successfully, the best matches being those with Cooper's Hill, which the famous half-back, W. Hutchinson, had then made into one of the strongest teams in England. At the end of the season an extra match was arranged with the Glasgow and Edinburgh Academicals, to come off after the International match at the Oval. The Scotsmen brought down no less than twelve of the Scotch Twenty in their fifteen, and after a grand game defeated Oxford by 2 tries to 1. This is the first recorded defeat of Oxford since the foundation of the club seven years before, and it is a noticeable fact that on the rare occasions on which Scotch teams have visited Oxford, they have generally proved a thorn in the side of the 'Varsity team, as the present writer has good occasion to remember. Two of the Oxford team had just played for England against Scotland—the full-back, A. H. Heath, then a freshman from Clifton, afterwards a cricket blue for four years, and now captain of Staffordshire, and F. H. Lee, who was noted as the best "follower up" of his day. In the International match he backed up a magnificent run of Hutchinson's, and secured the try which won the match for England. The 'Varsity match of this year was chiefly noticeable as being the first played with fifteen a-side, and as coming on the same day as the International match against Ireland in Dublin, a clashing of dates which has not been allowed since, as it prevented Michell from playing for Oxford, who, nevertheless, won by a try. The Oxford team consisted of:—

A. H. Heath, F. G. Champneys (backs), E. H. Nash (three-quarter back), H. Bourdillon, J. Forman (half-backs), W. H. Bolton (captain), F. H. Lee, H. D. Bateson, C. F. Harrison, A. Law, J. James, T. Johnson, T. W. Wall, H. Russell, and E. C. Fraser (forwards).

The Oxford captain, W. H. Bolton, could not play for England, because he hailed from Scotland, where he played for the West of Scotland Club, but he kept up the tradition of the Oxford captain being an International by getting his Scotch cap. He was the first of the many good Scotsmen we have had in Oxford teams.

The next season, 1876-7, was a disastrous one for Oxford. They lost three matches, including the Cambridge one, in which A. H. Heath was not able to play, and they had only one man playing for England, namely the captain, F. H. Lee. At the same time there was a team in Oxford which held an unbeaten record for two whole seasons. We allude to the St. John's College team —which was developed by the College Ties, started in 1875. They had a determined set of forwards, noted for their hard tackling and good passing, and several men behind who played for the 'Varsity, such as M. Shearman, F. W. Champneys, H. Brembridge, Lockhart Ross, and W. Giles. They won the Ties as long as they lasted, but these were soon abolished, because they were found to be making the College matches too bloodthirsty, and all subsequent attempts to revive them have happily been

A DRIBBLE.
(From an instantaneous Photograph by E. Alrey, Bradford.)

unsuccessful. The success of this forward team is alluded to in the Badminton series as an instance of how determined forward play can overcome superior combination behind the scrummage. The defeat of Oxford by Edinburgh University in 1885, referred to on page 292, is another example of the same. The Oxford team, which was beaten by Cambridge by a goal and 2 tries to *nil*, was :—

A. C. Sim, C. C. Atkinson (backs); R. W. Rücker (three-quarter back); J. Forman, F. W. Champneys (half-backs); F. H. Lee (captain), J. H. Bainbrigge, J. James, H. Brembridge, J. J. Mowbray, T. W. Wall, C. Phillips, M. Macmillan, W. H. Cornish, and R. Gaisford (forwards).

In 1877-8 Oxford had a very satisfactory season, as they lost only one match against the United Hospitals, who brought down a very strong team, including E. B. Turner and J. M. Biggs forward, and A. W. Pearson, W. J. Penny, L. Stokes, and A. H. Jackson behind, whilst Springman, Hirst, and A. H. Evans, Oxford's three best men behind, were on the sick list, and F. H. Lee had to play three-quarters for the occasion. The Cambridge match was won rather easily by 2 tries to *nil*. Cambridge had the heavier forwards, but Oxford played a loose dribbling game, and so gave their backs a chance of showing their superiority. H. Fowler, a freshman from Clifton, who afterwards got his cricket blue, was the best forward in the team, and he played against Scotland in the following spring. The Oxford captain, H. D. Bateson, was a very clever player in the open, but had rather a predilection for wing play; he secured his International cap the year after he had gone down.

The Oxford team was as follows:—

A. H. Heath, J. Ravenscroft (backs); P. Springman, E. T. Hirst (three-quarter backs); A. H. Evans, A. H. Vecqueray (half-backs); H D. Bateson (captain), H. Fowler, F. H. Lee, J. J. Mowbray, H. Brembridge, J. H. Bainbrigge, C. Phillips, T. W. Wall, J. James.

In 1878-9 H. Fowler, the International, was elected captain, and the rest of the committee were C. Phillips, E. T. Hirst, A. H. Heath, A. H. Vecqueray, T. W. Wall, P. Springman, and A. H. Evans. The names of the committee are by themselves sufficient to show that the Oxford team would be a good one; but, unfortunately, the 'Varsity match had to be postponed over Christmas for frost, and the team were not so well together after the vacation as they had been in November, when the present writer paid his first visit to Oxford and saw T. W. Wall place seven goals in succession against the Naval College. Wall went down at Christmas, and Crosby Burrowes lost his chance of his football cap by rowing in the 'Varsity eight in the following term. He and H. Brembridge and R. S. Kindersley used to play for Devonshire against Somersetshire in the days when H. Bourdillon, H. A. Tudor, C. F. Sanctuary, and the writer, formed the Oxford contingent of the Somerset team.

The team that eventually played a drawn game with Cambridge in February at the Oval was as follows:—

A. H. Heath, H. A. Tudor (backs); P. Springman, E. T. Hirst (three-quarter backs); A. H. Evans, A. H. Vecqueray (half-backs);

H. Fowler (captain), C. Phillips, A. Back, E. Branfoot, G. V. Cox, M. Shearman, G. O. Jacob, J. Ravenscroft, and J. J. Mowbray (forwards).

This was the last appearance of A. H. Vecqueray, who had done good service for Oxford at half-back; he was a brother of the Vecqueray who played for Oxford in 1873, and they were sons of the Rugby master of that name.

It is worthy of notice that several of the Oxford forwards were school three-quarters, who were not found good enough to play for Oxford in that position, but who nevertheless were made into excellent forwards. G. V. Cox was a Clifton three-quarter who had won the freshman's quarter at Oxford. Montague Shearman had played three-quarters at Merchant Taylors and for St. John's, and his marvellous sprinting soon earned for him the position of President of the Athletic Club. George Jacob had played three-quarters for Blackheath School, and J. Ravenscroft had played full-back for the 'Varsity in the previous year. Of these, Shearman afterwards played for the South, and Ravenscroft became an International.

In 1879-80 A. H. Evans was elected captain, but the 'Varsity match was again postponed for frost, and at Christmas he resigned the captaincy to C. Phillips, and gave up the game. He then took up Association as a gentler form of exercise, and became so good at it that he was offered his cap—an honour which he declined out of consideration for his old Rugby football friends. He was a wonderfully good all-round athlete, who more than justified the great reputation which he had at Clifton. He is the only man who has been captain of both cricket and Rugby football at Oxford. His place on the football field was half-back; but he could play three-quarters, and he once played as a forward for the South, and was picked as a forward for England v. Ireland, but the match was postponed for frost, and when it did come off Evans did not play. Springman also had to give up the game because of an injury to his knee. He was as good at three-quarters as Evans at half, and that is saying a good deal. He was very small and very fast, and had a wonderful knack of getting through his men untouched. They came up to Oxford in the same year, and it is probably safe to say that the 'Varsity team never secured a pair of freshmen of equal

s 2

value before or since. Springman was the second great player whom we received from Scotland, but he was of English birth, being a brother of H. H. Springman of Liverpool, who played against Scotland in 1879, and again in 1887 after an absence of eight years in the Colonies.

The loss of Evans and Springman was brought home to us in the 'Varsity match which we lost in February by 2 goals to 1. Maclachlan touched the ball when Finch dropped his goal, but Stokes and Gurdon, the umpires, did not see it, and Cambridge deserved to win, for the Oxford half simply gave them the try, from which H. Y. L. Smith placed a very fine goal.

The Oxford team was as follows:—

A. H. Heath, N. Maclachlan (backs); E. T. Hirst, H. A. Tudor (three-quarter backs); R. L. Knight, L. Watkins (half-backs); C. Phillips (captain), G. O. Jacob, E. P. Branfoot, M. Shearman, P. A. Newton, H. Vassall, J. G. Walker, A. R. Paterson, and C. F. Sanctuary (forwards).

This was the last match played at the Oval. Three of the forwards of the 1882 team made their *début* in it, and it was the last occasion on which some of the old lights appeared, such as the cricket blues, Heath and Hirst, the athletic blue, Shearman, and the captain, C. Phillips, who played against Scotland in the following month. C. F. Sanctuary and L. Watkins, by securing places in this team, maintained the tradition handed down to them by W. H. Game, H. A. Tudor, and R. T. Finch (the Cambridge captain), that the captain of Sherborne School should always get into the 'Varsity team—a tradition which we hope their successors have carried on to the present day. A. R. Paterson, J. G. Walker, and N. Maclachlan were all freshmen from Loretto School. After one more year Maclachlan had to give up football because of an injured knee, but he became captain of cricket; J. G. Walker got his cricket blue, and became a Scotch International; whilst Paterson became president of the O. U. B. C.; and this trio was only a sample, though certainly a good sample, of what was to follow from the same school.

It may be mentioned as a point of interest that the word "deliberately" was cut out of the Rugby Union law about "knocking-on" because of a dispute which occurred in the Richmond match of this season. Twynam knocked the ball on at the far end of a line out of touch, followed up his knock, caught the ball, and ran in unopposed. The Richmond captain, F. R. Adams, refused to admit that the knock-on was deliberate, and as there were no referees in those days, but only two umpires, a deadlock ensued, which finally convinced the authorities that the word should be cut out of the law.

In the season of 1880-1 P. A. Newton was elected captain. He had played half-back for Blackheath against Oxford the year before he came up, but he was made into a forward at Oxford, and afterwards gained his International cap in that position. The secretary for the term was R. N. Blandy, a very good forward from Cheltenham, who had been unlucky enough to hurt his knee after he had been picked to play against Cambridge the year before, and who was again unable to play in this his last year.

We lost one match before Christmas, *v.* Cheshire, who managed to snatch a victory by a dropped goal, and one after Christmas, *v.* Blackheath, who beat us by a try to *nil*, whilst we managed to make a draw of the Cambridge match, thanks to Bevan's dropped goal being disallowed by the umpires. It was claimed that the ball had never been properly in the scrummage, which only meant that the scrummage had not been started in the good old-fashioned way. A Cambridge forward had kicked the ball out at once to Don Wauchope, who passed to Bevan. Perhaps the umpires did not see what had happened, or perhaps they thought it unorthodox play, but we feel certain that any referee of the present day would have allowed the goal to stand. Oxford had a good team forward, thanks to the dribbling of the four Scotchmen, Paterson, Mackenzie, J. G. Walker, and A. Walker, but only a moderate lot behind, where H. A. Tudor, who was picked for the South that year, was the only one really up to form. We had a wonderful half-back in R. L. Knight, who was also a cricket blue, but he was injured before the 'Varsity match; he was very small and very fast, and he used to score at least one try in almost every match. He was offered a Welsh cap, but declined it. Had he been a little stronger in defensive play, he might have played for England. After Christmas he was elected captain and Vassall secretary for the rest of the season. In the 'Varsity match Knight's place was taken by the long-jumper, M. B. Peacock, who had come up from

Wellington with a great reputation as a three-quarters, but who was quite out of his place at half-back.

The Oxford team was as follows:—

N. Maclachlan, J. Booker (backs); H. A. Tudor, A. M. Evanson (three-quarters); H. Irwin, M. B. Peacock (half-backs); P. A. Newton (captain), H. Vassall, A. R. Paterson, J. G. Walker, A. Walker, A. O. M. Mackenzie, C. S. Sanctuary, C. F. H. Leslie, and W. M. Barwick (forwards).

In the following February the first England v. Wales match was played. One place amongst the English forwards was left to be filled from amongst the Englishmen in the Oxford team after their match with Blackheath. The place was given to Vassall, who scored 4 of the 16 tries of the match, and thereby secured his place against Scotland in company with the old Oxonians Fowler and Phillips. Two Oxford men played for Wales, the cricket blue, E. Peake, and the half-back, L. Watkins. In this year also there was a Manchester schoolboy, W. R. Richardson, playing for England v. Ireland. He came up to Oxford in the following October and at once became Asher's partner at half-back.

H. VASSALL.
(From a Photograph by Elliott & Fry, London.)

For the season 1881-2 Vassall was elected captain, and the committee consisted of Walker, Maclachlan, Paterson, Mackenzie, Booker, and Evanson; so that the Scotchmen were in a majority. There was plenty of good material for the new team, for, besides eleven old caps, there were Tatham and Strong amongst the seniors, and Asher, Allen, Richardson, Cave, and Tristram amongst the freshmen. The season opened well with a series of six wins, which included Blackheath and Richmond, and then came the memorable match with Edinburgh University on November 28th—memorable as being the last defeat to which Oxford had to submit for more than three years. The next defeat occurred on February 9th, 1885, at the hands of the same club, Edinburgh University, and was the only defeat of that season. These events have given a special interest to all matches between Oxford and Edinburgh Universities, and a résumé of them will show what close fights they have provided.

Edinburgh won the first by 2 goals to a goal and a try. Knight came up to help his old club for the last time, and scored both goal and try for Oxford. One of the Edinburgh's goals was from a fair catch made off a feeble kick of Allen's, just in front of his own goal. Oxford had their revenge in December, 1883, when Tatham took the Oxford team on tour for the first time, and defeated Edinburgh by a goal and a try to *nil*. Edinburgh then broke the Oxford record at Oxford in 1885 by 1 try to *nil*. In December of the same year Lindsay took the Oxford team to Edinburgh, and beat them by 2 goals to a goal and a try. In 1886 they paid another visit to Oxford, and once more won by a try to *nil*, and again in 1888 they won in Edinburgh by the same score, but the last match played in Christopherson's year in Edinburgh was won by Oxford by the comparatively large score of a goal and 2 tries to *nil*. Thus Edinburgh have won four matches, and Oxford three, but Edinburgh have only scored 3 goals and 4 tries to Oxford's 5 goals and 4 tries in the seven matches, so there has never really been very much to choose between the two teams.

In November, 1881, a new Rugby Union match was started under the title of the Universities *v*. London, nominally as an interesting match in itself, but really as a trial match for the South team. It had struck the Oxford captain that the 'Varsities were not getting their fair share of the places in the South team, so on the way back from the Scotch match in March, he proposed the new match to L. Stokes, who was then captain of England and of Blackheath, and who, by the way, had just dropped the most wonderful goal—a full 75 yards drop—against Scotland that the writer has ever seen. Stokes took up the idea of the match without any suspicion of the designs upon the London monopoly of the South team, and with the help of Rowland Hill got it accepted by the Rugby Union committee. The immediate result of the match was that whereas in the previous year the Cambridge captain, C. P. Wilson, was the only resident 'Varsity man in the South team, in this year there were five, A. S. Taylor, H. G. Fuller, H. Vassall, W. M. Tatham, and A. M. Evanson, and in the following year five more were added to these, as will appear in due course.

In the first of these matches, sixteen a side were played, so as to allow each 'Varsity to send eight men—for subsequent years it was settled that the odd man should come from the winners of the last 'Varsity match, unless the two captains agreed to the contrary. The captaincy was to go to each 'Varsity alternately, and the selection of the joint team was to be left entirely to the two captains — contrary to the usual method of procedure at the 'Varsities, where all teams are picked by the committee. We should be glad to see the system changed, as we hold very strongly that the captain ought always to have the final selection of the team for which he is responsible, and that committees ought only to pick the trial teams to bring men under the captain's notice. The Oxford half of the first joint team were H. Vassall, J. G. Walker, A. O. Mackenzie, W. M. Tatham, and C. F. H. Leslie (forwards), W. R. Richardson, A. M. Evanson, and E. R. Wethey (behind) : A. R. Paterson could not play, and all the full-backs except A. S. Taylor of Cambridge were injured, but, as two full-backs were still considered necessary, Wethey, who proved an efficient substitute, was given the place, and the match ended in a very even draw. It was in this match that the historic maul of five minutes' duration took place between C. Gurdon and Vassall, since which time the writer has always been a keen advocate for the total abolition of mauls.

W. M. TATHAM.
(From a Photograph by Stillard & Co., Oxford.)

The 'Varsity match was won fairly easily by 2 goals and a try to a goal, in spite of the dodgy runs of Don Wauchope and the deadly tackling of A. S. Taylor, which the writer has good cause to remember. The

Oxford forwards, who were just beginning to get into the game which made them famous for some years to come, carried all before them, and A. M. Evanson played better at three-quarters than he ever played before or since. It was he who kept the combination going throughout the match, and it must not be forgotten that in this match he had only one partner at three-quarters. The team against Cambridge was:—

H. A. Tudor, H. W. Cave (backs); A. M. Evanson, C. P. Allen (three-quarters); A. G. Grant-Asher, W. R. Richardson (half-backs); H. Vassall (captain), W. M. Tatham, J. G. Walker, A. R. Paterson, C. F. H. Leslie, A. O. Mackenzie, W. M. Barwick, E. L. Strong, F. W. Hodgson forwards.

As Leslie went down after this season, it may be well to mention here that he and Grant-Asher are the only two members of the Rugby team who ever represented Oxford in three different branches of athletics—Leslie in football, cricket, and racquets, and Asher in football, cricket, and long-jumping.

In the International matches of this year Oxford was represented by Tatham and the captain for England, and by Asher and the two Walkers for Scotland. These two brothers were two of the best forwards that Oxford has ever had. They were thorough proficients of the Scotch style of scrummaging, which means that they were the backbone of every scrummage formed.

The Welsh match of this year was against a North team. W. R. Richardson played for the North, and W. F. Evans and C. P. Lewis for Wales. Evans had been just outside the Oxford team of

A. M. EVANSON.
(From a Photograph by Byrne & Co., Richmond.)

1879, and Lewis, who captained Wales for three years, was an old Oxford blue, both for cricket and athletics.

For the season 1882-3 H. Vassall was elected to a second term of office as captain, but as he was known to be going down at Christmas, James Walker was elected deputy-captain.

Unfortunately he hurt his ankle badly in Scotland after playing for Scotland v. Wales, and was therefore unable to play in the following term, when Evanson was made captain for the rest of the season, and Tatham secretary. The rest of the committee for this year were Richardson, Mackenzie, Strong, and Asher.

Great things were expected of the team before the season began. Arthur Budd had written a magazine article for the special benefit of the Oxford captain, pointing out that there was no end to what might be done, given good material and plenty of opportunities for practice. Good material he certainly had, for besides twelve of the last year's team, which was no bad one, there were Wooldridge, Kindersley, Court, Moore, F. C. Mackenzie, Squire, to pick from amongst the forwards, Wade, Rotherham, and Tristram were there ready to be brought out, and Lindsay had just come up with a great reputation from Loretto, for he had already played in East v. West as a schoolboy. The workman must be bad indeed who could complain of such tools as those. Budd's second requisite for making a team invincible was constant practice, and here again Oxford is specially favoured. With excellent grounds in the Parks close at hand, and crowds of men ready to play six days a week if given a chance, the difficulty was rather to stop them from getting too much practice. The common thing was to play five times a week: one match, more rarely two, one "picked fifteens," one college match and a couple of Association college matches thrown in on off-days. In those days a good many colleges could not put an Association and a Rugby team on the field on the same day, consequently there was a good deal of overlapping, and nearly all the Rugby Blues used to play Association for their colleges, just to keep their feet in at dribbling. The Rugby team undoubtedly derived much benefit from this Association practice, but the "picked fifteens" were the centre of the whole system. There was great competition for a place in them, which carried with it the right of wearing the club jersey with the crown on it. The committee took infinite pains in picking the sides, and the games were as keen as games could be. Everybody with any sort of a reputation, either from his school or from his college, was given a chance of showing what he was worth; men were tried in new positions, three-quarters were made into backs or forwards (as, for instance, J. R. Deakin, who afterwards became captain of the Midland Counties as a forward), and, most important point of all, constant coaching was going on throughout the game. The result was thoroughly good football and thoroughly enjoyable football—far more useful to the team than the minor foreign matches. These practice games gave the committee a thorough knowledge of the play of all the best men in the 'Varsity, and made the task of picking the 'Varsity team comparatively easy to them. They also knew offhand who were the right men to play as substitutes for any member of the team who might be injured, or to fill up places in any visiting team which came down short-handed. We must not omit to mention that far the most valuable emergency man of the day was W. E. W. Collins, the fast bowler, who, though too senior to play against Cambridge, was always ready to fill a vacant place, and so well did he fill them that he was once offered the position of full-back in the South team, which his modesty alone made him decline. As we were debarred by our rules from presenting the Blue coat to anyone who did not actually play against Cambridge, we gave him the club cap in recognition of his services. Mention of the Blue coat reminds us that it was in this term, when eight of our men had just been picked to play for the South, that it occurred to T. H. French, the Association captain, that it was a good opportunity to claim the full Blue coat for the football teams. He asked the Rugby captain to write the letter, which was sent to A. R. Paterson, president of the O. U. B. C., as the chief representative of existing Blues, requesting him to convene a meeting of Blues representing boating, cricket, and athletics, to consider the application of the football clubs for admission to the sacred circle. The football clubs undoubtedly had a strong case; football was by this time universally recognised as the national winter game. Oxford football had always been of a high standard and was now approaching its zenith; the time had therefore clearly come for putting it on a level with the other three great branches of sport at the University. The athletic men had been admitted to the dignity of the Blue some years before, but not without a somewhat heated controversy. The football men were now admitted not only without opposition but with cordiality and good grace. The committee which admitted them to the fellowship of the Blue consisted of three dons and four undergraduates. The dons were Messrs. T. Case, C. N. Jackson, and W. W. Courtney, one for each branch of sport; and the undergraduates were G. C. Harrison, E. T. Wells, W. Cave, and the president, A. R. Paterson.

A. R. PATERSON.
(From a Photograph by Hills & Saunders, Oxford.)

The team improved steadily all through the season; only thirteen matches were played, but they were all won, and the score at the end of the season was 28 goals and 26 tries against 1 goal and 2 tries. The two tries were scored by Sandhurst in the first match of the season, before the team was properly together, and the goal was dropped by a forward for the Midland Counties in the last minute of the match, which Oxford won by 6 goals and 1 try to 1 goal. Ten of the Oxford goals were dropped by Cave, Lindsay, Wade, and Rotherham, and the tries were scored by no less than seventeen different men—a fact which will give some idea of the extent to which passing was developed. It was this development of the passing game which was the keynote to the success of the team. Short passing amongst the forwards had been adopted by other clubs before this date; but long passing, right across the ground if necessary, was a thing hitherto unknown. The team soon grasped the idea that passing, to be successful, must be to the open, and they learnt very quickly to back up in the open, and only to call for passes when they were in a better position than the man in possession. In this way they used to sweep the ball from end to end of the ground time after time, passing any length with such deadly accuracy that very often the whole team handled the ball in less than two minutes, and their opponents, who were not accustomed to these novel tactics, were completely nonplussed.

After the combined 'Varsities had beaten London, ten of their men were picked for the South team, which beat the North by 4 goals and 4 tries to *nil*; from Cambridge their full-back, A. S. Taylor, and their grand forward, H. G. Fuller, who fell into the Oxford style of play as if by instinct, and from Oxford, Rotherham, Evanson, Wade, Vassall, Tatham, Strong, Kindersley, and Wooldridge. We must not omit to mention that Asher, who was already a Scotch International, had strong claims to be Don Wauchope's partner at half-back for the combined team, but as the match was now recognised as a trial for the South, the Oxford captain, who knew what a treasure he had secured in Rotherham, felt bound to give him his chance of showing the authorities what he was worth. The extraordinary thing about Rotherham's sudden rise to the first rank is that he came from Uppingham School, where in those days they did not play Rugby Union rules, but mixed rules of their own, one feature of which was that the ball might never be picked up except on the first bound.

Wade's rise was quite as sudden, but, to our shame be it said, he had been in Oxford a year before we discovered him. From outside sources we heard that there was a great Australian player at Merton College, called Wade; at first we were somewhat disinclined to believe the report, as he had not been near the Parks the year before; but when we found that there was such a man rowing in the Merton boat, we sent him an invitation to play in "picked fifteens." We shall never

G. C. WADE.
From a Photograph by Hills & Saunders, Oxford.

forget the curiosity with which we watched his first appearance. He did not seem quite at home with the ball at first, and his kicking was a little faulty; but everybody who tried to tackle him retired from the attempt convinced that the rumour was true, and that we had secured a wonder, who only wanted a little practice to make him into the best three-quarters of the day. Against these discoveries must be set the loss of A. O. M. Mackenzie, who broke his leg in the United Hospitals match, and of E. L. Strong, whose injured knee alone prevented him from getting in that year the International cap, which he secured the year after.

In the Christmas vacation we suffered a still more serious loss owing to J. G. Walker's accident, and when the day finally came for the postponed 'Varsity match, Paterson was rowing in the 'Varsity eight, and Evanson and Cave had been injured in the Swinton match. Cambridge had also lost their captain, Don Wauchope, and others, so the match was robbed of much of its interest. It ended in a narrow victory for Oxford (by a clever try of Rotherham's to *nil*).

The team that played was:—

H. B. Tristram (back); G. C. Wade, G. C. Lindsay, C. P. Allen (three-quarter backs); A. Rotherham and A. G. Grant-Asher (half-backs); H. Vassall (captain), W. M. Tatham, C. S. Wooldridge, R. S. Kindersley, E. J. Moore, E. D. Court, G. F. Bradby, W. H. Squire, and F. C. Mackenzie.

It is a noteworthy fact that there were twelve Internationals in Oxford at this time, and that four more of this team became Internationals the year after. In order to put a fifteen of Internationals on the field, we should have had to play four three-quarters, a thing then unknown; but as a club team of Internationals is unique, we put it down on paper:—

H. B. Tristram (back); G. C. Wade, A. M. Evanson, G. C. Lindsay, C. P. Allen (three-quarters); A. Rotherham, A. G. Grant-Asher (half-backs); H. Vassall, J. G. Walker, W. M. Tatham, R. S. Kindersley, C. S. Wooldridge, E. L. Strong, E. J. Moore, E. D. Court, with W. R. Richardson as umpire.

But even if none of the men had been injured, and if four three-quarters had been the fashion, we should never have played this team exactly as it stands, for it does not include H. W. Cave (who, in spite of his bad eyesight, was a better man on that year's play than either Lindsay or Allen) and A. R. Paterson, who would have been one of the first men picked for England if he had been eligible. The Scotch authorities would not hear of him for Scotland, and possibly they were right, for the Scotch style of forward play was at that time very different from the Oxford style, and Paterson had not Walker's gift of adapting himself to both styles, but at his own game he was hard to beat. The other four Blues of that year, Bradby, Squire, and the two Mackenzies, though they never became Internationals, were quite sound players, fully worth their places.

Tristram had been improving all the season, and was the first full-back who played for us in that position by himself. He was not picked in the earlier big matches because A. S. Taylor had a start of him in reputation, but by the end of the season he was universally admitted to be the best full-back in England, and he played in that position against Scotland.

There were no less than seven of that year's Blues who came from Loretto School—Walker, Paterson, Asher, Tristram, Lindsay, and the two Mackenzies—a wonderful record for a school of the size of Loretto. Strong also came from a Scotch school, and Wade from Australia—the rest were from English schools, Rugby coming first with Cave, Allen, Court, Bradby, and Squire, Marlborough next with Vassall and Tatham, so that the two schools which practically monopolised the team ten years previously, now only provided seven men between them. Kindersley came from Clifton, Rotherham from Uppingham, Evanson from Oundle, Moore from Epsom, Richardson from Manchester, and Wooldridge from Winchester.

Uppingham rules did bear some resemblance to Rugby rules, but Winchester rules are absolutely *sui generis*, and most Wykehamists took to Association on leaving school, but the late G. W. Burton, of Blackheath, had gained an International Rugby cap as a fast forward, and Wooldridge was quite one of the best forwards of his day.

The double Blues in this team were Kindersley and Paterson, successive presidents of the O. U. B. C., Evanson, who put the weight, Lindsay, who ran in the quarter, and Walker, the cricketer; Asher's treble Blue has already been mentioned. Some of them were to be seen rowing for their colleges, such as Wooldridge, Mackenzie, Wade, and Cave, for at this time it was still considered possible to take up both rowing and football, though the breach between the two was always widening, and of late years has become rather marked, definite complaints being heard that football has robbed the river of much of its most promising material; and as a matter of fact, the only double Blue for rowing and football since the days of Paterson and Kindersley was C. R. Carter in 1885. We regret the quarrel, and should be glad to see the compromise of the early eighties restored. It certainly worked with very little friction then.

Besides all the Rugby International caps, there was a fair sprinkling of Association ones about this time in Oxford. The names of C. W. Wilson, P. C. Parr, R. S. King, and shortly afterwards of Bromley Davenport and M. P. Walters, occur to one as evidence that the football Blue was handsomely earned in both branches of the game. In the season 1883-4 W. M. Tatham was elected captain, and A. G. Asher secretary. Strong, Moore, Rotherham, Tristram and Wade completed the committee. There were 13 old Blues available, and the two new ones were C. W. Berry from Loretto, who became a Scotch International in the same year, and R. E. Inglis, a freshman from Rugby School, who played for England in 1886; so there was no falling-off in the quality of the material available for filling up vacancies. The natural result was that under Tatham's captaincy the team not only maintained but considerably increased its reputation. The record for the season was twenty matches won, one drawn, and none lost; and the score, 48 goals and 44 tries, against 4 goals and 4 tries. The

C. S. WOOLDRIDGE.
(From a Photograph by H. M. Salmon, Winchester.)

R. S. KINDERSLEY.
(From a Photograph by Hills & Saunders, Oxford.)

most noteworthy features of this eventful season were the decisive defeat of Cambridge, the Northern tour, and the Yorkshire match.

The team that played against Cambridge, and beat them by 3 goals and 4 tries to 1 goal, was as follows:—

H. B. Tristram (back); G. C. Wade, G. C. Lindsay, C. P. Allen (three-quarters); A. Rotherham, A. G. G. Asher (half-backs); W. M. Tatham (captain), E. L. Strong, R. S. Kindersley, E. J. Moore, E. D. Court, C. W. Berry, W. H. Squire, F. C. Mackenzie, and R. E. Inglis (forwards).

Bradby was unable to play, and Inglis took his place.

Immediately after the North v. South match, Oxford started on its first tour.

E. J. MOORE.
(From a Photograph by C. Gillman Oxford.)

They played Manchester on the Monday, Liverpool on the Tuesday, Glasgow Academicals on the Thursday, and Edinburgh University on the Saturday—a very fair week's work for any team. They whipped up a few of the last year's Blues to help them—namely, Walker, Paterson, Evanson, and Wooldridge; but Walker hurt himself again in the first match, and Evanson collapsed in the second. In the two remaining matches W. W. Ord came to the rescue; he was a useful man, who could play in any position, and who had often filled a place in the 1882 team. Contrary to the expectation of some of his friends, who thought that he was trying to get too much out of his men in a week, Tatham returned victorious, and well pleased to have wiped out the Edinburgh University defeat of 1881. At the beginning

A. COURT.
(From a Photograph by Hills & Saunders, Oxford.)

T

of the Easter term the team was very nearly caught napping by Gloucester County, who played them a drawn game in vile weather, but nevertheless they felt justified in challenging Yorkshire County at the close of the season. Yorkshire had not been beaten for three seasons, and a tremendous amount of interest was taken in the meeting of the two unbeaten teams of the day. In order to take a gate the match was played on the 'Varsity Running Ground in Iffley Road, and there were 6,000 spectators, who were rewarded by seeing one of the keenest and most even matches ever played. There was no score in the first half, but soon after change of ends Wooldridge secured the ball from a line out and passed to Rotherham, who dashed in, and Berry turned the try into a goal; and Oxford eventually won by this goal to nothing. Asher and Rotherham were the heroes of the day—in fact, Asher probably never played better in his life than he did in this match—Tatham, Kindersley, Wooldridge, and Court were most prominent among the forwards; and for Yorkshire, Bonsor, Wigglesworth, Fallas, Hutchinson, and the captain, G. T. Thomson, distinguished themselves especially. Eleven of this year's Oxford team were Internationals, viz., all the backs (Tristram, Wade, Lindsay, Allen, Rotherham, and Asher) and five of the forwards (Tatham, Strong, Kindersley, Berry, and Moore). In the next season, 1884-5, A. G. G. Asher was elected captain, A. Rotherham secretary, and the committee was filled up by Berry, Cave, Lindsay, and Squire. Cave had to give up the game this season, but his place was immediately filled by yet another acquisition from Loretto in the person of A. S. Blair, who soon proved himself fit to play in the wonderful company of backs in which he found himself—namely, Asher, Rotherham, Tristram, Wade, and Lindsay. He was very fast, as was proved by his winning the quarter for Oxford at Lillie Bridge in 1885; and if his football career had not been cut short by an injury to his knee early in the ensuing season, he would probably have played for Scotland. As it was, he had to content himself with serving them as secretary, and it was he who conducted the case for Scotland through all the troublous times of the International dispute.

In this year, then, Oxford was stronger than ever behind, but there was a sad falling-off amongst the forwards. By the time of the 'Varsity match only three of the old forwards (Berry, Squire, and Inglis) were available, and the new ones were of a different class altogether—indeed, some of them were quite bad players, and to this fact the ultimate downfall of the team was due. Their backs pulled them through most of their matches pretty easily, though there were two drawn games before Christmas, those against Manchester and Bradford. Bradford was one of the strongest clubs in the country this year, and made a bold bid to lower the Oxford colours; but, fortunately for Oxford, three of the old forwards were able to play on that day, namely, Kindersley, Moore, and Court, the last of whom was in his best form that year, and played for England later on in the season.

The 'Varsity match of this year was remarkable as an exception to the rule that backs cannot win a match if their forwards are hopelessly beaten. The Oxford forwards made no stand at all against the Cambridge ones. They were simply pushed all over the field and yet Oxford won by 3 goals and a try to a try; besides which, Wade and Lindsay both so nearly dropped goals that in each case the ball hit the post. This result can, of course, only be attributed to the exceptional excellence of the Oxford backs. At least four of them (Tristram, Wade, Rotherham, and Asher) were perfect in their respective positions, and the other two (Lindsay and Blair) were in their very best form. Rotherham and Asher on that day stood the hardest test that can be applied to half-backs, that of finding openings for your three-quarters when your forwards are being rushed. It was more than mortal man could do to stop Wade when he meant business, as he did that day; and whenever Cambridge did get the ball past the Oxford three-quarters, they still had to deal with Tristram, who was as safe as a house.

The Oxford team was:—

H. B. Tristram (back); G. C. Wade, G. C. Lindsay, A. S. Blair (three-quarters); A. G. G. Asher (captain), A. Rotherham (half-backs); W. H. Squire, C. W. Berry, R. E. Inglis, B. A. Cohen, A. B. Turner, P. Coles, H. V. Page, A. McNeill, and R. C. Kitto (forwards).

Of the new men, McNeill and Kitto came from Loretto as well as Blair; Cohen and Coles came from Rugby, Turner from Marlborough, and Page from

Cheltenham. McNeill was president of athletics at the time, and Page afterwards became captain of cricket.

Oxford began the next term with three wins, and then came their Black Monday, February the 9th, when they were beaten by Edinburgh University by a try to *nil*. The Scotch forwards were far too cunning to try to rush the scrummages, as Cambridge had done. They simply kept the ball tight, and the game was a long succession of scrummages. If the Oxford forwards had done nothing more than keep it loose, their backs would have won this match also; but they were never given half a chance of doing so, and Oxford had to taste defeat for the first time for over three years. During that time they had played 56 matches, won 50 and drawn 6, and had scored 108 goals and 101 tries against 8 goals and 9 tries.

In the season 1885-6 G. C. Lindsay was elected captain, and A. S. Blair secretary, the places on committee being filled by G. F. Bradby, P. Coles, H. V. Page, and R. C. Kitto. In this season Oxford had to make a fresh start, as all the members of the 1882 and 1883 teams had gone down except the new captain G. C. Lindsay; and G. F. Bradby and Coles, Page, and Kitto were the only other old Blues available, as Blair dislocated his knee in the first match. It was, therefore, no light task that Lindsay had before him—to form a team worthy to uphold the reputation gained for Oxford by the teams of the last four years, especially as Cambridge were known to be leaving no stone unturned in their efforts to break the run of Oxford victories.

By the time of the 'Varsity match Cambridge had been beaten by Blackheath and Richmond, and Oxford by Richmond and South Wales, but, unfortunately, Oxford lost their best half-back, the Marlburian, R. R. Mangin, who broke his collar-bone in the London Welsh match. He had played so well for the combined 'Varsities v. London that but for this accident he would certainly have been picked for the South team of this year.

The team that played against Cambridge was:—

J. G. B. Sutherland (Fettes) (back); G. C. Lindsay (Loretto) (captain), J. R. Wordsworth (Glenalmond), K. J. Key (Clifton) (three-quarter backs); E. A. Surtees (Haileybury), J. D. Hall (New Zealand) (half-backs); G. F. Bradby (Rugby), P. Coles (Rugby), R. C. Kitto (Loretto), H. V. Page (Cheltenham), F. C. Cousins (Finchley), P. H.

Blyth (Loretto), C. R. Carter (Cheltenham), J. D. Boswell (Loretto), C. R. Cleveland (Finchley) (forwards).

An unusual proportion of this team became schoolmasters; Bradby and Page are back at their old schools, Surtees at Repton, Carter, the rowing Blue, at Wellington, and Kitto at Llandovery.

Cambridge won the match by two tries, scored by Brutton and Leake, to *nil*, and thus started a series of victories which lasted until 1889, or just as long as the previous run of Oxford wins.

Immediately after the 'Varsity match the Oxford team started on their second northern tour, on which they had the satisfaction of beating Edinburgh University with their ordinary team—a victory chiefly due to Lindsay, who dropped a goal and scored a try. They were beaten by the West of Scotland, then, as usual, the champion team of Scotland, by 2 tries to 1, and then they came back to England and defeated the famous Bradford team by 2 tries to *nil*; but it is only fair to state that for this match Oxford had enlisted the services of the old Blues, Tristram, Wade, Rotherham, and Inglis, without whose assistance they could hardly have hoped to win. On the next day West Cheshire scored a lucky win by a dropped goal to *nil*, but no more matches were lost this season, at the end of which Lindsay and Brutton agreed to a rule, which ought to have been passed long before, to exclude fifth-year men from the 'Varsity match. In the following season, 1886-7, P. Coles was elected captain and R. C. Kitto secretary; the committee consisted of P. H. Blyth, F. C. Cousins, J. D. Boswell, and C. R. Cleveland. They took a very wise step in securing the services of C. N. Jackson of Hertford College as permanent treasurer for the club; and they passed a rule that no member of the team should be allowed to miss a club match for any other except an International, to which Champion County matches have now been added, on the application of L. J. Percival for leave to play for the Midland Counties *v.* Yorkshire.

Actual residence with a four years' limit was now made the qualification for the 'Varsity match, and the season opened with an excellent innovation in the shape of a freshmen's match on the lines of the freshmen's match at cricket.

The season was not a very successful one, as, although thirteen matches were won, including two on tour in Ireland against the Wanderers and Lansdowne, several of the most important matches at Oxford were lost, and Cambridge won at Blackheath by three tries to nil.

Team.—K. J. Key (Clifton) (back); J. D. Hall (New Zealand), P. Christopherson (Bedford), M. H. O. Ewing (Finchley) (three-quarter backs); L. R. Paterson (Keble), A. P. Koe (Haileybury) (half-backs); P. Coles (Rugby) (captain), R. C. Kitto (Loretto), F. C. Cousins (Finchley), C. R. Cleveland (Finchley), P. H. Blyth (Loretto), N. F. Henderson (Dulwich), J. D. Boswell (Loretto), H. H. Castens (Rugby), R. M. C. Harvey (Marlborough) (forwards).

PASSING THE BALL.
(*From an Instantaneous Photograph by E. Airey, Bradford.*)

Of these Cleveland, who was one of the best forwards ever produced by Oxford, played in all the International matches of the year, and as this was the last appearance of Henderson, it must be mentioned here that he played for Scotland five years later.

In the following season, 1887-8, R. C. Kitto was elected captain; J. D. Boswell, the future Scotch International, secretary; and Castens, Christopherson, and Harvey to the committee.

Oxford had a much better record this year than in the two preceding ones; no matches were lost before the Cambridge match, and the only one lost after it was that against Bradford at Bradford.

The brilliant successes of the Christmas term had led us to hope for a victory over Cambridge; but when the time came, Scott and Duncan proved far too good, and Oxford was badly beaten by a goal and 2 tries to *nil*. The team was:—

W. Rashleigh (Tonbridge) (back); P. Christopherson (Bedford), C. J. N. Fleming (Fettes), J. B. Sayer (Finchley) (three-quarter backs); W. G. Wilson (York), L. R. Paterson (Loretto) (half-backs); R. C. Kitto (Loretto) (captain), J. D. Boswell (Loretto), H. H. Castens (Rugby), J. M. Glubb (Bedford), E. P. Simpson (Wellington), D. W. Evans (Llandovery), R. O. B. Lane (Marlborough), C. C. Bradford (Clifton), R. D. Budworth (Brecon) (forwards).

In this team it should be noted that Rashleigh succeeded Key at full-back, and that since the time of these famous cricketers there have been no double Blues of any sort in the Oxford Rugby teams up to the present date.

There were no English International matches in this year, but Castens played for the South *v.* the North, and he turned out for the Cape against the English team that went out there in 1891.

But for the 'Varsity match itself the committee had every reason to be satisfied with the team they had selected; but it must always stand recorded against them that they entirely failed to discover the merits of F. Evershed as a forward. He used to play three-quarters for his college, and they tried him in that position for the next twenty against the first fifteen at the beginning of the season, but that was all. The next season he came to live at Burton, and was soon found to have the makings of a first-class forward in him. He played for England against the Maoris in that year, and by 1890 he was the best forward in England.

In the season 1888-9 the officers elected were P. Christopherson (captain), D. W. Evans (secretary), R. O. B. Lane, W. Rashleigh, and W. G. Wilson (committee-men). The team showed very in-and-out form up to Christmas, after which every match was won, but before Christmas they had lost as many matches as they had won—a record unprecedented in the annals of Oxford football, and due in part to the fact that they played far too many matches and consequently not enough " picked fifteens." Some of their victories, however, had been quite as startling as their defeats. Both Oxford and Cambridge had played drawn games with the London Scottish, then the champion team of the South, and Oxford had beaten Bradford, whereas Cambridge had just been beaten by them; but all who had hopes of winning the 'Varsity match were doomed to be disappointed once more at Queen's Club, where Cambridge won by a goal and 2 tries to *nil*. The team was:—

W. Rashleigh (Tonbridge) (back); C. J. N. Fleming (Fettes), P. Christopherson (Bedford) (captain), A. R. Lewis (Christ's Hospital) (three-quarter backs); R. F. C. de Winton (Marlborough), F. Morgan (Llandovery) (half-backs); D. W. Evans (Llandovery), R. O. B. Lane (Marlborough), R. D. Budworth (Brecon), J. B. Aldridge (Malvern), J. H. G. Wilson (York), E. H. G. North (Blackheath), T. Parker (Durham), R. S. Hunter (Fettes), W. T. Grenfell (Marlborough) (forwards).

It is noticeable that there was not a single Lorettonian in the team for the first time for ten years.

Once more there were no English International matches, but D. W. Evans played for Wales, and P. Christopherson played for the South.

In the following season, 1889-90, the following officers were elected:—R. O. B. Lane (captain), R. D. Budworth (secretary), C. J. N. Fleming, E. G. North, J. H. G. Wilson (committee).

Exceptional interest was taken in the 'Varsity match of this year, because the number of wins was now equal, and Cambridge had won for the last four years in succession. The freshmen's match did not produce much talent, Cochran of Loretto being the only freshman to secure a place in the team, but there were plenty of good men over from the year before, such as Percival, Bromet, Kay, Coventry, and Clauss, to fill up the vacancies in the team, and the committee spared no effort to produce a good team. On the day of the match both sides expected to win, but the Oxford forwards carried all before them, and Coventry played better than he had ever played in his life before. Percival scored a try in the first half, from which Fleming placed a goal, and De Winton scored another just before time; and Oxford thus won a more decisive victory than her keenest supporters had dared to hope for. The team was:—

P. Cochran (Loretto) (back); C. J. N. Fleming (Fettes), P. R. Clauss (Loretto), J. S. Longdon (Brecon) (three-quarter backs); R. F. de Winton (Marlborough), R. G. Coventry (Hereford) (half-backs); R. O. B. Lane (Marlborough) (captain), R. D. Budworth (Brecon), E. H. G. North (Blackheath), J. H. G. Wilson (York), R. S. Hunter (Fettes), L. J. Percival (Clifton), W. E. Bromet (Richmond), A. M. Paterson (Loretto), A. R. Kay (Fettes) (forwards).

After the match Oxford started on a disastrous tour in South Wales, which quite spoilt their record for the season, as every single match of it was lost. Four matches in a week is hard work for any team, and in this case an exceptional number of the men were injured, and Budworth and Lane had to go to Manchester for the South v. North match. This tour should serve as a warning to future secretaries not to arrange too large a programme, and to avoid playing matches on consecutive days. Apart from this tour Oxford lost only two matches in the season (those against Blackheath and the Harlequins), and won eighteen.

The Oxford men playing in the International matches of the year were Budworth and Evershed for England, Boswell for Scotland, and Evans for Wales.

In the ensuing season, 1890-1, the following officers were elected:—C. J. N. Fleming (captain), E. H. G. North (secretary), J. H. G. Wilson, R. S. Hunter, R. F. C. de Winton (committee), and after Christmas, P. R. Clauss (secretary). None of the men who played in the Freshmen's match secured their Blue in this year, but there were eleven Old Blues in residence and plenty of good men amongst the seniors such as Bonham-Carter, Rice-Evans, Wilson, and Caddell.

It soon became evident that the team of this year was an unusually good one, and when the time came for North v. South, the Rugby Union committee selected no less than five of the Oxford forwards, viz., North, Percival, Bonham-Carter, Kay, and Wilson, for the South, and would have selected a sixth, Caddell, if he had been an Englishman by birth. Of these, North, Percival, and Bonham-Carter secured International caps, whilst Rice-Evans played for Wales, and Clauss for Scotland. Percival was injured at the time of the Scotch match, in which Clauss scored the first goal for Scotland by a neat drop, and in which Fleming was to have played if Gregor McGregor had been too unwell to turn out.

The 'Varsity match was not played until March 3rd, as it had to be postponed no less than three times, on account of the fogs which prevail at Queen's Club. On one occasion we believe that Queen's Club was the only ground in London from which the fog did not lift. The match proved as uninteresting as it always has done when postponed, and ended in an even draw of 1 goal each.

The team, for which Percival and Cochran were unable to play, was as follows:—

F. J. Cowlishaw (Rugby) (back); C. J. N. Fleming (Fettes) (captain), P. R. Clauss (Loretto), W. H. Parkin (Sedburgh) (three-quarter backs); R. F. C. de Winton (Marlborough), R. G. Coventry (Hereford) (half-backs); E. H. G. North (Blackheath), J. H. G. Wilson (York), A. R. Kay (Fettes), A. M. Paterson (Loretto), E. Bonham-Carter (Clifton), W. Rice-Evans (Llandovery), S. E. Wilson (Liverpool), P. R. Cadell (Haileybury), and R. W. Hunt (forwards).

For the season 1891-2 the following officers were elected:—P. R. Clauss (captain), L. J. Percival (secretary), A. R. Kay, R. G. T. Coventry, and P. Cochran (committee).

There were seven Old Blues available, of whom three were Internationals. Fleming's place was taken by Conway-Rees, who became a Welsh International in the course of the year, and De Winton's place was filled by Wilkinson, who succeeded at last in playing through the season without getting injured. Carey, of Sherborne, was the only Freshman to secure a place, though Robson, of Edinburgh Academy, played in most of the preliminary matches.

Wakefield, of Charterhouse, shares with Aldridge, of Malvern, and Wooldridge, of Winchester, the distinction of getting a Rugby football blue without having been at a Rugby Union school.

The season opened badly with defeats by the London Scottish and the Old Merchant Taylors, who have always proved a thorn in the side of Oxford; but the form shown in the Blackheath match at Blackheath was so good that confident hopes were entertained of a victory over Cambridge. The hero of the Blackheath match was Percival, who played a first-class game throughout, and wound up with a rush all down the ground, and a punt over the full-back's head and a try. When the Varsity match came off, the Oxford forwards proved themselves superior to their opponents in the first half, but they played the wrong game and lost the match. They wore themselves out by tight scrummaging, and were unable to prevent Fforde and Neilson from running in in the second half. Cambridge thus drew level with Oxford once more in the score of wins, and in that interesting position we must leave them to fight it out in years to come.

The team was as follows:—

P. Cochran (Loretto) (back); P. R. Clauss (Loretto) (captain), J. Conway-Rees (Llandovery), J. F. Cowlishaw (Rugby) (three-quarter backs); R. G.

Coventry (Hereford), W. E. Wilkinson (Durham) (half-backs): L. J. Percival (Clifton), E. Bonham-Carter (Clifton), A. R. Kay (Fettes), F. O. Poole (Cheltenham), G. F. Cookson (Clifton), C. G. Baker (Sherborne), G. M. Carey (Sherborne), W. H. Wakefield (Charterhouse), E. Selby (Sedburgh) (forwards).

We append a complete list of Oxford Internationals in order of seniority of play:—

A. Davenport (Rugby).
W. O. Moberly (Rugby).
F. W. Isherwood (Rugby).
H. Freeman (Marlborough).
C. W. Boyle (Clifton).
E. R. Still (Rugby).
W. R. B. Fletcher (Marlborough).
M. J. Brooks (Rugby).
C. W. Crosse (Rugby).
A. T. Mitchell (Rugby).
E. H. Nash (Rugby).
E. C. Fraser (Blackheath).
A. H. Heath (Clifton).
F. H. Lee (Marlborough).
W. H. Bolton (Rugby).
H. Fowler (Clifton).
H. D. Bateson (Rugby).
C. Phillips (Rugby).
J. Ravenscroft (Rugby).
H. Vassall (Marlborough).
W. R. Richardson (Manchester).
E. Peake (Marlborough).
L. Watkins (Sherborne).
C. P. Lewis (Llandovery).
W. F. Evans (Sherborne).
P. A. Newton (Blackheath).
W. M. Tatham (Marlborough).
A. Walker (Loretto).
J. G. Walker (Loretto).

A. G. Grant-Asher (Loretto).
H. B. Tristram (Loretto).
A. M. Evanson (Oundle).
G. C. Wade (Parramatta).
A. Rotherham (Uppingham).
C. S. Wooldridge (Winchester).
E. J. Moore (Epsom).
R. S. Kindersley (Clifton).
E. L. Strong (Edinburgh Academy).
C. P. Allen (Rugby).
G. C. Lindsay (Loretto).
C. W. Berry (Loretto).
E. D. Court (Rugby).
R. E. Inglis (Rugby).
C. R. Cleveland (Finchley).
F. Evershed (Burton).
D. W. Evans (Llandovery).
J. D. Boswell (Loretto).
R. D. Budworth (Brecon).
P. R. Clauss (Loretto).
E. G. North (Blackheath).
W. E. Bromet (Bradford).
W. Rice-Evans (Llandovery).
P. Christopherson (Bedford).
L. J. Percival (Clifton).
E. Bonham-Carter (Clifton).
N. F. Henderson (Dulwich).
J. Conway-Rees (Llandovery).

Also a list of those members of Rugby football teams who have represented Oxford in any other branch of sport:—

W. H. Game (Sherborne), cricket.
H. Russell, athletics.
M. J. Brooks (Rugby), athletics.
M. Shearman (Merchant Taylors), athletics.
A. H. Heath (Clifton), cricket.
H. Fowler (Clifton), cricket.
E. T. Hirst (Rugby), cricket.
A. H. Evans (Clifton), cricket.
R. L. Knight (Clifton), cricket.
N. Maclachlan (Loretto), cricket.
A. R. Paterson (Loretto), rowing.
J. G. Walker (Loretto), cricket.
C. F. H. Leslie (Rugby), cricket and rackets.

R. S. Kindersley (Clifton), rowing.
A. M. Evanson (Oundle), athletics.
M. B. Peacock (Wellington), athletics.
A. McNiel (Loretto), athletics.
A. G. Grant-Asher (Loretto), cricket and athletics.
H. V. Page (Cheltenham), cricket.
A. S. Blair (Loretto), athletics.
G. C. Lindsay (Loretto), athletics.
C. R. Carter (Cheltenham), rowing.
K. J. Key (Clifton), cricket.
W. Rashleigh (Tonbridge), cricket.

CHAPTER XVI.

RUGBY FOOTBALL AT CAMBRIDGE.

By C. J. B. Marriott.

(Late Captain of Cambridge University F.C.)

IN 1861 a few old Rugby boys started their favourite game at Cambridge, and were looked upon as little less than madmen by the majority of Cantabs of that day. This we have on the authority of an old Rugbeian, a near relative, then resident at Cambridge, but now, unhappily, deceased. The great athletic revival was then beginning to spread over the kingdom, and in spite of the ridicule bestowed on it at Cambridge as being only fit for boys (the same argument, by the way, was urged against having Inter-'Varsity athletic sports), football made considerable headway and the number of players increased. In some of the first games played on Parker's Piece the spectators, from a misapprehension that the players were fighting, rushed on the ground to part the contestants. Soon other old public school men resident at Cambridge took up the sport, and in 1863 representatives of the different large schools met to arrange rules which should unite them all under one governing code.

Of the committee appointed to draw up these rules, the Rev. R. Burn, of Shrewsbury School, was chairman. Eton was represented by R. H. Blake-Humfrey and W. F. Trench; Rugby by W. R. Collyer and M. F. Martin; Harrow by J. F. Prior and H. R. Williams; Marlborough by W. P. Crawley; Westminster by W. S. Wright. From Mr. Alcocks's admirable handbook on the Association game we learn that these rules allowed a player touching the ball down behind the opposite line a free kick twenty-five yards straight out from the goal line. Though there was no mention of running with the ball, there was a stipulation allowing charging; but holding, pushing with the hands, tripping up, and running were strictly forbidden.

These Cambridge rules were shortly afterwards discussed at a general meeting of football men in London, and held by the metropolitan players to be, with a few alterations, worthy of adoption as embracing the true principles of the game with the greatest simplicity. As is well known, however, the Blackheath Club would not assent to the elimination of so many of the peculiar features of their game, and it was mainly on account of the Cambridge rules that they and their followers seceded from the Football Association.

This led those educated under the Rugby code to adhere to it at Cambridge, and the breach between the two games was further widened by the Cambridge Association being unable to get on a match with the Football Association unless they adopted the rules of the latter body. Things went on in this unsatisfactory condition until 1872, when a meeting was held in the rooms of the late R. P. Luscombe at Clare College to discuss the advisability of adopting the Rugby Union rules and bye-laws by those players who followed the carrying game at Cambridge. The outcome of this meeting was the formation of the Cambridge Rugby Union Club, and the adoption of the rules formulated by the Rugby Union in 1871. Among others who attended the meeting was R. S. Whalley, now a prominent member of the Union executive, then an undergraduate. Whalley played in several of the early matches for Cambridge before the Oxford match was instituted, and was instrumental with several others in obtaining possession of the field still known as the Amalgamation Ground. The University matches were, however, chiefly played on Parker's Piece before a mere handful of spectators. One of the first, if not the very first, matches played by the Cambridge University Rugby Union Football Club was against the United Hospitals. Unfortunately the books containing list of members, early meetings, etc., have, in passing through so many different hands, disappeared. This is much to be regretted.

Next season, 1873-74, the game had made such progress at both Universities that a match was arranged between them. This duly came off at the Oval on

THE CAMBRIDGE UNIVERSITY RUGBY TEAM, 1886-87.
(From a Photograph by Hills & Saunders, Cambridge.)

December 3rd, and resulted in a draw, 1 try-all—a surprise, as Oxford were expected to win easily. Twenty aside took part in the game, an account of which we reproduce from a contemporary report:—

"The play consisted chiefly in tight scrummages. For the first quarter of an hour the Oxford men had the better of the game, and A. T. Mitchell had a shot at goal from a fair catch after scrummaging right on the Cambridge line. W. H. Game then all but got over after a fine run, falling close to the goal post; but at length a fine drop by J. M. Batten, the Cambridge captain, who played back, relieved his side from the Oxford attack. Cambridge then gradually gained ground and got to the Oxford line, where Batten, having the ball passed to him, scored a try; his kick at goal, however, failed. After half-time Oxford, with a very slight wind in their favour, carried the scrummages, and by slow stages got to the Cambridge line. Here Mitchell got over. Moberley took the place, but failed to register a goal—the ball rolling. Nothing further was scored by either side, and the game ended in a draw of 1 try each, Cambridge having touched down twice. For the dark blues Moberley, Vecqueray, and Mitchell, back, and Still, forward, played well. For Cambridge Riley at half was best; while Lewthwaite, Baxter, Wace, and Margerison played well forward. We append a list of the Cambridge team:—G. W. Agnew, W. Lewthwaite, A. Baxter, R. Margerison, D. Pearce, A. S. Forbes, E. R. Dalton, J. W. Chapman, J. Hornby, G. A. Lewis, J. Bonham-Carter, H. Wace, W. Fairbanks, and another—forwards; H. Riley and R. P. Luscombe, half-backs; A. F. Smith, three-quarter back; H. A. Hamilton, W. G. Mitchell, and J. M. Batten (captain), backs." (E. T. Gurdon's name always appears in all accounts of this match as one of the team. This is an error, as, owing to defective train service, Gurdon, though all ready dressed for play, appeared on the ground too late to take part in the game. The name of his substitute has not been handed down.)

In 1874 the Oxford match again resulted in a draw, J. M. Batten, the old Haileyburian, for the second season captained the Cambridge team. The team was as under:—

J. M. Batten (captain), A. Jameson, and A. R. Lewis, backs; J. W. Loxdale and R. P. Luscombe, half-backs; W. Fairbanks, three-quarter back; R. Bealey, H. A. Bull, E. R. Dalton, E. T. Gurdon, A. Hopkins, J. Hornby, A. W. Moore, D. Pearce, W. Raikes, D. B. Roffey, A. F. Smith, C. J. C. Touzell, H. Wace, and A. Williams. (Of these, J. M. Batten obtained his International cap against Scotland, and was the first Cambridge man to obtain this distinction.)

Next season, 1875-76, the Oxford men were too strong for the Light Blues, and won the 'Varsity match by a try to *nil*. Though the Rugby Union authorities still adhered to 20 a-side in International matches, the 'Varsities, finding how much more open and interesting the game became if played by 15 aside, took the initiative, and this season reduced their teams to that number. Only one three-quarter back was played, thus allowing

10 men forward. E. T. Gurdon succeeded his fellow-Haileyburian, J. M. Batten, as captain of the team, which was constituted as follows:—

W. G. Mitchell, A. R. Lewis, backs; W. L. T. Dalton, three-quarter back; L. T. Williams and D. B. Roffey, half-backs; E. T. Gurdon, (captain), G. A. Lewis, C. M. Agnew, W. J. Darch, H. H. Child, R. Steward, W. H. Blake, C. J. C. Touzell, H. A. Bull, and J. Allen, forwards.

In 1876-77 Cambridge had a powerful team. E. T. Gurdon again filled the position of captain. Another conspicuous member of this year's fifteen was R. T. Finch, an old Sherborne boy. For four successive years this player was invaluable at half-back, and his dodging powers, which were especially dangerous on a wet ground, were long remembered by *habitués* of Parker's Piece. C. J. C. Touzell was the most brilliant of the forwards, and obtained his English cap. The then powerful Ravenscourt Park were defeated by a goal; but Blackheath, by kicking a goal, won by that amount to 2 tries. The Inter-University match was played at the Oval on December 11th, and won easily by Cambridge by a goal (kicked by Mitchell from a try by Finch) and 2 tries (gained by Finch and Allen) to nothing. Oxford showed but little dash, and the Light Blues were decidedly the better team all round. Lee for Oxford played well, while Finch's dodgy running, and Gurdon's forward play, were conspicuous on the winning side.

R. T. FINCH.
(*From a Photograph by Witcomb & Son, Salisbury.*)

Team.—W. G. Mitchell and P. H. Clifford, backs; L. Dalton, three-quarter-back; R. T. Finch, A. Williams, half-backs; E. T. Gurdon (captain), H. H. Child, C. M. Agnew, S. R. James, H. R. Clayton, J. Hornby, R. Steward, C. J. C. Touzell, W. L. Agnew, J. Allen, forwards.

The team in 1877-78 was not nearly so strong as in the previous season—no less than ten vacancies having to be filled up. Among others, D. Q. Steel, the cricketer, who also represented Cambridge in the Association match, played, as did C. Gurdon, the oarsman. The match with Oxford took place at the Oval on December 12th, 1877, the ground being in fair order for running and dropping. Oxford had the better backs, and, playing up harder, won by two tries—from runs in by H. Fowler (the cricketer) and Springman—to nothing. Springman showed good pace, and Bateson and Lee were well in the van of the Oxford forwards; for Cambridge, Finch, behind the scrummage, and C. Gurdon and Agnew,

A LINE OUT.
(*From an Instantaneous Photograph by E. Airey, Bradford.*)

forward, played hard. Other matches resulted as follows:—Richmond were defeated by two tries; Walthamstow by a try; Clapham Rovers, a draw; and Blackheath were victorious by one goal and one try to nothing.

No resident Cantab obtained an International cap this year.

The team v. Oxford was as follows:—

P. H. Clifford and C. E. Jeffcock, backs; C. S. Albright and D. Q. Steel, three-quarter-backs; J. A. Bevan and R. T. Finch, half-backs; S. R. James (captain), W. S. Agnew, H. R. Clayton, C. Gurdon, H. H. Browell, C. M. Kennedy, C. P. Wilson, C. H. Coates, P. T. Wrigley.

In 1878-79, Cambridge had a stronger team. H. R. Clayton filled the post of captain. Of the new men in the team, two were afterwards destined to be famous in the annals of Cambridge football; we allude to the now president of the Cambridge Rugby Football Club, H. G. Fuller, who, in the position of half-back, made his first appearance against Oxford, and E. Storey, the first of the long list of Cambridge footballers who have hailed from that nursery of the game, Fettes College.

Before the 'Varsities match, the Light Blues defeated, among others:—Walthamstow (1 goal and 1 try to 1 try), Gipsies (1 try to nothing), and King's College (by 1 goal and 3 tries to *nil*). They lost, however, to Blackheath (3 tries to 2 goals). The Oxford match was played at the Oval, on February 10th, 1879, having been postponed from the previous term through frost. The ground was in bad condition owing to heavy rain, and the attendance small. The match was very evenly contested, and neither fifteen obtained any definite advantage. A. H. Evans, for Oxford, and R. T. Finch, for Cambridge, were conspicuous. The number of scrummagers was this year reduced to nine, a second three-quarter being played by both teams.

No resident Cantab played in the International matches this year.

Team.—P. T. Wrigley and C. E. Boughton-Leigh, backs; E. Storey and P. H. Clifford, three-quarter-backs; R. T. Finch and H. G. Fuller, half-backs; H. R. Clayton (captain), W. S. Agnew, S. R. James, H. H. Browell, C. H. Coates, C. P. Wilson, J. E. Jones, H. Y. L. Smith, C. M. Kennedy, forwards.

In 1879-80, R. T. Finch was elected captain, and closed his brilliant Cambridge career by winning the match *v.* Oxford by dropping a goal.

J. H. Payne, afterwards well-known as the Lancashire and English half-back, made his appearance in the Light Blue team this season, as the associate of Storey at three-quarter. The team was a strong one all round, and proved their strength by drawing with Blackheath, which club had not suffered defeat throughout the season.

The 'Varsity match was played at the Oval, and won by Cambridge by 2 goals to 1. Finch—who played admirably throughout—dropped a goal and Smith kicked another for the winners. McLachlan dropped the Oxford goal.

Team.—P. T. Wrigley and A. S. Taylor, backs; E. Storey and J. H. Payne, three-quarter-backs; R. T. Finch (captain) and E. S. Chapman, half-backs; C. H. Coates, C. P. Wilson, H. G. Fuller, H. Y. L. Smith, F. L. Cox, R. M. Yetts, J. J. Gover, J. T. Steele, C. H. Golightly, forwards. Of these, C. H. Coates and R. T. Finch obtained well-deserved places in the English team.

In 1880 the writer commenced residence at Cambridge, and though debarred by a severely sprained ankle from playing football, he had the opportunity of watching the University matches attentively. C. P. Wilson, an old Marlburian, succeeded Finch as captain. This year one of the most dashing, and certainly the cleverest dodging half-back we have ever seen, appeared, meteor-like, in the Cambridge football firmament. We refer to the old Fettesian—A. R. Don Wauchope. Our first sight of this famous player was in this wise. When crossing Parker's Piece one day we noticed a considerable crowd congregated round one of the side pitches. Now, as the minor games in those days attracted little or no attention (the trial matches monopolising what spectators there were), we were induced by curiosity to learn what the cause of the gathering might be. And well were we rewarded. The match was between the Old Fettesians and Old Cliftonians, and Don Wauchope was treating the latter team to a taste of his quality.

C. P. WILSON.
(From a Photograph by Francis H. Elwell, M.A., London.)

How many tries he gained we cannot at this distance of time recall, but the way in which he dodged through his opponents, without their being able to lay a finger on him, is indelibly impressed on our memory. The following Saturday saw Don Wauchope in the University fifteen for the first time. The match was played on the John's ground, and the Old Fettes boy fully bore out the high opinion formed of his running and dodging powers. After a very successful season, the match with Oxford resulted in a draw—1 try each. Cambridge unfortunately had a dropped goal disallowed. The scene of the match was this year changed from the Oval to Blackheath.

The following represented Cambridge:—

P. T. Wrigley and A. S. Taylor, backs; E. Storey and J. A. Bevan, three-quarter-backs; A. R. Don Wauchope and E. S. Chapman, half-

U 2

backs; C. P. Wilson (captain), H. G. Fuller, J. T. Steele, H. Y. L. Smith, W. M. McLeod, E. Rice, R. M. Yetts, J. G. Tait, T. Pater, forwards. C. P. Wilson played for England v. Wales, and A. R. Don Wauchope represented Scotland in the match against England.

1881-82 showed a marked upward movement in the popularity of football mainly owing to the acquisition by the executive of the use of the Corpus ground for their games and matches. This step was imperative, owing to the action of the municipal authorities in debarring the Rugby game from being played on Parker's Piece as of old. It was alleged that the Rugby game damaged the turf, and henceforth townsfolk and collegians, possessing no ground of their own, have been compelled to play on the Piece under Association rules or not at all. H. Y. L. Smith, an old Wellingtonian, acted as captain, and a more painstaking one or a more conscientious player could not be found. The first match of this season was against the London Scottish, which the University won. The writer was a spectator of this game, but in the next match—that against Blackheath—he was lucky enough to get a place in the visiting team, who scored 4 tries to the Varsity's goal. The Blackheath forwards outplayed their opponents at all points, and their style made such an impression on the Cambridge authorities that they summoned a meeting of the Light Blues to discuss the desirability of modelling their forward play on that of the Blackheath men. To this meeting the writer, though he had never played for Cambridge, was invited to attend and give his opinion on the reason for the superiority of the Blackheath forwards. This was not a hard task, as the visiting forwards owed much of their success to the clever way in which, directly the ball was put down, they rushed it to one side or other of the scrummage, and broke away with it in a body. This style of play was new to the Cantabs, who knew of no other forward play than that learnt in the big side games at school, of pushing in the scrummage whether on the ball or not, and never dreaming of utilising the feet except to drive the ball through the centre of the packs to the opposing half-backs. The result of the match above-mentioned clearly showed these old-fashioned tactics to be useless when opposed to forwards clever with their feet and adepts at bringing the ball away at which ever side of the scrummage they chose. Efforts were made with some success, in the remaining matches of the season, to rely more on foot-work in the scrummage and on rushing the ball to the open side than on mere blind pushing.

Oxford, under Vassall, were already bringing their scrummage and passing play to perfection. This capable leader, with as fine a body of athletes under him as ever a captain led into the field, had revolutionised the style of play at Oxford. Combination was the one thing aimed at, and, as leader for two years of almost identical teams, the old Marlburian brought the game to a pitch of excellency and effect that has perhaps never been attained by any other fifteen. The men were taught to play a systematic game. At Cambridge, however, though there was plenty of individual excellency, coaching was unknown; each man played far too much for his own hand, and great ignorance existed about the fine points of the game. During this and the three succeeding seasons Cambridge were influenced by the Oxford movement, and attempted to assimilate their play to that of their rivals. Four successive defeats occurred before this end was attained, and Cambridge had to begin *de novo* before they could master the Oxford style. It was uphill work, but success at length crowned their efforts, and the Light Blues have during the past seven years only once suffered reverse at the hands of their rivals.

During the season under notice Don Wauchope was again in splendid form at half, and received support in the same position from J. L. Templer, who, though playing a thoroughly old-fashioned half-back game, possessed indiarubber-like qualities coupled with undeniable pluck. Of the other backs A. S. Taylor alone showed 'Varsity form; C. E. Chapman at times played well; but the other backs were weak and uncertain. Cambridge suffered no defeat up to the Oxford match, and there was really little to choose between the two teams on the day. The superiority of the Dark Blue three-quarters won the game for Oxford, the score at the finish being 2 goals and a try to a goal.

Tonbridge School, by the way, had as many as five candidates tried in the team, four of whom played in the Inter-'Varsity match.

It should be mentioned that the match between the

combined Universities and London, which has ever since had such an important bearing on the selection of the South team, was instituted in this season. H. G. Fuller obtained his English cap this year, and Wauchope again showed brilliant form for Scotland.

Team.—A. S. Taylor, H. F. Cooper, backs; C. E. Chapman, J. W. Dickson, three-quarter-backs; A. R. Don Wauchope, J. L. Templer, half-backs; H. Y. L. Smith (captain), H. G. Fuller, R. M. Yetts, T. Pater, E. Rice, C. J. B. Marriott, J. Hammond, R. M. Pattisson, R. Threlfall, forwards.

Next season, 1882-83, saw A. R. Don Wauchope assume the reins of office, being the first Fettes boy to occupy that position. Unfortunately, however, for Cambridge, this grand player had been badly hurt in Scotland at the close of the previous season, and was unable to play in many matches—notably that against Oxford. In the 'Varsity match both sides were weakened by the absence of several prominent players, Oxford suffering most in this respect. The veteran H. G. Fuller captained the Cantabs in Wauchope's absence. The game was a very even one, Oxford in the end winning by a try. H. Vassall in this match closed his long and valued leadership of the Dark Blue team. The season was marked by a new development in the game, three three-quarters and one back being played by both sides for the first time.

H. G. Fuller and R. M. Pattisson represented England. The team against Oxford was as follows :—

C. H. Sample, back; C. H. Ware, C. H. Newman, J. Gibbons, three-quarter-backs; J. L. Templer, E. A. Douglas, half-backs; H. G. Fuller (captain), R. M. Pattisson, C. J. B. Marriott, C. J. B. Milne, B. C. Burton, P. M. Lucas, W. M. McLeod, H. F. Ransome, J. G. Tait, forwards.

In season 1883-84 C. J. B. Marriott was elected captain, in which position he received much assistance from the old Rugbeian, B. C. Burton. Before the University match the team carried all before them, defeating, among others, Blackheath, Wakefield Trinity, and the London Scottish. Our improvement was in great measure due to the kindness of G. Rowland Hill in coming down to Cambridge to coach the team, and the writer will always remember with gratitude Mr. Hill's help and instruction to him when leader of the Light Blues. Our defeat by Oxford, in which match on our previous performances we were favourites, was a bitter pill, and never likely to be entirely forgotten. Up to half time we were winners, but after changing over our men fell away before the splendid play of the Oxonians, conspicuous amongst whom may be mentioned Tatham, Rotherham, and Wade.

Some idea of the strength of the Oxford team we met that year may be gathered from the fact that *thirteen* out of the fifteen players gained their International caps. We may perhaps be pardoned for reproducing the opinion of the hon. secretary of the Union which appeared in the annual for the year: "Amongst other clubs that Oxford defeated, the sister University should be numbered. This match always creates a large amount of interest. A close fight was anticipated. It was played early in December, and additional interest was excited from the fact that neither University had been beaten till the day of the match. Cambridge had just before defeated Wakefield, and had shown surprising good form during the term. Unaccountably on this occasion they played far short of their proper form. The result was a genuine surprise. The Cambridge men were all at sea, whilst their opponents were playing their very best. Previous to the match it was acknowledged that Oxford were much stronger behind and a more scientific team, but there was a suspicion of slackness amongst the forwards; whilst, on the contrary, the Cambridge team, though rather weak behind, displayed such energy and dash forward, that it was thought that the deficiency in one respect would be made up by the other. Up till this match no Cambridge team had ever done better."

The team was as under. The names, by the way, are wrongly given in the volume entitled "Inter-University Records":—

C. H. Sample, back; C. H. Chilcott, G. L. Colbourne, E. B. Brutton, three-quarter-backs; E. A. Douglas, W. B. Salmon, half-backs; C. J. B. Marriott (captain), C. J. B. Milne, H. G. Fuller, B. C. Burton, H. F. Ransome, R. Threlfall, J. Lees, G. B. Guthrie, and W. P. Richardson, forwards. From that year's team C. J. B. Marriott and H. G. Fuller obtained places in the English team.

In 1884-85 the late C. J. B. Milne, of Fettes, succeeded to the captaincy. The team was decidedly weak behind, but the forward division contained good material, and many of the scrummagers afterwards became prominent players. Up to the all-important Inter-University match the team showed by no means good form, sustaining a heavy defeat from Bradford, besides reverses from Blackheath and Richmond. Against Oxford the forwards played up splendidly, and gave promise of future excellence, which the next season confirmed. The splendid outside combination of the Oxonians, however, gave them the victory by 3 goals and a try to a try.

Team.—H. S. F. Adams, back; C. E. Chapman, C. H. Sample, J. Le Fleming, three-quarter-backs; E. A. Douglas, H. Neilson, halfbacks; C. J. B. Milne (captain), H. F. Ransome, G. L. Jeffery, V. C. Le Fanu, W. J. Plews, H. W. Sample, F. G. Swayne, L. E. Stevenson, E. P. Alexander, forwards.

No resident Cambridge man played in the International teams this year. Some account of the difficulties incurred in obtaining a full blue for the Association and Rugby teams may not be out of place here.

Towards the close of 1883, the Oxford teams, both Rugby and Association, having been granted their full blues in the previous season, it was thought that the Cambridge men selected to oppose them were worthy of similar honour. With this object in view, the writer, in company with H. G. Fuller and the Association captain, F. W. Pawson, had a lengthy interview with the presidents of the boat and athletic clubs and captain of the cricket eleven. These gentlemen, though dead against the football teams having a full blue, at length offered the suggestion that a certain number of full blues should be divided up among the two teams. This suggestion could not be entertained by the football authorities. Our delegates going out of residence at the end of term, the matter was left *in statu quo* until the next season, when negotiations were reopened with no better result. At length the Rugby players adopted the only course remaining open to them, viz., to take their full blue for themselves; and this they did, appearing for the first time in blue coats in the Rectory field, Blackheath, on December 10th, 1884. A great deal of discussion on the rights and wrongs of this course appeared in the public journals of the time. Public opinion was, however, on the side of the footballers, most people considering the representative exponents of such a popular and national game equally worthy of a full blue as a hammer thrower or weight

H. G. FULLER.
(From a Photograph by H. B. Salmon, Winchester.)

JOHN H. DEWHURST.
(From a Photograph by G. Glanville, Tunbridge Wells.)

CHARLES J. B. MARRIOTT.
(From a Photograph by H. E. Simpson, Toronto.)

W. R. M. LEAKE.
(From a Photograph by W. Hoat, Gipsy Hill, S.E.)

O. L. JEFFERY.
(From a Photograph by H. Erne, St. John's Wood, N.W.)

putter. The matter, however, was not done with yet. At the end of the Lent term, when interest in football is decidedly on the wane, the following motion was brought forward at the Union by the boating authorities:— "That this meeting regrets the resolution of the authorities of the C. U. R. U. F. C. and the C. U. A. F. C. to adopt the full blue against the decision of the committee to whom they had submitted the question, and trusts they will yet find it possible to bring themselves into harmony with those unwritten laws by which the social relations of this University are governed." The motion, it will be seen, was cleverly worded, so as to include amongst its supporters any who had a shadow of a doubt about the propriety of the action of the Rugby men. The result, however, was a grand triumph for football, the motion being lost by three to two. The scene and description of the meeting at the Union is thus described in a contemporary report:—

"It was an amusing sight. Never has the Union been so crammed before. Benches, gallery, floor, tables, crowded with men. Nearly half the 'Varsity recorded their votes. The appearance of Cobbold was the signal for a grand outburst of cheers, showing that football had a strong if not preponderating host of supporters. Milne, too, received quite an ovation. F. E. Churchill arrived at two minutes to eight, and was cheered, though less lustily, to his seat. The house were evidently curious to know their own mind, but the cheers and counter-cheers soon proved football to be in the ascendant. Lehmann made a rhetorical and moderate speech, though his funny remarks about the 'cerulean warbler' fell flat on the ears of an unsympathetic house; but he spoke well and courageously, though a little baffled by the uproarious cheers which greeted an accidental mention of Cobbold's name. He appealed to 'unbroken traditions,' etc., and suggested a compromise, *e.g.*, a 'full blue shirt;' but the general feeling was: 'This is too late; why was that not proposed before?' It would be dull to go through the pros and cons which are set forth in the columns of the *Field*. J. F. P. Rawlinson was throughout clear, good, and sensible; he made a home thrust when he remarked that the boat president had got his ideas of autocracy from his similar position at Eton. There seems no doubt that through negligence, or otherwise, the advice of committees was not fully taken. F. J. Pitman is not an orator, but he is justly respected, and his words were attentively listened to; he complained that one in thirty-three football players should be 'blues.' R. Threlfall (of Caius), an old Rugby Unionist, and also known as the 'Hercules' in 'The Birds' last summer, spoke with inimitable gruff good-humour, and time after time brought the house down by his wit. The half-hour during which he held the house was soon past. He was followed by a well-known athlete, Rev. C. H. Coates, a true *laudator temporis acti*. His views were stigmatised as antiquated by M. J. Randall, of Trinity, who also stated that the boating and football clubs had no antagonistic feeling. After several other speakers, L. J. Maxse (of King's), who described himself as a 'non-athlete,' made an exceedingly amusing and telling speech, which he started by reading a copy of the 'boat captain's' circular. One telling argument was this: If twenty-six new Blues swamp the existent twenty-nine, how is it that the eleven cricket Blues did not still more swamp the nine boating?"

Lehmann responded shortly, and confidently appealed to the support of the house. Then, amid intense excitement, the house divided, and returned to find the motion lost by the large majority of 241, the numbers being:—

For the motion	...	...	...	...	466
Against	...	...	...	...	707
Majority against	...	...	...	241

Thus ended this memorable discussion, and though, from the foregoing account, it may appear that the relations between the boating men and the footballers were at the time somewhat strained, the most amicable feelings have since existed between these two bodies of Cambridge athletes.

Season 1885-86 saw E. B. Brutton, an old Durham boy, elected to the post of captain. The team by no means showed to advantage before the Oxford match, suffering defeat from Blackheath, Richmond, and Wakefield Trinity. They, however, fully atoned for these reverses by at length turning the tide of Oxford victories. At Blackheath, on December 14th, the Light Blues, after four consecutive defeats, once more won the Inter-University contest. Two tries to *nil* was the score obtained.

Team.—H. S. F. Adams, back; E. B. Brutton (captain), J. Le Fleming, M. M. Duncan, three-quarter-backs; W. R. M. Leake, M. T. Scott, half-backs; G. L. Jeffery, V. C. Le Fanu, E. P. Alexander, L. E. Stevenson, F. G. Swayne, J. H. Dewhurst, F. W. Goodhue, W. P. Carpmael, J. A. Shirer, forwards.

Eleven of this team have gained International honours. Outside, the team was stronger than it had been for some years. Duncan proved a great acquisition at three-quarter, and played a capital game with Le Fleming and Brutton. Scott at times played brilliantly, and Leake was always cool and reliable. A glance at the names of the forwards will show that the team was a formidable one, and it is strange that they showed such poor form in the earlier matches.

This year an important and salutary measure was adopted by both 'Varsities, viz.—" a man may play for his University for four years from matriculation, provided he is a *bonâ-fide* resident in the University." This rule has effectually done away with an evil that had crept in of residents acting as warming-pans in the term matches for Old Blues who ousted them in the Oxford match.

This season, also, it was deemed advisable to have a president of the club who, by being in residence, would be better able to guide and assist the fresh executive of each year. A meeting for this object was held under the presidency of R. M. Pattisson (Fellow of Emmanuel), an Old Blue. For the important post to be filled a unanimous choice elected H. G. Fuller, than whom no better or more qualified man could have been picked.

In the following season, 1886-87, Brutton was re-elected captain, being the first Cantab since the days of E. T. Gurdon to captain the team for two years. Brutton was fortunate in having, with one exception, the same strong back team as in the previous season. Very few vacancies also had to be filled up among the forwards. The team, however, had to put up with several defeats, Bradford, Richmond, and Dublin beating them. The latter match was played at Dublin, being the first appearance of the Cambridge team in the sister isle.

At Blackheath, on December 15th, Oxford were defeated by three tries to nothing.

Team.—W. G. Mitchell, back; M. M. Duncan, E. B. Brutton, J. Le Fleming, three-quarter-backs; M. T. Scott, W. R. M. Leake, half-backs; V. C. Le Fanu, F. G. Swayne, E. P. Alexander, J. H. Dewhurst, F. W. J. Goodhue, W. H. Thomas, A. Methuen, A. Robinson, A. A. Surtees, forwards.

Of the above, no less than thirteen have at one time or other played in the International teams of their countries, thus equalling the number enjoying similar distinction in the Oxford team of 1882.

In 1887-88 M. M. Duncan (Fettes) captained the team, and by his play contributed much to their success. Very in and out form, however, was shown, as the result list shows. Dublin University, Liverpool, and Blackheath were defeated, while reverses were sustained from Leeds St. John's, Richmond, and Old Leysians. The forwards were a powerful and hard-working lot, while outside, such capital halves as Scott and Leake, for the third year in succession, gave them great advantage over most teams. Alderson and Morrison afforded their captain efficient aid at three-quarter. It is perhaps worthy of note that of the six backs who played this season five have at one time or other enjoyed International honours, as have four of the forwards.

The Oxford match resulted in a victory for Cambridge by 1 goal and 2 tries to nothing, being the first time Cambridge had scored a goal since December, 1883. After six years at Blackheath, the scene of play was this year shifted to the Queen's Ground, Kensington.

Team.—E. Bromet, back; M. M. Duncan (captain), P. H. Morrison, F. H. R. Alderson, three-quarter-backs; M. T. Scott, W. R. M. Leake, half-backs; A. Methuen, A. Robinson, W. H. Thomas, E. H. Wynne, J. W. Cave, F. J. L. Ogilvie, J. W. Fogg Elliott, W. Bevan, D. L. McEwen, forwards.

Of the above, four hailed from Fettes. England played no International matches this year, but A. Robinson was chosen in the representative English team.

In 1888-89, A. Methuen, of Fettes, led the Light Blues, who were again victorious over the Oxonians. Their supremacy lay in their backs, who were far and away superior to those representing the Dark Blues, and played a clever combined game. Forward they were much lighter than the generality of Cambridge teams. Cave was the best of the scrummagers; outside, Martin Scott and Wotherspoon made a strong pair at half, while Alderson, Todd, and Morrison were a thoroughly dangerous and capable trio at three-quarter. Their finest display during the season was the utter rout of Newport. Other victories were gained over the Maoris, Richmond, and Dublin University, while defeats were received at the hands of Bradford, Blackheath, and Richmond in the return fixture.

Queen's Club was again the scene of the Oxford match, and the Cantabs delighted their supporters by winning for the fourth time in succession. The score was identical with that of the previous year, viz., 1 goal and 2 tries to *nil*. Soon after the kick-off, Alderson, backing up a good run of Martin Scott's, got a try, but the place failed. Later on, Alderson made an opening for Todd, and the latter, when near the Oxford line, in turn transferred to Scott, who got in behind the posts. His place resulted in a goal. Nothing more was scored during the first half. After changing over, a brilliant run by Morrison added another try, but Bowhill's place failed. Fettes, by the way, again supplied four men to the Cambridge team, which was made up as under:—

E. Bromet, back; P. H. Morrison, F. H. R. Alderson, T. Todd, three-quarter-backs; W. Martin Scott, W. Wotherspoon, half-backs; A. Methuen (captain), J. W. Cave, A. Trethewy, E. C. Langton, J. W. Bowhill, W. N. Mayne, S. M. J. Woods, P. T. Williams, F. C. Bree Frink, forwards.

Of these, Scott and Cave played for England against the New Zealanders, and Methuen for Scotland in the matches against Wales and Ireland.

1889–90 saw P. H. Morrison, Loretto, elected to the post of captain. Morrison, by the way, is the first Loretto boy to obtain his football blue at Cambridge. Though defeated by Oxford, the team had a successful season—only three out of twenty matches being lost. At three-quarter the team was strong, as also at half. Scott was, unfortunately, not able to play v. Oxford, but his place was filled by an efficient and well-tried performer in P. H. Illingworth. Of the forwards, Woods was the best; but more scrummage work was needed among them, as was only too clearly demonstrated in the Oxford match. The latter game took place at the Queen's Club on December 14th, and after four successive reverses the Oxonians gained a well-deserved victory by a goal and try to nothing. Coventry, after a fine run, passed to Percival, who got over, and Fleming landed the goal. Then Cambridge played up better, but good passing between Coventry, De Winton, Fleming, and Clauss enabled the latter to make a fine run, which De Winton consummated by a try.

Three Cantabs — Aston, Morrison, and Woods— figured in the English team this season, and Gregor MacGregor in the Scotch.

Team.—Gregor MacGregor, back; P. H. Morrison (captain), R. L. Aston, C. E. Fitch, three-quarter-backs; W. Wotherspoon, P. H. Illingworth, half-backs; J. W. Bowhill, S. M. J. Woods, E. C. Langton, F. C. Bree Frink, P. T. Williams, J. Smith, J. C. McDonald, A. L. Jackson, T. W. P. Storey, forwards.

In 1890–91 W. M. Scott, Craigmount, was elected

captain, but unfortunately was only able to play about twice during the season. In the preliminary matches the Light Blues did well, and were generally expected to win against Oxford. After establishing a record in the way of postponements, the match resulted in a draw—one goal each. The better play of the Oxford forwards neutralised the superiority Cambridge possessed outside. Neither side played its full strength. Cochrane was incapacitated a few days previous to the match, while Cambridge was without Wotherspoon as well as Scott. Woods was far and away the best Cambridge forward, but the scrummage work was bad throughout the season. MacGregor always played grandly, as did Aston when sound.

Team.—Gregor Macgregor, back; P. H. Morrison, R. L. Aston, C. A. Hooper, three-quarter-backs; A. Rotherham, P. H. Illingworth, half-backs; S. M. J. Woods, T. W. P. Storey, F. C. Bree Frink, R. Thompson, C. P. Simpson, W. J. Rowell, H. W. T. Patterson, C. B. Nicholl, W. H. Thorman, forwards.

MacGregor and Woods played for Scotland and England respectively.

For the season just over T. W. P. Storey (a halfbrother of E. Storey) was the captain, thus making the fifth old Scotch schoolboy in succession who has filled that position. Only three Old Blues were available to take their places in the team—an unprecedented paucity. As in the immediately preceding seasons, Cambridge by no means showed consistent form in the matches prior to the Inter-'Varsity contest. Defeats were sustained from London Scottish, St. Thomas's Hospital, and Dublin University, while the form shown in several other engagements was by no means encouraging. Against Blackheath they did their best performance, and displayed fine all-round play. Two Internationals, Neilson (Scotland) and Montgomery (Ireland), obtained places at three-quarter, the trio in that position being made up by Fforde of Bedford. For the third season in succession Martin Scott was unable to take his place at half; a heavy loss to the Cantabs. A. Rotherham (a relative of the peerless A. Rotherham), who formed one of the Cape team, was one of the halfbacks, the other being J. C. Orr. The Union authorities, by the way, preferred the play of H. Marshall, who was passed over by the Cambridge executive, and awarded him the position of half in the North and South match. Two more cricket Blues, Wells and Douglas, took the places of MacGregor and Woods. Forward the Cantabs were by no means a good team.

Oxford were decided favourites for the match. Though defeated early in the season by London Scottish and Old Merchant Taylors, they had achieved some noteworthy victories over Swansea, Blackheath, Edinburgh Academicals, etc., and had, moreover, seven of the previous year's winning team in their ranks, including three Internationals. The result of the match was contrary to expectation, for although in the early part of the game Cambridge had much the worst of the scrummage play, and it seemed as if Oxford must win the match, yet, on changing ends, the Light Blue forwards played in such improved form that their backs were given a chance to demonstrate their capabilities. Fforde and Neilson obtained tries, and thus the Cantabs won by 2 tries to *nil*, making their record identical with that of Oxford. In the series of matches seven have been won by each University and five have been drawn. Cambridge have scored 8 goals and 16 tries; Oxford 11 goals and 13 tries.

The following constituted the team :—

C. M. Wells, back; A. B. Fforde, W. Neilson, R. Montgomery, three-quarter-backs; A. Rotherham, J. C. Orr, half-backs; T. W. P. Storey (captain), C. B. Nicholl, E. Mayfield, H. Staunton, A. E. Elliott, H. J. Craig, W. Cope, R. N. Douglas, B. F. Robinson, forwards.

Of the above, Nicholl and Neilson played this season for Wales and Scotland respectively.

Before concluding this article, it has been suggested to the writer to pick the strongest possible team to represent his old University. This is a somewhat invidious task. To make such a selection a feasible one we have divided Cambridge football into two periods: The first, from 1871 to 1880; the second, from 1881 to the present time.

The strongest team that could be chosen from the players in period one we select as follows :—

*A. S. Taylor, *J. M. Batten or P. T. Wrigley, backs; E. Storey, three-quarter-back; *R. T. Finch, L. T. Williams, half-backs; *E. T. Gurdon, R. S. Whalley, *C. Gurdon, *A. Budd, *C. J. C. Touzell, *C. H. Coates, *C. P. Wilson, C. M. Agnew, H. Y. L. Smith, S. R. James.

* Denotes the player also gained International Honours.

For period two:—

*C. H. Sample or *Gregor Mac Gregor, back; *M. M. Duncan, *R. L. Aston, *F. H. R. Alderson, three-quarter-backs; *A. R. Don Wauchope, *W. Martin Scott, half-backs; *H. G. Fuller, E. Rice, *R. M. Pattisson, *G. L. Jeffery, J. Hammond, *J. H. Dewhurst, *F. W. J. Goodhue, *S. M. J. Woods, *V. C. le Fanu.

Altogether Cambridge has furnished fifty-one International players.

We append a list of Cambridge Internationals:—

ENGLAND.

F. H. R. Alderson, Durham.
R. L. Aston, Tonbridge.
J. M. Batten, Haileybury.
E. B. Brutton, Durham.
A. Budd, Clifton.
J. W. Cave, Wellington.
C. E. Chapman, Stoney Stratford.
C. H. Coates, Finchley.
J. H. Dewhurst, Mill Hill.
R. T. Finch, Sherborne.
H. G. Fuller, Finchley.
E. T. Gurdon, Haileybury.
C. Gurdon, Haileybury.
P. F. Hancock.
G. L. Jeffery, St. John's Wood.
W. R. M. Leake, Dulwich.
J. Le Fleming, Tonbridge.
C. J. B. Marriott, Tonbridge.
W. G. Mitchell, Bromsgrove.
P. H. Morrison, Loretto.
R. M. Pattisson, Tonbridge.
J. H. Payne, Manchester.
A. Robinson, Cheltenham.
C. H. Sample, Edinburgh Academy.
M. T. Scott, Craigmount.
W. M. Scott, Craigmount.
A. S. Taylor, Merchant Taylors.
C. J. C. Touzell.
C. P. Wilson, Marlborough.
S. M. J. Woods, Brighton.

SCOTLAND.

A. R. Don Wauchope, Fettes.
M. M. Duncan, Fettes.
F. W. J. Goodhue, Merchiston.
A. Methuen, Fettes.
W. Neilson, Merchiston.
C. J. B. Milne, Fettes.
L. E. Stevenson, Edinburgh Academy.
J. G. Tait, Edinburgh Academy.
W. M. McLeod, Fettes.
Gregor MacGregor, Uppingham.
W. Wotherspoon, Fettes.

WALES.

E. P. Alexander, Brecon.
J. A. Bevan, Grossmont.
N. Biggs, Cardiff.
C. H. Newman, Newport.
E. J. Lewis, Llandovery.
C. B. Nicholl, Llandovery.
W. H. Thomas, Llandovery.

IRELAND.

V. C. Le Fanu, Haileybury.
J. C. Macdonald, Armagh.
R. Montgomery, Queen's College, Belfast.

Also a list of those members of Rugby football

* Denotes the player also gained International Honours.

teams who have represented Cambridge in any other branch of sport.

- E. B. Brutton (Durham), athletics.
- G. L. Colbourne (Oundle), athletics.
- A. R. Don Wauchope (Fettes), athletics.
- R. N. Douglas (Dulwich), cricket.
- C. Gurdon (Haileybury), rowing.
- J. Le Fleming (Tonbridge), athletics.
- A. R. Lewis (Blackheath), athletics.
- G. McGregor (Uppingham), cricket.
- W. G. Mitchell (Bromsgrove), athletics.
- C. B. Nicholl (Llandovery), athletics.
- D. B. Roffey, Association.
- E. Storey (Fettes), athletics.
- D. Q. Steel (Uppingham), Association and cricket.
- L. E. Stevenson (Edinburgh Academy), athletics.
- C. H. Ware (Hereford), athletics.
- C. M. Wells (Dulwich), cricket.
- C. P. Wilson (Marlborough), cricket and bicycling.
- S. M. J. Woods (Brighton), cricket.

CHAPTER XVII.

METROPOLITAN FOOTBALL.

By a Londoner.

THE best definition of Metropolitan county football would furnish a very appropriate subject for a prize competition. To call it "county football" is a misnomer: it is rather a travesty of it, which has been played for so many winters that both the managers, performers, and public are getting heartily sick of it, and are at the eleventh hour beginning to consider whether it would not be advisable to substitute something more realistic in the place of this threadbare burlesque. Every species of galvanism has been applied to the unfortunate patients in the hope of restoring vitality, but the sufferers have failed to respond to the stimuli. Hard-working secretaries have worn out their pens, boots, and energies in the vain endeavour to collect a representative team of Middlesex or Kent to journey to Yorkshire or Lancashire, but their efforts have generally resulted in the scratching of the match "through inability to raise a fifteen." Middlesex, it is true, has been fairly successful when opposed to Northern counties, but then without consulting the archives of the past it is a tax on one's memory to recollect when last she did meet a Northern opponent. It must be recorded to the credit of Surrey that she has always kept her engagements at home and abroad, and has arranged yearly a representative list of fixtures, while Kent and Middlesex have generally contented themselves with the unambitious programme of garden-party games between each other and Surrey. As champion of the South-Eastern group last season Kent did manage to take a team to Yorkshire, but came back with an ignominious record of goals and tries scored up against her.

MIDDLESEX TEAM V. SOMERSET: WESTON-SUPER-MARE,
DECEMBER 28, 1889.

W. G. CLIBBORN. E. G. FINCH.
F. C. GORDON, J. H. HEDDERWICK, R. O. B. LANE, H. B. LAWRELL, T. W. LOCKWOOD, A. REED, J. H. MULLIGTON.
A. A. SURTEES, A. J. GOUTH, W. E. MACLAGAN, L. G. BONHAM CARTER, G. C. LINDSAY.
L. LAWELL. C. P. SIMPSON. F. BONWICK.

The reason of the failure of county football in the Metropolis is not difficult to diagnose. It is simply that Middlesex, Kent, and Surrey are not from a football point of view counties *per se*, but that the three form an aggregate London. An old legal maxim teaches us that the lesser estate is merged in the greater, and in this instance the three counties have become merged in the Metropolis. Here county football is played by a hotch-potch of players sorted out in accordance with the relation of their birth, or domicile to Charing Cross, and until they are informed by a county secretary, or have studied a map of London, a great many of them would not be able to tell you which county they were qualified to represent. As a consequence, nobody cares a sixpenny-piece whether Middlesex beats Kent, or Kent Middlesex—in fact, the essence of London football may be said to lie in club rivalry and county indifference. The keenness between Blackheath and the London Scottish is intense, but when in a Kent and Middlesex match, five or six Heathens or five or six Scots find themselves representing Middlesex against five or six fellow-clubmen with whom they play every Saturday, but who are now opposed to them in the Kent fifteen, the anomaly is too extravagant to permit of the kindling of even the smallest spark of rivalry or enthusiasm. The game, of course, resolves itself into the purest farce, and only serves the purpose of bringing Metropolitan county football into ridicule and contempt.

A great Kent enthusiast—a veritable *rara avis*—formulated a scheme whereby, as in Yorkshire and Lancashire, and other Northern counties, the county was to have a first call on a player's services in preference to his club; but his proposals met with great disfavour and scorn, and in some quarters indignation—a fact which serves to illustrate how completely paramount is the *esprit de corps* for club rivalry in London.

Such, then, is the nature of the disease, and the question remains as to what the nature of the remedy shall be.

Two remedies suggest themselves: (1) Allow the *locus in quo* of the ground of a club to confer a county qualification; (2) consolidate Middlesex, Kent, and Surrey into a district, "the London counties."

Both of the above reforms were proposed many years

ago by Messrs. Budd and Vassall, but were not received with favour. It is possible, however, that the melancholy experience of ten years may have modified the opinions of those who were formerly so strongly opposed to a change, and that when they have carefully studied the humiliating records of their counties, these Rip Van Winkles will awake to the reality that they must either linger on in decrepitude, or submit to an operation of some sort or the other.

Under the first of these schemes a man who played for Blackheath, whose ground is situated in Kent, would be eligible to play for that county; and a Richmond, or London Scottish, player, whose grounds lie in Surrey, would be qualified to play for her. This proposal would entail the extinction of Middlesex as a county, but as, with the exception of Rosslyn Park, there is not, I believe, any prominent club who has a ground in that county, there can be no real objection to the scheme. The enormous advantage of it is that it preserves the club rivalry, which is the substratum of London football, and gets rid of the anomaly of fellow-clubmen playing against one another, when representing a different section of the Metropolis.

I need not, of course, say that in working out the details of such a scheme it would be necessary to accurately define what constituted *a player* for a club— *i.e.*, what length of play could confer a qualification.

The second scheme, the consolidation of the three into the London counties, would do a wonderful deal towards infusing vitality into London football, which is in none too vigorous a condition at present. There would be no longer any difficulty in getting a team to go afield, and, better still, it would put an end to the monopoly which Lancashire and Yorkshire seem likely to retain in the County Championship contest.

The scheme, I must admit, does not find favour with most of the country counties on the ground that it would furnish too powerful an organisation for them to cope with; but they should remember that not one of them, unless things greatly alter, will ever have a chance of defeating Lancashire or Yorkshire in the County Championship, the final for which, unless this scheme is adopted, is likely to resolve itself into an annual duel between these two to all time. Further, they have admitted the precedent in the case of the Midland and Eastern counties, the case of the former being an exact analogy to that of the Metropolitan counties, the only difference being that in one instance Birmingham and in the other London is the centre of the counties. Oddly and inconsistently enough, the Eastern counties, who are consolidated on these same lines, are perhaps the strongest opponents to the Metropolitan counties enjoying a similar advantage. After all, winning the championship is a very secondary consideration. What we want to do by these contests is to promote football, and the good which would be done to, and the enthusiasm which would be infused into, London football by the acceptance of this scheme would be incalculable. The fact must not be lost sight of that, with the exception of Yorkshire and Lancashire, there are more players in London than in any other three counties combined, and that, therefore, it is important that every attention should be paid to the welfare of so large a body.

That something must be done is perfectly plain, and, though either scheme has no doubt its objections and faults, I respectfully submit them to consideration as the only possible solutions of this very difficult question.

The London Football Clubs.

As it is impossible in a volume of this character to review every London club, the more prominent ones have been selected for detailed notices, which appear elsewhere—I propose here merely to offer a general criticism on London Club football considered as a whole.

If we take the play of Northern clubs as a standard, I am afraid that we have to confess that our average of play is an uncommonly low one—in fact, Blackheath and the London Scottish were the only Metropolitan fifteens last season who could compete with a crack Northern fifteen with any hope of success.

Now, the cause of failure of Metropolitan county football is, as I have said, easy of diagnosis, but here the mischief is a much more complex and obscure one.

I will, of course, admit that minor clubs are greatly handicapped, when they come to recruit, by the gravitation of the best players from the provinces and the

SURREY COUNTY RUGBY FOOTBALL TEAM V. YORKSHIRE: DECEMBER 8, 1890.

(YORKSHIRE — 2 GOALS 5 TRIES.   SURREY — NIL.)

(From a Photograph by R. T. Watson, Hull.)

Universities to the most successful London club. A man who plays on a really good side is bound not only to gain a better chance of notoriety than one who plays with an unsuccessful team, but he is bound also to become the more scientific player.

Unfortunately, as we are situated in London, with a huge mass of clubs belonging to one city, and very few of them imbued with any local *esprit de corps*, it will be found impossible to prevent this gravitation; and, even if you could do so, I believe that the standard of South football would be lowered, for it is only in the best London teams, where you get a collection of expert recruits, that we see anything approaching scientific football exhibited. But apart from this advantage, which I admit the premier clubs enjoy, it is extremely difficult to explain the mediocre form of the generality of London clubs.

The majority of Yorkshire fifteens are composed of working men, who have only adopted football in recent years, and have received no school education in the art. The majority of members of London clubs have played it all their lives, yet when the two meet there is only one in it—the Yorkshireman.

How is it, then, that the latter, despite his want of school tuition in the game, can beat the former, who has learnt it with his Latin grammar? The only reason I can assign is a want of keenness, a want of condition, a want of pride in the record of one's club, and a want of energetic club management, without which, neither of the other three qualities are engendered. Football rivalry in the North and in some clubs in the South has reached such a pitch that if you hope to succeed you must have three things: (1) An able and indefatigable secretary; (2) fifteen men who are keen for the club's prestige; (3) a captain who insists on his men getting and keeping fit.

One reads with amazement of villages in Yorkshire, whose names one cannot discover in Bradshaw, springing up like mushrooms as formidable fifteens, and tussling with the best for the cup. They receive no recruits from without. How is it done? Why, by converting the indigenous talent into an enthusiastic machine, and by insisting on the fact that that machine is always in working order.

Is it not astounding that with our plethora of players we have only two half-backs of any class in London, and that both of these are University men?

To all this a great many would answer, "Well, if that's so, it must be so; we can't be bothered with your training—we play for pleasure, and if we get beaten, we get beaten," and so on.

The man who makes this kind of remark has never been, and never will be, of any service in building up or sustaining the fabric of a football club. The day is at hand when, if you play football at all, you must play it in earnest. The sooner your masherdom is banished from the game the better.

And after all, getting and keeping in condition for young active men is a very small task. If you have not time for prolonged exercise, condense it. Ten minutes with a skipping-rope, and ten with the dumb-bells or clubs daily, will suffice, with a modicum of walking and two sprints of a hundred yards each to keep a man in very fair trim.

I sincerely hope that in the coming season our London clubs will shake off their lethargy. What can be done in a Yorkshire village can surely be done here, and if nothing else will, at least the Tyke yokel forging further and further ahead ought to touch our pride and galvanise our energies.

THE BLACKHEATH FOOTBALL CLUB.

The Blackheath Club is the oldest of all Rugby football clubs. Of this fact Blackheathens are justly proud. But the traditions of the high-class football always played by this club are still more honourable than the bare fact of Blackheath being the first legitimate club organisation to adopt the Rugby game. The president of a prominent Northern club once designated Blackheath as "the home of standard English football," and such title rightly describes the principles that have guided its players on the field of play, and its officials in the council chamber. The influence of the Blackheath Club has been enormous, and has been gained notably by the excellence of its officers, by the success of the club, but also in no small degree by the style of game played by the team.

The club was started in the year 1860 by four boys

of the Blackheath Proprietary School. Their names were W. Burnett, Frank Campbell, Gower, and Alexander Sinclair. The club was known as the " Old Blackheathen Football Club," and consisted entirely of old Blackheath Schoolboys. W. Burnett was the captain, but after two years' trial, it being found impossible to get up teams without the aid of boys who had not been to Blackheath School, the name was altered to the " Blackheath Football Club." The early matches seem to have been played by just a few schools, Army-crammer teams, and pick-up games.

The names of the captains since the formation of the club are: W. Burnett, Moore, Cooper, W. C. Scott, J. Paterson, F. Stokes, G. W. Pearson, A. Hill (1875-76), L. Stokes (1876-81), G. W. Burton (1881-83), P. A. Newton (1883-84), H. Vassall (1884-85), C. J. B. Marriott (1885-87), A. Budd (1887-88), G. L. Jeffery (1888-89), A. E. Stoddart (1889-91), P. Christopherson (1891-92).

The most successful of these was Lennard Stokes. The following is the record of the club during his captaincy.

	Matches Played.	Won.	Lost.	Drawn.	Goals for.	Tries for.	Goals against.	Tries against.
1876-77	18	14	1	3	25	19	0	5
1877-78	20	15	2	3	35	25	3	1
1878-79	16	15	1	0	54	30	1	4
1879-80	16	14	0	2	41	37	2	1
1880-81	13	10	2	1	23	25	3	0
Total	83	68	6	9	178	136	9	11

With the exception of one of these eighty-three matches, viz., that against the R. M. C. Sandhurst in 1880 (when he acted as umpire), Stokes played in all, and during the period gained fifty-six tries for his club, besides dropping many goals. He was well backed up by such players as A. W. Pearson, who could both drop and place a ball well, and as full-back was the most deadly tackler who has played in London; G. W. Burton, who was very fast in the open and a great scorer; A. Budd, who was very similar in style to Burton; G. F. Vernon; G. O. Jacob; F. L. Pattisson; P. A. Newton, and Aubrey Spurling, among the forwards; H. H. Taylor, A. H. Jackson, and H. Roberts as half-backs; with a selection from G. Stokes, H.

Bradley, A. Poland, W. N. Bolton, or W. J. Penny as full-backs. At this period, and for some time later, the Blackheath Club seldom played a match without a Spurling or a Stokes in the team. As the Hewitts, the Frys, and the Hills were the guiding spirits of Queen's House, so the Spurling and the Stokes families are intimately connected with the Blackheath Club. Aubrey was the most famous of the Spurlings as a player, being a genuine scrummager of the old-fashioned order, and able to adapt himself to the passing system, when that style came into fashion. An enthusiast in the game, a club patriot in his affection for the club, no member of the same has worked more enthusiastically, earnestly, and unselfishly, to further the interests of the Blackheath Club. To him the writer is indebted for facts and statistics regarding the club. A diligent recorder of the game, Aubrey Spurling has done good service to the historian by preserving accounts of the early games played by the Blackheath Club.

A. SPURLING.
(From a Photograph by T. Fall, Baker Street, W.)

The record of the club subsequent to the captaincy of Lennard Stokes is as follows:—

	Captain.	Matches.	Won.	Lost.	Drawn.	Goals for.	Tries for.	Goals against.	Tries against.
1881-82	G. W. Burton	20	15	3	2	24	42	5	1
1882-83	G. W. Burton	18	14	1	3	17	25	3	3
1883-84	P. A. Newton	21	12	6	3	27	39	5	7
1884-85	H. Vassall	20	16	1	3	42	23	5	4
1885-86	C. J. B. Marriott	13	9	2	2	18	20	3	2
1886-87	C. J. B. Marriott	18	12	6	0	18	31	3	6
1887-88	A. Budd	19	9	9	1	23	20	10	9
1888-89	G. L. Jeffery	22	11	10	1	36	25	24	14
1889-90	A. E. Stoddart	23	15	6	2	34	18	5	9
1890-91	A. E. Stoddart	20	12	8	0	29	34	19	13
1891-92	P. Christopherson	21	16	3	2	39	47	7	7
	Total	215	141	55	19	307	324	89	75

When the club was formed they used to play on Blackheath, and continued playing there until the end of the season 1876–77. The match against Richmond, on January 20th, 1877, was the cause of the club quitting the heath for a private ground. In this match the spectators assembled in such numbers, and were so unseemly in their behaviour, that the game was brought to a premature conclusion. Towards the finish the game might almost be described as the spectators being in the centre and the players on the touch-lines.

The first private ground occupied by Blackheath was Mr. Richardson's field, which he kindly lent to the club for the nominal rent of £10, a sum believed to be assigned for the benefit of the St. John's Schools, Blackheath. The first match played on this field was against Guy's Hospital, October 20th, 1877. The Oxford v. Cambridge matches of 1880–81–82 were played there, and it was the birthplace of the London v. Oxford and Cambridge matches. On December 2nd, 1882, the North v. South took place here, but the only International match ever played on Richardson's field was the first contest between England and Wales, February 19th, 1881. It was in this match that L. Stokes threw the ball halfway across the ground to R. Hunt, giving him an easy run in, but the ball was ordered back by the umpires, their decision being that such a long pass was not football.

In the winter of 1882–83 the field was bought by a building society, but the club were fortunate enough to obtain the use of the Rectory Field in January, 1883. Guy's Hospital were again the first opponents on this ground, January 17th, 1883. It has been the venue of four International matches:—England v. Scotland, March 1st, 1884, in which the unfortunate dispute occurred; England v. Wales, January 2nd, 1886; England v. Ireland, March 15th, 1890; and England v. Wales, January 2nd, 1891. The following North v. South matches have been played:—December 20th, 1884; December 18th, 1886; February 4th, 1888; and December 15th, 1888.

The present Blackheath Cricket, Football and Tennis Company was formed in 1885. The Morden Cricket Club in 1884 found it was impossible to keep a decent wicket on Blackheath as the heath authorities would not allow them to re-turf and keep in order their own ground as they had done heretofore, so that M. J. Druitt, the secretary, and A. Poland, the treasurer, negotiated with G. W. Burton, the secretary, and Aub. Spurling, the treasurer of the Blackheath Club, with the result that a meeting of residents of Blackheath was called, the present company formed, and a lease of the Rectory Field obtained for twenty-one years.

It is impossible to give a detailed record of each season of the club, but the following incidents in the history of the games may be of interest. In the season 1880-81 only two matches were lost, viz., against Manchester and against the Marlborough Nomads. The match with Manchester was the first fixture with that club, and was won by Manchester by 2 goals to 2 tries. One of the Manchester goals was dropped by R. Hunt, and the ball just touched the tips of the fingers of a Blackheath back, who said nothing about it till after the game, so of course there was no appeal. The back did not know the rule, and his only complaint was that the ball had nearly taken his finger-nail off. The Marlborough Nomads won by a goal to 2 tries. H. Vassall scored the try from which the goal was kicked; the tries for Blackheath were gained by W. N. Bolton and L. Stokes. Bolton was playing full-back, and obtained his try by taking the ball from a long throw-in from touch by Stokes.

JOHN F. HAMMOND.
(*From a Photograph by Elliott & Fry.*)

In the same season in the match *v.* Clapham Rovers on Wandsworth Common, December 17th, 1881, the day was so rough that it was impossible to keep the goal posts standing up, so it was arranged to score by tries only. A forward in *dribbling* the ball against the wind kicked a little to the right, and the ball was blown back twenty yards. There were eight spectators to see the match. Twenty-one trees were blown down on Wandsworth Common the same day.

Against Guy's Hospital on the 19th October, 1878, L. Stokes placed 10 goals from 11 tries.

Against the Royal Naval College on November 24th, 1877, P. Brunskill, playing for Blackheath, ran against the goal-post, and although he knocked it over failed to obtain a try.

John Hammond holds the record of appearances in the Blackheath and Richmond fixtures, having played nineteen times. He commenced playing for Blackheath in the season 1882-83, and up to the end of 1890-91 had played 135 times, and is still playing. He has represented the South on four occasions, and has frequently been first reserve for the English team, but, unlike many players much his inferior, has not had the luck to obtain his cap through one of the original choices falling out. He was one of the Cape team in 1891, and played in every match through the tour. Hammond has been a most consistent player, as the above record will show. Had he been taller, a large share of International honours might have fallen to his lot. The same cry has always been raised, "Oh, Johnnie Hammond is a real good man, but he is not tall enough for the English team"; and so he has been passed over for men his inferior in every way except stature.

The following were the officials and the rules of the Blackheath Club in 1862 :—

CAPTAIN: W. Burnett.   TREASURER: F. M. Campbell.
SECRETARY: W. L. Gower.
COMMITTEE: R. E. Gower, F. H. Moore, L. P. Sueur.

RULES:

1. That the ball be started from the centre of the ground by a place-kick.
2. A fair catch is a catch direct from the foot, or a knock-on from the hand of one of the opposite side; when the catcher may either run with the ball or make his mark by inserting his heel in the ground on the spot where he catches it; in which case he is entitled to a free kick.
3. It is not lawful to take the ball off the ground, except in touch, for any purpose whatever.
4. A ball in touch is dead, and the first player who touches it down must kick it out straight from the place where it entered touch.
5. A catch out of touch is not a fair catch; but may be run off.
6. Running is allowed to any player on his side if the ball be caught or taken off the first bound.
7. Any player holding the ball unless he has made his mark after a fair catch may be hacked; and running is not allowed after the mark is made.
8. No player may be hacked and held at the same time; and hacking above or on the knee or from behind is unfair.

9. No player can be held or hacked unless he has the ball in his hands.

10. Though it is lawful to hold a player in a scrummage, this does not include attempts to throttle or strangle, which are totally opposed to the principles of the game.

11. A player whilst running or being held may hand the ball to one of his own side, who may continue to run with it; but after the ball is grounded it must be hacked through, not thrown or lifted.

12. When a player running with the ball grounds it, it cannot be touched by anyone until he lifts his hand from it.

13. If the ball goes behind the goal it must be kicked out by the party to whom the goal belongs from in a line with the goals; but a catch off a kick from behind goal is not a fair catch, but may be run off.

14. No player is to get before the ball on the side furthest from his own goal; but if he does he must not touch the ball as it passes him until touched by one of the opposite side, he being off-side.

15. A goal must be a kick through or over and between the poles, and if touched by the hands of one of the opposite side before or whilst going through is no goal.

16. No one wearing projecting nails, iron plates, or gutta-percha on the soles or heels of his boots be allowed to play.

Uniform.—Dark blue serge trousers, black and scarlet striped jerseys and socks.

BLACKHEATH v. RICHMOND.

Aubrey Spurling gives the following as the record of the matches between these famous clubs:—

'67	Jan. 26	Richmond Green	Drawn: R., 1 try.
'67	Feb. 9	Blackheath	Drawn: B., 1 try.
'67	Mar. 2	Richmond Green	R. won by a dropped goal to *nil*.
'67	Dec. 14	Richmond Green	Drawn: R., 1 try.
'68	Feb. 15	Blackheath	R. won by a goal to *nil*.
'68	Nov. 21	Richmond Green	Drawn: A try each.
'69	Feb. 20	Blackheath	Drawn: R., 1 try.
'69	Dec. 4	Richmond Green	R. won by a goal to *nil*.
'70	Nov. 19	Richmond Green	B. won by 1 goal, 2 punts-out to *nil*.
'71	Mar. 4	Blackheath	B. won by a goal to *nil*.
'72	Nov. —	Richmond Green	R. won by a goal to *nil*.
'73	Feb. 15	Blackheath	Drawn: B., 1 try.
'73	Nov. 8	Old Deer Park	Drawn: Nothing scored.
'74	Feb. 14	Blackheath	Drawn: B., 1 try.
'74	Dec. 12	Old Deer Park	Drawn: Nothing scored.
'75	Jan. 16	Blackheath	B. won by a goal to *nil*.
'75	Nov. 13	Old Deer Park	Drawn: Nothing scored.
'76	Feb. 5	Blackheath	B. won by 2 goals 4 tries to *nil*.
'76	Dec. 16	Old Deer Park	B. won by a goal to *nil*.
'77	Jan. 27	Blackheath	Drawn: Spectators stopped the game.
'78	Jan. 19	Richardson's Field	Drawn: Nothing scored.
'80	Jan. 17	Richardson's Field	B. won by a try to *nil*.
'80	Dec. 11	Old Deer Park	Drawn: Nothing scored.
'82	Jan. 14	Richardson's Field	B. won by a try to *nil*.
'82	Dec. 9	Old Deer Park	Drawn: Nothing scored.
'83	Jan. 13	Richardson's Field	B. won by a goal and a try to *nil*.
'83	Dec. 7	Old Deer Park	Drawn: One try each.
'84	Jan. 12	Rectory Field	R. won by a goal to a try.

'84	Dec. 6	Old Deer Park	Drawn: Nothing scored.
'85	Jan. 19	Rectory Field	Drawn: Nothing scored.
'85	Dec. 5	Old Deer Park	B. won by a goal and a try to *nil*.
'86	Jan. 30	Rectory Field	B. won by a goal and a try to *nil*.
'86	Dec. 4	Old Deer Park	R. won by a try to *nil*.
'87	Jan. 29	Rectory Field	R. won by a try to *nil*.
'87	Dec. 3	Old Deer Park	R. won by a try to *nil*.
'88	Jan. 28	Rectory Field	B. won by a goal to *nil*.
'88	Dec. 1	Old Deer Park	B. won by 2 goals and a try to *nil*.
'89	Jan. 26	Rectory Field	B. won by a goal and a try to *nil*.
'89	Nov. 30	Athletic Ground	R. won by a try to *nil*.
'90	Jan. 25	Rectory Field	B. won by a goal and a try to *nil*.
'91	Mar. 21	Rectory Field	B. won by 4 tries to *nil*.
'91	Nov. 28	Rectory Field	B. won by 3 goals and 2 tries to *nil*.
'92	Jan. 23	Athletic Ground	B. won by 5 goals and 2 tries to 1 try.

Matches played, 43. Blackheath won 17, Richmond won 9, drawn 17. Blackheath, 22 goals 28 tries; Richmond, 5 goals 10 tries.

The Richmond Football Club.—This club from its early formation has a great history at its back, which its progress and present position in the football world have maintained. It was started by one who, in the year 1861, found himself located in Richmond, after spending his early days in a town in Surrey, where the old custom still remained of playing football in the public streets on Shrove Tuesday. Thus being inspired with a boyish love of the game, nothing would suffice but that a football club should be started in the town of Richmond, and consequently the same was done in the above-mentioned year.

The Richmond Club is unique in one respect, namely, in having been guilty (like some of our greatest statesmen) of changing its creed—or in this case, its rules. It was started, as perhaps few may know, under the rules then known as the Harrow rules, which resembled somewhat the Association rules of the present day. Disaster attended its early efforts, as the writer well remembers when he himself took part in the games at Barnes, Walthamstow, and elsewhere.

Later on, a change in the captaincy occurred, and a suggestion was then made to alter the game to Rugby rules, a suggestion adopted and pursued with marked success. From this date the club went apace amazingly, and its only formidable opponent at that time was the older established Blackheath Club, and to these two clubs the Rugby Union game, in a very great measure, owes its present popularity and prosperity as a national pastime. The first ground of the Richmond Club has a history in itself as well as being historical from a football point of view. In the early days there was no other place available for the game in the town, and consequently the originator of the club, nothing daunted, duly had the goal posts erected on a village green. Hence it was that the game was played there for many years after, to the delight of the then village crowd of spectators, and it is only in quite recent years that it has been found out that all games but cricket and bowls were strictly prohibited in this royal enclosure, by order of that all important personage, the Ranger.

This incident is rather a singular one, as it was long after the Richmond Club had migrated to its first ground in the old Deer Park that the above-referred-to prohibition of football on the Green was found to exist. Referring to its first captains, it is recorded that F. Morris held the reins of office in the field in its "*Harrow rule* days"; E. C. Holmes followed in its first days under Rugby rules (pure and simple); then in the following order, E. C. Holmes, C. D. Heatley, the Honourable H. A. Lawrence, F. R. Adams, E. T. Gurdon, W. G. Clibborn, F. C. Cousins, and W. G. Mitchell, of present day renown.

There seems to be no very accurate record kept of the secretaries, but writing from memory the first secretary and originator was Edwin Ash (and then W. Wallace), and afterwards A. D. Melladew (one of the first, strangely enough, to welcome the English team at the Cape), H. P. Gardner and W. E. Clifton, J. C. Groome and W. K. Arber filled the post at various times.

H. P. Gardner particularly did an immense amount for the club, at a time when it was very difficult to preserve financial equilibrium.

The Richmond Club lays claim to have done two important things in the interest of football: the first being on the occasion of a match with Blackheath on Richmond Green, when on account of fog the game had to be abandoned. Both teams were weakened through many men being laid up from injuries received in previous matches through the hacking system, and there and then a resolution was unanimously passed in favour of the abolition of hacking, which ultimately resulted in its universal abolition.

The second important step accomplished was that

conjointly with the then Blackheath secretary, the Richmond secretary of that day (E. Ash) wrote a letter to the newspapers suggesting the formation of the present Rugby Union. As recorded elsewhere, Ash was the first hon. secretary to the Rugby Union. E. C. Holmes, the Richmond captain of that day, and L. J. Maton took an immense amount of labour in drafting the original rules, which form the nucleus of the present code of laws.

As the game increased in popularity and Richmond in population, the number of spectators at the matches seriously interfered with the game, and after a successful career on the "old Green" a private ground had to be sought for, and the Richmond Club were extremely lucky in obtaining so excellent a one as the Old Deer Park. Two years ago they were in fortune's way once more in securing a still better ground, viz.—that of the Richmond Athletic Association.

W. O. CLIBBORN.
From a Photograph by the London Stereoscopic Company, Cheapside.

It would take up too much space to refer in detail to the past performances of the club, but mention must be made of the brilliant *régime* of E. T. Gurdon, who captained a fifteen in 1886-87 which was as strong as, if not superior to, any club fifteen which ever entered the field. This team, which was unbeaten for a season, included such famous players as W. G. Mitchell (back), G. C. Wade, A. J. Gould, and A. M. Evanson (three-quarter), A. Rotherham and J. Roberts (half), J. H. Dewhirst, W. G. Clibborn, J. S. Ward, and F. G. Swayne (forward). Twynam and W. A Evanson, two of the finest halves that ever played, and Frank Adams, the captain of the English team, were bulwarks of the club in the past. At the present time Richmond is suffering from one of those periods of depression which every club has to face one day or the other. The retirement of the Gurdons, Wade, Evanson, Rotherham, and Roberts *en masse* was undoubtedly the cause of decadence, which everybody hopes will be but shortlived, and none more so than its oldest friend, the writer.

The London Scottish Football Club.—The London Scottish Football Club has now entered upon the fourteenth year of its existence, and, considering its comparative youth, may be said to have made for itself a very creditable position in Metropolitan football circles.

During the year or two before it sprang into life, the idea of forming such a club had been revolving in the patriotic breasts of a few Scotsmen in London, who, when they foregathered, were wont to deplore this apparent aching void in London football. Suddenly, in April, 1878, a more definite expression was given to this feeling by the calling together of a few loyal Scots to reasonably consider the important question.

At this meeting, convened, if memory is not at fault, by Messrs. Neil McGlashan, D. Begbie Gibson, and George Grant, the London Scottish Football Club was enthusiastically founded.

The writer remembers the preliminary and most burning question to have been that of the ground upon which to play our matches. It was eventually placed in the hands of a small committee to spy out the land, and during the summer of 1878 that committee scoured the environs of London with great ardour, but with so little success that the club had to open its career on an odd corner of Blackheath Common. It was there the team played its first match, beating Ravenscourt Park, once strong and well-known, but then rather on the decline. This success rather intoxicated us, and we rushed the following Saturday on to our fate in the shape of a beating from Queen's House; Sydney Ellis, one of that club's foremost players, being the first Sassenach to cross our goal line. Since then the Scottish have won and lost many matches, but our wild joy at our first win and the despondency attending our first defeat are still fresh on the writer's memory. At the beginning of its career, and, indeed, for some short time afterwards, the club was regarded by some as a venture which would die an early death of its own accord, or be wiped out of existence in a few years' time at the hands of its rivals. But the maternal care and nurture of one or two of the committee did much to keep the little precious life in its body, and now, in 1892, those of the original members who are still to the fore affectionately regard the club as an organisation with every symptom of health and strength in it for years to come.

The club received a great fillip when W. E. Maclagan came South and joined its ranks. It must be considerable satisfaction to him to know that his part in the history of the club stands out by itself, and that his services have been fully appreciated by everyone of his fellow-members. His name off the field largely helped to attract to the club any Celtic resident in Modern Babylon who was worth a place in the team. Of his merits as a player it would be waste of time and space to write; they are too well-known by everyone who has any pretence to a knowledge of football, but it was always a recognised fact among his fellow-players that when this splendid three-quarter was on the field his team played with a confidence and dash they never had were he absent. Among those whose names figured for years in the club records, D. J. Macfarlan, three-quarter, and J. F. Smith, half-back, did much to bring honour and glory to the club. Their loss to the Scottish when the former left for India and the latter retired from football was most keenly felt, more especially as they were at their best when they left us.

The Scottish has had five captains during its career—Messrs. D. Begbie Gibson, Robert Arnot, W. E. Maclagan, D. J. Macfarlan, and G. C. Lindsay, who is still at his post.

Among the past and present members of the club a number have gained the Scottish national cap. This fact reflects considerable credit and lustre on the London Scottish, when it is considered how far the club is from the Scotch official headquarters, and it also shows that the talent here is fully recognised by our Northern brethren.

During the whole life of the club, and up till the close of 1890-91 season, the London Scottish first team have played in all 207 matches, with the following results:—138 won, 40 lost, and 29 drawn.

Against Bradford, the North of England cracks, we have only played twice, both times on their ground; the first match we won and the second was left drawn.

It was a matter of general regret to all Metropolitan football circles when the once famous Queen's House broke up and its name disappeared from the weekly chronicles of matches played. Perhaps more regretful to the London Scottish than to others, for in the five matches played the "Canny Ones" were never able to snatch a victory.

True, a draw was once obtained, but the wearers of the white jersey with the blue crown finished off with four matches against us. It may be that for a short time after that club had ceased to exist some of us were inclined to resent its decease from a personal point of view, as we could never in consequence have a chance of retrieving our losses. Had we even but once won a match, it is probable we should have regarded the demise still with regret for the disbanding of some good sportsmen, but with a chastened spirit containing "more of sorrow than anger."

Unlike the leopard the London Scottish has frequently changed its spots. Beginning with several different sites on Blackheath Common we retired to a more sequestered nook near Clapham Junction. From this ground the rapacious appetite of London builders ousted us and we took refuge at Lee. In some respects this was a capital ground, but in wet weather a trifle soft, and the writer remembers the surprise which made itself apparent in the faces of our opponents when one wet day before starting the game we had to chase from the centre of our pitch some ducklings that were swimming about in an unconcerned manner.

From here we tried Hampstead, but the heavy clay soil made play impossible in damp weather, and, for a fortunately short time, we had fears of a nomadic existence. At this juncture the Old Deer Park Ground at Richmond was offered to us, and it is unnecessary to say that we joyfully accepted the offer. Here our lines are cast in pleasant places, and we have hopes that the cordial relations existing between our lessors, the Richmond Cricket Club, and ourselves, will ensure a prolonged and comfortable tenancy. In closing this article the writer would like to place on record the thanks of the London Scottish Club for the courteous attitude assumed by Southern rivals towards it, standing as it does by itself in the heart of English football. It recognises, of course, that keen rivalry will always exist between good clubs, and this is rendered more striking where some slight national feeling is unavoidably present. It is, however, a fact, and happily so, that every principal football club in the South of England is actuated by the true English love of sport for sport's sake.

R. H. HEDDERWICK.

Two Famous Clubs of the Past.

The Gipsies Football Club.—During the summer of 1868, three "old Tonbridgians," F. Luscombe, J. A. Body, and W. J. Parker, all very keen on football, and who belonged to no London club, thought they knew a sufficient number of men who would be pleased to play the game if chance presented itself, and so they arranged a card of matches for the season 1868-69. After the two first matches had been played they called a meeting of their friends on the 17th of October, 1868, when it was decided to form "The Gipsies Football Club," F. Luscombe being elected as hon. sec., and H. H. Batten, J. A. Body, J. Brewer, W. J. Parker, and J. N. Streeten as the committee.

The result of the first season's matches—7 won and 11 drawn—showed that the founders were not wrong in their ideas. During the next season, 1869-70, the club continued to prosper, as the result of matches shows, viz.: played, 18; drawn, 13; won, 3; lost, 2.

Subsequently the club continued its existence with varied success, being at times one of the strongest playing the running game, but unfortunately most of its records have been mislaid, and it is not, therefore, possible to furnish the details of each season. However, many hard battles were fought with the leading clubs of those days—to wit, Blackheath, Richmond, Oxford and Cambridge Universities, Ravenscourt Park, Marlborough Nomads, Woolwich, Sandhurst, Cooper's Hill, St. Andrews Rovers, Clapham Rovers, West Kent, etc.

When strong behind the scrummage the Gipsies were formidable opponents, for their forwards were always a good lot. In December, 1872, *Bell's Life* wrote:—"The Gipsies have played and beaten Guy's Hospital, the Civil Service, Oakfield (Croydon), Ravenscourt Park, and have also fought a very hard and equal game with the Marlborough Nomads, and are better than ever this year, and are sure to win most of their matches": and further on in the same article referred to Blackheath, the Gipsies, and Ravenscourt Park, as the three crack clubs. The club can boast of such well-known names as F. Luscombe, the two Shearmans, Pickering, Clarke, Billy Barker, C. J. B. Marriott, W. B. and R. M. Pattison, and J. T. Ward. The Gipsies Club was disbanded twelve years ago.   W. PARKER.

Queen's House.—At one time one of the most formidable clubs in London, and in its best day decidedly the most difficult to beat, as the London Scottish know to their sorrow and chagrin. It owed its creation to the co-operation of the brothers Hill, Rowland and his elder brother Edward, and the families of Hewitt and Fry, who all lived in Greenwich, and its name, "Queen's House," to the domicile where our present Rugby Union secretary took his first breath of life. Cameron Hewitt played back, Tom and Fred Fry, three-quarters, and Sidney, half. Forward, Walter Hewitt, the International and famous oarsman, Malcolm, his brother, and Sidney Ellis, were the most prominent of a physically powerful lot; probably as strong a set of scrummagers as were ever got together. They did not go in for a fast or showy game, and were never great scorers, but their defence was wonderfully strong, and it is doubtful whether any team ever had a finer lot of tacklers. Their great rivals were their neighbours, Blackheath, with whom they played the closest and most exciting matches. The emigration of Cameron Hewitt and Fred and Sidney Fry to Canada, with the retirement of Tom Fry, took away the nucleus of the team, and it was decided to disband the club in the height of its prosperity sooner than risk the probability of a decadence. Tom Fry, Sidney Ellis, and Walter Hewitt played for England.

W. W. HEWITT.
(From a Photograph by Fradelle & Young, Regent Street, W.)

Old School Clubs.

The Marlborough Nomads.—The Nomads were started in the year 1868 by James Bourdillon, of the Indian Civil Service, and the writer, who was the first secretary, and after some two or three years became the captain. The next secretary was H. Stanhope Illingworth, a sportsman well-known in football as also on the running path, but now, alas! dead for some years. The very first match was played in 1868, at Richmond, *v.* Richmond, when such old players as E. C. Holmes and the two Rutters played against us, and we got a rather disappointing hiding by about three goals. We, however, took on all the best clubs, and for many years used to have really good matches with Blackheath, culminating in or about 1882 by our beating them, thanks principally to A. Kaye Butterworth and Harry Vassall. Amongst our opponents, besides Blackheath and Richmond, we counted West Kent, The Gipsies, Ravenscourt Park (all now deceased), and it can fairly be said that we played every good club. We progressed favourably, and in 1871 A. St. G. Hamersley played for England, at Edinburgh, *v.* Scotland. In 1872 we had four of our men in the English team *v.* Scotland: Fred Mills, back; Harold Freeman, three-quarter; and A. St. G. Hamersley and F. I. Currey, forward. Hamersley, Freeman, and Mills also played in 1873, and in 1874 Hamersley captained England, and at the same time we had Sydney Moore and W. H. Milton playing for England, while H. M. Hamilton, one of our best three-quarters, played the same year for Scotland. Besides the above men we have had R. W. B. Fletcher, H. Vassall, and W. M. Tatham, all Oxford Blues, the last two Internationals, and amongst others A. Kaye Butterworth, C. M. Wilkins, F. Thuresby, who are pretty well-known, besides the present captain, Rowell, and A. J. Hill, the Cantab cricketer, now playing. Tatham captained us after leaving Oxford. We have (as all school clubs must) had our ups and downs, at one time being literally at the top of the ladder, and at another very low down; but up to the present we have never desponded, and during the season just past we have picked up very well (winning eight and losing eight matches). Illingworth was followed in the secretaryship by R. F. Isaacson, and he by the late J. D. Vans Agnew, both in their time well-known men. We used for many years to play on Blackheath, on the opposite side of the road to the B.F.C., except when the latter had a match away, when, like the magpie, we prigged their nest. Of course, the ground was unenclosed, and the spectators were a most accursed nuisance in the way they trespassed on the ground. For several years past we have had a private ground at Surbiton. We have played both our old school, and also Haileybury College, for the last *twenty-four* years without a break, which is about a record.

Hamersley, Freeman, A. K. Butterworth, Vans Agnew, and F. I. Currey have been on the committee of the Rugby Union, and the latter held the secretaryship in 1874, during Guillemard's temporary absence abroad.

Many well-known authorities rather disapprove of old school clubs; in this the writer does not agree, but rather holds the opinion that they do much good to the school, and are very useful in keeping men together and inspiring *esprit de corps*.

I may add that with the exception of three clubs the Nomads are one of the oldest Rugby clubs in existence, and, except the Old Etonians, the oldest school club.

F. I. CURREY.

Old Leysians.—This club—a comparatively modern one—has in the last few years tasted the sweets and bitters of fortune with a vengeance. Its members are old boys of the Leys School, Cambridge, and three years ago, when A. L. Brooke was at his best, with the two MacArthurs, A. R. Richards, one of the best of modern half-backs, J. H. Gould, and a hard-working team to help him, the premiership of the Metropolitan clubs lay between them and the London Scottish. During the last two seasons they have experienced a series of disasters. This has been due to two reasons: several of the best men have been laid up with accidents, and A. L. Brooke, their great scorer, has lost a good deal of his brilliant form. They may, possibly, be able to retrieve their losses, but the vicissitudes of Old Boys' clubs, as we have seen them in London, leads to the reflection whether after all they are good institutions.

The Old Merchant Taylors.—This club was formed some ten years ago, and for several seasons has been very

steadily coming to the front, until to-day it is
certainly about the strongest of the Old Boys' clubs,
its card including all the chief Metropolitan clubs,
the Universities, Gloucester, and the three leading
Welsh clubs. Its strength lies mainly in its forwards,
who are not afraid of hard work, and are, in addition,
clever with their feet. The club owes very much to the
hon. sec., L. H. Gunnery, who has worked very hard for it
since its formation. Among the more prominent backs
who have played for the Old Merchant Taylors may
be mentioned M. Shearman, Lockhart Ross, Wells, W. S.
Buck, and B. S. Cave. H. H. and A. S. Taylor are both
Old Merchant Taylors, but the club was hardly started in
their playing days. The Pearsons, Green, Prescott, Disbrowe, and others, have been among their best forwards.

Mention should also be made of such Old Boys' clubs
as the Old Cheltonians and Old Paulines, but their
existence is chiefly with a view to the sentimental end
of playing football every Saturday with old school chums.
By thus having to represent the old school club Saturday after Saturday, a great many good players are
prevented from joining other clubs.

Kensington.—This club has for many years been able
to show a respectable record, which it has maintained,
not so much by the brilliancy of its players as the
thoroughness of its forward game, albeit, of a rather
old-fashioned type. It has always been notorious as a
difficult club to beat. Last season they were the only
London club who defeated the London Scottish. The
forwards atoned for the lack of pace and style by honest
grit and hard work. Dix, a very dangerous runner when
he gets off, has been of inestimable value to the team, which
may be described as a stopping and not a scoring one.
The veteran Elliott, who still plays, Gardner, the brothers
Currick, all noted boxers, have contributed an immense
amount of muscle to the physically powerful team.

Harlequins.—One of the oldest of London clubs,
and numerically one of the strongest. Any Saturday
they can put three teams in the field, and with such
materials at hand they only require some Yorkshire
stingo to place them far higher in the scale of success.
They have always been able to take away teams to meet

clubs out of London. A couple of years ago, when the
brothers Surtees were at their best, and Leake was at
command, the team was a really strong one. It is one
of the few London clubs which is endowed with a large
amount of *esprit de corps*, and can boast of having
evolved Stoddart and Jeffery, who afterwards migrated
to Blackheath. The great services of W. Burnand, now
in Russia, and Cipriani, who still plays, call for special
mention.

Middlesex Wanderers.—Originally founded by Trimmer
and others, from a nucleus of Old Rugbeians: have had
a fairly successful career, but not an even one. A few
years back they had a very consistent forward team, but
have never had pace or style enough to rank in the first
class. With Hooper, Miller, and Orr behind the scrummage they are still formidable, but until they can
command a regular set of forwards with a determined
and definite style, they will never obtain the success
which their straightforward style of play is entitled to.

St. Thomas's Hospital.—During the last five years this
hospital has played a prominent part in Metropolitan
football, and may be said to be the only hospital which
has so far mastered a scientific game, or which has been
able to hold its own in first-class company. For three
years they have carried off the Inter-Hospital Challenge
Cup, and amongst other notable achievements, beat
Cambridge in the past season. F. J. Goodhue and J. H.
Dewhirst, both International players, are the best known
of their forwards, while behind the scrummage, W. E.
Bromet, sen., and P. Northcote have contributed largely
to the successes of the club.

Cooper's Hill.—Fifteen years ago the engineering
college at Egham was very nearly at the top of the tree.
In the past it has brought out such famous International
players as Finney, Price, Hutchinson, Macleod, Fowler.
At the present time the team is of medium strength, but
a long way behind the form of old days. It may be due
to boys leaving school earlier than they used to, but the
fact remains that their recent fifteens are composed of
very much smaller men than of old, and not to be compared in physique to their predecessors. They have

lately been fairly successful against minor clubs, but cannot hold their own in first-rate company.

The Clapham Rovers.—This club holds a unique record in the football world. From the foundation in 1869 the club has been a leading organisation both in the Association and in the Rugby games. Its prowess under the Association code is evinced by the success of the team in 1879 and in 1880. In the former year the Clapham Rovers were the runners-up for the Association Cup, and in the latter they won the trophy. This peculiar feature in the constitution and history of the club obtained for the Rovers the sobriquet of the "Hybrid Club," a title bestowed somewhat in ridicule, but, as events have turned out, destined to be the most honourable appellation that could have been selected for this remarkable organisation.

The club was formed on the 10th August, 1869. The circular calling the meeting was issued by W. E. Rawlinson, who, on the formation of the club, was elected hon. secretary. It was agreed to play under both codes, Association rules to be played one week, and Rugby the other. The first match was played on the 25th September, 1869, against the Wanderers, at that time the strongest Association playing club. The Rovers won by one goal to none, and were much complimented on their splendid organisation by C. W. Alcock, the Wanderers' captain.

They were equally successful under Rugby rules, and by January, 1870, the membership was sufficiently strong to enable the club to play two matches every Saturday, one under each code. At the close of the season only two matches had been lost, one under each rules, and in both instances the return match was won, viz., under Rugby rules, with the Marlborough Nomads; and under Association, with Charterhouse School.

W. E. Rawlinson continued to hold the office of hon. secretary and treasurer till the end of the season 1873, and it is in a great measure due to his indefatigable exertions that the club owe their successful start. For many seasons they more than held their own with the best clubs in the Metropolitan district, and though the club has not in the last few seasons won so many of its matches as heretofore, it still ranks as one of the best clubs. From 1870 to 1881 the club played 151 Rugby games, winning 80, losing 30, and drawing 41.

In the second season, 1871-2, R. H. Birkett was captain, and with the assistance of his brother, L. Birkett, Crampton, and Walker made about the strongest combination of the time behind the scrummage. C. C. Bryden played this season, and, like R. H. Birkett, was found playing the Association game almost as often as Rugby. The club played Richmond for the first time on the 21st October, 1871, and won the match by 1 goal and 2 tries. R. H. Birkett (2 tries), C. C. Bryden (1 try). Three Birketts and two Brydens played in this match. At the end of the season the club, who so far had played on Clapham Common, moved to a field at Balham, where they continued to play till 1876, when they moved to Wandsworth, where they still play.

R. S. WHALLEY.

Rosslyn Park.—As a club which has been steadily making its way to the front rank, Rosslyn Park deserves a brief mention. Founded in 1879 with about a score of playing members, and with the modest ambition of vanquishing the second fifteens of such clubs as Hornsey and the Arabs, the club is now able to get matches with both the Universities and all the strongest Metropolitan organisations. For this success it has mainly to thank a succession of devoted officials, of whom C. C. H. Miller was the first, and A. Reid, who has recently resigned his post to J. B. Jackson, the last. It was about two years ago that a third fifteen of Rosslyn Park first boasted a regular fixture list and that Rosslyn Park men found their way into the Middlesex fifteen. Reid, who as secretary has been the life and soul of the club, has also been of great use to his side in the field, playing equally well at full-back and at three-quarter. His chief virtues as a player are the coolness and judgment which are born of long experience, and a remarkable amount of steady courage which is particularly valuable in defence. This quality he has shown in county matches, and by it he gained his Middlesex cap. E. Figgis, a dashing and clean forward, C. Nicholas, a hard worker of somewhat fine physique, and J. Lamont, a fair half-back, have also been selected for similar honours. The other regular half-back of the team, R. F. Chaldecott, has frequently played for Surrey. Chaldecott is a sturdy and fast player, who in anything below first-class company never fails to distinguish himself, and invariably requires watching. He cannot be said to have a genius for the passing game, but even in this respect is not inferior to the average half-back of the best London clubs. Among the three-quarters must be mentioned H. C. L. Tindall, the champion quarter-miler, who two or three seasons back rendered the club good service; it can also occasionally reckon on the assistance of D. G. Anderson and G. C. Lindsay, the London Scottish players, who are both on the roll of members. But it is principally to sterling forward play and fair combination throughout the team that the Rosslyn Park Club has owed its success up to the present, and to search for "stars" among its players is to render scant justice to the fifteen. The ground of the club is now at Acton, but it is worthy of note that it was originally a North London club playing at Gospel Oak, whence, after draining the ground for the benefit of its successors, it was in 1885 evicted mercilessly. That football clubs are so few in the Northern suburbs is doubtless due partly to the great difficulty of renting fields at a reasonable price, and partly to the outlay that is necessary to make a deep and heavy clay soil suitable for use in winter. The clubs which have triumphed over these obstacles have been very few, and that Rosslyn Park has been one of them, may be put down in no small measure to the activity of A. Reid, the only surviving member who was among the original founders.

CHAPTER XVIII.

COUNTY FOOTBALL.

THE COUNTY CHAMPIONSHIP.

CURIOUSLY enough county football dates from an earlier period than even the Rugby Union. The first contest between two counties was the encounter between Lancashire and Yorkshire at Leeds in the year 1870, whereas the Rugby Union did not come into existence until the year 1871, and the first International match was played in the same year. But whilst International matches have been conducted with regularity since their institution, county football has been of a fluctuating nature. True, the Lancashire and Yorkshire match has been an annual and regular fixture, but as regards other counties there have been periods of spasmodic vitality followed by cycles of inactive torpidity. This has been pre-eminently the case as regards Southern counties, and more especially in respect of the Metropolitan counties. The reasons are not far to seek. With reference to football in and about London, the county fixtures do not contain the same exciting elements as exist in club matches.

But, notwithstanding many unfavourable influences in the South, county football has been fostered and has flourished. The Middlesex player, whilst having little interest in an encounter with Surrey or Kent, has been fired with the spirit of rivalry as between North and South, when meeting the two great northern counties of Lancashire and Yorkshire; and the absence of annual fixtures between these two counties and Middlesex has been due to other causes than lack of enthusiasm on the part of the Southern player. The gate-money

YORKSHIRE (CHAMPION COUNTY) TEAM v ENGLAND: HALIFAX, FEBRUARY 23, 1889.

(ENGLAND—3 GOALS. YORKSHIRE—NIL.)

J. W. SYKES. M. NEWSOME (President). J. TOOTHILL. F. W. LOWRIE. G. JACKETTS. J. A. MILLER (Hon. Sec.). H. WILKINSON.
W. STADLER. R. E. LOCKWOOD. F. BONSOR (Capt.). H. BEDFORD. J. H. JONES. E. HOLMES.
J. W. SUTCLIFFE. A. L. BROOKE. D. JOWET.
J. DODD.

(From a Photograph by R. T. Watson, Anlaby Road, Hull.)

x

taken at Southern county matches is insignificant compared with the ample funds at the disposal of the Northern executives. Hence financial difficulties have been a great factor in the inability of Southern counties to meet their more fortunate (in a pecuniary sense) rivals of the Northern counties on equal terms. It is true, that grants have been made by certain Northern counties to Southern teams to enable them to carry out their fixtures, but this is not a satisfactory method of conducting county football.

Whilst thus alluding to the Metropolitan portion of Southern football, it is satisfactory to note that the Western counties have exhibited much more consistency and regularity in bringing off county fixtures. Devonshire, Somersetshire, and Gloucestershire have been noteworthy for managing their county clubs with much greater enthusiasm than that evidenced in the London district. The Midland counties, too, have not been backward in turning out teams representative of football in the Midlands. Naturally it has been impossible for either the Western or Midland counties to meet *all* rival counties, nor is it desirable that such should be the case. It is not so in cricket. Nottinghamshire, Surrey, Lancashire, Yorkshire, and other counties would find it impossible to arrange cricket fixtures with every other county in England. And if this is the case in cricket, it is more so as regards football. County football to a great extent calls upon clubs to let off their players from club matches to assist their county, and a plethora of county matches would lead to either the formation of a county fifteen, the members of which would play only occasionally for a club, or the abandonment of county fixtures through the unwillingness and inability of clubs to allow their players to assist in the county fixtures. No doubt a visit made by a Middlesex, Lancashire, or Yorkshire team to the Western or Midland counties is most attractive and exceedingly beneficial to football; but from the nature of the game in which club is the principal factor, and which is fostered and developed by club interests, it is manifestly impossible to arrange such a series of county fixtures as would practically compel a player to abandon the interests of his club, in order to place his services unreservedly at the disposal of the County Committee.

It is in the North that county football reigns supreme. Lancashire, Yorkshire, Cheshire, Northumberland, and Durham have for many years kept up an unbroken series of county matches, and of late years Cumberland has been coming to the front. In these counties there is a genuine and sustained interest in county games, and the rivalry is both healthy and of great service to the game. The County cap in Yorkshire is a coveted honour, and players contend eagerly with one another for a place in the ranks of the county fifteen. As a rule, clubs are eager to place the services of their players at the disposal of the county executive. Many a member of the Yorkshire County Committee has found himself in bad odour with his Club Committee, because he has failed to obtain a place in the county team for a player whom the supporters and enthusiasts of his club consider to be far more skilful than some who have been more fortunate than he in being selected for the team. This is a healthy sign. Of course, in one sense it is ridiculous. Very often it means calling a goose a swan—in fact, the absurd one-sided partisanship, which biases the judgment and colours the opinions of the average club supporter in Yorkshire and Lancashire, cannot be realised save by those who have had the amusing experience of fraternising with these enthusiasts and of hearing them (generally in the vernacular of the particular district) express their sentiments with respect to the player in question, and also their flattering (?) opinion with regard to the selecting body. But still that the feeling exists is a healthy sign. The gentleman player may at times be inclined to regret that the popularity of the game has resulted in the introduction of a class of players who may not be the equal socially of the player of former days. The workingman has made the game his own, and has clearly demonstrated his ability and skill, and so has earned his place in county and international teams. It is therefore greatly to be rejoiced at that such is the enthusiasm and keenness of the workman player, that he is prepared to sacrifice work and wages for the coveted distinction of a County, Northern, or International cap. One, and that not the least, of the benefits to the game by county football in the North has been the effect which it has had in placing before the working-man a goal of ambition, which requires for attainment high and lofty motives, and which entails upon the successful aspirant a certain amount of sacrifice. The opposite has been the case in the Association game. There is no eager competition for places in the North and South, County and Association matches. On the contrary, the player being better paid for a club match feels no inducement to quit the club ranks in order to participate in a county match; whilst the club whose existence is dependent upon success in order to obtain the public support necessary to provide the funds to carry on club affairs is reluctant to grant permission to the player to assist his county or district association. This is very significant, and in commenting upon any point of the Rugby Code and comparing the same with the Association game it will be found that there is one very safe rule to follow. Has any particular feature shown a tendency to decline in the Association game, whilst at the same time it has continued to flourish and develop under Rugby rules? Then the observer may safely conclude that the fact of decline in one case, and growth in the other, is distinctly to the advantage of the Rugby game. And on this point—viz., the eagerness of players and clubs to support the county games—the Rugby Union may rest the confident expectation of the advancement of the best interests of the game in the Northern counties.

But such support has not always been given to the County Committee by clubs and players. The first notable instance in Yorkshire was on the occasion of the match with the Midland counties at Wakefield on November 18th, 1882, when J. Dodd and A. Wood of the Halifax Club were retained by their own club when chosen to play for Yorkshire. On that occasion the County Committee were content to apply moral suasion only, and, in writing to the Halifax Club reprimanding them for "assuming (what think ye of that word, ye Southern Clubites?) the right to keep men at home to play in their own club matches when their services are required for the county," went no further than intimating "that in the future players so doing will endanger their chance of being selected to play in any subsequent county match." This threat proved sufficient till November 22nd, 1884, when the Bradford Club, being on tour in the South of England, and playing a match with the Marlborough Nomads, declined to allow their players to take part in the Lancashire and Yorkshire match on the same day, and compelled them to go South with the rest of the Bradford team. Such conduct might have been passed over with a reprimand had victory smiled upon Yorkshire, but smarting under defeat at the hands of their ancient rivals, and influenced by the fact that Bradford, who scored against the Nomads no less than seven goals and four tries to nothing, would have won their match even without the aid of the county selections, the Yorkshire Committee dealt with the offence in a decided and decisive manner. As usual, punishment in future cases was to be inflicted through the medium of the Challenge Cup competition.

That such declarations and actions on the part of the Yorkshire Committee have been possible and effectual, conclusively shows in how different a light county football is regarded in the North compared with the South. Indeed, county football was organised for years ere it received official recognition from the governing body, and it was not till the season 1883-4 that rules of qualification for county players were adopted.

The institution of the County Championship marks a distinct era in county football, and may possibly galvanise into life the torpid energies of the Metropolitan counties. It is only since the season of 1888-9 that the title has received official recognition from the Rugby Union authorities. But the natural feeling of rivalry has caused counties in the past to put forward their claims to be considered the leading county of the year. Practically only three counties have by their achievements been able to put forward a legitimate claim for such distinction. Middlesex in the South, Lancashire and Yorkshire in the North, have exhibited form so markedly superior to other counties, that they only need be referred to when discussing the subject of County Championship during the years previous to the official institution of the same.

Of these Middlesex are practically placed out of court

by their own action in playing so few matches, and those at irregular intervals. This county, though able at all times to put a first-class team in the field, cannot for any period advance any substantial claim to be considered champion county. Lancashire may, therefore, be considered to have fairly established their pretensions to the position during the first decade of county matches. But in '81, '82, and '83, Yorkshire had a wonderful series of successes, and during those years were not beaten by any other county team, though in the spring of '84 they succumbed to the powerful Oxford team, which defeated them by a goal. For those years Yorkshire may fairly be considered champion, especially so for the season '83-'84, when Lancashire, Cheshire, Durham, Midland Counties, and Northumberland in turn succumbed to them. In '84-'85, Lancashire recovered their lost laurels, for not only did they defeat Yorkshire, but were also successful against Cheshire, Northumberland, and Durham. In '85-'86, Yorkshire, though defeating Lancashire, lost to Middlesex, so that the championship for that year may be considered in abeyance. In '86-'87, Lancashire drew with Yorkshire and defeated Middlesex, losing the match with Somerset. Middlesex defeated Yorkshire and lost to Lancashire. Yorkshire drew with Lancashire, lost to Middlesex, and defeated Somerset. In this cross calculation the partisans of the respective counties may be allowed to settle the premiership to suit their respective and special fancies. In '87-'88, Middlesex won all matches, defeating Durham, Yorkshire, Somerset, and Lancashire, thus establishing themselves as unquestionably the champions of that year. This season is also marked by the great advance of Somerset, who, though defeated by narrow margins by Lancashire and Middlesex, completely outplayed Yorkshire at Weston-super-Mare.

In '88-'89, the Rugby Union officially recognised the title of Champion County. Several causes conduced to this step. The dispute with the Unions of Scotland, Ireland, and Wales had led to the abandonment of International matches as far as the English Union was concerned. And so in '89 there had been a huge blank as regards the great matches of the year. England had been boycotted by the other Unions, and that year presented the unusual spectacle of an English International team being selected, and caps awarded, without the players having an opportunity of displaying their prowess against the picked players of the other counties. The Rugby Union depends for a main part of its funds upon the profits made upon the International matches of the year. The committee therefore were faced by two difficulties: on the one hand they were likely to have a deficit on the year's working, and on the other English players were deprived of the excitement and sport of the great matches. How were these difficulties to be met? It was suggested that two additional matches should be played, viz., a second North and South match, and that the Rugby Union should declare a champion county, which county should play the Rest of England. The suggestion was eagerly received and accordingly carried out.

The County Championship was inaugurated upon a very simple principle. As soon as the county matches for the year were played, the committee of the Union were to examine results and declare the county which they considered had the best record. In '88-'89 there was no difficulty in arriving at a conclusion which met with general approval. In that season Yorkshire had an extraordinary record, and won all their six county matches against Northumberland, Durham, Lancashire, Cheshire, Surrey, and Somerset, with consummate ease and by overwhelming scores. On Lancashire they inflicted a crushing defeat by 4 goals and 2 tries to nothing, exactly the great score obtained by Lancashire against them in '81. So superior were the form and combination of the Yorkshire players, that no less than eleven of them found places in the North team against the South. Further proof of the excellence of the Yorkshire team was furnished in the match against the New Zealand team at Wakefield, when the Maoris sustained the most decisive defeat of their tour, being vanquished by no less a score than that of 5 goals and a try to a goal and a try. In treating of the champion team a criticism of their play cannot be omitted, though any praise of their achievements must not be construed into neglect to appreciate the merits of their rivals and opponents. Yorkshire in '88-'89 had a wonderful team, and it is open to dispute if any county, at any time, put a fifteen into the field which could have lowered the colours of the champions of that season. Eleven members of the North team and seven Internationals is a record without precedent in the modern days of the Rugby Union, when clubs and players have so increased in numbers. Vassall's Oxford team is the only combination that in recent times can boast of more brilliant achievements in the gaining of International honours. The forwards were exceptionally heavy and fast, and their combined rush was almost irresistible. Their keenness in following up and their quick play generally made the "Yorkshire rush" almost proverbial. They had successfully developed the system of not going back to help their backs, but of waiting to have the ball returned. In this they were materially assisted by the marvellous kicking of Sutcliffe, the centre three-quarter, who, by his long and accurate drops and punts into touch, invariably saved the forwards and rendered the system possible. Bonsor, Stadden, and Wright, all Internationals, furnished a trio of half-backs who, whilst scorers themselves, were thorough adepts at the passing game, and thus enabled Sutcliffe, Lockwood, and Brooke, at three-quarters, to make full use of their undoubted abilities. But when pitted against the Rest of England, at Halifax, on February 23rd, 1889, the Yorkshiremen failed to maintain their reputation, and were easily defeated by 3 goals to *nil*. The credit of the victory lay mainly with F. R. H. Alderson, A. E. Stoddart, and F. Evershed. Alderson's display at centre three-quarter was a most finished and scientific exhibition, and even the Tykes were compelled to admit that on that day's form he ought to have represented England against the Maoris instead of J. W. Sutcliffe. The latter's play was tame in the extreme, and his failure to exhibit his real form was a main cause of Yorkshire's defeat. Frank Evershed had every opportunity of breaking away in his own particular style, and his play quite electrified the spectators, who were unanimous in awarding the speedy Burton man the palm as champion forward of the year. The defeat was a great blow to the Yorkshiremen, who had regarded victory as a certainty, but there can be no doubt that the better team on the day won, and that the champion county was not seen quite at its best. The record for Yorkshire in the season 1888-89 was as follows :—

YORKSHIRE MATCHES, 1888-9.

	Yorkshire. G. T.	Opponents. G. T.
Nov. 10.—*v.* Northumberland	4 3	0 1
Nov. 17.—*v.* Durham	3 1	0 0
Nov. 24.—*v.* Lancashire	4 2	0 0
Dec. 3.—*v.* Surrey	0 3	0 0
Feb. 9.—*v.* Cheshire	3 3	0 1
Feb. 16.—*v.* Somerset	2 3	0 1
	16 15	0 3

Played, 7; won, 7; lost, 0; drawn, 0.

*Dec. 12.—*v.* New Zealand Team	1 3	2 4
Jan. 19.—*v.* New Zealand Team	5 1	1 1
Feb. 23.—*v.* England	0 0	3 0

It is a matter of regret that Yorkshire in this season did not meet Middlesex.

In 1889-90 Yorkshire were again to the fore, but, though undefeated, they could not boast of the brilliant record of the previous season, and draws with Middlesex and Cheshire were unsatisfactory items in the season's records. Lancashire, Durham, Northumberland, Surrey, Kent, and Somerset were defeated, but the great scores of the previous year were conspicuous by their absence. As some explanation of the draw with Middlesex it should be remembered that early in the game M. Wise, of Otley, half-back, was incapacitated by a strained knee. Middlesex had far the best of the play, and Yorkshire, thus handicapped, were exceedingly fortunate in making a draw of the game. The Rugby Union had no difficulty in awarding the championship, and the match was played at Bradford on February 22nd, 1890, when, contrary to expectation, the Rest of England were defeated by 1 goal and 3 tries to a goal and a try. Thus Yorkshire with a weaker team than in the previous year completely reversed the verdict, and not only won the match by so decisive a score, but also had much the best of the game. England certainly were not so strong as the year before, several men being unable to take part in the match. Naturally, as the match does not entitle a player to wear the England cap, men are not so keen in getting off to play as they would be were the match an International match proper. But Yorkshire were weaker comparatively.

* This was only a second team of Yorkshire.

YORKSHIRE (CHAMPION COUNTY) TEAM V. ENGLAND: BRADFORD, FEBRUARY 22, 1890.

(YORKSHIRE—1 GOAL, 3 TRIES. ENGLAND—1 GOAL, 1 TRY.)

(*From a Photograph by R. T. Watson, Aulaby Road, Hull.*)

Lockwood was unable to play through illness, and Lowrie, damaged, was also compelled to stand down, the place of centre three-quarter being taken by S. Eastwood, of the Brighouse Rangers. D. Jowett, who had been placed on the reserve, the result of slack play in previous matches, took the place of Lowrie, and right well did the giant justify his right to form one of Yorkshire's premier fifteen. England early took the lead, and with a goal, dropped by Crompton, and a try to the good, it seemed as if the result of the match would be as in the preceding year, but the Yorkshire forwards pulling themselves together gave a most finished exhibition of determined forward play. Time after time the England backs made ground by kicking or running, only to see their forwards lose the advantage through the irresistible rush of the Yorkshiremen. The Yorkshire forward play was a revelation to the Rugby Union magnates who were watching the game, and though Stadden at half passed well, and Dyson of Huddersfield ran brilliantly, their efforts would have been of no avail had not the forwards so completely routed the opposing forces. But the Yorkshire victory was of more than passing or of local moment. Gratifying as it was to the champion county to find its representatives capable of defeating the Rest of England, the result of the match was most important to the interests of the English team. The match between the Champion County and the Rest of England was sandwiched between the International matches with Wales and Scotland. '89-'90 saw the renewal of International fixtures, and the Saturday previous to the champion match England had met Wales at Dewsbury and been defeated. Consternation had seized upon the Rugby Union Executive. Scotland was to be met in a fortnight. How were the English forwards who had been routed by the Welshmen to be depended upon to meet the sturdy, strong play of the Scotsmen? If ever England desired to win the Scotch match it was on this occasion when the International dispute was arranged. On the evening after the Welsh match everything pointed to the victory of the Scotsmen. The Yorkshire triumph of the succeeding Saturday was like a gleam of sunshine breaking through the lowering clouds. As rush succeeded rush bearing back the England forwards with irresistible onslaught, it was apparent that in the Yorkshire team were to be found the men capable of stemming the Scotch forwards, and if Scotland could be held in check forward the English backs could be depended upon to win the day. Accordingly Yorkshire furnished no less than five of the forward brigade: Dyson, of Huddersfield, being chosen as three-quarter, and Bonsor as half-back, the champion county thus supplying seven of the International fifteen in *the* match of all International matches. And right well did the Yorkshiremen acquit themselves, though Bonsor, through a sprained knee, was unable to play. How magnificently the Scotch forwards strove in the last twenty minutes to gain a point to reverse the verdict, and how sturdily the English forwards met these mighty efforts! England were leading by a goal and a try to nothing, yet so persistently did the Scotsmen keep up the attack in English quarters that hope did not desert the Northmen, nor anxiety depart from the Englishmen till the call of time. Had there been any flinching on the part of the English forwards, the stern determination of the Scotsmen would have triumphed and have altered the issue of the match. The defeat of England by Yorkshire, March, 1890, will always be remembered as having resulted in the victory over Scotland by revealing the merit and determination of the forward contingent of the Yorkshire team.

The record of the champion county for the season '89-'90 was as follows:—

YORKSHIRE MATCHES, 1889-90.

	Yorkshire.		Opponents.	
	G.	T.	G.	T.
Nov. 9.—*v.* Durham	4	1	0	1
Nov. 16.—*v.* Northumberland	1	4	0	1
Nov. 23.—*v.* Lancashire	1	0	0	0
Dec. 9.—*v.* Middlesex	0	0	0	0
Dec. 16.—*v.* Surrey	2	4	1	1
Jan. 4.—*v.* Somerset	0	1	0	0
Jan. 6.—*v.* Kent	2	2	0	0
Feb. 8.—*v.* Cheshire	0	4	1	1
	10	16	2	4

Played, 8; won, 6; lost, 0; drawn, 2.

| Feb. 22.—*v.* England | 1 | 3 | 1 | 1 |

In the season '90-'91, Yorkshire was deposed from the place of proud pre-eminence. But ere this took place a change had taken place in the conditions of the County Championship.

Yorkshire submitted a scheme for the regulation of the County Championship which was unanimously accepted at the October meeting of the Union. Of course, the simplest and easiest method would have been to declare so many counties first-class counties and to leave them to enter the contest for the championship; but this plan met with the expressed disapproval of so many counties who saw themselves by it entirely cut off from any chance of championship honours that it had to be abandoned, and so the problem to be solved was rendered somewhat complex, the three main principles being as follows:—First, it was absolutely necessary for a genuine competition which should guarantee that, as far as possible, the best county should come to the front, that no arrangement should be arrived at which would give any advantage to any particular county. Secondly, such was the eagerness evinced by different counties to enter the competition that provision for all counties must be made. Thirdly, the geographical position and financial condition of the counties had to be considered, whilst at the same time an enormous increase of county matches would practically render the scheme impossible. Keeping these three principles in view, Yorkshire proposed the division of the counties into four groups: the North-Eastern, North-Western, South-Eastern, and South-Western, and that the counties in each group should play amongst themselves to decide the leading county of the group. This was to be the first stage of the competition. The second stage was then to be fought out between the respective group winners, the most successful of which was to be declared champion county.

In 1890-91, Lancashire were indisputably the champion county, and their record was almost without precedent. This year, the first season under formal rules for the championship, was marked by surprises. Middlesex, defeated by Surrey, were unexpectedly deprived of the position of group winner in the South-Eastern section. Gloucester, after playing an undecided match with Somersetshire, by defeating that county were returned winners for the South-Western group. Lancashire and Yorkshire were the winners of the North-

Western and North-Eastern groups respectively. Practically the championship was decided by the defeat of Yorkshire by Lancashire at Whalley Range on November 29th, 1890, for with only Surrey and Gloucester to meet in the other groups, the success of the Red Rose was a matter of almost absolute certainty. In their encounter with Lancashire, Yorkshire were undoubtedly unfortunate in very early losing the services of their full-back, S. Mawson, who broke his collar-bone in tackling Valentine, but this accident cannot be quoted as accounting for the Yorkshire defeat. The Lancastrians won by superior combination, especially amongst the forwards and in the half-backs as a link between the forwards and the three-quarters. The Yorkshire eight fought manfully against the opposing nine in the first half of the game, at the conclusion of which Yorkshire were leading by a try; but numbers and combination told at the finish, and Lancashire won handsomely by 2 goals 1 try, to 1 try.

The record of the competition for the County Championship for the season is appended.

COUNTY CHAMPIONSHIPS, 1890-91.

PRELIMINARY SERIES.

(1) NORTH-WESTERN GROUP.

	Lan.	Ches.	Cum.	West.	W.	L.	D.	F.	A.
Lancashire	—	w.	w.	w.	3	0	0	35	2
Westmorland	L.	—	w.	—	1	1	0	4	16
Cheshire	L.	—	—	—	0	1	0	0	7
Cumberland	L.	—	—	·	0	1	0	2	16

(2) NORTH-EASTERN GROUP.

	Yks.	Dur.	North.	W.	L.	D.	F.	A.
Yorkshire	—	w.	w.	2	0	0	14	1
Durham	L.	—	w.	1	1	0	3	6
Northumberland	L.	L.	—	0	2	0	1	11

(3) SOUTH-EASTERN GROUP.

	Mid.	Sur.	Kent.	Sus.	W.	L.	D.	F.	A.
Surrey	w.	—	w.	—	2	0	0	8	4
Middlesex	—	L.	w.	—	1	1	0	11	5
Kent	L.	L.	—	—	0	2	0	1	11
Sussex	—	—	—	—	0	0	0	0	0

(4) SOUTH-WESTERN GROUP.

	Som.	Dev.	Glou.	M.C.	W.	L.	D.	F.	A.
Gloucestershire	D.W.	—	—	w.	2	0	6	8	0
Somersetshire	—	w.	D.L.	—	1	1	6	7	3
Midland Counties	—	w.	L.	—	1	1	0	13	8
Devonshire	L.	—	—	L.	0	2	0	3	20

SECOND SERIES.

	Lanc.	Yks.	Sur.	Glou.	W.	L.	D.	Points. F.	A.
1. Lancashire	—	w.	w.	w.	3	0	0	35	1
2. Yorkshire	L.	—	w.	—	1	1	0	12	7
3. Surrey	L.	L.	—	—	0	2	0	0	25
4. Gloucestershire ...	L.	—	—	—	0	1	0	0	14

LANCASHIRE MATCHES, 1890–91.

	Lancashire. G. T.	Opponents. G. T.
Nov. 8.—*v.* Cheshire ...	2 1	0 0
Nov. 15.—*v.* Northumberland	3 6	0 1
Nov. 22.—*v.* Westmorland	4 4	0 0
Nov. 29.—*v.* Yorkshire ...	2 1	0 1
Jan. 10.—*v.* Devonshire ...	2 5	0 2
Jan. 24.—*v.* Durham ...	1 4	0 1
Feb. 15.—*v.* Surrey ...	3 5	0 0
Feb. 28.—*v.* Cumberland ...	3 3	0 1
Mar. 14.—*v.* Gloucestershire	4 2	0 0
	24 31	0 6

Played, 9; won, 9; lost, 0.

Mar. 9.—*v.* Ulster ...	3 2	0 0
Apr. 18.—*v.* England	1 0	1 1

Such figures speak for themselves, and conclusively show that the championship was fairly earned by Lancashire in 1890-91, and yet only three Lancastrians, J. Berry, R. P. Wilson, and T. Kent played for England, though D. Gwynn and W. McCutcheon figured as Welsh Internationals. Lancashire's strength in 1890-91 lay in their combination and evenness. Though only Wilson and Kent, as forwards, were selected for England, it is doubtful whether their play was much superior to the worst forward of the nine. A more hard-working, evenly-balanced set of forwards has rarely been combined in the same county team. Berry and Cross behind them were an excellent pair of halves in a winning game, and by feeding Gwynn in the centre enabled the Lancashire three-quarters to indulge in the modern scientific passing game to perfection. The advent of Berry and Cross from Westmorland, and the happy circumstance that caused Gwynn and McCutcheon to locate themselves in Oldham, furnished Lancashire with the needed addition to the strength of their team, and caused that county to be represented in 1890-91 by the most finished combination amongst county teams in recent times.

The match *v.* the Rest of England, played at Whalley

LANCASHIRE (CHAMPION COUNTY) TEAM v. ENGLAND: MANCHESTER, APRIL 18, 1891.

(ENGLAND—1 GOAL, 1 TRY.   LANCASHIRE—1 TRY.)

(From a Photograph by R. T. Watson, Hull.)

T. CRAVEN,   T. ROTHWELL,   J. BERRY,   W. MCCUTCHEON,   J. PYKE,   T. KENT,   J. STRAND,
E. H. FLOWER,   T. WHITTAKER,   J. VALENTINE (Capt.),   W. ATKINSON,   T. MULLADEW,   T. COOP.
E. BULLOUGH,   D. GWYNNE,   W. CROSS,   H. P. WILSON.

Range on April 18th, 1891, was confidently looked upon by Lancastrians as likely to result in a win for the county. Nothing would have better suited the partisans of the county team than to record a success against England, and by that to put themselves on a par with their rivals of Yorkshire the season previous. The result of the match was a severe blow to their aspirations. For England Mitchell was unable to appear as full back, whilst Christopherson, three-quarter, and Leake, half, were also absentees; but, despite these defections, England put a strong team into the field, comparatively much stronger than the one which opposed Yorkshire in 1889-90, so, had the Lancastrians been successful, their victory would have been specially meritorious. The Lancashire combination told at the start, and they early obtained a goal from a try by Valentine. Pressing England strongly, there were but few who anticipated the defeat of the county. But the England forwards getting more together as the match proceeded gave their backs more opportunities, and at the close England had won by a goal and a try to a goal. The feature of the match was the ubiquitous character of the game played by Alderson, the English captain, who, but for a decided tendency to press the wing three-quarters near touch ere passing to them, gave a perfect exposition of centre three-quarter play. Lancashire may attribute their defeat to sheer hard luck, for McCutcheon, dropping at goal, kicked the ball over the bar, but to his mortification found that the officials decided that it had touched Alderson in its flight. Then some informality in taking the ball out for the second England try was also overruled. Had either of these points gone in Lancashire's favour, as they well might have done, the verdict of the match would have been reversed.

The season of 1891-92 saw Yorkshire recover her lost laurels. The group winners were Lancashire, Yorkshire, Midland Counties, and Kent, the latter county overcoming Middlesex in a close match, remarkable for the plucky manner in which the Kent men pulled the game off in the last few minutes. Had Middlesex won in the South-Eastern group the second stage would have been more interesting, as the Kent team proved to be no match for Yorkshire when these counties met at York, and so, as in 1890-91, the County Championship was virtually decided

Y

YORKSHIRE (CHAMPION COUNTY) TEAM *V.* ENGLAND: LEEDS, FEBRUARY 20, 1892.

(YORKSHIRE—2 TRIES. ENGLAND—*NIL*.)

J. TOOTHILL. E. DEWHIRST. W. NICHOL. D. JOWETT. F. WOOD. W. GOLDTHORPE.
H. BRAMSHAW. H. VARLEY. W. E. BROMET. A. BROADLEY. E. REDMAN. BARRON KILNER (*President*).
A. BRIGGS.   J. DYSON.   R. E. LOCKWOOD.   A. GOLDTHORPE.

by the Lancashire v. Yorkshire match. For the first time a county match was decided by a penalty kick, the Yorkshiremen having the good fortune to kick a goal from a free kick allowed for an infringement of the rules by the Lancashire full-back delaying to play the ball when tackled. As Lancashire had had two free kicks allowed them, both of which had failed, it would seem that the fortune of war was rather in favour of Yorkshire. The weather was unfavourable, and the ground very heavy, but despite all these disadvantages the game was fast and open, and most evenly contested, though the Tykes were slightly the better team. At this period of the season Lancashire and Yorkshire were very evenly matched, but as the season progressed the Yorkshire team, through judicious changes and constant practice, improved considerably, and when England were met at Leeds outplayed their opponents, and won by 2 tries to *nil*, a score which does not adequately represent their superiority over the Rest of England. As a consequence, eight Yorkshiremen played against Scotland, viz., Dyson and Lockwood, three-quarters; Varley and Briggs, half-backs; and Bromet, Toothill, Nichol, and Bradshaw, forwards. This selection is proof of the all-round calibre of the Yorkshire team. Again, as in 1890, were the Yorkshiremen the backbone of the England team v. Scotland, and once more after Yorkshire had beaten the Rest of England, did England score a victory against the Scotsmen. In the four years that the championship has been instituted Yorkshire have been successful three times, and have twice beaten the Rest of England.

The following is the record for the year :—

COUNTY CHAMPIONSHIP, 1891-92.

PRELIMINARY SERIES.

(1) NORTH-WESTERN GROUP.

	Lan.	Ches.	Cum.	West.	W.	L.	D.	Points. F.	A.
Lancashire	—	w.	w.	—	2	0	0	19	5
Westmorland	—	w.	L.	—	1	1	0	7	27
Cheshire	L.	—	w.	L.	1	2	0	11	25
Cumberland	L.	L.	—	w.	1	2	0	35	25

(2) NORTH-EASTERN GROUP.

	Yks.	Dur.	North.	W.	L.	D.	Points. F.	A.
Yorkshire	—	w.	w.	2	0	0	49	7
Durham	L.	—	L.	0	2	0	7	21
Northumberland	L.	w.	—	1	1	0	4	32

RUGBY FOOTBALL.

(3) South-Eastern Group.

	Mid.	Sur.	Kent.	Sus.	E.Cts.	W.	L.	D.	Points. F.	A.
Surrey ...	L.	—	L.	w.	w.	2	2	0	... 42	22
Middlesex ...	—	w.	L.	w.	w.	3	1	0	... 58	17
Kent ...	w.	w.	—	w.	w.	4	0	0	... 46	18
Sussex ...	L.	L.	L.	—	w.	1	3	0	... 7	32
Eastern Counties	L.	L.	L.	L.	—	0	4	0	... 7	71

(4) South-Western Group.

	Som.	Dev.	Glou.	M. C.	W.	L.	D.	F.	A.
Gloucestershire	...	w.	—	L.	1	1	1	... 9	9
Somersetshire ...	—	w.	D.	L.	1	1	1	... 16	2
Midland Counties	w.	w.	w.	—	3	0	0	... 18	2
Devonshire ...	L.	—	L.	L.	0	3	0	... 2	32

Second Series.

	Lan.	Yks.	Kent.	M.C.	W.	L.	D.	F.	A.
1. Lancashire ...	—	L.	—	w.	1	1	0	... 4	3
2. Yorkshire ...	w.	—	w.	w.	3	0	0	... 38	5
3. Kent ...	—	L.	—	—	0	1	0	... 5	27
4. Midland Counties ...	L.	L.	—	—	0	2	0	... 0	12

Yorkshire Matches.

	Yorkshire. G.	T.	Pts.		Opponents. G.	T.	Pts.
v. Durham ...	3	1	17	...	1	1	7
v. Northumberland ...	4	6	32	...	0	0	0
v. Lancashire ...	1	0	3	...	0	0	0
v. Somerset ...	3	2	19	...	1	1	7
v. Devon ...	1	5	15	...	0	0	0
v. Kent ...	3	6	27	...	1	0	5
v. Cheshire ...	2	1	12	...	1	4	13
v. Midland Counties ...	1	2	8	...	0	0	0
	18	23	133	...	4	6	32

Played, 8; won, 7; lost, 1.

| v. England ... | 0 | 2 | 4 | ... | 0 | 0 | 0 |

CHAPTER XIX.

COUNTY FOOTBALL: LANCASHIRE.

By A. M. Crook.

NO work on Rugby football would be complete without some record of the important part played by this County Palatine in the history of the game, and although it is very little more than a quarter of a century since the introduction of the Rugby Code into Lancashire, its rise and progress have been of so remarkable a character that space will only allow a passing reference to the principal events and topics of interest during that period. Under the circumstances, attention is drawn more particularly to county and early club football.

LANCASHIRE COUNTY.

In dealing with this subject it is necessary to refer back to the year 1870, when the first match arranged for the county of Lancashire took place, at Leeds *v.* Yorkshire, and this fixture, which has been arranged annually ever since that time, has done more to encourage and advance the popularity of the Rugby game in the North than any other combination of circumstances, for to-day the "Battle of the Roses" is considered the "blue ribbon" of Northern football, and to be included in the team of either county is the ambition of young players, for it is looked upon as the high road to International honours.

In the earlier matches from 1870 to 1881 the government and arrangement of county matches in Lancashire were vested solely in the hands of the committee of the Manchester Football Club, who constituted themselves the recognised authorities for the selection of players, etc., although there appears to have been a mutual understanding between themselves and the Liverpool

Club. It is true that the management of county affairs had been attended with conspicuous success, but as new clubs sprang into existence and county matches became more frequent, it was soon apparent that the easiest and most effectual way to obtain county fame was by membership and obligation created by playing for the club who had these honours at their disposal; and complaints were loudly raised by younger organisations that they were powerless to prevent the migration of their players into the ranks of the premier club. Nor could the player be altogether blamed, for if he wished to gratify his ambition and advance himself in the football world, it was the soundest policy he could adopt. Such was the position of affairs in 1881, when this monopoly of power in the opinion of many had become so intolerable, that in the early part of that year an agitation was commenced by W. Bell, the hon. secretary of the Broughton Football Club, with the object solely in the first instance of securing for some of the leading clubs a voice in the selection of county teams. Although W. Bell initiated the movement, he was assisted and supported in the preliminary stages of the agitation by an informal committee consisting of the following gentlemen:—G. C. Lindsay (Manchester Rangers), A. M. Crook (Free Wanderers), F. C. Hignett (Swinton), Hunter (Birch). These representatives met the representatives of the Manchester Club by arrangement, and appealed through them to the Manchester Committee to take the initiative in forming a representative committee. The Manchester authorities, however, declined, and on the 10th March, 1881, the Manchester secretary wrote stating "that it was the opinion of his committee that the interests of county football would not be better served by forming a general committee and disturbing the existing arrangement." From the very commence-

WM. BELL.

ment the movers in this matter had been careful to avoid even the appearance of opposition to the Manchester Club. Doubtless the motives which actuated the Manchester Committee in opposing the movement were a natural disinclination to transfer the government of county football (of which they were undoubtedly the founders) to an elected and representative body without being fully assured of its ultimate success. Be this as it may, after the refusal of the Manchester Club to co-operate a general meeting was called, and the following extract from a local newspaper of May 4th, 1881, will best describe the progress of affairs:—" Last Tuesday evening a meeting was held at the Mitre Hotel in this city, the purposes of which gathering are fraught with concerns of the utmost interest and importance to the Rugby Union game of football in the county of Lancaster. The meeting was called by five gentlemen (referring to those whose names have been mentioned) officially connected with the Manchester Rangers, Birch, Free Wanderers, Swinton, and Broughton, to take into consideration whether or not it is desirable to form a County Committee for the Palatinate, and all organisations which are affiliated with the Rugby Union received invitations to send a couple of delegates."

At this meeting a deputation was appointed to again wait upon the Manchester Club, and discuss the proposals which had been submitted, but the delegates met with little or no encouragement, and the interview was considered so unsatisfactory that it was determined to call another general meeting of Lancashire clubs for the 17th May, 1881. At this meeting the following clubs were represented:—Manchester Rangers, Free Wanderers, Broughton, Swinton, Walton, Rossendale, Oldham, Manchester Athletic, Rochdale Hornets, Chorley Birch, Cheetham. W. Bell reported that the deputation appointed at a previous meeting had met the Manchester Committee with a view to securing the co-operation of the Manchester Club, and a letter was read from J. MacLaren, declining on behalf of the Manchester Club to take part in the movement.

It was then moved by W. Bell, seconded by G. C. Lindsay—

> That a Lancashire Football Union be, and hereby is, formed, the Union to consist of the clubs represented at this meeting, together with

any other clubs, members of the Rugby Union, who may signify their intention of joining the Lancashire Union within three months from this date.

Carried unanimously.

The following gentlemen were subsequently elected officers of the Lancashire Football Union:—

COMMITTEE:
T. S. Farr, A. Collier, H. Wyles, J. A. Berrington, H. Sheriff. W. Bell, hon. secretary. G. C. Lindsay, hon. treasurer.

A code of rules was adopted, and two county matches were actually arranged altogether apart from the Manchester Club, viz., *versus* the Midland Counties and Lanarkshire (Scotland).

The hearty response to the movement and the determined attitude shown by a majority of the Lancashire clubs ensured its success, for shortly afterwards the Manchester Committee recognised that opposition was useless; they bowed to the inevitable, opened negotiations, and issued a circular inviting the different clubs to send "a representative" to meet their committee to consider a scheme which they had prepared for the formation of a county club. This Manchester proposal did not appear, however, to satisfy the Lancashire Union, for W. Bell was instructed to issue a circular "recommending the clubs not to send a representative to the meeting which had been called without the knowledge or consent of the Lancashire Football Union," and pointing out "that as the Manchester Executive consist of fifteen gentlemen, and the other clubs are asked to send one representative each, the Manchester Club would have practically the control of the meeting, even if every club responded to the invitation."

The circular concluded as follows:—

As the Lancashire Union has been in existence upwards of six months, and has taken over the management of the county affairs on a representative basis, the action of the Manchester Club in this matter seems to be unreasonable. Although I do not wish to go into the matter of the proposed scheme, I must call your attention to Rule 6, by which the Manchester representatives would have power to elect the entire County Committee from their own club.

(Signed) W. BELL, hon. secretary.

As might have been expected, the clubs in the Union intimated their intention of absenting themselves from the meeting.

The following letter from James MacLaren, who

had taken an active part in the negotiations, will be read with interest, as it signalises what may be appropriately called the closing scene in the controversy:—

[COPY.]
LANCASHIRE COUNTY FOOTBALL.
December 19th, 1881.

MY DEAR SIR,—You will have heard no doubt of the meeting in connection with above on Wednesday evening last.

To this meeting your Union, as an organisation subscribing to the Rugby Union, was invited. You declined on behalf of the Union, and also issued notices to the different clubs belonging to your Union asking them not to be present.

As the Union and the Manchester Football Club are supposed to be working to the same end—the success and efficient management of county football—do you not think it would have been better to come to the meeting and hear what was said and allowed the other clubs to do the same? You could then have decided whether to join the county club, which, I am glad to say, is in a fair way to be established.

On behalf of the club we again ask your attendance on Thursday. And as the avowed object of your Union is now accomplished—the formation of a county club—we hope to see you, as representing the Union, and the other clubs belonging to your Union at the meeting on Thursday evening.

I am, dear Sir,
On behalf of the Committee of the Manchester Football Club,
(Signed) JAMES MACLAREN.
Wm. Bell, Esq., hon. secretary, Lancashire Football Union.

It is perhaps hardly necessary to state that after having received this conciliatory letter, together with a draft scheme, the clubs were advised to attend a meeting on December 22nd, 1881, at which meeting the scheme as proposed by the Manchester Club was discussed, and, after some alterations and amendments (particulars of which are given in the following copy), was finally agreed to, and Lancashire for the first time had a duly constituted and representative governing body.

Copy of Scheme agreed to by the Manchester Football Club and the Lancashire Union, December 22nd, 1881.

1. That the name of the club shall be THE LANCASHIRE COUNTY FOOTBALL CLUB.

2. That the officers shall be president, vice-president, hon. secretary, hon. treasurer, and a committee of ten, five to form a quorum.

[This law was amended so as to read, "That the officers shall be president, two vice-presidents, hon. secretary and treasurer (to be held by one person), and a committee of ten, five to form a quorum."]

3. That any Lancashire club member of the Rugby Union shall be eligible for membership, having been

duly proposed and seconded by two other clubs members of the County Club.

4. That the annual subscription shall be 10s. 6d., with an entrance fee of 10s. 6d., etc. etc.

5. That general meetings be held in October and March of each year.

6. The president, vice-president, treasurer, and secretary shall be elected from the Manchester Club, and also two members of committee, and the remaining eight names shall be elected by ballot.

[This law was amended so as to read, " The president, a vice-president, the hon. secretary and treasurer shall be elected from the Manchester Football Club, a vice-president and a member of committee from the Liverpool Club, the remaining eight names to be elected from clubs other than the Manchester and Liverpool clubs."]

7. That all Home County matches shall be played on the ground of the Manchester Football Club.

8. That in consideration of the Manchester Football Club having handed over the management of the affairs to the County Club, Laws 6 and 7 are not to be altered for the next *three* seasons without the consent of the Manchester Football Club.

[This law was amended so as to read, " That in consideration of the Manchester *and Liverpool* Clubs having handed over the management of the affairs to the County Club, Laws 6 and 7 are not to be altered for the next *two* seasons, etc. etc."]

The remaining Laws, 9, 10, and 11, simply referred to matters of detail.

The following is a list of the first officers and clubs elected to represent the newly-formed Lancashire County Football Club:—

PRESIDENT:
James MacLaren, Esq. (Manchester).

VICE-PRESIDENTS:
W. Brierley, Esq. (Manchester); E. Kewley, Esq. (Liverpool).

HON. SECRETARY AND TREASURER:
W. Grave, Esq. (Manchester).

COMMITTEE:
Manchester, Liverpool, Broughton, Cheetham, Preston, Manchester Rangers, Rochdale Hornets, Oldham, Swinton, and Free Wanderers.

The new committee cancelled the fixture with Lanarkshire, but confirmed the match with Midland Counties, which was played at Coventry on March 26th, 1882. On December 27th, 1881, the following team (the first under the auspices of the County Club) was

LANCASHIRE TEAM V. MIDDLESEX: OVAL, MARCH 12, 1887 (CHARITY MATCH).

(LANCASHIRE—1 TRY. MIDDLESEX, NIL.)

(*From a Photograph by E. Hawkins & Co., Brighton.*)

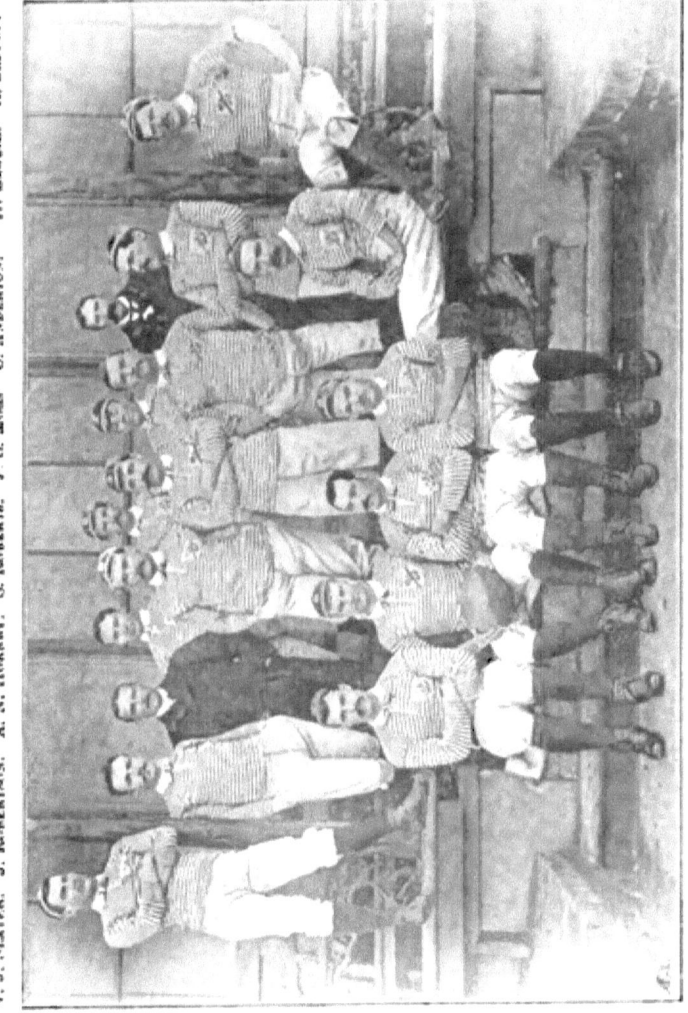

chosen to represent Lancashire v. Northumberland on December 31st:—

W. W. Higgin (Cheetham), full-back; E. Beswick (Swinton), T. Farr (Swinton), H. C. Rowley (Manchester), three-quarter-backs; J. H. Payne (Broughton), W. R. Richardson (Manchester), half-backs; T. Blatherwick (Manchester), E. Wood (Cheetham), W. S. Hulse (Free Wanderers), J. T. Hunt (Manchester), C. Horley (Swinton), J. A. Brodie (Walton), W. S. Butterworth (Rochdale Hornets), J. B. Rye (Oldham), A. B. Rowley (Manchester), forwards.

This match was subsequently cancelled.

Under the management of the new club, county affairs worked smoothly and successfully; and nothing of any great importance occurred until October 17th, 1883, when W. Grave resigned the position of hon. secretary and treasurer, and J. H. Payne was elected his successor. On October 1st, 1884, James MacLaren resigned the office of president, and W. Brierley that of vice-president. A. N. Hornby as president, and R. Walker as vice-president, were unanimously elected their successors.

On October 1st, 1886, E. Kewley was succeeded in the office of vice-president by F. A. Grover, of the Swinton Football Club.

In the year 1887, a movement was set on foot in London for two popular matches under Rugby and Association rules to be played upon the same day at Kennington Oval, to commemorate the Jubilee of Her Majesty's reign, the proceeds to be devoted to charities. Lancashire was specially honoured upon this occasion, for the matches ultimately arranged were between Middlesex and Lancashire (Rugby), and Corinthians v. Preston North End (Association). Both games were played upon the afternoon of the 12th of March in the presence of a vast concourse of spectators, and under the immediate patronage and presence of H.R.H. the Prince of Wales. The Rugby match will always be looked back upon as a red letter day in the annals of the county, for although opposed by a team composed almost entirely of English, Scotch, and Welsh Internationals, contrary to all expectation, after a most remarkable and desperately fought game, Lancashire won by a try, gained by V. Slater (Salford), to their opponents' *nil*. At the conclusion of the game both teams were invited to the front of the royal enclosure, when J. H. Payne and E. T. Gurdon, the respective captains, had the honour of being presented to the Prince.

Although the now all-important official the "Referee" was established by the Rugby Union in the year 1885, it was not until the year 1888 that a formulated scheme for the appointment of referees under the direct management of the County Committee was adopted. Previous to the adoption of this scheme, the difficulties which secretaries of clubs experienced in obtaining referees were enormous, and added greatly to the labours of those self-denying gentlemen who, when all goes right with a club, get scanty praise; but if the slightest hitch occurs in the most trivial arrangements, well, woe betide them—"a secretary's life is not a happy one." It was the energetic secretary of the Warrington Football Club (E. Warren) who at a general meeting suggested that the honorary secretary of the county might relieve club secretaries by sending some well-known authority to act as referee when requested by a club. To this J. H. Payne replied, "That's rather a large order, but I will endeavour to frame a scheme to submit to the committee." The outcome of this was that a "Referees' Committee" was formed which to-day is one of the most useful and important branches of the County government.

In April, 1888, the sum of £100 was voted from the club funds to the medical charities of Manchester and Liverpool—viz., £75 to the Manchester and Salford Hospital Saturday Fund, and £25 to the Liverpool Hospital Saturday Fund.

In February, 1889, a very important proposal was made by W. Lees, of Mossley, involving a change in the constitution of the club. Hitherto the Lancashire County Club had been governed by a president, two vice-presidents, hon. secretary and treasurer (held by one person), and a committee of ten—five forming a quorum; all past presidents and vice-presidents being *ex-officio* members of the committee. It was now proposed to substitute for this rule the following :—

That the officers shall be president, two vice-presidents, secretary and treasurer (one person), and a committee of fifteen, nine to form a quorum; that the county shall be divided out into five districts with three representatives each, and that such districts be Manchester, Liverpool, South-East Lancashire, West Lancashire, and North Lancashire.

It was resolved, "That a sub-committee of representatives of five clubs outside the members of the County Committee should consider the constitution of the County Club, along with the committee and the secretary, J. H. Payne, and submit the result of their deliberations to the general meeting in September." The following five gentlemen were appointed a sub-committee by the meeting:—Lees (Mossley), Warren (Warrington), Broomhall (South-East Lancashire), Clegg (Wigan), and W. G. Thomson (St. Helen's Recreation).

This sub-committee appointed J. H. Payne chairman, and after a friendly discussion requested him to prepare a scheme, which was subsequently accepted by them, and being approved by the general committee was passed at a special general meeting of the club held 26th day of August, 1889.

The principal alteration effected in the constitution of the club was a scheme of district instead of club representation on the committee. For this purpose Lancashire is divided into four divisions. The north comprising all clubs north of and including Preston; the south comprising all clubs south of the Manchester Exchange; the north-east comprising all clubs north-east, and the north-west all clubs north-west of the Manchester Exchange. The committee is composed of twelve representatives—the north having one, the south four, the north-east three, and the north-west four. In addition to the new rules passed at this meeting, a new code of rules was passed enlarging the powers of the Referees' Committee. This committee meet every week for the purpose of appointing referees, also for the purpose of adjudicating upon disputes, etc., and have certain powers delegated to them by the Rugby Union and the County Committee which relieve these bodies from an immense amount of labour.

This brings us down to the season of 1890-91, when under an elaborate scheme carefully prepared by Yorkshire, and passed by the Rugby Union, for regulating the County Championship, Lancashire had the satisfaction of lowering the colours of every county they met, their record being exceptionally brilliant, not a goal being scored against them in any of the county matches they played.

Having thus gained the position of champion county, a match was arranged v. the Rest of England, on the 18th of April, 1891, the popularity of which fixture may be imagined when it is stated that tickets corresponding to the accommodation of the ground were all sold beforehand, and not one single penny was taken at the gates. The proceeds, after deducting expenses, amounted to nearly £600, which amount was distributed amongst the medical charities of the county. The match itself is alluded to elsewhere.

In the season of 1891-92 the good fortune which attended the efforts of the county team in the preceding season appeared to have deserted the Red Rose, for Lancashire having somewhat easily disposed of all opponents, were unluckily defeated by Yorkshire, who placed a goal from a penalty kick allowed by the referee for an infringement of the rule which deals with players who when tackled with the ball do not immediately put it into play. Such are the fortunes of war; this proved to be the only point scored in the match, and Yorkshire (who had upon more than one occasion been penalised during the game), by a successful place kick, won a hard-fought game, and so wrested the championship of England from Lancashire.

The following clubs are members of the Lancashire County Football Club:—Aspull, Askam, Barrow-in-Furness, Blackley Rangers, Blackley, Boothstown, Broughton, Broughton Rangers, Bury Broughton Park, Crompton, Failsworth Free Wanderers, Leigh, Liverpool, Liverpool Old Boys, Lancaster, Manchester, Manchester Rangers, Morecambe, Mossley, Oldham, Owens College, Pendleton, Radcliffe, Rochdale Hornets, Rochdale St. Clements, Salford, Stalybridge, St. Helen's, St. Helen's Recreation, South-East Lancashire (Rugby Union), Southport, Swinton, Tottington, Tuebrook, Tyldesley, Ulverston, Walkden, Warrington, Werneth, West Lancashire (Rugby Union), Widnes, Wigan.

In the foregoing list of clubs reference is made to two affiliated Unions, viz., West Lancashire and South-East Lancashire and Border Towns Rugby Union. These organisations have been the means of bringing several players and junior clubs into prominence, and have proved a useful auxiliary to the Lancashire County Club.

The West Lancashire Union was formed in 1884, and has a membership roll of twenty-three clubs, whose interests are watched by a representative committee, of which F. T. Parry is the hon. sec. During the season of 1890-91 and 1891-92, clubs within this Union have furnished four International players, viz., J. Berry (Tyldesley), J. Pike (St. Helen's Recreation), T. Coop (Leigh), and E. Bullough (Wigan). A Challenge Cup has been instituted to be competed for on similar conditions to the Yorkshire Cup, and since the formation of this Union upwards of £700 have been presented to charitable institutions.

The South-East Lancashire Union was formed in 1877, and consists of forty-one clubs. It has now two cups, senior and junior, the competition being worked on similar lines to the Yorkshire competition. This Union, like its rival in the West, has been successful in stimulating Rugby football, particularly amongst second-class clubs, and much of its success is due to the efforts of the hon. sec., Wm. Broomhall, Manchester.

The first thought likely to strike a casual observer is the comparatively small number of clubs in membership with Lancashire County as compared with the Yorkshire Union. This, however, is easily explained. There are scores of junior clubs in Lancashire who would become members of the county if they held out the same advantages as Yorkshire. In Lancashire the membership is entirely optional; whereas in Yorkshire, in order to be eligible to compete for the Challenge Cup, it is necessary to become enrolled as members of the Rugby and County Unions; and as cup ties are exceedingly popular and profitable, young clubs are only too anxious to join, for there is the possibility of being drawn against a first-class or leading club, and whatever the result of such match may be, a large gate and consequent acquisition of funds is assured. The Lancashire authorities have always opposed a County Challenge Cup: but whatever arguments are advanced against this policy, one thing is certain—it has had a stimulating influence on Rugby football in Yorkshire.

CLUB FOOTBALL.

In reviewing club football it is necessary to revert in thought to about the year 1870, when properly constituted organisations in Lancashire could almost have been counted upon the fingers of the hand, and when in many instances, with a free and open gate, fiercely contested matches were often played before a mere handful of spectators, these being for the most part friends of the combatants. Gate-money, the most demoralising factor of modern football, in those days was

A PLACE KICK.
(*From an instantaneous Photograph by E. Airey, Bradford.*)

almost an unknown quantity, and members, in addition to their annual subscriptions, were expected to pay the whole of their expenses when playing home or foreign matches, and it was no uncommon occurrence for an extra call to be made at the end of a season to make up a deficit caused by the inevitable "balance due to treasurer." Some of the minute books of the earlier clubs would be a revelation to those of a more recent date; the question then was not as to how much a member could get out of a club, but rather as to how much the privilege of being a member would cost him. Omnibuses, for instance, were looked upon as luxuries to be provided for outside the club funds, and although the deliberations of the committees at the time referred to would be looked upon by our modern clubs as absurdly trivial, they were subjects of importance to those who

z

had to provide the "wherewithal." Nor could the business of our earlier clubs be said to have been conducted in a careless or flippant manner, for an extract from the minutes of a meeting of one of the leading clubs records, "That the news that the farmer from whom they rented the field had destroyed himself was received by the committee with due decorum"; also, "That a certain well-known player having promised to play in a match and having failed to put in an appearance was severely reprimanded by the chairman" —a somewhat depressing kind of meeting, one would imagine. It is not recorded in what terms the reprimand was administered by the chairman: but those who have had the misfortune to take part in an important match where perhaps their best player has failed to turn up can imagine the expressions of feeling indulged in by the remainder of a short-handed team. If the player in question is not suffering "eternal combustion," the momentary hopes and wishes of the disappointed ones have not been fulfilled.

Space will only permit a short sketch of some of the earliest "Rugby" clubs in Lancashire, of which the following are selected:—Manchester, Liverpool, Free Wanderers, Manchester Rangers, Birch, Rochdale Hornets, Swinton, Preston and Broughton Wasps, for what little interest was manifested in the game by the public was chiefly centred in these clubs. To obtain a notice in the daily newspapers was a special favour, for hitherto the press could not be described as having looked with favour or given encouragement to this now popular branch of sport.

MANCHESTER.

This club, whose founders may justly be described as the pioneers of the Rugby game, not only in Lancashire, but also in the North of England, was organised about the year 1867, although it could not be considered to be in full operation until two years later. Still, from that time until the present, unlike other organisations with which it is surrounded, a certain amount of prestige has always been attached to the club, doubtless owing to its representative title, for there are amongst the supporters of the Rugby code those who consider the honour of the city is at stake when "The Manchester" is opposed by any other city or town club.

The city of Manchester has a reputation as a sport-loving community, but the following resolution from the Manchester Lete Roll, dated October 12th, 1608, will come as a surprise to many who imagine the popularity of football is of recent date.

(COPY.)

"That whereas there has been heretofore great disorder in our toune of Manchester, and the inhabitants thereof greatly wronged and charged with makinge and amendinge of their glasse windows broken yearlye and spoiled by a companye of lewd and disordered psons vsing that unlawful exercise of playing with the ffote-ball in ye streets of ye s{}^d toune, breakinge many mens windowes and glasse at their pleasures and other great enormyties, Therefore wee of this Jurye doe order that no manner of psons hereafter shall play or use the footeball in any street within the said toune of Manchester subpoened to evye one that shall so use the same for evye time XII{}^d."

It is an extraordinary thing how history repeats itself, for in 1892 in almost every bye-street in Manchester during what is known as the "dinner-hour," the youth of the city is engaged in playing some kind of football, generally without a ball, but with a handful of rags tied up with string, which makes a suitable substitute. Our business, however, is not to deal with ancient history, but to compare the popularity of Rugby football in Manchester twenty-five years ago and the position it holds to-day. Originally commenced by public schoolmen and confined to a select few, Rugby football has gradually become a "people's game," and is probably more popular amongst the working-classes of this great city than any other branch of national sport.

In order to give our readers an idea of the Rugby game at its commencement in Manchester and the opinions of the public, some extracts from the press at this period will be read with interest.

In the early part of 1872 a local newspaper describes a match between Manchester and Liverpool as follows:—
"A struggle for superiority of the two strongest clubs in the North of England. The Manchester Club on this occasion made a charge of sixpence for admission to the ground, which was staked round with rope, and kept the spectators from crowding upon the players. The committee generously left one end of the ground open so that anyone who did not feel disposed to pay for admission could see the game from the road." On the

z 2

Manchester side Grave, Wooley, MacLaren, Burbury, Greg, Pilkington, and "Roger" (referring to Roger Walker), are singled out for special recognition, whilst Hay Gordon and Tobin appear to have done the lion's share of the work for Liverpool. Referring to the game, the report proceeds to relate "how the pack rushed up, and a line is formed, the ball is thrown in, C. Pilkington catches it, and rushes over the Liverpool goal-line amidst loud applause. A *punt-out* is resorted to, and a shout was heard of 'Now, Roger, look out,' but Roger had evidently forgotten to use his napkin at luncheon, and would you be surprised to hear, let the ball slip to the ground, which was eagerly picked up by Tobin," etc. etc.

Another match which caused considerable excitement in the football world was Manchester v. District, and was the first big side match ever played in the locality of Manchester. The game was arranged for fifty players on each side, and nearly that number put in an appearance. One report describes two runs made by C. W. Blacklock (Free Wanderers), one of the best half-backs in Lancashire, who on this occasion assisted the District, and winds up by stating "that a big side is not the game to show the abilities of half-backs, as there are too many 'stragglers' on the look-out for them to get very far away; also that the *bell* rang for hostilities to cease, and a rush to the pavilion announced the game over, a game which was a grand sight; but for showing the quality of players commend us to witness a *twenty-aside* match."

In the early days of Rugby football it was no uncommon occurrence to hear of a match being played under what was called "Strict Rugby" rules, which meant "full hacking," but, thanks to the Rugby Union, this barbarous fashion of enjoying a "friendly game" has been prohibited. An account of a match between the Manchester Club and the Free Wanderers will serve to show one style of play which was indulged in at this period :—

"The Rugby game was played, which means of course that each side may kick his opponents whenever he gets the chance, and judging from the play we should think there would be some sore shins, although the Manchester Club were the heaviest and appeared to have an advantage in the shin-kicking department. We could distinctly hear the heavy thuds of the meeting of leathers and shins, and thanked our stars we were merely spectators without assisting at the ceremony. A spectator cried out, 'Go it, Roger,' as that individual was pegging away right and left and seemed to smack his lips at the kicks he got in return, not very sweet things we should imagine."

Another graphic description of a match, Manchester v. Preston Grasshoppers, relates

"how at times all the pack were down, which elicited roars of laughter as they began to sort themselves out, and a few claret-dyed noses were plainly visible during the play. A. N. Hornby, by his fine play, proved a tower of strength to his brother Grasshoppers, as also did C. G. Hulton."

Again, in a match, Manchester v. Clarendon,

"the friends of each side can be heard shouting, 'Go in, Reds,' 'Knock him over, Blues,' 'Take it through, Reds,' 'Oh!' 'Well played,' etc. All the pack can be covered with a sheet so close are they, and the steam rises in clouds from their midst whilst the players are puffing and blowing like so many porpoises. The palm must be awarded to D. B. MacLaren for his real sterling play, although Jackson, Burbury, 'Catch me quick,' Grey, and J. Maclaren for the Reds distinguished themselves, as also did Ward, Inchle, Mellor, and Wooley for the Blues."

Although in 1871 county matches had been played between Lancashire and Yorkshire, a match was arranged in that year, and was played at Whalley Range, with the unassuming title of Lancashire v. The World. The world, however, does not appear to have extended far beyond the municipal boundary of Manchester at this period. Describing this game, one newspaper reports that

"each side continued to struggle for supremacy, and with such spirit that one would think their existence depended upon their success. Here there would be a severe collision between two antagonists, and one or other would surely come to grief. Surely no electrician's services are required, as the shock is so great as to loosen every joint. Here was a player who had omitted to put on the tight-fitting jersey of the club and was playing in his woollen shirt, or rather part of it, for his enemies soon found out where a good handful was to be had, and before the game was over that gentleman was minus half a shirt. Another cried out, 'This is lively,' as he exhibited a front tooth which had just parted company from his gums; he had evidently experienced a collision."

These extracts of the early Manchester matches which have been furnished by J. Turner, who was for many years a familiar figure in connection with the Manchester Club, serve to show the first impressions of the Rugby game upon the public. To-day the numerous and intricate points are watched with the keenest interest by thousands of spectators every Saturday. To attempt to detail the history of the Manchester Club would in the small space at disposal become an impossibility. Suffice it to say that after an honourable and successful career, extending over a quarter of a century, the "Manchester Club is still regarded as the premier club"; its roll of membership never was stronger, and in these days of veiled professionalism it can be confidently asserted that nowhere is the Rugby game played more for the love of sport in its purity than in the ranks of this time-honoured club. What list of celebrated players from one organisation will compare with the "old warriors" who have passed through the ranks of the Manchester Club? Amongst the foremost exponents of the game, the names of such men as Grave, J. Hulton, Openshaw, Richardson (half-backs), A. N. Hornby, "Bob Hunt" (as he was familiarly known, and who will be remembered as one of the finest dropkicks in the country), Campbell Rowley, and more recently E. Storey, as three-quarter backs; also in other departments of the game, the MacLarens, R. Walker, Marriott, Fowler, Genth, Bulteel, Greg, Todd, Thorp, Schofield, Aitken, Blatherwick, Bleackley, the Cleggs, the Macnivens, and scores of others, are amongst the number who have contributed in no small degree to the present successful and proud position of the club.

LIVERPOOL.

This club enjoys the distinction of a long and honoured career, dating its origin to about the same time as its oldest rival, the Manchester Club. Allusion is made elsewhere to the interest taken in the annual encounters between these old opponents; also to the part which Liverpool took in the formation of the Lancashire County Club, for any history would be incomplete that did not recognise the invaluable services which this club has rendered to Rugby football, especially during the earliest stages of the game. Despite all the changes that have taken place in the conditions under which the Rugby game is now played, it is with no small degree of pleasure that we chronicle the fact that the Liverpool Club still occupies a foremost position amongst the organisations of Lancashire. Space only permits of a passing reference to a few of the most prominent players, of whom the name of E. Kewley stands out most prominently, although A. Lyon, C. W. H. Clarke, the Hon. S. Parker, J. R. Hay Gordon, Tobin, C. L. Verelst, C. W. Carver, H. Springmann, and more recently A. T. Kemble, have done yeoman's service for their club.

FREE WANDERERS.

One of the oldest clubs in the county dates its existence previous to the year 1870, when matches were arranged and played by a team under the above title, and these players, principally "Old Boys" of the Victoria Park and Chorlton High Schools, formed the nucleus of the present club, which may be said to have been incorporated in the year 1870. For many years the Wanderers held a position in the very front rank, though latterly they appear to have been gradually going down, and are now making a hard struggle for existence. The club appears to have been unfortunate in locating themselves on the southern side of Manchester, for here the Lacrosse champions hold undoubted sway, and since the introduction of that game the popularity of Rugby football has steadily declined. This club has produced some prominent exponents of the Rugby game, notably the Brothers Massey, C. W. Blacklock, who at one time was considered one of the best half-backs in the North of England, A. M. Hammerton, R. Mellor, F. Williams, the brothers Adams, W. H. and J. Young and F. and E. H. Inchle, the latter an old Rugby boy and an exceptionally fine drop-kick, J. W. and W. S. Hulse, the Ledwards, and C. Anderton. A singular fact is recorded by a local newspaper in connection with this club—viz., that in 1876 twelve out of the original team in 1870 had played regularly that season.

In the year 1880 the Free Wanderers amalgamated with a neighbouring club, the Fallowfield Rovers, which brought them a large acquisition of playing members.

As Rugby football is undoubtedly the popular game throughout Yorkshire (Sheffield excepted), the following account, copied from a Sheffield newspaper, may perhaps to some extent account for the success of the Association game in that district:—

FREE WANDERERS v. SHEFFIELD (GARRICK).

This match was played on Saturday afternoon on the Garrick Ground at Machon Bank. The Manchester Club played Rugby rules, and it was arranged that each club's rules should be played on its opponent's ground, so that a novelty was provided for the lovers of football in Sheffield, the Rugby rules being played here for the first time. In about a week's time three distinct sets of rules have been exhibited in the town —viz., the Sheffield Association, the Football Association (London), and Rugby. With the merits or demerits of the two former codes our football readers are doubtless cognisant, the two rules providing against the use of the hands, and making it *foot*-ball in a literal sense of the word. Penalties are also imposed for foul play, such as charging behind, hacking, tripping, etc., and everything done to promote skill and judgment in preference to brute force. In the rules played on Saturday, however, a marked contrast to this is shown, as the heaviest and roughest side will invariably have the advantage. What little skill is required is good drop-kicking and ability to dodge through your opponents with the ball to secure a touch down. The peculiarity of these rules is that it is next to impossible to give a foul, as a player can pick up the ball and run with it, knock it on, kick it, or throw it to another when likely to be tackled. If, however, he has the ball in his possession, an opponent seizes him round the neck, legs, or any portion of clothing that first presents itself to his grasp. Others then come up, and unless he cries out " Have it down," he is quickly prostrated and rolled on or sat on, as the case may be. Several cases of deliberate hacking, or, in other words, kicking at an opponent's shins as he is running with the ball, did not convince either us or the spectators of the superiority of the Rugby over Association rules. They are quite suitable for schoolboys, who are proverbially impervious to accident, but we should have thought adults would prefer a game with more skill and less roughing. The above remarks may look prejudicial, and might be modified if two first-class teams were witnessed contending together, but certainly on Saturday a decidedly unfavourable opinion of the Rugby rules was formed by the spectators. Play was commenced at 3.30, Garrick having won the toss and kicking down hill, the wind also favouring them. It was quickly apparent that the Sheffielders were ignorant of the rules, and before they had time to obtain an insight into them a goal was scored by Manchester. To effect this a touch-down must be obtained behind the enemy's goal line, no easy matter with even sides, as the strict off-side rule is played, and a player has to run the gauntlet of his opponents before this consummation can be reached. From this they have virtually a free kick for a goal, the ball being taken some distance in the field and the defending side stationed behind the goal line. The ball is placed by one and kicked by another player, and a goal is scored when it is sent directly over, not under the bar as in Association rules. Hammerton obtained the try or touch-down, and F. Inchle kicked the goal. Ends were then changed, and a detailed account of the play is simply impossible, consisting as it did of wrestling, strangling, running with the ball under one arm and striking opponents in the face with the disengaged hand, splendid drop-kicking by Manchester, and plucky but utterly futile efforts by Garrick to turn the tide in their favour, although they showed a marked improvement towards the latter part of the game. B. Tingle was particularly useful in the tackling department, and W. Horton played pluckily and dodged his opponents surprisingly. T. Buttery also played well. The ball was almost continually at the Garrick end of the field, and after playing about forty minutes the resisting teams were credited with three goals, the try for the second of which was obtained by C. Smith, and Blacklock kicked the goal. The third try was excellently obtained by Chamberlain, and the goal kicked by Young. No side was called at five o'clock, Manchester being victorious by 4 goals 3 tries and 17 rouges to 0.

MANCHESTER RANGERS.

Although at the present time an entirely new organisation have adopted the name of "Manchester Rangers," the club above referred to has unfortunately passed out of existence. The club was first formed about 1870 by Messrs. C. W. Smith, T. R. Sutton, and a few members of St. Michael's Church, Hulme, who became the leading spirits of the then unknown St. Michael's Choristers Football Club. In 1872 the name was changed to the "Moss Side Rangers"; and in 1873, having to change their ground, they again changed their name and assumed the title of "Manchester Rangers." This alteration seems to have been coeval with the advanced influence and popularity of the club, for they had an amount of success which brought them prominently before the public. The names of E. T. and C. W. Smith, the Suttons, Colliers, Markendale, Stancliffe, Lindsay, Fletcher, and the Andrews, will long be associated with what once was one of the strongest combinations in the North of England.

ROCHDALE HORNETS.

The Rochdale Hornets must certainly be included amongst the early pioneers of the game in Lancashire, and are to be congratulated to-day in occupying a front place amongst the chief clubs in the county. Twenty years ago in this densely populated county of Lancashire the only towns outside Manchester and Liverpool that could boast of anything like strong clubs were Preston and Rochdale, and the Rochdale Hornets worked honourably and industriously to obtain this position, and many clubs in the neighbourhood of Manchester have reason to remember the struggle for supremacy in those early days. Of individual players, Andrew Irving, Wilfred Butterworth, J. Sellars, C. M. Taylor, Goulbourne Davies, and E. Healey, are amongst those who have upheld the honour and reputation which the club has so justly acquired.

SWINTON.

This wonderful club, although previously playing Association football, dates its existence as a Rugby club from about the year 1870, and certainly no organisation in England has enjoyed a more singularly uninterrupted run of success. The game is exceedingly popular in the "colliery village," and is not likely to languish from want of recognition by the inhabitants of its own locality. Nothing succeeds like success, and probably their continued success makes the natives so proud of the achievements of their club. The height of the ambition of Swinton was gratified when they met the premier club (Manchester) at Whalley Range in the year 1878, and after a memorable game retired the victors by a try to *nil.*

Referring to individual players, it is extremely difficult to particularise where all have done so well; one curious fact, however, may be mentioned—viz., that at one time four of the Brothers Farr played with the club, H. J., better known as "Buck," Farr perhaps being the most prominent. The names of W. Longshaw, the Dornings, Ogden, Barker, Beswick, C. Horley, S. Roberts, J. Marsh, and last, but not least, Joe Mills and Jim Valentine, will long remain associated with an organisation which to-day occupies the foremost position in the list of Lancashire clubs. Swinton may assuredly contemplate with satisfaction the career of its very plucky club, which has worked so successfully for so many seasons, for it must not be overlooked that the annual fixtures are arranged with the strongest opponents in the country.

Birch.

This club, now defunct, was one of the earliest established in Lancashire, and, like several others, it originated by playing Association football for one or two seasons, ultimately adopting the Rugby code.

For many years the Birch occupied a very high position amongst the principal clubs, and the match v. Swinton was regarded as one of the most attractive and popular fixtures in the Manchester district. Quoting from an article which appeared in a football annual in 1876, the writer states. "That the Birch Club, one of the most successful in the North, is entirely composed of young fellows who have had to acquire what they know of the game within the last two or three years, and so rapidly and thoroughly have they become possessed of the knowledge as to be a fit match for any club in the country. Their list of members will number nearly 200, and if necessity arose they could place four teams in the field with a great chance of each being successful against opponents of average strength."

Unfortunately, this club, which appeared to have such bright prospects, is now broken up, still the names of Nicholson, Cass, the brothers Heggs, J. Glossop, W. Emery, T. Hunter, R. and W. Macfarlane will live in the memory of those who remember the Birch Club in its palmy days.

Preston Grasshoppers.

Established in 1869, and at one time one of the strongest organisations playing Rugby football in the North of England, is now unhappily dissolved. This club bid fair to have a long run of success, including amongst its players such names as A. N. Hornby, R. Hunt, J. T. Hunt and W. H. Hunt, C. Hulton, etc. By some means or other these gentlemen found their way into the ranks of the Manchester Club, and having, in addition to desertion by their members, to struggle against the growing popularity of the Association game, the interest in Rugby football began to wane, and although the Preston Club made a gallant effort to retain the amateur code of football in the town they were unsuccessful, and, all things considered, it is not surprising that we have to chronicle the extinction of the club.

BROUGHTON WASPS.

This club, now known as the Broughton, was originally formed by members of a club known in 1869 as Broughton College. After playing two or three seasons on the Broughton Cricket Ground they changed their title to the Broughton Wasps, under which name they played many a hard-fought game and won many a well-earned victory against some of the strongest opponents in the North. In 1877 the Wasps amalgamated with a very smart club of schoolboys, which established itself in the Broughton district, called the Wellington, who were the first club to introduce the passing game into Lancashire, and brought it to such perfection, that, in spite of their youth, they succeeded in beating many of the principal clubs of the district. Since that period the Broughton Club has continued on its prosperous career, and whilst several of their old opponents have been compelled to dissolve, it is a pleasure to record the fact that this club is in a flourishing condition.

Amongst the many prominent players hailing from this club the names of the brothers Sawyer, J. H. Payne, H. Mallalieu, F. Moss, T. Deane, Sockett, the Dennetts, E. Jordan, and E. H. Flower are the most conspicuous.

Thus, as has already been stated, space only permits of a brief history of the introduction of Rugby football into Lancashire and a reference to the first few clubs. To attempt to do justice to those of a more recent date would exhaust the pages of this volume; suffice it then to say that clubs such as Salford (with its upwards of 2,000 subscribers), Wigan, Oldham, Warrington, Barrow-in-Furness, Liverpool Old Boys, Lancaster, St. Helens, St. Helen's Recreation, Widnes, etc., to-day form the "backbone" of the Rugby game in Lancashire.

In this review of Lancashire Rugby football no reference has been made to the rival code, "the Association game," of which this county is undoubtedly a stronghold. Both codes are extremely popular, although the conditions under which they are played are *supposed* to be as wide as the poles. In short, the Football

Association have legalised professionalism, whilst the Rugby Union declare it to be illegal. Notwithstanding the combined efforts of the governing body, by means of special legislation, etc., to preserve the amateur conditions of the Rugby game, the dark shadows of professionalism have latterly unmistakably manifested themselves, and the all-absorbing topic at the present time amongst those who have the welfare of the old game at heart is, What is to be the future of Rugby football? To some minds it may be questionable whether there can be any reason why remuneration for playing should not be permitted to football players as well as to cricketers and others who pursue for profit the numerous and varied forms of popular sport. All we can reply in Lancashire is that the lesson taught by the legalisation of professionalism in the Association game is not encouraging, for not only does club patriotism appear to be destroyed by talent becoming a marketable article, but the richest clubs become the strongest, and betting, with its accompanying evils, is the inevitable result of a system which it is extremely improbable will ever receive the approval or sanction of the Rugby Union as at present constituted.

James Maclaren.—There is no more prominent personage in Northern Rugby football circles than J. Maclaren. Since his connection with the Manchester Football Club, of which he was one of the founders, he has taken the liveliest interest in the game, both as a player and an official, and much of the prestige and success of Lancashire as a football county must be attributed to his indefatigable efforts. Maclaren was one of the earliest Northern members elected on the Rugby Union Committee, where his services were recognised by his election as president in the season of 1882-1883. His elevation to this important position marked a new departure from the traditions of the Union, for hitherto this honour had only been conferred upon Southern members. In his capacity as a past-president of England, Maclaren is an *ex-officio* member of the Union, and occupies a seat on the International Board. Maclaren has filled the position of president of the Manchester Football Club, and was the first president of the Lancashire County Football Club, his interest in the latter body being as keen as ever. He is also hon. treasurer of the Lancashire County Cricket Club, in which he takes a great interest.

A. N. Hornby, the popular president of the Lancashire County Football Club, was born at Blackburn on February 10th, 1847, and was educated at Harrow School. As a youth he was an ardent lover of field sports, showing at a very early age exceptional proficiency as a cricketer. He ultimately became associated with his native county club, and has for over twenty years rendered invaluable service to the Lancashire eleven,

A. N. HORNBY AND W. H. HUNT.
(From a Photograph by J. Moffat, Edinburgh.)

during the greater part of which period he has been the "skipper." In the football field he has been equally successful, and has figured in innumerable County, North and South, and International matches, and has not only captained his County, but he occupies the unique position of having captained England in International engagements both at cricket and Rugby football.

Hornby is one of the Lancashire representatives on the English Rugby Union, and at the present time there is no more enthusiastic supporter of the Rugby game.

R. WALKER.
(From a Photograph by Burrowl, Liverpool.)

Roger Walker.—Amongst the many distinguished Lancastrians, probably no old player is more popular or better known in connection with Northern Rugby football than this gentleman. His connection with the Manchester Club (of which for seven years he was captain) has been of such long standing that in the oldest football records his name is continually in evidence. Walker was a most useful and hard-working forward, and in addition to playing in many county matches, he has played five times for the North v. the South, and has been included in the English International fifteen on five occasions—viz., against Scotland in 1874, 1876, 1879, 1880, and against Ireland in 1875.

E. KEWLEY.
(From a Photograph by Robinson & Thompson, Liverpool.)

Walker's retirement from football as a player has not prevented him from taking an active interest as an official in all that appertains to the welfare of the game. He is at the present time president of the Manchester, Bury, and Southport Football Clubs. He is a Lancashire representative on the English Rugby Union, of which body he is a vice-president, and is also a vice-president of the Lancashire County Football Club.

R. HUNT.
From a Photograph by N. McNeel, Blackburn.

William Grave was born at Manchester, in the year 1848, and is the second son of the late Mr. Alderman Grave, ex-Mayor of Manchester. He was one of the first members of the Manchester Football Club, for which he played for several seasons. As a half-back he was possessed of great trickiness and wonderful drop-kicking powers, as many old opponents of the Manchester Club have reason to remember. He was one of the twenty who played in the first County v. Yorkshire, in 1870. He has also been included in the North team v. the South. Grave was for many years hon. secretary of the Manchester Football Club, and was also the first hon. sec. of the present Lancashire County Football Club.

J. T. HUNT.
(From a Photograph by Arthur Winter, Preston.)

E. Kewley.—This celebrated player was born at Farnham Royal, Bucks, on the 20th June, 1852, and was educated at Marlborough College, where he was included in the XI. and XVI. of the club. After completing his education, Kewley identified himself with the Liverpool Football Club (of which he has always been a staunch supporter), and played for Lancashire in several of the early county matches v. Yorkshire, making his first appearance for the county in 1871. In addition to North and South matches Kewley has played in no less than seven International engagements—viz., v. Scotland in 1874-75-76-77-78 (captain, 1877-78), and v. Ireland in 1876-77 (captain, 1877). Kewley was best described by a Southern annual of 1878 as follows:— "For the second year captain of the English fifteen, and a most successful and popular leader. An admirable forward, always playing on the ball with the greatest pluck and spirit: one of the best dribblers and followers-up in the three Kingdoms, and can also run well."

On the formation of the present county club Mr. Kewley was elected a vice-president, and although now retired from the active list, as a past-president of Lancashire he still retains a connection with the governing body as an *ex-officio* member.

William Henry Hunt, who may appropriately be styled "one of the boys of the Old Brigade," was born on May 11th, 1854, and is a native of Preston, for which club he played for many seasons. Possessed of great strength, which he knew how to use to advantage, he proved himself an exceptionally useful forward, his weight telling in the scrummages, whilst his height (6 feet 3 inches) gave him exceptional facilities for securing the ball when thrown out from touch. He first played for Lancashire v. Yorkshire in 1876, and was selected the same year for the North v. the South, and so well did he acquit himself in that match that he was included in the International Twenty v. Scotland. In 1877 he played against both Ireland and Scotland, and again v. Ireland in 1878. He is the eldest of the four brothers, who have all distinguished themselves at the Rugby game, viz., R. Hunt and J. T. Hunt (Lancashire County and International), and Thomas Howard Hunt (Lancashire County in 1884). W. H. Hunt was a prominent supporter of the "Preston Grasshoppers" and Manchester Football Clubs, and, as the representative from Preston, occupied a seat on the Lancashire County Committee for several seasons. Since retiring from football W. H. Hunt has devoted his spare time to Volunteer Artillery, and at the present time has the honour to be in command of the strongest position corps of Volunteer Artillery in the United Kingdom, viz., the Fifth Lancashire Artillery Volunteers. At the Royal Military Tournament, open to the whole of the British Forces, held at Islington on June 26th, 1889, Hunt won:—

First prize, Lance v. Sword . . . } Mounted
Second prize, Sword } Competitions.
v. Sword . . . }

C. M. SAWYER.
(From a Photograph by Kay, Southport.)

Robert Hunt.—This sterling three-quarter back was born at Preston, on January 12th, 1856, and was educated at Preston Grammar School and Owens College, Manchester. During his brilliant football career he has played for the "Preston Grasshoppers," Manchester, and one season with the Blackheath Football clubs. He was a splendid tackler, with great pace, and as a drop-kick was unrivalled; measures 6 feet in height, and when playing scaled 12st. 4lb. R. Hunt made his first appearance for Lancashire in 1878 v. Yorkshire. In the following years, 1879-1880, he was selected to play for the North v. the South, and in 1880 gained International honours, playing v. Ireland. In 1881 he played for England v. Scotland and Wales (the latter match being the first International match between the two countries), and again in 1882 for England v. Ireland. He is now in practice as a medical man at Blackburn.

James Thomas Hunt, a brother of W. H., Robert, and T. H. Hunt, originally hailed from the "Preston Grasshoppers," but, as a member of the Manchester Club, to which he also belonged, he first played for Lancashire v. Yorkshire in 1880, when he scored one of the tries obtained in the match. He also played for the North v. the South in 1880 and 1881, and obtained International honours in the match v. Ireland on February 6th, 1882, and so far justified his selection as to be included in the English fifteen v. Scotland. In 1883 he again played for the North v. the South, also appearing in the International fifteen v. Wales in 1884. On this latter occasion J. T. Hunt had the distinction of being the only Northerner selected for a place in the team.

C. M. Sawyer, one of the most powerful three-quarter backs that Lancashire has produced, was born in Manchester, in the year 1856. Early in his football career he became associated with the Broughton Wasps, which, after amalgamation with the Wellington Club, was known as the Broughton Club. To this latter organisation he was a "tower of strength," and, for a man of his physique, was exceptionally fast, a strong tackler, and, with the ball in his opponents' "25," was considered almost irresistible. He first played for Lancashire in 1877, and in this and

H. C. ROWLEY.
(From a Photograph by J. Huff, Penrith.)

many subsequent county matches he rendered valuable assistance. In 1880 he was selected in the North team v. the South, in which match he created such a favourable impression that he was the same year included in the International fifteen v. Scotland. In the following year (1881) he also played for England v. Ireland.

Hugh Campbell Rowley (born March, 1854).—Those who remember this celebrated player will agree that he was one of the best all-round men who ever played the Rugby game. He was originally a member of the Bowdon and Lymm Club, where his value was speedily recognised, and he was selected to play for Cheshire v. Lancashire in the first match between the two counties (February 24th, 1877), and was fortunate enough to score the first try. Cheshire had thus the satisfaction of scoring the first point of importance against their formidable opponents. Subsequently, Rowley became a member of the Manchester Club, and in 1879 played for Lancashire, and it would be impossible to overestimate the efficient services which for several years he rendered to that county. He also played in several North v. South matches, and has been included in the English International fifteen on no less than nine occasions—viz., v. Scotland, 1879-80-81-82; Ireland, 1879-80-81-82; Wales, 1881.

Campbell Rowley was one of the most useful of football players, very strong and fast, was never done with, could play any position in the field equally well, and had his whole heart in the game.

H. H. SPRINGMANN.
(*From a Photograph by Morell & Morrison, Liverpool.*)

Hermann Henry Springmann.—In the long list of Lancashire representatives there have been few more consistent players than Springmann, who was born at Liverpool in the year 1859. He was educated at Craigmount, Edinburgh, and eventually associated himself with the Liverpool Football Club. His abilities were speedily recognised, and in 1879 he was selected to play in the Lancashire fifteen, and acquitted himself so creditably that in the same year he played for the North v. the South, and again for England v. Scotland. Shortly afterwards Springmann left for America, only to reappear again upon the scene in 1886, when it was soon discovered that he had lost none of his old form, for in that year he assisted the county team v. Cheshire and Yorkshire. Once more he was selected to play for the North v. the South, and finally was included in the English team v. Scotland, which match was played at Manchester, March 5th, 1887. One journal, commenting on the merits of the different players in this match, stated that "Of the Northern forwards Springmann was the pick, and most creditably in this great match closed his brilliant career."

J. H. PAYNE.
(From a Photograph by Lafosse, Manchester.)

John Henry Payne, the popular honorary secretary and treasurer of the Lancashire County Football Club, was born at Broughton, in the year 1858, and is the eldest son of the late Mr. J. B. Payne, who will long be remembered as a prominent cricketer and supporter of the Broughton Cricket Club. J. H. Payne was educated at the Manchester Grammar School and St. John's College, Cambridge, where in 1881 he took his degree as Bachelor of Arts. In early life it was apparent he inherited a love for field sports, more particularly cricket and Rugby football. He first played for his school and the Wellington Football Club, which was absorbed by the present Broughton Club, and it was during his connection with the latter that he obtained International honours, playing half-back v. Scotland in 1882. In 1883 he played against Scotland, Ireland, and Wales ; in 1884 against Ireland ; and in 1885 against Ireland, and Wales. In the *Football Annual* of 1885 he was appropriately described as " A most scientific half-back, good at every department of the game ; picks up pluckily, and passes unselfishly and with great judgment." J. H. Payne also obtained his Blue for Cambridge University, and captained Lancashire County successfully for many seasons.

As a cricketer he has rendered efficient service to the Broughton Club, where having shown exceptional proficiency as a wicket-keeper, he was selected to play in the Lancashire County eleven. In his official capacity, both as county secretary and as a Lancashire representative on the English Rugby Union, he has rendered valuable service, and has taken a leading part in many reforms introduced into legislation for the purification and improvement of Rugby football.

Alfred Teggin, a native of Manchester, was born in the year 1860. He was a member of the Broughton Rangers F. C., and was one of the most sterling forwards in England. In 1883 he played for Lancashire and for the North v. the South. In 1884 he played for England v. Ireland; in 1885 he appeared for England v. Wales; and in 1886 and 1887 he was included in the English International teams against both Scotland and Ireland.

Edward Beswick, a prominent Swintonian, who rendered efficient service to his club as a three-quarter back, was included in the Lancashire County team which played v. Cheshire, Nov. 29th, 1879. He also played in many subsequent county matches, and was selected in 1881 in the North team v. the South. In 1882 he obtained International honours, playing for England in that year against both Ireland and Scotland.

A. T. KEMBLE.
(From a Photograph by Bradshaw, Hastings)

Arthur Twiss Kemble was born in Cumberland in the year 1862, and is the third son of the Rev. N. F. G. Kemble, of Allerton, Liverpool. He is prominently identified with the Liverpool Cricket and Football clubs, and has held official positions in both organisations. As a football forward he soon made his mark, being particularly smart in the open, and always on the ball. He was first chosen to play for Lancashire in 1883, and for several seasons rendered valuable aid to the county, of which at one period he was the captain. In 1884 he played for the North v. the South, and gained his International cap in 1885, playing against Wales and Ireland. He also played v. Ireland in 1887. Not only in football circles has Kemble distinguished himself, for he is probably more widely known in connection with the cricket field, having succeeded the late Richard Pilling as wicket-keeper for Lancashire county. It is well known how successfully this popular sportsman has acquitted himself in this department of the game.

JAMES VALENTINE.
(From a Photograph by Brown, Barnes & Bell, Liverpool.)

James Valentine, another player who hails from the football stronghold of Swinton, near Manchester, was born on the 29th July, 1866. As a three-quarter back he soon proved himself a worthy successor of his noted predecessors, the Brothers Farr and E. Beswick. He was first selected to play for Lancashire in 1884, and has taken part in most of the county engagements since that time. Although a most proficient player, it was not until 1890 that he actually played for England, although in 1888, when International matches were suspended, a team of England was selected, and International caps were presented to the fifteen, J. Valentine being amongst the number. It was in no small degree owing to his

TOM KENT.

fine play in the season of 1890-91 that Lancashire obtained the distinction of champion county, for, in addition to scoring sixteen tries in county matches, he captained the team with great judgment.

Thomas Kent was born at Nottingham on June 19th, 1864. He became associated with the Salford Football Club in the season of 1887-88, and proved himself to be such a strong, sterling, hard-working forward that he was promptly recommended for county honours, which he obtained in the match Lancashire *v.* Somersetshire, on the 21st January, 1888. Since that time he has figured conspicuously in almost every county match. He was selected in the North team *v.* the South which was played at Richmond, February 1st, 1890. In 1891 he gained his International cap, and played against Wales, Ireland, and Scotland, a distinction which he also achieved in the season of 1891-92.

CHAPTER XX.

COUNTY FOOTBALL: YORKSHIRE.

"YOUR Yorkshire County Committee is a wonderful creation." So writes one of the leading spirits of the Rugby Union. But "creation" is not the right term to apply to the continuous phases of development which have led to the establishment of the present Yorkshire Rugby Union, an institution of which the followers of Rugby football in Yorkshire are justly proud. To trace the inception and development of this powerful organisation may be interesting, as exhibiting, in the successive stages of the progress of the committee, a history in miniature very similar to that of this nation perfecting its constitution and always maintaining its freedom. At first governed by five clubs, all independent, owing no allegiance save that of their own will, and bound by no ties save their desire to promote county football, this period, that may well be termed the Pentarchy of Yorkshire football, has been followed by vicissitudes that may be likened to the successive periods of agitations in the history of our own land as the "Wars of the Barons," "The Rise of the People," and the admission of all classes to the franchise. In no county has there been presented the spectacle of oligarchic rule developing into democratic government in any manner to compare with the history of the Yorkshire County Committee.

It has often been stated that the original executive was self-elected, but the term is rather wide of the mark. The origination of any committee (if the managers of Yorkshire football could at that time be termed a committee) arose out of the match with Lancashire in 1870. J. G. Hudson, then secretary of the Leeds Club, has the honour of being the leader of the movement. It was he who conceived the idea of Yorkshire playing a match with Lancashire. The first match was played at Leeds, and Howard Wright, the captain of the Leeds Club, led the Yorkshire team. From this crude beginning dates the foundation of the Yorkshire committee. Leeds, Bradford, Huddersfield, and Hull took up the management of county affairs, simply because there was none to dispute their right to govern. But the only work to be done was in connection with picking the teams, and this task devolved almost entirely on the captain, who was always the representative of the club whose ground had been selected for the match. Thus Howard Wright led the team at Leeds, Alfred Bradley at Huddersfield, and Harry Garnett at Bradford; and when the matches took place out of the county, Hutchinson of Hull held the reins, and decided pretty much his own way as to who should play or be left out.

It is generally supposed that H. W. T. Garnett was the first to call a proper committee meeting together prior to the Lancashire fixture of 1874 at Bradford, but Garnett's own version of his joining the committee is somewhat different. "My first match with the Yorkshire team was against Durham at Darlington in 1873. It was the first match we played with that county, and we played a return match the same season (on March 21, 1874). When we went to Durham they neither met us at the station nor gave us a luncheon. When the return match was to come off at Leeds, I wrote to J. G. Hudson, the secretary, asking for a seat on the committee. I was invited to attend, and proposed the following resolution, 'That we should entertain Durham to luncheon at the Queen's Hotel, drive them to the ground in a four-in-hand, entertain them to dinner afterwards, and send them all home drunk.' We successfully carried out the programme with the exception of the latest clause. We had to guarantee the expenses amongst ourselves, and I can remember I undertook to guarantee £5, and actually had to pay £3 10s. as my share of the deficit."

From 1874 the committee began to meet fairly regularly, and this again at the instigation of Garnett, who called the captains of the Leeds Athletic, Bradford, Hull, York, and Huddersfield clubs to meet at the Queen's Hotel, Leeds. The first members were B. Cariss

H. W. T. GARNETT,
President, 1876-1884.
(From a Photograph by Appleton & Co., Bradford.)

A. K. HUDSON,
President, 1884-1886.
(From a Photograph by Sister, Llandudno.)

BARRON KILNER,
President, 1891-1892.
(From a Photograph by G. and J. Hall, Wakefield.)

J. A. MILLER,
President, 1892-1893.
(From a Photograph by Hoskins, Leeds.)

M. NEWSOME,
President, 1888-1890.
(From a Photograph by Valentine Blanchard, Dewsbury.)

REV. F. MARSHALL,
President, 1890-1891.
(From a Photograph by J. E. Shaw, Huddersfield.)

THE YORKSHIRE PRESIDENTS.

(Leeds Athletic), H. W. T. Garnett (Bradford), W. Hodgson (Hull), Christison (York), and H. S. Brook (Huddersfield). In 1877 Garnett was formally appointed captain of the team, and held the post till his retirement in 1880. Garnett and Arthur Hudson were virtually the founders of the present Yorkshire committee. To Arthur Hudson Yorkshiremen owe the origination of the Yorkshire Challenge Cup. His influence on Yorkshire football was very great, and the late successes of Yorkshire players in the field are mainly due to the wise counsels and far-seeing legislation of one whose memory will ever be venerated by all Yorkshire football enthusiasts.

Arthur E. Hudson never was a football player, and his enthusiasm for the game dated from his stay in Manchester in 1874-75, when he took an interest in the Manchester Club. On his return to Leeds he took an active part in Yorkshire football. Whilst in Manchester he had observed that the Lancashire county players were selected mainly from the Manchester Club. He came to the conclusion that the combination in the team arising from this circumstance was a great factor in the run of success which fell to Lancashire in the matches with Yorkshire, for up to that time Yorkshire could claim only one victory in eight matches. Accordingly, he conceived the idea of founding a club which should play the same part in Yorkshire as Manchester was doing in Lancashire, and hence arose the Yorkshire Wanderers Club. This was raised on the ashes of the Leeds Athletic Club and Potternewton, or perhaps it would be kinder to say on the ashes of the former and the amalgamation of the latter. Originally it was termed the Leeds Club, but it afterwards became known as the Yorkshire Wanderers, for whom such noted players as the following appeared: Rev. E. H. Dykes, C. W. L. Fernandes, Ben Cariss, C. H. Coates, A. J. Forrest, T. A. Naylor, R. H. Fowler, A. R. Atkinson, Cecil Atkinson, Gilbert Harrison, E. T. Hirst, C. Scharf, H. W. T. Garnett, and others.

But Arthur Hudson had further ideas for the development of football in Yorkshire, and, in conjunction with H. W. T. Garnett and F. Schutt, originated the Yorkshire Challenge Cup. This was the real basis of the committee's rule in Yorkshire. The idea thus mooted by the gentlemen named above was taken up by the five clubs, who formed themselves then and there into a business-like assembly for conducting the entire affairs of the county. Nothing could have been more fortunate, as things have turned out, than the idea of the Cup being made the pivot round which the whole machinery of state had to turn. It has held the fabric together ever since in a manner that could not have been achieved any other way. The refractory, the rebellious, and the wavering have all been brought to their senses by having the Cup dangled before their eyes by the committee as occasion required, and to-day finds the spell just as potent as ever. The names of the executive at the period of the institution of the Cup in 1876 were as follows: H. W. T. Garnett (Bradford), who became president, A. E. Hudson (hon. sec.), F. Schutt (Leeds), E. Glaisby (York), H. Huth (Huddersfield), W. H. H. Hutchinson (Hull). It is popularly supposed that the Cup was presented and paid for by the five clubs. Such idea is erroneous. The names of the five clubs founding the competition are engraved upon the Cup, but the Cup was purchased out of the proceeds of the final tie in the first year of the competition.

It will be seen that at the origination of the Cup contests the quintette of clubs that had had the management of county football formed the first committee. But the numbers and method of election of the committee soon underwent changes. The first great agitation for reform arose at the end of the season 1879-80, when general dissatisfaction was expressed at the exclusive constitution and management of the then existing committee, which was composed as follows: H. W. T. Garnett (Bradford), president; H. Huth (Huddersfield), G. Harrison (Hull), G. T. Thomson (Halifax), and A. E. Hudson (Leeds), hon. secretary and treasurer. York had lost its seat, and Harrison, though coming from Hull, did not sit as a representative of that town. The Huddersfield Club, though directly represented on the committee, took the initiative. The movement was supported by the Wakefield Trinity, Dewsbury, Halifax, Huddersfield, Leeds St. John's, Bradford Rangers, and Kirkstall Clubs. B. Schofield, of Huddersfield, acted as secretary to the "agitators." The agitation was vigorously conducted, and excitement was great in the county. Seats on the committee were offered to the Wakefield Trinity and Dewsbury clubs. The former accepted the offer and, along with the Halifax Club, retired from the agitation, but the Dewsbury Club, having pledged themselves to "united action," refused the proffered seat unless the invitation was further extended. Feeling ran high, and the committee further increased the strength of the opposition by refusing to receive a deputation on the subject. But wiser counsels prevailed, and ultimately the following gentlemen—J. Watkinson (Huddersfield), B. Schofield (Huddersfield), H. H. Doe (Leeds St. John's), M. Newsome (Dewsbury), and W. Peat (Kirkstall)—attended at a meeting of the committee on the 11th August, 1880, to explain the views and state the grievances of the agitators. John Watkinson was chief spokesman on behalf of the deputation, and preferred the case in moderate language but with strong argument.

After full discussion the committee decided to invite representatives from the Dewsbury and Leeds St. John's clubs to join their body. They also departed from the principle of absolute self-election, by proposing "to submit the names of their nominees to the approval of the clubs to which such nominees individually belong." These concessions gave temporary satisfaction, and matters were amicably settled. Subsequently the York Club was asked again to send a representative, and at the commencement of the season 1880-81 the committee consisted of the following members:—H. W. T. Garnett (Bradford), president; H. Huth (Huddersfield), G. T. Thomson (Halifax), G. Harrison (Hull), C. T. Baldwin (Wakefield Trinity), A. Newsome (Dewsbury); J. B. Ogden (Leeds St. John's), hon. sec.; and A. E. Hudson (Yorkshire Wanderers, late Leeds), hon. treasurer. J. B. Ogden thus took the place of A. E. Hudson as hon. secretary, who was compelled to resign that office through pressure of business. "Joe" Ogden was one of the leading spirits of the Leeds St. John's Club from its formation in 1869 by his brother, T. J. Ogden. Though a county player, he achieved greater fame at the game of "La Crosse," in which he gained International honours, being a member of the English La Crosse team against Ireland at Belfast in 1881. No more genial or more popular fellow exists than the facetious "Joe," who is all sport, and a

Yorkshireman to the backbone, relieved with Leeds trimmings, for his attachment to the Leeds St. John's—now the Leeds—Club is pre-eminent. He took a leading part in the great agitation in London in 1882.

J. D. OGDEN.
From a Photograph by Dinnie, Leeds.

Ogden was succeeded at the end of 1881-82 by his club mate, T. Glover. Like Ogden, Tom Glover was a Leeds St. John's man, and, curiously enough, he also was more famous at La Crosse than at Rugby football. In 1881 he was chosen in the English La Crosse team which met Ireland at Belfast, and scored two goals out of the four obtained by the Englishmen.

But though the agitation of 1880 was not successful in obtaining all the points claimed, the committee were evidently cognisant of the feeling in the county, and proceeded to frame a constitution for the government of Yorkshire football. The constitution was published on January 15th, 1883, and though a great advance on the previous system of election of the committee, retained the management in the hands of certain clubs and left the selection of representatives practically in the power of the retiring committee.

And so, on the publication of the constitution, the Yorkshire clubs commenced to agitate for the election of the committee at an annual meeting of Yorkshire clubs in the Rugby Union.

T. GLOVER.
(From a Photograph by Brown, Barnes and Bell, Regent Street, W.)

A requisition to this effect was drawn up, and a deputation attended a meeting of the Yorkshire committee on May 7th, 1883, but the committee decided they could not accede to the wishes of the requisitionists, though they would at an early date take into consideration the advisability of increasing the number of representatives on the committee. Accordingly, on May 21st, the committee decided to accord a seat to the Hull Club, W. J. Close being elected their first representative.

In August, 1883, the Thornes Club was elected to membership in the place of the Yorkshire Wanderers. It is generally supposed that Thornes earned their seat under the rule that " the holders of the Challenge Cup, if not already represented, shall have a seat on the committee," but this is not the case; the Thornes club was elected on August 8th, 1883, whereas the rule having reference to the Cup holders was not adopted till August 30th. It was under this rule that the Batley Club were received after winning the Cup in 1885; that club is the only club that has been accorded a seat under the rule referred to, though doubtless the circumstance that the Thornes club were the winners of the Cup in 1882 was the chief cause of the election of that club to a seat on the committee in 1883. No further change took place in the constitution of the committee for a considerable period (though the decadence of Thornes caused that club to be voted off the committee in 1886), for the simple reason that, the principal clubs in Yorkshire being all represented, any agitation would necessarily fail for lack of leadership. Guided by past experience, the committee were inclined to voluntarily include any rising club; indeed, the rule referring to the holders of the Challenge Cup was expressly intended to afford an opening by which a club could, through merit, earn representation on the executive. So, with the exception of according a seat to the Spen Valley clubs at the end of the 1886-87 season, no further change took place till 1888, though Arthur Hudson advocated the claims of the Manningham Club to representation when that club rose to prominence. The next change came from circumstances outside the committee, and not from any action by the Yorkshire clubs. But previous to this there were alterations in the *personnel* of the committee. In 1884 Garnett retired from the presidency, and was succeeded by Arthur Hudson, who held the office till his death in 1888. Mark Newsome then became president, and has the honour of being the last president of the Yorkshire County Committee, and the first president of the Yorkshire Rugby Union. In November, 1884, T. Glover resigned the secretaryship, and his seat on the committee was accorded to J. A. Miller, who was also elected to the office of secretary, a post which he held till June, 1892, when he was elected president in succession to B. Kilner, who had succeeded the Rev. F. Marshall in 1891.

The season 1887-88 saw the great change from the Yorkshire County Club to the Yorkshire Rugby Union, and, with this change, the placing of the election upon a popular basis. And June, 1888, saw the first meeting of a representative body, comprising the clubs in Yorkshire, members of the Rugby Union. By the new constitution adopted at that meeting, it was specifically enjoined that all clubs joining the Yorkshire Union thereby became members of the Rugby Union, and were admitted without further subscription to take part in the competition for the Yorkshire Challenge Cup. Thus the bait of the Cup was made use of by the Yorkshire committee to obtain votes at the general meetings of the Rugby Union. And now the Yorkshire Union is the most powerful organisation in the country. It has a membership of 150 clubs, or about three-sevenths of the entire number in affiliation with the Rugby Union. At first clubs were indiscriminately elected to seats on the committee, but latterly the Union has been divided into districts, a seat being assigned to each district, and this is the present arrangement.

The future legislative problem is the relationship between the Yorkshire Union and the Rugby Union. The latter representative of the varied interests in the different districts in which the Rugby game is played is threatened with the undesirable contingency that one district by its preponderate voting power may arrogate to itself the control of the destiny of the game. Such contingency can be averted only by increased interest and vigilance in other districts, by well-advised concessions on the part of the Rugby Union to the legitimate proposals of Yorkshire, and by the Yorkshiremen adopting wiser counsels and more moderate methods. But the history of the Yorkshire committee, with its serious agitations and club interests so markedly manifest in every discussion, does not give much hope that Yorkshiremen will be moved from their steadfast purpose of claiming what they consider their just right according to their voting power.

Yorkshire Clubs and Players.

Sheffield is certainly the oldest football town in Yorkshire. The dribbling game was being played there in the "fifties," and the Sheffield Football Association was formed long before the Londoners assumed their authority over the sport in 1863. The Sheffield Club claims to be the oldest football organisation in the kingdom. It was started in 1855. Its minute book for 1857 is still in existence. There were some excellent Rugby players living in Sheffield about 1869, and they were asked to play for Yorkshire in the first county match arranged with Lancashire on March 28th, 1870. These men probably hailed from the Sheffield Association, as

J. G. HUDSON.
(From a Photograph by Rushy, Leeds.)

there cannot be found a trace of a separate Rugby club existing in the cutlery town at that time, anyhow there was none in membership with the Rugby Union, when that body sprang into existence a year later. Sheffield had five men in the Yorkshire county team, but even that impetus failed to establish Rugby principles in the town as against the overwhelming influence of the Associationists, and Sheffield, as a Rugby centre, never had any existence at all.

The institution and progress of clubs has been carried out in two opposite ways. There have been clubs founded by public school boys anxious to play Rugby football after their school career had closed, and there have been clubs founded in a general way by the sport-loving public in the various towns. Of the former, Bradford, Hull, and Huddersfield are notable examples,

B B

whilst the Leeds Athletic Club is an instance of a club taking its beginning from an appeal to the sportsmanship of the general public in a large town. One of the principal leaders in the movement was J. G. Hudson, of Leeds, whose attention was drawn to the following advertisement appearing in the *Leeds Mercury* of March 7th, 1864 :—

"FOOTBALL.—Wanted a number of persons to form a football club for playing on Woodhouse Moor for a few days a week from 7 to 8 o'clock a.m. Apply K 99, Mercury Office."

K 99 turned out to be Henry Irwin Jenkinson, then a clerk at the North Eastern Railway Goods Department. He will be better known as the writer of a "Guide to the English Lake District." Hudson and Jenkinson, along with R. O. Berry, now a carting agent in Leeds, and W. Dickenson, now manager of a savings bank in Sheffield, were the founders of the club and formed the committee. Their first proceedings were to buy a ball and provide themselves with boundary flags and goal posts, these latter consisting of broom handles with pieces of cotton nailed on as flags. Their ground was Woodhouse Moor, and they arranged to play at half-past six every morning of the week. Games also took place in the evening. The head-quarters of the club were at Manor House Hotel, kept by one Strickland, who undertook to take charge of the goal posts and the ball. The hour, 6.30, was somewhat early both for Strickland and the players, but punctuality was ensured by the infliction of a fine of sixpence, rigidly enforced, upon a late player.

The rules of the game were on a par with the primitive posts. They called it Rugby football, but the players were not allowed to run with the ball, though they could handle it, make a fair catch, and were compelled to observe the law of on-side. A goal was scored, however, whenever the ball passed between the posts, irrespective of height, there being no cross-bar. Their ideas of the size and shape of the ball were similarly crude. They seem to have experimented with the balls, imagining that the bigger they had them the better, and at one time actually played with one fourteen inches in diameter.

The initiation of members proceeded upon a simple but effective plan. If an individual came upon the Moor and took an interest in the play, Hudson would accost

FRED. BONSOR—1884-1889.
(From a Photograph by Bradge and Smith, Bradford.)

J. L. HICKSON—1880-1891.
(From a Photograph by R. C. Clifford, Bradford.)

GILBERT HARRISON—1883-1888.

E. HOLMES—1891.
(From a Photograph by Robinson and Sloves, Bradford.)

W. F. BROMET—1891-1892.
(From a Photograph by Gilman & Co., Oxford.)

FIVE YORKSHIRE CAPTAINS.

him and ask, "Will you be a member?" If the reply was "Yes," there followed a demand for a shilling as a subscription, and if he paid he became a member, and was put to play on one side or the other. The club grew and soon numbered about 500 members, and the morning and evening practices became the sight of Leeds. There were any quantity of players on a side, and 150 players in an evening and sixty in a morning was no unusual thing. In a month or two some fairly good players joined the club, and it was dubbed the "Leeds Athletic Club." The first captain was Howard Wright, afterwards captain of the Yorkshire team in the first match against Lancashire at Leeds in 1870. The first match was in the year 1864 against Sheffield. It was played at Sheffield, and must have been under the Sheffield code of rules, which at that time admitted of a player being on-side, so long as the goal-keeper was between himself and the goal. These tactics nonplussed the Leeds men, who suffered a severe defeat, though they managed to turn the tables in the return match at Leeds.

In 1865 Manchester was challenged and a match arranged which took place at Fieldhouse, near Huddersfield, on a ground lent by Edward Brooke. The goalposts and flags were taken over to Huddersfield, and the match was played under Rugby rules. The club continued to play its games on Woodhouse Moor for about two years, and then took a ground in the Horticultural Gardens, where it flourished for some time under the name of the "Leeds Athletic Club."

As has been already stated, the five clubs inaugurating the Yorkshire Challenge Cup were Hull, Leeds, Bradford, Huddersfield, and York. These were practically the only organisations existing in the county at the end of 1869, when the sport was beginning to be publicly recognised. For several years after this period Hull was looked upon as the premier club in Yorkshire, and was the first Yorkshire club to join the Rugby Union immediately after the foundation of the same. Bradford was the next to become a member, viz., in 1874, following which a number of clubs joined simultaneously. Doubtless there were two or three additional organisations being founded at the beginning of the year 1870, but they had no sort of standing beside the quintette mentioned above, who comprise the "early clubs" of Yorkshire football. It may be of interest to mention the names of a few minor local clubs, that followed pretty closely in the wake of these early pioneers, viz., Chapel Allerton, Chapeltown, Doncaster, Harrogate, Ripon, Ravensthorpe, Mirfield. This list does not, of course, include the whole of the second division existing at the period referred to, but it about comprises the list of those which were known to the five elect, beyond which there could be hardly any existence to speak of.

The Hull Club.

The first Hull club was formed in the autumn of 1865. The chief promoters were W. H. H. Hutchinson, C. B. Lambert, F. A. Scott, E. Waltham, and H. J. Wade, all of whom played in the early Yorkshire teams against Lancashire. The club soon had a membership of forty to fifty members, and played on the Rifle Barracks parade ground. The game played was neither the regular Rugby nor the Association game, but one something resembling Rugby, though running with the ball was only permissible after a catch. The first matches were in 1867, against Lincoln, both of which were won, and until 1870 three or four matches were generally played in each year with Bramham College, St. Peter's School, York, Louth (Lincolnshire), Newark, and perhaps one or two others in which the Hull Club was usually victorious.

In 1870 a ground was taken at Ferriby. Here Leeds were met twice, each club winning one match, but owing to the distance between Hull and the West Riding clubs in 1871 a ground was rented at Selby, where the Hull men met Leeds, Bradford, and Huddersfield, and beat them all, though the win against Huddersfield was a very lucky one. Club colours were commenced, at that time pink and white stripes. About this time the three Hodgsons, William, Richard, and Edward, joined the club, and also some good men from the public schools—viz., E. A. Hollingbery and F. O. Moss from Rugby, and E. W. Harrison from Cheltenham, all of whom played for the county.

Until 1877 the club continued to play the chief of the Yorkshire clubs with fair success on the whole, though often let down through being short of men when playing from home. The ground during that time was first at Newland, near Hull, and afterwards on the Anlaby Road, Hull. In 1877 the Hull Club, after beating Mirfield and Heckmondwike, was defeated in the Challenge Cup ties by York, and at the end of the season virtually broke up, almost all the old players, the Hodgsons, Wade, Walter Harrison, Hutchinson, Moss, and others dropped out, and there were very few young ones to take their places. The club continued under different management for three or four years longer, when it became amalgamated with the Hull White Star Club, and has since continued under its present management. The first captain was Edward Waltham, who was followed by Beevor Lambert, but the man best known in the early days of Hull and Yorkshire football was W. H. H. Hutchinson, a fine strapping forward familiarly known to all his friends as "the Baron." He was considered a great authority on the game in his day, and as a scrummager he had certainly no superior. Up to 1876 he was the recognised captain of the Yorkshire team in matches played outside Yorkshire, and was the first Yorkshireman to gain the distinction of being selected to play for England. He retired from the captaincy of the Yorkshire team in 1876.

W. H. H. HUTCHINSON.
(From a Photograph by Sarony, Scarborough.)

Gilbert or "Gillie" Harrison was another famous player who hailed from Hull, and like Hutchinson acted as captain for Yorkshire. He commenced playing for the county in 1875, and from that date formed one of the Yorkshire team in almost every match up to the end of the season 1887-88. In 1878-79 Harrison played against Scotland and Ireland, and in the following season played against Scotland, but was unable to take the journey to Ireland. His name does not again appear in an International team till 1884-85, when he played against Wales. This selection after so long a gap is a wonderful testimony to the ability and staying powers of the Hull player. His connection with his county team extended over no less than fourteen seasons. Harrison was a lithe forward, an honest scrummager, but specially notable for coming through the pack and dribbling in a very clever manner. The honour of captaining Yorkshire came late in the day, when Harrison was beginning to slow down after ten years' hard service. Amongst the later Hull players may be mentioned the Calverts, Jacketts, Iveson, Bell, and Oxlade.

THE BRADFORD CLUB.

The Bradford Football Club is given in the *Football Annual* as founded in 1868, but it is really an offshoot of the Bradford Cricket Club, which was founded in 1836, and is still one of the best known clubs in the North. It is recorded, on the authority of "Nomad," a local writer on sporting topics, that for many years prior to 1868, a party of young men, who had been initiated into the game in their school days at Steeton Hall and Bramham College, were in the habit of playing football in the winter months on the Bradford cricket ground, which was then situated in Horton Road, about a quarter of a mile from the present enclosure, now known in all cricket and football circles as "Park Avenue." The football meetings of the young men can be traced back to 1863, and they framed a code of rules for themselves, the Rugby Union not having then come into existence. The game played was a cross between the present Association and Rugby rules. Oates Ingham was the earliest leader. This was the foundation of the B. F. C. Shortly after the commencement of the club leave to play on the Bradford ground was withdrawn on account, it is assumed, of damage done to the cricket pitch; and the club then went through various vicissitudes, occupying various grounds in succession, such as Manningham, Peel Park, and Girlington, and finally settled at Apperley Bridge, a few miles out of Bradford, until Park Avenue became available.

In or about 1875 the cricket club had to leave the ground in Horton Road, and took a lease of a larger area of land in Park Avenue. Shortly after this negotiations were commenced with the object of amalgamating the cricket and football clubs, and the end was successfully attained in 1881, when on the new field a special enclosure was prepared and reserved for the football section of the club. It was a long time before fixtures could be arranged with other teams, Leeds being the first to meet Bradford, then Huddersfield, Hull, and York in the order named. Some members of the team in 1869-70 were A. Haley, A. Firth (captain), A. Holmes, W. Haley, F. Hargreaves, A. Lassen, C. Lonsdale, F. Adcock, G. Bateman, O. Ingham, M. Dawson, Greenwood, and Bateson.

The Bradford Club can point to two particular periods of success, and curiously those periods are separated by the space of ten years. 1873 - 75 saw Bradford at the top of Yorkshire football. At that period Garnett, F. Schutt, R. Mills, F. S. Tetley, and J. Richardson were picked to play against Lancashire. Reggie Mills was *the* halfback for Bradford of his day.

F. S. TETLEY.
From a Photograph by Appleton & Co., Bradford.

Tetley played either halfback or three-quarter, and filled either position equally well. He was a hundred yards' runner and often competed at athletic sports. His speed combined with his weight made him an awkward customer to tackle. His handing-off was very powerful, and he was also a fair drop, but he is best summed up in the words "speed and strength." He gained his England cap against Scotland in 1876.

Harry Garnett, pre-eminently connected with the Bradford Club, is the man above all others who has founded County football in Yorkshire. Captain of the Bradford Club from 1874 to 1881; captain of the Yorkshire Fifteen from 1877 to 1880; a member of the County Committee for some eighteen years, for seven of which he filled the post of president; an International player, and president of the Rugby Union 1889-90, no

BRADFORD:
WINNERS OF THE YORKSHIRE CHALLENGE CUP, 1884.

(From a Photograph by R. T. Watson, Hull.)

H. ROBERTSHAW, N. August 4TH.

W. P. CARTER, A. R. PERKINS, J. W. BOTTOMLEY, F. T. RITCHIE, T. ATKINSON, F. B. HOLMES, F. BOOTH, J. BARKER, J. WRIGHT, E. CRITCHLEY, S. MAJOR.
R. H. BUSOR, J. W. MARSHALL, J. L. HICKES, F. BOSOR (CAPTAIN), E. WILKINSON, R. ROBERTSHAW, J. POTTER.

man has done more service for his club, his county, and his country than Harry Garnett, of Otley, and the clubs of Yorkshire perpetrated an act of ingratitude when they deprived past presidents of the Yorkshire Union of the right to sit on the committee as *ex-officio* members, and thus severed Garnett's official connection with Yorkshire football. As a player he was always conspicuous on the field as playing barelegged, without stockings or shin guards, having whilst a schoolboy learnt to despise a hack. He had many sides, for he was the heavy forward, the fast dribbler, and the long kicker by turns. He could also play a fair game at three-quarter, and was a splendid coach to young players, whose blunders were always treated by him from the humorous side. He had a perfect knowledge of the game and was a stickler for having it played "according to Cocker."

"The second period, 1883-84-85, saw Bradford at the zenith of their fame, and at that time their successes over the strongest clubs in England and Scotland, combined with the efficient management of the club, raised Bradford into the position of being in many ways the premier club of England. Much of the credit of these achievements is due to the capable captaincy in 1882-83 of A. B. Perkins, of flag-wielding fame and Yorkshire Committee and Rugby Union renown, who was a born general, and knew exactly how to keep a team together. He was fortunate to be captain at a time when the team was acquiring strength almost weekly. Fred Bonsor had become a regular member of the team in 1881-82, which season also was the beginning of Frank Ritchie's connection with the club. Edgar Wilkinson, Laurie Hickson, and Herbert Robertshaw joined in 1882-83; the following season saw Rawson Robertshaw develop as a centre three-quarter. Individual brilliancy, combination, and scientific passing caused the Bradford team of this period to be the most accomplished fifteen that has ever done duty for any single club in Yorkshire.

Fred Bonsor and J. Wright were the half-backs, and both men gained International honours. The latter was a sturdy, safe, defensive player, and a much better man than many more showy players who were supposed to be his superiors. Bonsor was without doubt the best half-back that Yorkshire has produced. Limby, with a clutch like that of an octopus, he always grassed his man, whilst possessed of weight, speed, and strength, combined with dodging powers, he was a most dangerous player on the attack. His feeding of the backs and judgment in play were of the highest order. Fred Bonsor at his best was the half-back of an age. He is the only Yorkshireman who has acted as captain of an England team.

Edgar Wilkinson was a brilliant forward in the open,

Rawson. Percy. Herbert.
THE BROTHERS ROBERTSHAW.
(From a Photograph by Bridges & Son, Bradford.)

but not much of a scrummager. He and Herbert Robertshaw were the two flying men of the Bradford forward division, and the most dangerous men near the goal line. A good dribbler, a fast follower up, and always at hand to take a pass, Edgar Wilkinson had a share in most of the many brilliant victories gained by the Bradford Club during the period that he was in the ranks of its team. In 1886 he played in all the International matches of the season, scoring a try against Wales, and in the following month obtained the only try scored in the Irish match at Dublin. In the following season Wilkinson played against Wales and Scotland.

Rawson Robertshaw first appeared in the Bradford

team as a forward, but on being placed at centre three-quarter he speedily evinced such peculiar talent for that special position that he became the acknowledged "centre" of his time. His style is often referred to as the perfection of centre three-quarter play, and by common consent he has been dubbed "the Prince of Centres," a title which he fairly earned, for he can claim the distinction of being the initiator of modern centre play. He possessed all the physical qualifications for the post with which his name is thus associated. Strong, active, fearless, and decisive, he was unsurpassed in his ability to stop a dribble or a forward rush. But it was in attack chiefly that he revolutionised back play. He linked the three-quarters into harmony and made them a component part of the machinery of the game. He could take or give a pass with the greatest ease, and his picking up and dropping into touch were notably clean and accurate.

His brothers, Herbert and Percy, worthily upheld the family name. Herbert was the first to earn fame as a forward, and was quite the most brilliant man in the Bradford team, and it was only because he had the misfortune to shine in a year remarkable for a plethora of fast forwards that he failed to secure an England cap.

Percy Robertshaw was the youngest of the three brothers, and played full-back for Bradford, occasionally appearing as centre. On the retirement of Rawson he was elected to fill the vacancy at centre. He was a sound player, his kicking being especially good. He was awarded his England cap in the season 1888, when England played no International matches owing to the dispute.

John Lawrence (Laurie) Hickson came from the Bingley Club to Bradford in 1882 and immediately came into prominence. In addition to being a regular glutton for scrummage work, Hickson was always a fair kicker both at drop and place and had good pace into the bargain. He was a rare scorer, and used to beat the best backs of the day whenever a chance presented itself near the goal line. Laurie succeeded Gillie Harrison in the captaincy of the Yorkshire team, and it used to be his boast that he had never been on the losing side against Lancashire in seven years of fixtures (he was on tour with Bradford when the Red Rose won in

1884), but his record was spoilt at Whalley Range in 1890, when Squire Mawson had his collar-bone smashed.

Another Bradford crack and English International was J. J. Hawcridge. In 1876, along with others, he formed the Manningham Albion Club, and already his dodging powers had become noticeable. Then playing amongst the forwards, he was known as the "Waddling Duck," and his sinuous runs were described as "the trail of the serpent." Later on, when playing at three-quarters, he came to be styled "the Artful Dodger," and certainly few backs were more difficult to stop. Running with a peculiarly stealthy stride, and a marvellous swerve, he seldom failed to elude the grasp of the would-be tackler. In 1878 the Manningham Albion took the name of Manningham, and the present Manningham Club is the result, so the credit of bringing Hawcridge out belongs to the Manningham Club, whose prominence as a club really dates from the period Joe Hawcridge began to play with them. It was in

J. J. HAWCRIDGE.
(From a Photograph by R. C. Clifford, Bradford.)

1884-5 that Hawcridge joined Bradford. He had two magnificent props in Fred Bonsor and Rawson Robertshaw, and with their assistance and his own inimitable dodging he totalled 38 tries that season. In the famous match between Oxford and Bradford in this season, which ended in a draw, the Oxford back team included H. B. Tristram, A. S. Blair, G. C. Lindsay, A. G. Grant-Asher, and A. Rotherham, and yet opposed to these players Hawcridge made a sensational run which nearly won the match for Bradford. It is believed that his play in this match earned him his England cap, for he appeared in the teams against Wales and Ireland, scoring a try in each match.

Among the later players J. Toothill, who also came to Bradford from the Manningham Club, is a forward of the old type, and has been for some years the centre of the Bradford pack, and one of the mainstays of the Yorkshire scrummage. A determined player, with no undue roughness, and with any amount of pluck and capacity for hard work, Toothill is a grand specimen of a Yorkshire forward, and has done great service for England against Scotland in 1890 and 1892. J. Richards, a speedy forward, A. Briggs, and C. Emmott, half-backs, have been the latest addition to England teams from the Bradford Club, which club has in all furnished thirteen International players. E. Holmes, a genuine forward, always working, and playing a most unselfish game, hails from the Manningham Club.

LEEDS.

This club must not be mistaken for the Leeds Athletic Club already described in this chapter, nor for the present Leeds Club playing at Headingley. It is the club founded by the late Arthur E. Hudson. It was afterwards known as the Yorkshire Wanderers. The present Leeds Club, which had nothing to do with the promotion of the Challenge Cup competition, is in reality the old St. John's Club, which was founded in 1870 in connection with the Leeds St. John's Sunday School, and for the first year membership was confined exclusively to the scholars. The founder was T. J. Ogden, now at Malvern, who was the first captain; and who was succeeded by John Gordon, now a vice-president of the Leeds Club. J. B. Ogden, T. Glover, and J. A. Miller, successive county secretaries, were all prominent members of Leeds St. John's. The first ground of the Johnians was in the Militia Barracks, where they played on the cinders for several seasons. They subsequently migrated to Cardigan Fields, the scene of many notable conflicts for the Yorkshire Cup. Some three years ago several Leeds gentlemen conceived the idea of securing a first-class ground for cricket, football, and other pastimes. The present unrivalled enclosure at Headingley was the result of their efforts, and the Leeds St. John's Club was invited to join and supply the football team. The "Saints" generously decided to abandon the name under which they had won fame, and to throw in their lot with the new undertaking, and to take the name of the Leeds Football Club.

R. H. Fowler, of the old Leeds Club, was the first Leeds man to gain International honours in the year 1877. He was a heavy, powerful forward, ran straight and pushed men out of the way—the usual style of heavy-weight forwards in his day. Charles Hutton Coates, an old Cambridge player, was a member of the Yorkshire Wanderers in 1880-81. He was an energetic and hard-working forward, and was especially good at the line-out. He gained International honours in 1879, 1880, and 1881. He played for the South in 1879, and for the North in 1881. Charles Walker Luis Fernandes, of Wakefield, was also a member of the Yorkshire Wanderers. Some good judges consider Fernandes to have been the best forward who ever played for Yorkshire. He was very fast, tackled splendidly, and never tired. He obtained his county cap in 1879, and played against Scotland, Ireland, and Wales in 1881. Fernandes is constantly to be seen at the big matches, and in connection with this played for the North at Blackheath on December 15th, 1888.

C. W. L. FERNANDES.

The Yorkshiremen had to pass through Wakefield on their way to London. Fernandes was on the platform to see the "boys" off. Garnett and Kilner insisted on his accompanying them, and literally hauled him into the carriage, and he was landed in London with neither scrip nor baggage. A. L. Brooke was delayed by a fog, so that after the match had proceeded some twenty minutes, Fernandes was pressed into the forward ranks. His condition was so good that he was able to do his full share of the work, and his tackling was as keen and effective as ever. Thus, after having retired from football seven years, Fernandes once more became entitled to a North cap, a distinction gained by accident, but genuinely merited by the form he displayed in the match.

HUDDERSFIELD.

The Huddersfield Athletic Club was founded in 1864, but the earliest records of football date no further back than 1869, when a few football enthusiasts agreed to have

Frank.   Harry.   Fred.

THE BROTHERS HUTH.

(*From a Photograph by Seltman & Co., Huddersfield.*)

a little practice at the game, and as Percy Learoyd of "The Grove" was one of their number, he suggested that the practices should take place in the extensive grounds attached to that residence. This was acted upon. Fred Learoyd was appointed president, and H. B. Dransfield secretary. The meetings used to be held in the saddle room at "The Grove." After a few weeks Edward Brooke, of Edgerton, originated a match, Liberals *v.* Conservatives, and this took place at Fieldhouse in 1869. A return match was played in March, 1870. At that time the organisation could scarcely be called a club, as the teams were of a scratch character, but the above mentioned matches caused so much interest that it was decided to arrange a match or two with other clubs. Before long Leeds Grammar School was met, and afterwards Hull. Thus a proper playing team was got together. To defray sundry small expenses a subscription of 2s. 6d. was levied because the Athletic club did not see its way to take over the management of such a section, although most of the players were members of the club; but when later on it was evident that the game was becoming more popular, and that it was necessary to have a proper organisation, the committee of the Huddersfield Athletic Club decided to have football teams, to rent the field at Trinity Street, (the Rifle field) for winter as well as summer, and to provide players with goal posts, etc., all other expenses being defrayed by the players themselves. This state of affairs existed until the amalgamation with St. John's Cricket Club at Fartown in 1879. The following are some of the early players who attended the practices at "The Grove," and these formed about the first team: A. Bradley, who afterwards captained Yorkshire, H. S. Brooke, Yorkshire captain, G. S. Brooke, H. Beardsell, C. W. Beardsell, Thomas Holt, Percy Learoyd, Edwin

E. WOODHEAD.

J. DYSON.
(*From a Photograph by F. Bradley, Huddersfield.*)

HUDDERSFIELD.
WINNERS OF THE YORKSHIRE CHALLENGE CUP, 1890.

(From a Photograph by R. T. Watson, Hull.)

J. Pyman, G. Harrop (Hon. Sec.), W. H. England, L. Littlewood (Umpire), W. Hirst (Hon. Sec.), H. C., and A. C's
J. Pyman, G. Harrop (Hon. Sec.), W. H. England, F. W. Humphries, J. H. Shaw, J. W. Thewlis, T. H. England, J. P. Crosland (President).
G. Mitchell, P. Jackson, H. Archer (Captain), O. Franey, J. Schofield.
J. Kaye, F. Watkin, W. Longmans, A. L. Brooke.

Learoyd, George Brooke, J. B. Vickerman, C. Steward A. Calvert, H. B. Dransfield, John Riley, H. Sheard Conacher, W. Wimpenny, George Beaumont, Whiteley Tolson, C. E. Freeman. Later on at the Rifle field came E. Mallinson, T. P. Crosland, R. Welsh, Harry and Frank Huth, C. M. Sharpe, A. Schofield, R. P. Savery, B. Schofield, F. and H. Watkinson, Frank Walker, and others. C. E. Freeman, A. Bradley, and H. Beardsell were the Huddersfield stars of the early period, the first named being a wonderfully clever all-round player, who was always worth watching; Harry Beardsell, since so well known in connection with athletics, scored the first goal obtained against Lancashire in 1871. Yorkshire did not score a goal again till 1883.

Harry Huth was the first member of the Huddersfield Club to play for England. He and his two brothers, Fred and Frank, all three played for Yorkshire, appearing in the same team against Cheshire in 1878. The time of the Huths forms a distinct epoch in the history of the Huddersfield Club, and is often styled "the palmy days of the Huths." Certainly upon the retirement of the three brothers, the fortunes of the Huddersfield team were under a cloud until the recent resuscitation culminating in the winning of the cup in 1890. The characteristics of Harry's play were his wonderful dodging powers. He was a very powerful runner, and handed a man off in a peculiar way, with a jerk back of the shoulder, and a thrust of the body, eluding the tackle. He played against Scotland in 1879. Frank and Fred both played either as forwards or backs, and there can be little doubt that the latter, a powerful, clever forward, did not gain the honours to which his merits entitled him.

Ernest Woodhead, who played against Ireland in 1880, was a tall, clever forward. At Edinburgh University he played as a three-quarter, but subsequently as a forward. He was essentially a dribbler, and from his practice at three-quarter was very dangerous as a runner when he got possession of the ball. He shone particularly in loose play, but did not earn the reputation of being a genuine scrummager.

J. Dyson obtained his cap in 1890, appearing against Scotland in the famous match of 1890, and scored a try. He did not play again till 1892. Dyson is an exceedingly fast and strong runner, being very difficult to stop, and is the most dangerous scoring three-quarter of the present day. At one time he was regarded as a mere sprinter, but he has shown that he can dodge, kick, and tackle in the most finished manner. He has yet to rid himself of two defects in order to become a model three-quarter. He is inclined at times to wait for work to be given him, and to be slack in making openings for himself. He is also apt to fumble a pass, and knock the ball forward if the ball comes to him low.

YORK.

The football club of this ancient city dates its foundation about the year 1872-73, and at that time the ground was on the historic Knavesmire. Afterwards arrangements with the Yorkshire Gentlemen's Cricket Club secured the use of their ground. Amongst the early players in the York team, the name of Charlie Wood, of county fame, stands out most prominently, and that player is still remembered by the old school of players as the champion half-back in Yorkshire of his time. There may be mentioned the brothers Christison, Dr. Nicholson, F. Glaisby, T. Jolly, MacKenzie, Singleton, Harris, J. B. Shaw, Maugham, and Braithwaite. In 1884 the York Club and the York Melbourne Club were merged into one under joint management. At this time the fortune of the York team was on the wane, and it was thought by the infusion of new blood the prestige of the old York Club might be upheld. York has suffered much through lack of a good ground, and from the loss of good players, whose term of service to the club has been brief, either owing to injury or migration. It was about 1875-76 when York were at their best, and it was in that season they commenced playing matches with Bradford and Leeds regularly. They were defeated in the final round of the first year of the Challenge Cup by Halifax, the score being 1 goal 1 try and 9 touch-downs to *nil*.

HALIFAX.

On November 1st, 1873, the following advertisement appeared in the *Halifax Guardian* :—

"Persons desirous of joining a football and athletic club are requested to meet on Thursday next, November 6th, at 8.30 p.m. at the Upper George Hotel."

The advertisement was due to S. Duckitt, late vice-president of the Yorkshire Rugby Union, M. Brown, and J. Pearson, who have since held prominent positions amongst the officers of the Halifax Club, Alfred Walsh, the first captain, and A. Nicholls, who was chosen as hon. secretary. The above gentlemen were all present at the first meeting, which was attended by two others, truly not a very encouraging beginning. With a membership of ten the first game was played on the Trinity cricket ground on December 6th, 1873. The following season, 1874-75, was commenced with a membership of sixteen, and with this small number Leeds Athletic, Wakefield Trinity, and Wakefield, amongst others, were met. The record at the end of the season showed that 7 matches had been played, of which 3 had been won, 1 lost, and 3 drawn.

The following season, 1875-76, however, may fairly be said to have laid the foundation for future success of the club, for having been deprived of the use of the Trinity cricket ground, the club, after playing one or two matches at Ovenden, had recourse to Skircoat Moor (now known as Savile Park.) This was open to the public free of charge, and great crowds used to assemble to watch the play. There can be little doubt that the opportunity of seeing the Halifax Club play their matches there was the beginning of the interest taken in the play which has caused the Rugby game to be so popular in Yorkshire. Halifax was the first club who could claim to have any considerable number of supporters. At Skircoat Moor it was that George Thomson, residing near the ground, first watched the play, and then made his début as a player. In 1876-77, an amalgamation was entered into between the cricket and football clubs, and a new ground opened at Hanson Lane, where the club had their headquarters till they purchased and laid out the present ground at Thrum Hall.

The Halifax team has always taken a prominent part in the tussle for the cup. By winning in the first year of the competition, when they defeated Bradford at Apperley Bridge, they demonstrated that the enthusiasm and energy of the self-taught player was sufficient to successfully cope with the scientific knowledge of the school trained expert in the game. 1886 again saw Halifax winning the cup, and the club repeated the performance in 1888. Amongst the early players were S. Duckitt, M. Brown, and A. Walsh, but the accession of Thomson to the team was greatly instrumental in raising the standard of play, and in waking enthusiasm among the followers of the game. George Thomas Thomson was a strong, slashing player, especially good at the line-out and in the open, being a very strong runner, and generally going straight, and having but few tricks; he was a most difficult man to stop, handing an opponent off well. The match against Wakefield Trinity in 1877, in the first season of the cup, is still remembered for the manner in which he literally ran over the two Hayleys and scored the winning try. Of a most genial disposition, he was the idol of Yorkshire up to his removal to the south of England in 1885. His grand physique, and kind handsome face, but above all, his winning manners, endeared him to all alike, no matter whether friends or opponents. His popularity in Yorkshire has never been exceeded, and his name is still the subject of veneration amongst all footballers of his generation. Joining Halifax in 1875, he played for Yorkshire in 1877, and for England in 1878, appearing in nine International matches. On the retirement of H. W. T. Garnett, in 1880, Thomson was elected captain of the Yorkshire team, and filled the post till 1884. For many years he was a prominent member of the Yorkshire

G. T. THOMSON.
(From a Photograph by J. F. Beaumont, Heptroyd.)

H. WILKINSON.
(From a Photograph by Bates & Son, Halifax.)

Committee. He became a member of the Rugby Union Committee in 1882, and was elected as vice-president, but was compelled to resign in 1888, being ordered abroad for the sake of his health ; but it was too late, the voyage had been put off too long, and Thomson arrived in Australia only to die within a few days from landing.

Albert Wood, the most celebrated of a numerous family, who all did good service for the Halifax Club, was also an International, taking part in the match against Ireland, in 1884. He was a dashing forward of great speed. Later on Harry Wilkinson gained his cap against the New Zealand team in 1890. He was a quick, energetic forward, a sterling worker in the pack, from which he broke quickly away, and an excellent dribbler. T. L. Scarborough and E. Buckley were also Halifax stars, but Halifax's most serviceable player was James Dodd. Joining the club in 1876, he continued to be a regular playing member of the team till the close of 1890-91, and has played in every position in the field for his club, and also as half-back, three-quarter, and full-back for his county and the North, but was never fortunate to get his International cap.

Wakefield Trinity.

The Trinity Club was formed in the year 1873, from among the members of a Young Men's Society in connection with Holy Trinity Church, of which T. O. Bennett was the secretary. The club was for the first few years confined to members of the society only, but immediately before the institution of the Yorkshire Cup this restriction was removed. Heath Common was the first scene of their play. The field in the borough market was then obtained ; later the club migrated to Belle Vue on the opposite side of the road to the present field, and where the first cup ties were played. In the following year a move was made to the present field. The first captains were T. O. Bennett, 1873-74-75-76-77, A. Hayley, 1877-78-79, C. T. Baldwin, 1879-80, and B. Kilner, 1880-81.

The best team that Trinity ever put into the field was probably that beaten in the cup ties of 1884 by Heckmondwike in a mud hole on the Heckmondwike ground by a goal to 2 tries. The first year, 1879, that Trinity

WAKEFIELD TRINITY, WINNERS OF THE YORKSHIRE CUP, 1879.

(From a Photograph by G. and J. Hall, 26, Westgate, Wakefield.)

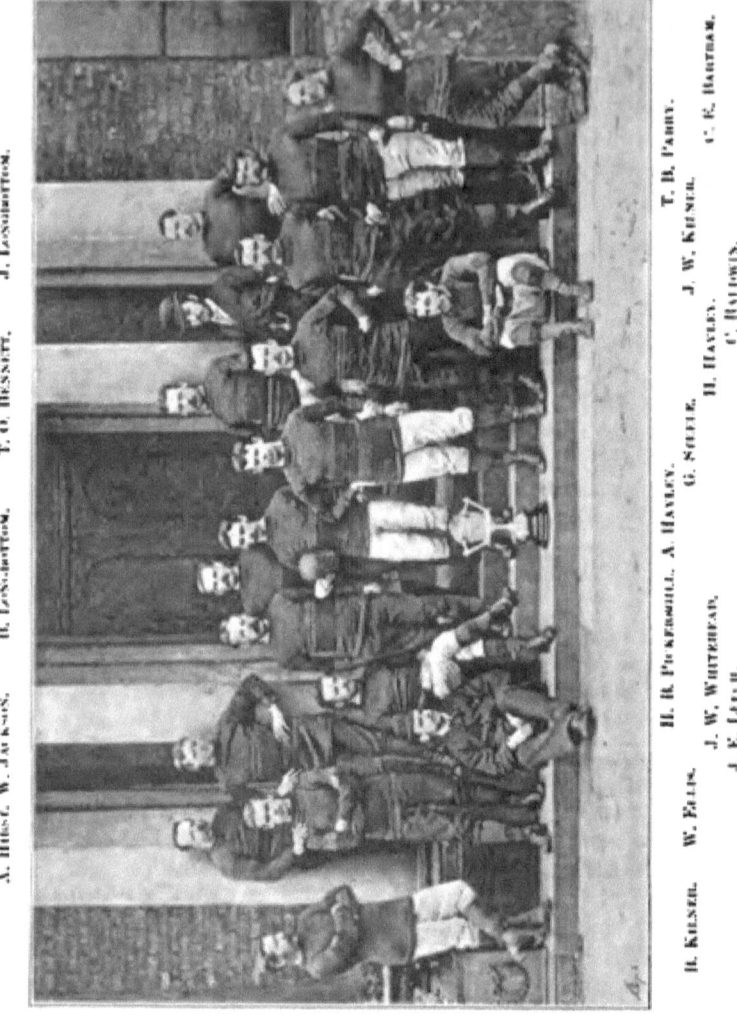

won the cup they had only three touch-downs registered against them.

Trinity are noted for playing a cup tie game. They have brought to perfection the science of obtaining little advantages and keeping them. They have developed a most clever method of working the ball steadily towards their opponents' goal by scrummage work and the use of touch. The style is not pretty but it is very clever, and nonplusses the opposing side. Their victims are loud in their outcry against the style, but repeated defeat may somewhat colour the spectacles through which envious rivals view the Trinity performances.

Of the early players may be mentioned T. O. Bennett, J. Longbottom, Harry and Arthur Hayley, E. J. Spink, J. W. and Barron Kilner, and C. T. Baldwin. Later on G. Steele, C. E. Bartram, Herbert Hutchinson, J. Latham, H. Fallas, and J. H. Jones have been prominent in upholding the fame of the club. Barron Kilner was a sturdy scrummager, and a very fast forward for 40 yards. He was a most dangerous man when close to the line, for then he used to put his head down and go straight for goal at full speed, when his weight and speed, combined with his sturdy build, rarely failed to carry him over. In the year 1883 he scored 26 tries for the Wakefield Club, a wonderful record for a forward. In this he was assisted by his clubmates, who invariably gave him chances when near the goal line. Wakefield Trinity are best known in connection with the Yorkshire Challenge Cup. Out of the first 25 rounds played in the cup ties Kilner played in 23, for during the first six years of the competition, Wakefield were in the final round no less than five times, and won the cup on three of those occasions. The object of his ambition at that time was to have his name engraved on the Yorkshire Cup as the captain of the winning team. He captained Wakefield in the years 1881 and 1882, when they worked their way into the final round, only to be defeated by Dewsbury in 1881 and Thornes in 1882, and it was exceedingly tantalising to Kilner to find his hopes thus dashed to the ground, especially as in 1883, when George Steele was captain, Wakefield easily defeated Halifax in the final.

Kilner's record in cup matches is however exceeded by that of his clubmate Herbert Hutchinson, a clever half-back whose merits did not receive just recognition, who played in no less than six final ties—viz., 1880-81-82-83-87-88, and wore the same jersey on all occasions. In the later matches the faded jersey was a conspicuous object on the field.

Kilner played five years for Yorkshire, and played against Ireland in 1880. He was early elected a member of the Yorkshire Committee, and also served on the committee of the Rugby Union. At one time he resigned his connection with both, declining to serve as a mere delegate of his club. In 1887 he again became a member of the Yorkshire Committee, and in 1889 once more joined the Rugby Union. He was elected vice-president of Yorkshire in 1888, and President in 1891.

Herbert Fallas, the only other Trinity man who has obtained his cap, was a dodgy three-quarter of good kicking powers, but Trinitarians always aver that the best man who played for the club was C. E. Bartram, who in his day attracted much attention in Yorkshire. He will be best remembered for his inventive genius in discovering loopholes in the laws, especially as regards the trick of picking up and dropping at goal after a try obtained in an unfavourable position. He was a speedy man and an exceedingly fine and accurate kicker. When tried in the North team he was past his best form.

DEWSBURY.

The Dewsbury Club, the club of the Newsomes, was established October, 1875, the founders being W. B. Atkins and W. H. Heys, both of whom played for the club for several seasons; the former was secretary for over seven years, resigning in 1884; the latter has gained considerable notoriety in Yorkshire as a handicapper. The club dates its rise from the time of the Newsomes joining the club. Accident had somewhat to do with this fortunate episode in the club's history. The Leeds Caledonians appeared at Crown Flats short-handed, and Mark Newsome, then just leaving school, who happened to be present as a spectator, was pressed into service for the visitors. This was practically the beginning of his football career and subsequent success. He was elected a member of the Dewsbury Committee and offered the captaincy of the club, and it is not too much to say that it is almost entirely due to the splendid play of the brothers Newsome in the field, and their abilities as legislators, along with C. Marsden, that the Dewsbury Club has attained its present high position. Mark Newsome was a splendid captain, always keeping his men well to their work. His running powers were above the average, as his numerous prizes testify. He was a safe tackler, picked up cleanly, and was in his best day the longest drop-kick in Yorkshire. He became President of the Yorkshire Committee on the death of A. E. Hudson in 1887, and was the first President of the Yorkshire Rugby Union, being elected in the seasons 1888-89, 1889-90. For some years he has served on the Rugby Union and as a member of the International Board. Alfred Newsome was a strong dashing runner, never going out of his way when making for the goal line, but handing off right and left and changing the ball accordingly. He never had his equal, at least in Yorkshire, at this style of play; he certainly was a terror. He was also a good kicker, excelling in punting.

A. NEWSOME.
(From a Photograph by Brown, Barnes and Bell, Regent Street, W.)

His clever left foot drop won the cup for Dewsbury in 1881, his brother Mark having put the club into the final tie by dropping a goal against Halifax in the previous round. C. Marsden, a clever, unselfish half-back, particularly good at passing, H. Purdy, W. K. Fisher, E. Wolstenholme, J. Garforth, Joe Naylor, and W. Stadden, the Welsh International, have all done yeoman service for the Dewsbury Club.

It is manifestly impossible in the present work to allude in detail to the clubs that have risen into prominence of late years, such as Manningham, Batley, Castleford, Liversedge, Brighouse, Hunslet, Otley, Pontefract, Holbeck, Leeds Parish Church, and others. Indeed, to do any justice to Yorkshire football and the clubs and players of that county would require a special volume. It may be that this may be done in the future, but in the present chapter the writer cannot go further than allude to one or two notable Yorkshire players who have earned the England cap, and have not been members of the clubs referred to above. Foremost of these is Richard Evison Lockwood, formerly of Dewsbury, and now of the Heckmondwike Club, and unquestionably the finest all-round wing three-quarter of the present day.

R. E. LOCKWOOD.
(*From a Photograph by J. E. Shaw, Huddersfield.*)

Comparisons with the veterans of old, who played under different conditions, cannot well be made, but all good judges admit the superiority of Lockwood over all the players of his time, as combining in one person in the highest degree all the essential qualities of a wing three-quarter. One of the smallest men who ever played for England, Lockwood may be best described as a "big little one," being powerfully built, and one mass of muscle. Taken at every point of the game he is in the first class. A speedy runner, a good dodger, an accurate kicker, both place and drop, an unfailing tackler; both on attack and defence, he is equally ahead of any contemporary. Of almost infallible judgment, always turning up at the right time, and invariably being at the right spot, he always does the right thing, whether in passing, running, or kicking. Whether seeking work for himself or being at hand to take a pass, or it may be in getting back to assist the defence, Lockwood's play for the past few seasons has been the theme of admiration of his friends, and has called forth the eulogiums and encomiums of critical observers. By common consent he is regarded as *the* player of his time. Lockwood first played for England in 1887. His clubmate, Donald Jowett, is a good-tempered, easy-going fellow, who, when he chose to exert himself, was a terror amongst the forwards, and possessing good pace in the open, was a dangerous scorer. It was no unfrequent sight to see him careering along grasping the ball in one huge hand, whilst with the other he brushed would-be tacklers aside as if they were so many flies in his path. He is a

DONALD JOWETT.
(From a Photograph by J. E. Shaw, Huddersfield.)

huge kicker, and the manner in which he landed the ball over the bar in the Scotch match of 1890 will always be regarded as a feature of that memorable game. Fred W. Lowrie, of Wakefield Trinity, and then of Batley, was a rare good forward, possessing speed, strength, and dash. Injured against Wales in 1890, he seemed to drop out of first-class fixtures prematurely, as in club matches he displays all his old cleverness and resource. He made a good companion to Harry Bedford, of Morley, and the pair brought off many a try in conjunction. Bedford was a heavy, dashing forward, and no more genuine, honest, hard-working player has appeared for England; but the fast game of the present has somewhat displaced such players as Harry, who, though only twenty-six, has increased in bulk, and cannot live the pace with the more active of his fellows.

W. E. Bromet, of Tadcaster, an old Oxford player, and the present captain of Yorkshire, is an ideal forward. In the season 1890-91 his play was almost perfect, for hardworking and untiring in the scrummage, and fast as a three-quarter in the open, he approached the acme of perfection as a forward. Like most of the Cape team his play in the season 1891-92 showed signs of deterioration, but he was still one of the leading forwards of England. The latest additions to International ranks from Yorkshire have been A. Briggs and C. Emmott, of Bradford, already alluded to, with W. Nichol, of Brighouse, and H. Bradshaw, of Bramley; the former a clever, fine, forward, and the latter a thorough bulldog in determination, and a glutton for work. Lastly, H. Varley, of Liversedge, playing against the Rest of England at Leeds, was chosen to partner Briggs at half-back against Scotland. In all, nine Yorkshiremen played for England in the season 1891-92.

Since the institution of the Yorkshire Challenge Cup £11,816 10s. has been distributed in charity, principally amongst the medical charities. The sum is thus made up:—1879, £100; 1880, £180; 1881, £300; 1882, £350; 1883, £552; 1884, £760; 1885, £900; 1886, £1,000; 1887, £800; 1888, £1,200; 1889, £903 10s.; 1890, £2,000; 1891, £650; 1892, £2,121.

The Winners of the Yorkshire Cup.

		G.	T.	T. D.		G.	T.	T. D.
1878	Halifax	1	1	9	beat York	0	0	0
1879	Wakefield Trinity	2	1	7	beat Kirkstall	0	0	0
1880	Wakefield Trinity	3	6	7	beat Heckmondwike	1	0	2
1881	Dewsbury	1 (d)	0	0	beat Wakefield Trinity	0	0	4
1882	Thornes	1	0	5	beat Wakefield Trinity	0	1	5
1883	Wakefield Trinity	1	2	11	beat Halifax	0	0	0
1884	Bradford	1	4	5	beat Hull	0	1	3
1885	Batley	0	0	8	beat Manningham	0	0	2
1886	Halifax	1	0	2	beat Bradford	0	0	2
1887	Wakefield Trinity	2	0	2	beat Leeds St. John's	0	0	2
1888	Halifax	0	2	2	beat Wakefield Trinity	0	1	1
1889	Otley	1	1	4	beat Liversedge	1	0	4
1890	Huddersfield	1	0	1	beat Wakefield Trinity	0	0	3
1891	Pontefract	1	1	4 pts.	beat Wakefield Trinity	0	1	1 pt.
1892	Hunslet	3	3	21 pts.	beat Leeds	0	0	0 pt.

CHAPTER XXI.

COUNTY FOOTBALL: RECOLLECTIONS OF NORTHUMBERLAND FOOTBALL.

By William Cail.

MY first recollection of football was Yorkshire. My grandfather had a place in the North Riding, where we went during the summer months for several years; each year my father invited the chief inhabitants, from the vicars downward, of two neighbouring villages, and chief of the afternoons' entertainments was football, one village against the other; that was long before the days of either Rugby or Association, and all of one village kicked down a large field, while those of the other kicked up; and if the ball hit the hedge at either end a goal was scored, and ample time for refreshment allowed.

My recollections then carry me to the valley of the Neckar, where many of us English lads, some from public schools finishing their education at Stuttgart, some at the schools at Cannstadt, used to meet weekly and play our Rugby game. From there the scene changed to North Germany, where about a dozen English had taught sufficient Germans to play to make up two teams, and regularly we had our game followed by a row on a neighbouring lake; these always took place on the Sunday mornings, so easily do we learn to do as the Romans when in Rome. I mention all these points to show that even before the game was organised, reported upon, lunched, saloon-carriaged, and dinnered, it was beloved.

On my return to Newcastle I found one football club, the Northumberland, while our neighbour Durham had Sunderland, still to the fore, Darlington—since given up to Association—and soon afterwards Bensham, afterwards partly merged in North Durham; against these we had many a fine game, games played in the best of spirit, where the dressing-room was often a hedge side and the spectators someone disappointed of a place in one of the teams.

In those days two county matches were played annually by the combined forces of Northumberland and Durham: one played in the name of Durham, and was v. Yorkshire, wherein Yorkshire generally had to be content with defeat; the other in the name of Northumberland and was v. Cumberland, which latter never scored a win against us. The last of these was played at Hexham about 1875 or '76, when Northumberland ran up a big score; Lowthian Bell being simply unholdable, going through the Cumberland team, time after time, with his peculiar teetotum-like motion.

After this new clubs rapidly sprang into being. The Tynemouth commenced playing in October, 1874; the Elswick—changed some three years later to Northern, and chiefly an offshoot from the Northumberland—about Christmas of the same year; Tynedale later on in the same season, and Gosforth early in the next.

At first the old Northumberland club more than held its own; at length it was beaten by Gosforth, the week following by Northern, and from that time ceased to be prominent in play. Towards the end of 1879 the ire of the county was raised when a match which the old club lost to York City was reported in the papers as Northumberland County; after letters in the public press the committee of the old club was induced to take the initiative, and call a meeting for the purpose of forming a county club. This meeting was held in Newcastle on 1st March, 1880, the six leading clubs—Northumberland, Tynemouth, Northern, Gosforth, Tynedale, and Percy Park—being represented. Mr. J. F. Ogilvie, of Tynemouth, was appointed chairman, and myself *ad interim* secretary. The first general meeting was held in the following April at which rules were passed: Sir M. W. Ridley, Bart., M.P., was elected president, and Messrs. Joseph Cowen, M.P., and T. E. Smith, M.P., vice-presidents; I being elected hon. secretary and treasurer. The former post was held by me until 1887, when I was elected president in succession to Sir M. W. Ridley. The latter office I still hold.

NORTHUMBERLAND TEAM V. YORKSHIRE, NOVEMBER 21ST, 1891: NEWCASTLE.

(YORKSHIRE—4 GOALS 6 TRIES. NORTHUMBERLAND—NIL.)

(From a Photograph by R. T. Watson, Anlaby Road, Hull).

J. A. WILLIAMSON, H. T. WHITELEY, W. YOUNG, A. SPEAS, H. ANGER, E. EMLEY, A. HENSON, W. CAIL (President).
(H.-u. Sec.) J. BOUTHWAITE, G. HOLMES, N. BRETTON, J. GREENWELL, P. H. MORRISON.
(captain).
H. HARRIS, T. NICHOLSON, E. W. TAYLOR, T. F. ALEXANDER.

D D

In 1880 I proposed that a Challenge Cup should be instituted, and this was at once accepted and acted on. An old hundred-guinea racing cup, weighing over 100 ounces, was bought and nearly paid for by private subscription, the County ultimately paying £23, while the members of the Northern subscribed £16, and those of Northumberland £8.

The match list for the first season showed fixtures v. Durham, Cumberland, and Dumfriesshire—all won. The selected team to play v. Cumberland at Whitehaven was: J. Cowper and S. F. Prest, backs; J. Lowthian Bell and W. Farr, three-quarter-backs; J. V. Rutherford and J. McConnell, half-backs; W. Ridley, D. Fawcus, W. Dickenson, S. Oliver, J. G. Burden, J. H. Richardson, D. M. Dodd, W. Pattinson, and C. Gibson, forwards; R. H. Robb, one of our present vice-presidents, ultimately getting his place in the team. Our second match was v. Dumfriesshire. Again we played two full backs. This match we won by 4 goals to nil, not a single minor being scored on either side. Ridley, now Dr. Ridley, again got his place, as also did Coward, and perhaps no two of our forwards have been better known outside their county than these: both kept their places and played regularly for years, and both ultimately captained the team. J. S. Crawford, our present senior vice-president, played among the forwards in the match.

The first match in which we played three three-quarters was v. Edinburgh University in February, 1881.

In November, 1881, we played our first match v. Yorkshire, when they beat us by 1 goal to nil, we having to play half the game with fourteen men, Jack, now Dr., Rutherford, getting a couple of ribs broken in stopping one of the Yorkshire rushes.

In the season 1881-82 Symington first played for Northumberland, and a more honest and hardworking player never donned jersey. There will doubtless be many Yorkshiremen who remember his superb collaring at Bradford in February, 1885, while playing v. Yorkshire. When at full speed he collared a player with one arm, just as that player had given a short pass to a neighbour. Like lightning he caught the second player with his other arm, hugged the two to his breast, his momentum carrying him and them several yards. The cheers from all parts of the ground I shall never forget.

But how the mighty fall! Shortly after this he got a good appointment as manager of an Indian tea-garden. After some years' residence there he caught the Indian paralysis, and is now to be seen at Eastbourne wheeled about in a bath-chair. Poor Symington!

In March, 1883, the first special train ever run in Northumberland or Durham in connection with football was run from Hexham to Newcastle, Tynedale playing in the final for the Challenge Cup. About this time I, on behalf of my County, took a great interest in attempting to arrive at a definite qualification for County players, and in the November attended a meeting of County representatives. L. Stokes, as representing Kent, was voted to the chair, and, after discussion, the laws, nearly as they are now, were framed. I afterwards proposed in the Rugby Union Committee that the Rugby Union should adopt them, but the then committee thought it was outside their jurisdiction, and it was not until a couple of years ago that they were adopted by the Union. How different now, when the Rugby Union have the whole supervision of County championship!

On the 26th January, 1884, we first played Cheshire, the match becoming an annual one until this season, when Cheshire had to give it up owing to the new engagements forced on to her by the championship. The first two matches were played at Leeds at a half-way house, Mr. Glover, the then Yorkshire secretary, making the arrangements. Since then they have been home-and-home fixtures. The first match we won by 3 goals and 2 tries to *nil*, I think.

In the spring of 1884, I, in the joint names of the Durham County secretary and of myself, called a meeting of all club secretaries in Northumberland and Durham, to arrange fixtures for the next season. This has since been an annual gathering held alternately in Durham and here.

In 1884 we first paid the rail fares of our players; before then every man not only paid his own, but also his share of any entertainment given to visiting teams. This latter was continued two years longer, since which the County, like all others, has undertaken all expenses in connection with their matches; and the present generation of players have to thank the self-sacrifices of those of the past, that the County is in its present financial position.

In this season we instituted a Junior Challenge Cup, and had 17 entries from junior clubs having a membership of 645. Also in this season Dr. Ridley first captained his County; and E. A. Bainbridge, a most promising young three-quarter, first played for the County; he appeared to have a brilliant football future before him, but after his first term at Cambridge started on a trip round the world, and was killed by the memorable volcanic eruption at the hot wells in north New Zealand.

In November, 1885, Finney and Gill, two three-quarter backs, who in future years did good service for the County, and who both afterwards captained their club teams, first played for the County. At one time Gill used to be both a sure place and drop; when he first played for Northern II., there was seldom a match without a dropped goal from him. I remember one Wednesday match, when Northern II. turned up weak and short at Sunderland to play the II. team of that club—reinforced for the day by several of their first team—Sunderland scored 9 tries, three behind the posts; but failed at each attempt at goal. Just before the call of time, Northern got a try close to the touch line; Gill took the place, landed a goal, and won the match.

In November, 1885, Mason Scott, who is now touring round the world to recruit after his severe illness of last winter, was first elected to play for us. For one match— that v. Cheshire—playable that winter, we had a grand back team: Sample, back, Brutton, V. Rutherford, and C. Gill, with Mason Scott and W. R. Gray at half. Unfortunately frost stepped in. Gray was a very reliable half; when at Cambridge he played off and on for the 'Varsity, but never got his blue. In this I very decidedly think the 'Varsity captain was at fault in his judgment.

In 1885 our present County secretary got a seat on the committee, but lost it the following year when the number was reduced.

In February, 1887, in the Durham match Alderson first played at half-back for Northumberland, and did much towards winning. Durham had just previously played up well v. Lancashire, and came confident of success, very long odds being offered by their more ardent admirers; however, they retired beaten by 1 goal and 1 try to *nil*. We Northumbrians felt very keenly when Alderson left the county of his birth and first played for Durham in 1890, and were inclined to think the Durham rule, which prevented him playing in the cup ties for his new club (Hartlepool) if he played for his own County, a very unsportsmanlike one.

In 1887-88 we changed our jerseys from green to black and white; we affiliated the junior clubs to our Union. In this season, Willie, or—as the majority of players other than Northumbrians know him—Martin Scott was first chosen for the County; and during the same season Coward first captained the County. In that season we had to play Northamptonshire, but they put the match off. We had a hot back team ready for them, including Alderson, Morrison, Gray, Mason and Martin Scott—four Internationals.

I think this brings my records within the memory of the youngest of our "futters"; but, as a summary, I may say we are a County without internal quarrels. Our rivalries between clubs are not so keen as in places where big gates are the order of the day; we have not a trace of professionalism among us—this is probably because all our efforts have been in vain to give the Rugby game a root among the working classes. Turning to the game itself, up to this season our forwards have always been able to hold the scrummage against all comers, although undoubtedly not so clever in the open nor so fast—though able to use their feet, they have never learned to use their hands, and the short passing game—so deadly on a dry day—appears yet a thing beyond their comprehension; in fact, they have a too sincere admiration for one another, and if one gets the ball and attempts a run, the others, instead of backing him up and spreading out for chances, stand with open mouths to admire the prowess of their *confrère*. At least, this was the experience of our last match—that disastrous one against Yorkshire.

Turning to our backs, we have been successful in producing some of the best men of recent years, but owing to the lengthened sojourn of many at the Universities—Cambridge in particular—we could seldom get them to play for us except in the holidays, when

W. M. SCOTT.　　　　　　　　　MASON T. SCOTT.
(From Photographs by R. H. Lord, Cambridge.)

J. L. BELL.
(From a Photograph by Marshall Wane, Edinburgh.)

C. H. SAMPLE.　　　　　　　　　E. B. BRUTTON.
(From a Photograph by L. Sawyer,　(From a Photograph by Debenham & Gould,
Newcastle.)　　　　　　　　　　　Bournemouth.)

FIVE NORTHUMBRIAN INTERNATIONALS.

a County fixture was rare. When they left the Universities they either left off playing, as Sample and Brutton; took to other sport, as Morrison is now doing, by sailing up the Mediterranean in his yacht; broke down, as the Scotts have done; or deserted us, as Alderson. I think there yet remains one whom we think will gain International honours: I allude to Taylor, who last season played half for the Rest of England v. Lancashire.

Before concluding, a short sketch of our Internationals may be interesting.

J. Lowthian Bell, the crack Northern half-back of the "'seventies," is a Northumbrian, though from playing so frequently with Durham County his name has been associated, though not quite correctly, with the latter County. Like all half-backs of his day, he played for his own hand, and was very difficult to stop, for whilst being a clever dodger, he ran with a peculiar teetotum-like motion, seeming to spin out of the clasp of the tackler, and rendering it exceedingly difficult to accurately gauge the exact whereabouts of his person. For Durham v. Yorkshire in 1873, a match memorable as being the first occasion of "fifteen a-side" in County fixtures, Bell ran in the only three tries scored during the game, a performance which has seldom been beaten in a great match. He obtained his England cap against Ireland in 1878.

C. H. Sample played twice for the Universities v. London—in 1882 at back, and in 1883 at three-quarter; three times for Cambridge v. Oxford, twice at back and in 1884 at three-quarter; three times in North and South matches—in 1883 back for the South at Manchester, in 1884 at three-quarter for the North at Blackheath, and in 1885 back for the North at Bradford (the first Union match where flags and whistle were used); and three times for England at back: in 1884 v. Ireland in Dublin, in 1885 v. Ireland in Manchester, and in 1886 v. Scotland in Edinburgh. Two brothers of his, William and Harold, played forward for Cambridge and Northumberland.

E. B. Brutton—now the Rev. E. B.—having a year previous played for Northumberland, went to Cambridge in October, 1883, and in his first college match (Jesus v. Trinity Hall) scored 5 tries, and was at once put in the

'Varsity team. In his first match he scored 5 tries out of 7—rather a brilliant start. In 1883 he was chosen for Oxford and Cambridge, but could not play on account of a broken bone; but in that season he played for Cambridge v. Oxford. In 1884 he did not play in the 'Varsity match, but at Christmas went on tour in Yorkshire with his college team and scored every point the team got, namely, 1 goal and 1 try v. Leeds St. John, 2 goals and 1 try v. Hudddersfield, and 1 dropped goal and 1 try v. Bradford. In 1885 he captained both his college and his 'Varsity, and in that year played v. Oxford, when Cambridge won after six successive defeats. In 1885 he was selected both for the South and North, but, of course, played for his native heath. In 1886 he again captained Cambridge, and played for England v. Scotland at Edinburgh—about his last appearance on a football field.

Mason Scott was, in his day, one of the safest and most unselfish of halves. Went to Cambridge in the autumn of 1884, and played v. Oxford in 1885, 1886, and 1887; three times for England, namely, v. Ireland in Dublin in 1886, v. Wales in Dewsbury in 1890, and in the same year v. Scotland in Edinburgh: one of his best days out, as it was also for two other Northumbrians, was in 1889 for the Rest of England v. Yorkshire, when he and his brother Martin at half and Alderson at centre three-quarter fairly smothered the Yorkshire backs.

F. H. R. Alderson did not go to Cambridge till October, 1886, and did not play v. Oxford till 1887, when he played wing-three-quarter, which place he retained till he left. In 1887 he played half for the North at Manchester, and in 1889, as above mentioned, for the Rest of England. In 1890 he was not elected in the North team, but was subsequently chosen centre three-quarter and captain for England, which position he kept all through the season, playing v. Wales, Ireland, and Scotland.

P. H. Morrison, after leaving Loretto in 1887, went to Cambridge and at once got his place in the 'Varsity team, which he retained for four years, captaining it in 1889. In both 1889 and 1890 he played for the South v. North, in latter year in all three International matches and for Rest of England; in 1891 he played v. Ireland.

W. M. Scott played for Northumberland in 1887; in October, 1888, went to Cambridge, and, like Morrison and Brutton, at once got his place in the 'Varsity team, and captained it the next season. In 1889 he played v. Yorkshire for the Rest, and in March of the same year for England v. New Zealand; this is the only time he has played for England, as since the resumption of International matches he has always been the victim of some accident when his country required his services; thus the most brilliant half who ever played has, from an International point, or, perhaps, from an English point, been useless.

Durham.

It is a matter of some difficulty to fix upon the exact date when Rugby football was introduced into the County of Durham. The first recorded County match between teams representing Durham (including some Northumberland players) and Yorkshire, dates as far back as 1873, and at that time the number of clubs playing in Durham would not exceed half-a-dozen. Darlington claims to be the oldest club under Rugby rules in Durham County. In the seasons 1865-66 and 1866-67 the team of that club played on the present Feetham's Ground, but then called the New Cricket Field. Before that time they used to play at Woodside Park, in the grounds of Mrs. Gurney Pease. Tom Watson was one of the founders of the club. The Football Club amalgamated with the Cricket Club in 1865, and as the football matches were played on the Woodside ground for at least two seasons before the amalgamation, the Darlington Club dates as far back as 1863, if not earlier. At present the Association game is the popular form of football at Darlington. Sunderland, one of the oldest constituted clubs, was formed about 1870, and for at least ten years subsequently they continued to take the lead in all football matters. They formed the nucleus of the first so-called County teams which held their own, and for a time more than their own, against Yorkshire. They were the first club in the district to inaugurate annual tours into the neighbouring County of Yorkshire, whilst at home they found themselves at least the equals of all opponents. They supplied the first president of the County Union, in the person of Arthur Laing, and the late C. Kidson, of the

Sunderland Club, was the first gentleman in the far North to have a seat on the Rugby Union of that day. He was mainly instrumental in establishing the Durham County Challenge Cup in 1880, and it was the Sunderland Club who first held possession of the much-coveted trophy. Among the chief players in the Sunderland Club in its early days may be mentioned Henry E. Kayll, one of the finest back players of his day. Kayll, Lowthian Bell, and Kidson were prominent in the early band of players who assisted Durham County to defeat Yorkshire, in the first years of the matches with that County. Playing for the North in 1877, he represented England against Scotland in 1878. He was a very fine runner and jumper, winning prizes at 100 yards, quarter-mile, 220 yards, and over hurdles. His best performances as a jumper were 19ft. 3in. for the long jump, and 5ft. 7in. for the high jump at Sunderland in 1876. In the same year he won the championship for pole jumping at Lillie Bridge, clearing 10ft. 3in. This height he exceeded at Ilkley in 1877, getting over the bar at 11ft. 1in. In later years Charles Henry Elliot, of the Sunderland Club, played against Wales in 1886. Educated at Repton in the Association code, he excelled as a dribbler. He was a very keen player, and captained the County for several seasons. In the Welsh match he specially distinguished himself by a foolish piece of play which luckily proved to be the winning point of the match. Following hard up, he caught the ball from a bad screw kick of the Welsh full-back and made his mark, instead of going for the try. That style of play might win applause in Durham, but it met with emphatic and forcible expressions of disapproval from the English captain and the "finished" players of the South. Stoddart took the place kick and scored a goal, so the laugh at the finish was on Elliot's side.

About the years 1873-74 we find several other clubs, which afterwards obtained notoriety in the County, springing up. Durham School (already noted for its oarsmen) was playing the old 20 a-side game, and the University was following suit. A natural consequence was the formation of a "Town" club, and to this day the City F.C. (as it is known throughout the County) holds its own amongst the foremost clubs of the North. Westoe, Houghton, Darlington, and Bensham all sprang into existence about

DURHAM TEAM V. YORKSHIRE, NOVEMBER 14TH, 1891: HULL.

(YORKSHIRE—3 GOALS 1 TRY: 17 POINTS. DURHAM—1 GOAL 1 TRY: 7 POINTS).

(From a Photograph by R. T. Watson, Anlaby Road, Hull).

T. M. SWINBURNE, J. LAVELLE, G. F. BRAGEY, A. BURN, J. LINDSAY, J. HUDWORTH, W. VIRGO, A. HILL.
(President)   T. FAULKNER, W. H. BELL, F. H. R. ALDERSON, R. C. P. CROW, W. TAYLOR, (Hon. Sec.)
                                                        (Captain).
                A. HILL,   J. MARSTON,   T. A. F. CROW,   A. C. NOTT.

this time. Westoe and Houghton still survive, though they have fallen to a second-rate position. Darlington has gone over to Association, whilst Bensham, which collapsed about 1875-76, supplied the materials which afterwards helped the North Durham Club, formed in 1875, to come to the front. With this club is associated the name of T. M. Swinburne, the present president of the County, who was the first captain of the club, and who attained the height of his "club" ambition when he captained the team which won the Challenge Cup in 1882-'83. Swinburne still takes an active part in the management of the club.

A season or two later a club was formed at Hartlepool, and a second club, Sunderland Rovers, at Sunderland. Both these clubs are now extinct. In 1874 P. B. Junor, of the Glasgow Academicals, came into Durham, and his advent marked a new era in local football. Junor played as half-back, and during his career the Durham County team was at its best, compared with Yorkshire. A fine player, his influence on the game has been most marked, and also most varied. He first commenced to play with the Glasgow Academicals, assisting in the foundation of that club. Then removing to Edinburgh he was chosen for Scotland in 1873, but could not play owing to business engagements. In 1873 he went to Houghton, and established the club there. In the following season he was at Durham, where he captained the Durham City Club. Later on in 1883 he removed to Spennymoor, where his genius for founding clubs was exercised in the formation of the Tudhoe Club (of which he is president), which has won both the first and second County Challenge Cups in the season 1891-92. In his days the Durham County team, with himself, Lowthian Bell, the late R. F. Boyd, Tom Watson, the master of the Darlington Harriers, the Kaylls, the Laings, and Kidson were more than a match for Yorkshire.

About 1877 the various clubs of the County combined, and formed themselves into the present Union, with A. Laing, of Sunderland, as president. In this movement Dr. Sanday, principal of Hatfield Hall, Durham, now of Cambridge, J. H. Brooks, Kidson, and Junor were the leading spirits. The only County matches played then were those against Yorkshire, but about

C. H. ELLIOT.

H. F. KAYLL.
(From a Photograph by Mendelssohn, Newcastle-on-Tyne.)

T. M. SWINBURNE.

F. H. R. ALDERSON.
(From a Photograph by T. Braybrook, West Hartlepool.)

P. B. JUNOR.

W. YIEND.
(From a Photograph by T. Braybrook, West Hartlepool.)

1878-79 Northumberland County was met for the first time. The institution of the Challenge Cup in 1880 marked a notable change in the history of football in Durham. Before a couple of years had passed clubs were springing up all round, and each year saw increased interest in the game. About the year 1881-82, a club was formed which was destined to play an important part in Durham football. "The Hartlepool Rovers" only ranked as a junior club at the outset of their career, but they gradually gained ground, and in the year 1883 an amalgamation with the old Hartlepool Club was effected, whereby the groundwork of the strongest and most powerful club the County has ever owned was established. Sunderland had won the Challenge Cup in 1880-81, only to be defeated by their old rivals Houghton the following year, whilst the latter were ousted by North Durham in 1882-83. In the final tie of 1883-84 the Hartlepool Rovers, after a memorable struggle, wrested the cup from the holders, and since then have lost possession of it only on three occasions, twice succumbing to Durham City, and the third time being beaten by Tudhoe in 1891-92 after a drawn game. The success of the Hartlepool Rovers during the past few years has been most marked, and they rank at the present moment amongst the foremost clubs of the North of England. Amongst their prominent players, F. E. Pease, W. Yiend, and F. H. R. Alderson have gained International honours. Pease, who played originally with the old Darlington Club, obtained his cap against Ireland in 1887. He was a fast forward of the modern school, and having learnt his football at Harrow became a thorough master of the art of dribbling, and carried the lessons learnt at the famous school into effect in the Rugby game. W. Yiend, a Gloucestershire man by birth, has played for both North and South. One of the gamest and most hardworking of forwards, he has earned the sobriquet of "Pusher" from his ability to do the hard work of the pack. He tries to map out the course of tactics to be followed by the forwards in a most elaborate and scientific manner, holding the theory that combination and method are as essential among the forward brigade as among the back division. He can theorise eloquently and with knowledge, and can put his theories into practical effect. He was one of the

English team against the Maories in 1889, and played in all the International matches of 1891-92, being selected in a rather singular manner. Yiend was not selected for the North team, and, much to the surprise of the public, his name was afterwards included in the Southern list. This was to many the first intimation that he was a Southerner by birth. The South were weak in forwards, and the Southern members of the Rugby Union, finding Yiend left out of the North team, chose him to strengthen the forward rank. In the match he not only shone as the centre of the pack, but exhibited a turn of speed hitherto unappreciated in one of his size and weight. In the Welsh match of 1892 he was responsible, along with Evershed, for the prettiest try of the day.

F. H. R. Alderson, a Northumbrian by birth, has done much for Durham County. He is a great advocate for the four three-quarter system, and has introduced it into his club and into the County team. So far the experiment has not met with the success prophesied for it, probably because the system is not yet thoroughly understood, nor is Durham sufficiently rich in back players to give it a fair chance; though when the eight Durham forwards held the Yorkshire nine at Hull in November, 1891, it seemed as if the new arrangement would give the Durham men their longed-for victory over their powerful rivals. The calibre of the Yorkshire three-quarters saved their County from defeat.

Amongst other noted players may be mentioned B. Cox, C. T. B. Wilkinson, the Crowes, J. Sowerby, H. Brooks, W. H. Bell, and Arthur Hill. For several seasons the Rev. C. H. Newman, the famous Welsh International and Cambridge "half-back," who came into the County in 1874, captained the team with signal success, and lately Durham has been honoured in having her captain, F. H. R. Alderson, who came from Cambridge in 1888, chosen to captain the English team in the matches in which he has played.

The most notable features of late years have been the rise of the Tudhoe Club, already alluded to, and the introduction of the four three-quarter system. Should this arrangement of players be generally adopted, Durham will then be able to fairly claim to have had a large share in introducing it into English football.

CHAPTER XXII.

COUNTY FOOTBALL : CHESHIRE.

By J. W. H. Thorp.

CHESHIRE was one of the earliest of the smaller Counties to form a Union under Rugby rules: Macclesfield and Crewe had joined the Rugby Union before the season 1875-6, the same year as Bradford, and only two seasons after Manchester, Liverpool and Hull. In 1874 S. Fynney of Crewe had played in the first North *v.* South match at Rugby, and Sale claimed to have a club under Rugby rules in 1861. In 1875-6 J. W. H. Thorp attempted to get up a County team from old 'Varsity and public-school players who, although resident in Cheshire, had naturally been drawn into the powerful clubs of Liverpool and Manchester; but it was not until the end of the season 1876-77 that, by the energy of H. M. Blythe (Birkenhead Park), the first president, and A. E. Ward, of Sale, the first County match was played against Lancashire at Sale, a trial match between East and West Cheshire having first been played. Lancashire won by 1 goal 2 tries to 1 try, the latter being obtained for the home County by H. C. Rowley, the International player. E. C. Kendall was captain, and W. H. Wallace and J. W. H. Thorp, the present secretary and president, played in the match. E. Kewley was the Lancashire captain, and Hulton, Knowles, Hunt, and Greg were in the team.

In February, 1878, when the two Counties met for the second time, Lancashire won easily by 3 goals and a try to *nil*. A. N. Hornby was captain of the Red Rose team, with R. Hunt three-quarter back, and that wonderful dribbler Openshaw at half. Cheshire wore the wheatsheaf jersey for the first time, Kendall, Thorp, and Middleton playing again; but in March, when Cheshire met Yorkshire for the first time at Sale, the home County won by 3 tries to a try, chiefly by the aid of Percy Shaw, Kendall, and Stewart. All the Huths played for Yorkshire, with Garnett, captain, and that sterling forward Fernandez, and E. Mann, the old "Rug," in the team. At the autumn meeting of the Rugby Union in 1878, the Cheshire president was elected to a seat on the committee. In the season of 1880-1 West Cheshire had beaten the Manchester Club, and the County had beaten Oxford University, but meeting Lancashire at Broughton, Cheshire were beaten by 2 goals and a try to nil. The Internationals Phillips and Ravenscroft were among the Cheshire forwards. In March, 1881, Cheshire beat Yorkshire at Dewsbury by 1 goal to nil. At a meeting of the Cheshire County Committee in April, 1881, it was resolved "That the cup ties be discontinued as detrimental to the best interests of the game in Cheshire, and tending to promote bad feeling between clubs"—the valuable silver Challenge Cup being left in the custody of Birkenhead Park Club, the winners for that season.

In September, 1881, W. H. Wallace was elected hon. sec. for the County in succession to G. Stewart. At the annual meeting in September, 1883, H. M. Blythe resigned and J. W. H. Thorp was elected president. After the season 1885-6 the sum of £40 was voted to Cheshire charities, and £50 to the same purpose in the next year.

In November, 1884, at the ninth meeting of the two Counties, Cheshire obtained the summit of their ambition by beating Lancashire at Liscard, chiefly by the aid of a dropped goal from Marsland; by a coincidence Thorp, the captain, who had played in every previous match, gave up active part in the game just before this success.

Cheshire arranged a fixture with Durham for the first time in December, 1887, at Birkenhead Park, which the home County won by 2 goals and a try to 1 try. The later matches with Yorkshire have been unusually interesting, and no County has a record against the mighty Tykes that can compare with that of Cheshire since 1888. In that year Yorkshire were smartly beaten by a goal to a try. In 1889 we suffered a crushing defeat at Dewsbury. The match in 1890 was drawn under circumstances of great excitement. Close upon time Cheshire were leading by one point, when Naylor for Yorkshire scored between the posts.

E E

The place-kick failed, and thus the match ended in a draw. The like result occurred at Huddersfield in 1891, when two cleverly-dropped goals caused the Cheshire score to equal the goal and 3 tries obtained by Yorkshire. 1892 saw Cheshire win at Birkenhead after another exciting game, the Cheshire men obtaining a try just on call of time, and thus converting what looked like a defeat into an unexpected victory. In justice to Yorkshire it should be mentioned that on several occasions prominent Bradfordians have been absent from the team selected to meet Cheshire in order that their club might meet Blackheath with their full strength.

The chief feature of late years in Cheshire football has been the rise of the Runcorn Club, composed chiefly of working men, who by combination and keen interest in their practice games have reached first class rank, beating Bradford in 1892. Stockport Club also has made great progress lately. The County kept on the even tenor of its play, losing to Midlands and Lancashire but winning its matches with Durham, Yorkshire, and Cumberland. Nine clubs compose the Union.

CUMBERLAND.

By R. Westray.

As a County, Cumberland has always enjoyed a high reputation in the world of athletics. The dalesmen in this part of northern England have for a long period practically held their own against all comers in most field sports. Such men as Steadman, Jamieson, Lowden, Clark, Rickerby, Wright, and a host of others whose feats in the wrestling ring have gained them a reputation that extends to the Antipodes, being but the type of a class who possess all the muscle and physique necessary to a successful career in any department of athletics. We believe that so far back as 1870 the Carlisle Club claims to have been devotees at the Rugby shrine, having played nearly twenty-two years under the code laid down by the Rugby Union. In the year 1876 Whitehaven appears to have formed a Rugby Club, followed a year later by Workington, after which several in different parts of the County followed in rapid succession. In the early part of 1882 a few of the principal adherents of the game in the western division of the County determined upon an effort to give it an impetus, and in a very short time a subscription, amounting to about £30, was invested in a handsome silver Challenge Cup, for which some half-dozen clubs were induced to compete. The organisation which, under the title of a "County Club," was formed for the purpose of promoting and conducting this competition, must therefore be accredited with having laid the basis of what has now developed into a well-ordered and successful County Union. Amongst those who took an active part in the initiatory work of this period must be included J. E. Birkett, of Workington, and E. G. Mitchell, of Maryport, both of whom have up to the present time given a support which Cumberland must ever recognise with gratitude. Having appointed as its first president the Rev. J. W. Wainwright, of Aspatria, the newly-formed club set about establishing a relationship with other Counties, the result of which was an arrangement of fixtures with Northumberland, Furness, Durham, and Westmorland. From a record of its proceedings at that time we find that the County Union consisted of about seven clubs—viz., Carlisle, Aspatria, Eden-Wanderers, Maryport, Workington, Whitehaven, and Cockermouth, who were, in consequence, the only competitors for the Challenge Cup and the sole contributors to the County team. In 1885 Millom, Wigton Penrith, and others appear to have cast in their lot with the County club, but in the following year (1886) the withdrawal, amongst others, of Carlisle, Eden-Wanderers, and Whitehaven, representing three of the best organisations in the County, caused a difficulty, which for a time was the source of much anxiety.

With only a small credit balance in each of the preceding years, the County Executive had also to accept a series of defeats in the field—a circumstance that is not to be wondered at considering the narrow limit of their playing resources.

This unfortunate state of affairs it was hoped would find a satisfactory solution at the annual meeting of May, 1887, when mutual explanations would enable the County body to resume their work under more promising conditions.

CUMBERLAND COUNTY *V.* LANCASHIRE: WHITEHAVEN, FEBRUARY 27, 1890.

LANCASHIRE—7 POINTS. CUMBERLAND—NIL.

E. G. MITCHELL, C. J. LEWTHWAITE, J. E. BIRKETT, W. SELKIRK.
R. WESTRAY (*President*), W. HOLMES.
J. SIMPSON, J. BUCKETT, J. HYLAND, J. J. MITCHELL.
W. ARMSTRONG, G. CUTHEL.
D. N. PAPE, J. MURCHIE, J. MOORE, J. PENDER.
G. LOWRIE, W. DAVIDSON, M. HUMPHREYS

In this, however, they were to be disappointed. The time appointed for the holding of the annual meeting having passed over without any sign of its being held, an old supporter and friend of the cause (C. J. Lewthwaite) summoned an informal meeting of those interested in the Rugby game to consider what step ought to be taken towards carrying forward the work of the County club. The necessity of some effort being made was still further emphasised by an intimation that owing to feeble health the president (Rev. J. W. Wainwright) had tendered his resignation, while for other reasons (which need not be referred to here) the hon. sec., J. C. Nicholson, had also relinquished the duties of his office. This meeting was held in September, 1887, the result of which was the appointment of R. Westray, Carlisle, as president; and C. J. Lewthwaite, of Cockermouth, as hon. sec.: with J. E. Birkett, of Workington, and E. G. Mitchell, of Maryport, as vice-presidents.

This meeting happily proved the turn of the tide in Cumberland football. The new Executive not only realised the importance of immediate and vigorous action, but instituted the policy by themselves entering energetically into the work. From this time the advance of the Rugby game has not only been rapid but substantial. Having succeeded in getting the local operations of the County Union upon a sound footing, attention was next turned to Cumberland's claims for recognition by other Counties, and an exhaustive research into the position and strength of those Counties yielded a somewhat unexpected result. Taking the recognised clubs of the various Counties as a standard of claim to representation, it was found that Cumberland possessed an equal (and in some instances a greater) number than the great body of Counties already enjoying representation on the Rugby Union, and that two Counties only—Lancashire

R. WESTRAY.
(From a Photo by White, Carlisle.)

and Yorkshire—were numerically stronger. Upon these statistics, representations were made to the Executive of the Rugby Union, setting out the claim to admission into the fraternity of Counties appearing at their board. That the appeal was complete and well-founded may be inferred by the prompt and generous action of the Rugby Union in communicating their intention of recommending the admission of Cumberland to the National Council. In September, 1888, just one year after the appointment of their new Executive, Cumberland had, therefore, the satisfaction and the honour of being for the first time acknowledged as a member of the Rugby parliament.

Since then Cumberland has steadily improved her position; the system of management and discipline observed by the Executive being not only effective, but receiving a ready and hearty support from the clubs generally, while the ambition and enterprise of her players find ample scope in the fixtures now established with Lancashire, Cheshire, Northumberland, South of Scotland, Westmorland, and Cambridge University, and an annual "Colts" engagement with South-East Lancashire.

The meagre list of members composing the County organisation in 1887 has been increased to twenty-six; while the scanty purse from which the County's expenditure had to be met has given place to a reserve fund of nearly £200, with a margin in addition sufficient to meet current expenses.

In dealing with the marked advance of the Rugby game in Cumberland during the past four years, it is impossible to overlook or over-estimate the assistance rendered by Lancashire. Without a name or prestige to recommend her, at the very outset of a new career, when a conquest over her could give no promise of honour to the victor, Lancashire generously responded to her appeal for a fixture, and to this unselfish display of true sportsmanship Cumberland must largely ascribe the advantages she has since reaped in that improvement of her players by contact with a County who has so worthily held the position of champion County.

The Challenge Cup around which the interests of the County were first centred has steadily gained in importance, until the number of the competitors is now more than double that of earlier years. In 1889 a Challenge Shield was introduced for the encouragement of junior players, with the most satisfactory results, no less than twenty teams having entered the competition for the present season. Altogether it must be agreed that the Executive of the County, who received their appointment under the cloud of 1887 and have continued to hold office up to the present time, have faithfully discharged the duties with which they were entrusted, in doing a lot of hard and valuable work, and if the policy initiated by them is continued by those who follow in their footsteps, Cumberland may with confidence look forward to a promising future. With a view of strengthening their position still further, the Executive appointed for 1892-93 has received two additions, the officers now being: R. Westray, president; E. G. Mitchell (Maryport), C. J. Lewthwaite (Cockermouth), Watkinson (Millom), J. Twiname (Broughton), vice-presidents; Dr. Dudgeon (Workington), treasurer; and J. E. Birkett (Workington), hon. secretary. The following is the result of the challenge competitions up to date, viz.—

CUP.				SHIELD.			
Aspatria	...	...	... 1883	Millom	...	...	... 1889
Whitehaven	...	...	... 1884	Egremont	...	...	... 1890
Aspatria	...	...	... 1885	Millom	...	...	... 1891
Carlisle	...	...	... 1886	Millom	...	...	... 1892
Millom	...	...	... 1887				
Millom	...	...	... 1888				
Millom	...	...	... 1889				
Egremont	...	...	... 1890				
Aspatria	...	...	... 1891				
Aspatria	...	...	... 1892				

WESTMORLAND.

By G. Webster.

Westmorland County football is of comparatively recent date. The County club was formed at a meeting held at Windermere on March 2nd, 1886, which meeting was promoted and attended by representatives of Ambleside, Kendal, Kendal Hornets, and Windermere clubs. At the present time, Kirkby Lonsdale takes the place of the Windermere club. With such a scarcity of clubs, it is much to the credit of the Westmorland officials that they have been able to organise and successfully carry out a series of County matches with the neighbouring Counties of Lancashire, Cumberland, and Cheshire. They have had to encounter many difficulties, not the least being the inability at times to put a representative team into the field, owing to an important club fixture taking place on the same date. In a County where the clubs are numerous such incident may not materially weaken the fifteen; but when the choice of players is limited to four clubs, it is evident that the defection of one club may cause the County fifteen to be seriously weakened.

The history of the County of Westmorland presents an instance of the difficulty under which the less important Counties labour in their inability to put forward the claims of their best players to higher honours than those of club or County. It would be absurd to advance the theory that the minor Counties should always furnish a contingent of players to the North, South, or England teams. Manifestly in the North the two great Counties of Lancashire and Yorkshire must always provide the bulk of the northern team. But Westmorland being unrepresented on the North Selecting Committee, and in consequence not on the Rugby Union Committee, are placed at a great disadvantage in having no representative to urge the merits of any of their players. The geographical position prevents the Manchester authorities from obtaining personal knowledge of the abilities of the Westmorland players: and so whilst R. Westray for Cumberland has been able to obtain places in the North team for such players as J. Holmes of Millom, and Davidson of Aspatria, there is no record of a Westmorland player, whilst a member of a Westmorland club, being selected on a North team. Two Kendal men, viz., J. Berry and W. Cross, have played for the North, and Berry played in all three International matches in the season 1890-91; but they were then members of Lancashire teams, Berry living at Tyldesley, and Cross at St. Helens. Directly these two players qualified for Lancashire their merits were recognised. They were equally expert in the game whilst in Westmorland, but their capabilities were not appreciated because there was no representative for Westmorland County who could press their claims to the notice of the selecting body. The Westmorland authorities argue very forcibly that it is impossible for a County unrepresented on the Rugby Union to develop its resources to the fullest extent, inasmuch as that County is being continually robbed of good players, who naturally prefer to play for a County (if they are qualified) in a position to bring their merits before the Rugby Union. In the season 1886-7 Westmorland played four matches, defeating West Lancashire, Cumberland, and North Lancashire, and drawing with West Lancashire: a most satisfactory inauguration of the County club. In 1887-8 four matches were played, North Lancashire were defeated; drawn games were played with Cumberland and West Lancashire, and the first match with West Lancashire was lost. The season of 1888-9 was disastrous, the County being defeated both by Cheshire and Northumberland, and also by the Maori team, the latter winning by a dropped goal to a try. In 1889-90, though losing to Cheshire and Cumberland, Westmorland were enabled to defeat Lancashire by the score of a goal and 2 tries to 2 tries, a feat of which they are justly proud. The team that achieved this signal distinction were:—

WESTMORLAND TEAM v. LANCASHIRE.

Back: W. G. Hoggarth (Kendal). *Three-quarter Backs*: J. Armstrong (Kendal Hornets); J. Berry (Kendal Hornets); J. K. Robinson (Kirkby Lonsdale). *Half-Backs*: W. Cross (Kendal Hornets); W. Ewan (Kendal). *Forwards*: R. Nicholson (Kendal); R. Moreton (Kendal); P. Ireland (Kendal); G. Graham (Kendal); G. Machell (Kendal); J. Carradus (Kendal); R. C. Beard (Kendal Hornets); E. Wilson (Kendal Hornets); R. Winskill (Kendal Hornets).

Berry and Cross were both playing for Westmorland. In the following season when the two famous Kendalmen were enrolled in Lancastrian ranks, the Lancashiremen inflicted a crushing defeat upon the Westmorland players—4 goals and 4 tries to nothing being the score. Lancashire were the victors in the County championship that season, and there can be little doubt that the defection of Berry and Cross from Westmorland and their joining Lancashire clubs, was a main factor in the success of Lancashire. Sorry consolation, however, for the poor Westmorland men to see the men, who should have been assisting Westmorland, thus contribute to raise Lancashire to the proud position of champion County! Though it was Westmorland men who were doing it,

KENDAL HORNETS.

WINNERS OF THE NORTHERN COUNTIES CHALLENGE CUP, COMPETED FOR AT BARROW-IN-FURNESS, 1888.

Players:—J. ALLEN, J. ARMSTRONG, G. BATTERSBY, R. C. BEARD, J. BERRY, W. CROSS, W. J. WALKER, J. WILKINSON, E. WILSON.

(From a Photograph by F. Armstrong, Kendal.)

it was Lancashire who were claiming and receiving the credit.

The season 1891-92 saw an extraordinary incident. Westmorland began badly by being severely defeated at Maryport by Cumberland; a fortnight later they surprised the football world by defeating Cheshire. They had then only Lancashire to meet in the North-Western group. The Kendal Hornets had an important fixture in the North Lancashire League on the same day as the Lancashire match. The County Committee selected four only of the Hornets' Club, but from one cause or another none of them were able to play. Suddenly the Kendal Town Club withdrew their players from the team and their club from the County club, and with a fifteen thus weakened the Westmorland authorities decided to abandon the match.

The future of Westmorland County football rests in the loyalty of its few clubs. It may be very interesting to enter into a League, and exceedingly profitable to the exchequer of the clubs that take part in League matches; but the interests of the County should be superior to the League contests, which, though they may be interesting, are selfish in their nature and, inasmuch as gate-money is their avowed and foremost object, destructive of the main principle—viz., amateurism, that is at the foundation and root of Rugby Football. At the present moment County football in Westmorland is passing through a crisis. If the clubs stick manfully together and insist upon the League fixtures not interfering with County matches, Westmorland may yet occupy a fairly good position in the North-Western group.

CHAPTER XXIII.

COUNTY FOOTBALL: THE MIDLANDS.

By E. B. Holmes.

BURTON can claim to be the oldest Rugby football club in the Midland Counties, being instituted in the year 1870. Thus the Rugby game has been played in the Midlands for about twenty years. It has not taken such a hold upon the public as the Association game, and in consequence the clubs have been comparatively few in number, though for the past few years Coventry, Leicester, Burton, Rugby, and Moseley have all been able to put fairly strong teams into the field. In the 'seventies Handsworth, The Crusaders, Old Edwardians, and Wolverhampton were all well-known clubs playing under Rugby rules. But in the early days so difficult was it for the Moseley Club to obtain fixtures without having to travel a long way from home, that they arranged matches with the Wednesbury Strollers, an Association club of some repute, on the understanding that a game under Association rules should be played at Wednesbury, and that in the return match at Moseley Rugby Union rules should be adhered to.

The Burton Club, founded in 1870, has supplied such players as S. H. Evershed, who gained a place in the North team, and was on the reserve for England, Frank Evershed, J. L. Mayger, who has played for the South, and Ward; whilst Coventry has been the club of the Ratliffs and the Rotherhams.

Coventry is one of the oldest clubs in the Midlands. As early as 1870-71 a club was started by some gentlemen at Stoke, near Coventry, playing originally only scratch matches under Association rules, but after a season or two the handling code was preferred. In

1873-74 a ground was taken in Coventry in the Old Bull field, and the Coventry Football Club came into active existence. Under the able captaincy of the late Harry Ratliff, who at three-quarters was a host in himself, great success attended the early efforts, so much so that in the season 1875-76 only one match was lost, and in the two following seasons every match was won. Of late years the Rotherhams have been the prominent players for Coventry.

But the club that has attained the highest renown in the Midlands is the famous Moseley Club, and had it not been for their extraordinary and well-deserved success it is more than probable that the interest in the Rugby game in the Birmingham district would have declined considerably. The club was formed in October, 1873, by certain members of the Havelock Cricket Club with the object of keeping their members together during the winter months. In the season 1873-74 a few matches were played under the name of the "Havelock Football Club," but in the following season the name was altered to the "Moseley Football Club," and the colours "red and black" were chosen. Among the earliest members were S. H. Deakin (the first captain), D. Gibson (his successor), T. A. Burt, and W. J. Chatwin, but the most successful period was that under the captaincy of Albert Smith. With him were associated A. S. Tyler, W. Breedon, F. Tyler, F. Fowler, G. B. Jones, and others. Albert Smith had much to do with the successes of Moseley in the early part of the "eighties." He was a strong runner, an excellent tackler, and combined good drop-kicking with accurate place-kicking. The club record from 1879-82 is worthy of record. For three out of these four seasons Moseley were undefeated. They played 54 matches, won 48, and drew 6, scoring 81 goals 118 tries, as against 2 goals and 7 tries. At that period they were without doubt the champion club of the Midlands.

In later years J. H. Rogers and his brother, A. Rogers, have conferred further distinction on the Moseley Club. J. H. Rogers is a strong, sturdy forward, working hard in the scrummage, and displaying plenty of dash in the open. He is a good stayer, working hard throughout the game, and is always to be found in the thick of the fight, but often mars his play by coming blundering through without the ball.

The inauguration of the Midland Counties Football Union is due to E. H. Richards, of the Derby Wanderers, a club long since defunct. It was formed in September, 1879, and comprised the Counties of Derby, Worcester, Warwick, Stafford, Northampton, and Leicester.

Sydney Evershed, M.P., of Burton (father of Frank Evershed), was the first president, E. H. Richards, hon. secretary, and G. Gill, of Leamington, hon. treasurer, which post the latter gentleman has filled to the present time. On the departure of E. H. Richards to Africa, he was succeeded by the present secretary, C. A. Crane, then of Wolverhampton, now of Pershore. In the year 1889, E. B. Holmes was president, followed two seasons later by H. Vassall, the old Oxford captain, now holding a mastership at Repton School. Of late years S. E. Herd has officiated as hon. match secretary. It was H. Vassall who suggested the match London v. Midland Counties. He also spotted Frank Evershed's talents whilst that player was acting at three-quarter, remarking "what a good forward he would make!" The great Oxford captain's judgment was correct, for at the present day Frank Evershed ranks as the most dangerous forward playing. He cannot be described as a scrummager, though he does more work in the pack than he is given credit for, but as a try-getter, and as a player quick to snap opportunities, Evershed is unrivalled. Amongst his most brilliant achievements are a try obtained against Yorkshire in 1889, and one against Scotland in 1890. In 1892 Evershed repeated the feats against Ireland and Wales. He attains full speed almost in an instant with a peculiar stride that disguises his pace, and with a quick swerve he appears to get past opponents before they are aware that he is off. He makes straight for the goal line, and every yard traversed is so much ground gained.

J. H. ROGERS.
(From a Photograph by H. J. Whitlock, Birmingham.)

The newly constituted County Union immediately commenced playing County matches. The history of those matches may be divided into three stages, characterised by ambition, consolidation, and development respectively. In the early days Yorkshire, Lancashire, Oxford University, and Wales were encountered, and though the first match against Yorkshire, who sent a weak team, was won, the subsequent reverses were of so decisive a character that the vaulting ambition of the young Union received such a check that in 1885 the authorities considered it wise to abandon these fixtures till their players had obtained greater experience in the game. In these matches the Union were often without the services of the Moseley players, who in consequence of important club fixtures or for other reasons, held aloof from the Union's matches. H. Ratliff, of Coventry, was the first captain of the Midlands team, and was succeeded in 1881 by S. H. Evershed, of Burton. During this period the game was but scantily attended and poorly supported by the public, and for some years the Union were practically without funds. On the second occasion that Yorkshire visited Birmingham the committee resolved that, as the Midland players had been treated so well in Yorkshire, a dinner should be provided for the visitors on this occasion. As the balance brought forward from the previous season was 6s. 2d., and the gate money taken at this match was just over £8, the dinner could not be provided out of the funds at the disposal of the Union, so four committeemen held themselves responsible for £10 each.

F. EVERSHED.
(From a Photograph by H. J. Whitlock, Birmingham.)

During the next few years the Midlands confined their efforts to meeting such Counties as Surrey, Northampton, and Gloucestershire; occasionally matches have been played with Middlesex and the Universities of Oxford and Cambridge. In these the balance of success has been fairly even. Surrey have been defeated thrice, and have won one match. Against Northamptonshire the record is four to three in favour of the Midlands; the Gloucestershire matches are evenly divided with three victories, three defeats, and one drawn match. Only one match has been played with Middlesex, when the Midlands won by 1 try to *nil*. The Universities have generally been too strong for the Midlanders.

During this, the consolidation period of the Midland Union, the cup competition had roused the enthusiasm of the public and the players. More clubs joined the Union, and the play of the different teams improved. Moseley no longer held a position pre-eminently superior to the other clubs; Burton, Leicester, Coventry, Rugby, and the old Edwardians had raised themselves till they were on a par with the famous Birmingham Club, if, indeed, they were not superior to them. But it was reserved for H. Vassall to propose the scheme which has had such an effect in developing the resources of the Midland clubs. Formerly the Midland player's road to distinction was through the North team to International honours. But such was the supply of strong candidates from Yorkshire and Lancashire that there was little chance of a good Midlander gaining the favourable notice of the Northern selectors, for the failure of the Union to play matches with the two great Northern counties was a step fatal to the chance of any Midland player catching the eye of the Selecting Committee. S. H. Evershed has been the solitary representative of the Midlands chosen for the North team. Accordingly it was suggested that the Midlands should be transferred from the North to the South, and that Midland players should henceforth be eligible to play in the Southern teams instead of for the North. Then in 1889 a match was arranged between the Midland Counties and London. To the surprise of the Londoners they were defeated by a goal to a try, and after the good front shown by the Midlanders several of their men were chosen to play in the Southern trial matches. Finally, J. H. Rogers, of Moseley, F. Evershed, and J. L. Mayger, of Burton, were selected to play for the South against the North, Rogers and Evershed obtaining their International caps, whilst Mayger played for England against the champion County, Yorkshire. A. Rogers, a younger brother of J. H. Rogers, also played centre three-quarter for the South in December, 1891, and filled the same position for England against the champion County, Yorkshire, at Leeds, in February, 1892.

The contest for the County championship has also had a great effect on the game in the Midlands. In the grouping of Counties the Midlands were assigned to the South-Western division. A defeat by Gloucester effectually extinguished their chance of being returned the winner of that division for the season 1890-91. But in 1891-92 the Midlands, under the captaincy of J. H. Rogers, exhibited form indicative of such marked progress, and excited such interest with the public as to warrant the anticipation of a still further growth of the increasing popularity of the game, even in a district so devoted to the Association code. They commenced the season by defeating Cheshire by 4 goals (eighteen points) to a try (two points). Following this up by a victory over the Western Counties they defeated Devon, Somerset, and Gloucester, in succession, and were returned the winners in the South-Western division. But these successes, though most gratifying, did not furnish so decisive a testimony to the advance in play amongst Midland clubs as was evinced by the close contests with the two great football Counties, Yorkshire and Lancashire. True, the Midlands suffered defeat in each match, but they made so good a fight and displayed such excellent all-round form as to warrant their enthusiasts in expecting a still further improvement in the position they have now attained. Much of this advance has been due to the Midland Counties' Challenge Cup, which was instituted in the season 1881-82. During the eleven years of the competition the cup has been won six times by Moseley, twice by Burton, once by the Old Edwardians, and twice by Coventry. The records of the final ties are as follows:—

March 14, 1882, at Coventry, Moseley beat Leamington by 3 goals and 3 tries to *nil*.
April 3, 1883, at Coventry, Burton beat Moseley by 2 goals to 1 goal and 2 tries.
March 22, 1884, at Rugby, Moseley beat Coventry by 1 dropped goal to 3 tries.
March 28, 1885, at Coventry, Moseley beat South Warwickshire Rovers by 4 goals, 1 try to *nil*.
April 10, 1886, at Coventry, Moseley beat Rugby by 3 touch-downs to *nil*.

F F

MIDLAND COUNTIES TEAM v. YORKSHIRE: MOSELEY, FEBRUARY, 10, 1892.

YORKSHIRE—1 GOAL 2 TRIES (8 POINTS). MIDLAND COUNTIES—NIL.

W. A. MARRIS.　　J. P. WARD.　　A. SULLEY.　　W. P. NICHOL.
H. STAUNTON.　H. W. T. PATTERSON.　E. B. LYCETT.　A. H. FRITH.　A. ROTHERHAM.
L. J. PERCIVAL.　　F. EVERSHED (Captain).　　J. H. ROGERS.
A. GORTON.　　A. ROGERS.　　W. RICE.

(From a Photograph by R. T. Watson, Hull.)

April 2, 1887, at Coventry, Moseley beat Rugby by 2 goals 1 try to *nil*.
April 7, 1888, at Rugby, Burton beat Coventry by 2 goals to *nil* (after having played a drawn game the previous week).
March 23, 1889, at Coventry, Moseley beat Leicester by 2 goals to *nil*.
March 22, 1890, at Coventry, Old Edwardians beat Burton by 1 goal to 1 try.
March 28, 1891, at Rugby, Coventry beat Leicester by 2 goals 2 tries to *nil*.
April 2, 1892, at Leicester, Coventry beat Moseley by 2 goals 2 tries (13 points) to *nil*.

2nd TEAM CUP instituted 1890).

March 29, 1890, at Moseley, Rugby beat Coventry by 1 try to *nil*.
April 4, 1891, at Leamington, Coventry beat Rugby by 2 tries to *nil*.
April 9, 1892, at Moseley, Coventry beat Burton by 2 goals (9 points) to 1 try (2 points).

GLOUCESTER.

Gloucester County football has been dependent mainly upon two clubs, viz., Clifton and Gloucester City, for the supply of players. The Clifton Club was founded in 1872, and for several seasons in the early days of Rugby football was a very strong organisation, being acknowledged to be the strongest club in the South, outside the London district, with the exception of the two Universities. In the season 1875-76, the Clifton Club supplied both full-backs (J. D. Miller and E. J. Taylor), and two forwards (J. A. Bush and M. Curtis), to the South team that played at Whalley Range. Their motto might now be "Quantum mutatus ab illo." Evidence of their pristine influence on the game in Gloucestershire is furnished by the fact that up to the close of the season 1889-90 the Clifton Club had supplied all the County captains.

But it is to the Gloucester Club that the County is most indebted for the successful manner in which the County engagements have been carried through. Founded in 1874, this club has for many years played an important part in the history of the County Union, so much so that during the last few years the very existence of the Union has depended upon the support of the City Club, and for this reason its progress is a matter of interest in Gloucestershire football. In its early days the club was exceedingly fortunate in possessing an admirable captain in J. F. Brown, who for seven seasons held the post, and under whom in 1882-83 the club was able to boast of an unbeaten record. An almost equally brilliant record was that of the following season, when H. J. Boughton (now president of the County Union) was captain, when of 20 matches played 18 were won. A slight falling off was noticeable during the next few seasons. This was due to the loss of many of the old players, but in 1888-89, under the captaincy of T. G. Smith, the club regained its high position, for out of a total of 23 matches, only 3 were lost, while the crack Welsh clubs, Newport, Cardiff, and Swansea, were amongst those defeated. The record of the season 1890-91, when 23 matches were won out of a total of 27 played, 2 being lost and 3 drawn, and the performances of the team during the past season are the best proofs of the excellence of the team now captained by T. Bagwell.

The Gloucestershire County Rugby Football Union was formed at a meeting held at Gloucester in September, 1878, the clubs represented being Clifton, Gloucester, Royal Agricultural College, Cirencester, Rockleaze, Stroud, and Cheltenham White Cross. The first officers and committee were: captain, J. D. Miller (Clifton); hon. secretary and treasurer, J. H. Dunn (Clifton); committee, J. F. Brown (Gloucester), A. J. Denison (R. A. C.), M. Cartwright (Stroud), G. G. Pruen (Cheltenham), T. R. Pakenham (Cheltenham).

The Union owed its formation mainly to the efforts of J. D. Miller, J. H. Dunn, and J. F. Brown; while its playing strength depended almost entirely on the Clifton and Gloucester Clubs. The newly-formed Union displayed great vigour in its early days, and in the first five seasons lost only 2 out of 17 fixtures in Inter-County matches. Its merits were early recognised by the Rugby Union Committee, and in 1880 J. D. Miller was elected to represent the West of England on the central executive.

But the early successes were not followed by a continued effort, for the game gradually degenerated in the Bristol division, and from 1883 to 1889 the Gloucestershire record was very poor and the outlook somewhat gloomy. During that period, extending over six seasons, only 10 Inter-County matches were played, and of these 6 were lost, 3 drawn, and only 1 won. With only one first-class club in the County such variableness is easily explainable. The strength of the Gloucester City team is the estimate of the strength of the County team, and success of the County is regulated by the success of the Gloucester Club. Reverting to the doings of that club as already recorded, it will be found that its palmy days in the olden times culminated in the season 1882-83, and so for that season the record of Gloucester County was most favourable. As the City Club deteriorated so the fortunes of the County Union declined, and as, again, the City Club improved its record, so once more did victory grace the efforts of the County fifteen, for in the seasons 1889-90, 1890-91, 1891-92, Gloucestershire lost two matches only. Those seasons have been the period of the revival of the strength of Gloucester City, and the figures quoted prove most conclusively that the City Club has been the main-stay of the Union for years, and that without its support the whole scheme must have collapsed. It has been no uncommon occurrence to find the City Club represented in the County fifteen by twelve or thirteen players, including all the backs.

It should always be remembered in estimating the strength of this Union that where, through illness or accident, any of the chosen team cannot play, it is almost impossible to get any adequate substitute, except perhaps among the forwards. A notable instance of this occurred in 1891, in the match *v.* Lancashire, when A. F. Hughes, the Gloucester full-back, had to play for the County, although in extreme ill-health. If a substitute is now needed outside the scrummagers he has usually to be taken from the City second fifteen.

Somerset, Devonshire, and the Midland Counties have been the regular opponents of Gloucestershire, and those Unions now form the South-Western group in the Championship scheme. In the first year of the County Championship (1890-91) Gloucestershire were the winners in the South-Western group; but in the match against Lancashire in the second series they met with a crushing defeat, being vanquished by the score of 4 goals and 2 tries to *nil*. In the past season they succumbed to what one of their officials designates " the huge combination entitled the Midland Counties." Much of this later success has been due to the efforts of H. V. Page, the old Oxford University forward, now captain of the Gloucester City Club.

At the end of the season 1890-91, a successful attempt was made to improve the standing of the Union, the prime mover in the matter being H. J. Boughton (Gloucester), the present president of the Union. New rules were drawn up, and all clubs of any note were invited to join. The new constitution was ratified at a General Meeting held in November, 1891. The Union now consists of ten clubs, viz., Gloucester, Clifton, Royal Agricultural College, Cirencester, Bristol, Cheltenham, Lydney, Sharpness, Dursley, Stroud, and Gordon Wanderers (Gloucester). The weakness of the Union consists in the paucity of first-class clubs, for of the above-mentioned, only Gloucester can be classed in the first rank. This is most conclusively shown by the fact that last season the Gloucester City second team beat the first teams of Bristol and Clifton. But with the Union now on a better footing, increased interest is being manifested by the smaller clubs, and better things may be expected; while the great improvement shown this year by the Bristol team gives great encouragement to all well-wishers of Rugby football in Gloucestershire, and may be a sign of increasing vigour and interest in that part of the County.

HIATT C. BAKER.
(From a Photograph by Elliott and Fry, Baker Street, W.)

Of Gloucestershire players, J. A. Bush, W. O. Moberly, and H. C. Baker played for England, whilst S. H. Nicholls, J. Watts, and G. Rowles are Welsh Internationals, H. L. Evans (Clifton) and H. F. Chambers (Cheltenham) have worn the Scotch Jersey. James Arthur Bush was educated at Clifton College, and afterwards played with the Clifton Club, for which he often figured at three-quarters, though his place was forward. He was a tremendously strong worker

J. D. MILLER.
(From a Photograph by Villiers and Quick, Bristol.)

GLOUCESTER COUNTY TEAM *v.* LANCASHIRE: MANCHESTER, MARCH 14, 1891.

LANCASHIRE—4 GOALS 2 TRIES (14 POINTS). GLOUCESTERSHIRE—NIL.

(From a Photograph by R. T. Watson, Hull.)

A. F. Hughes, G. J. Witcomb, A. Cromwell, H. S. Simpson (Hon. Treas.), A. Collins, G. Williams, R. C. Jenkins, T. Collins, T. G. Smith (Hon. Sec.)
H. T. Boughton (Umpire), S. H. Nicholls, T. Bagwell, H. V. Page (Captain), W. George, S. A. Ball, C. A. Hooper.
W. H. Taylor, W. Jackson.

and runner, and his tackling was terrific. He journeyed five times to London to play in small matches before being selected to play for England, so difficult was it in those days for a provincial player to gain the favourable notice of the selecting body. Bush played for England against Scotland in 1872, 1874, 1875, 1876, and against Ireland in 1875. In 1873 he was in Australia playing cricket with W. G. Grace's team.

W. O. Moberly was educated at Rugby and Oxford. He always played three-quarter, but was picked as a full-back for England. He was a clever runner, could drop with either foot, and was a good shot at goal.

Hiatt C. Baker was a huge forward, doing a power of work in the scrummage, and took the ball excellently out of touch. A very strong runner, he led a pack of forwards admirably by direction and example. He played against Wales in 1887.

J. D. Miller was somewhat of Lockwood's build, a very short but excellent full-back. Very long and certain kick, and could stand any amount of wear and tear. He was the first representative of the Western Counties on the Rugby Union Committee.

SOMERSET.

Somerset County matches date back as far as the year 1875-76, but the present organisation was not inaugurated till the year 1881-82. The first match was played against Devon in the season of 1875-76, when Willmott, of Weston, acted as captain. The match was won by Devon, the score being 1 try. As a proof of the slight beginning of the County organisation, it may be mentioned that the "gate" taken at the matches during the first season amounted to £5 3s. 9d.; that the travelling expenses paid out of the County funds were 14s. 3d., and that the total income from all sources was £22 5s. 1d.

Of the second season there appears to be no record. In the third season, 1877-78, the late H. Fox acted as captain and hon. secretary. During this season the names of H. Vassall and H. G. Fuller appear in the teams.

In 1880-81, H. Fox was succeeded in the posts of

SOMERSET TEAM *v.* YORKSHIRE: BRADFORD,
JANUARY 24, 1892.

YORKSHIRE—2 GOALS 1 TRY (7 POINTS). SOMERSET—NIL.

(*From a Photograph by R. T. Watson, Hull.*)

G. ALLAN. C. R. STACK. R. M. P. PARSONS. G. FOWLER. P. F. HANCOCK. W. H. MANFIELD. S. M. J. WOODS.
C. J. VERNON. H. MERRY. F. H. FOX. H. BOUCHER. F. C. DUCKWORTH.
N. H. STOCK. C. F. MERCHANT. F. SHINE.

hon. secretary and hon. treasurer by A. A. Michell, of Bridgwater, under whose guidance the present organisation was started. At present the following clubs are members of the Somerset Union, viz.:—Bath, Bridgwater, Taunton, Wellington, Weston, Wiveliscombe, Yeovil, Wells, Highbridge, Cheddar Valley, and Crewkerne. In 1883-84 F. H. Fox was elected hon. secretary and treasurer. He retired in 1891, and was succeeded by his brother, G. Fox.

The claims of the Western Counties to representation on the Central Executive were early admitted, and in 1882-83 J. D. Miller, of Clifton, was elected a member of the Rugby Union Committee. He continued to serve until the season 1886, when H. Fox, of Wellington, was appointed. On the melancholy death of the latter in the Caucasus in 1888, he was succeeded by his cousin, F. H. Fox, also of Wellington, who still represents his County and the West of England.

The earlier matches were played against the neighbouring Counties of Gloucester and Devon, and it was not till the formation of the County Union in 1881-82 that matches were arranged with Counties outside the western district. In that year Middlesex was encountered, and the West-countrymen had the satisfaction of defeating the powerful London combination by 2 goals and a try to a goal. Indeed, the recently established Union had the satisfaction of winning all the County matches in that season, defeating Devonshire, Middlesex, and Gloucestershire. Matches were also arranged with the London Hospitals, and the Universities of Oxford and Cambridge. The first of the series was won, but against both Oxford and Cambridge defeats were incurred. At that period both Universities were exceptionally strong, and would have been doughty opponents for even the crack County of the season—viz., Lancashire. Hence defeat by the Dark and Light Blues respectively was no discredit to the rising County.

The four following seasons contained nothing eventful, the matches, with the exception of a solitary fixture with Blackheath, consisting simply of fixtures with the neighbouring Counties of Devon and Gloucester. Of these matches Somerset won all three against Devon, and beat Gloucester twice, suffering defeat once from that County. In the season 1886-87, Somerset began to take a leading position among the Counties, and by her achievements in that and the two following seasons established her claims to rank with Middlesex, Lancashire, and Yorkshire as the four leading Counties in the football world.

The season began in a startling fashion. Devon were met and completely routed by the crushing score of 6 goals and 6 tries to *nil*. Curiously, exactly the same score was made in the same match in the following year, and this extraordinary coincidence may well rank among the curiosities of football. Lancashire were then defeated by 1 goal and 2 tries to 3 tries. A defeat was incurred in the Yorkshire match, and the match with Gloucester was drawn. This progress was due partly to the energetic management of the committee, and to the inclusion in the teams of many players much above the average.

In 1887-8 Somerset ventured upon a much enlarged programme, and this season marks an epoch in the history of Somerset football. The two western Counties were defeated in a ridiculously easy fashion, for neither Gloucester nor Devon scored a point against the Somerset men, who ran up a large score on each match, Gloucester being defeated by 2 goals and 4 tries to *nil*, whilst Devon had the mortification of seeing the gigantic score of 6 goals and 6 tries of the previous season again recorded. Lancashire just pulled off the match by 1 goal to 1 try, but Yorkshire were completely overthrown at Weston-super-Mare. Superior forward play, aided by the speed of Glass, Ashford, and Smith at three-quarters, completely beat the Yorkshiremen, who on the day were decidedly the inferior team. This victory revealed the merit of the West-countrymen, and clearly established the calibre of their style, exhibiting their players as good individually and also as united in combination. So favourably were the Rugby Committee impressed by the play of the Somerset team that no less than seven Somerset men were chosen for the South team in the second North and South match, viz., B. W. L. Ashford, S. C. Smith (selected but could not play), and R. A. Glass, three-quarter backs, F. H. Fox, half-back, and P. F. Hancock, S. M. J. Woods, and R. M. Parsons, forwards. The result was that the South won by a goal and a try to a try, the previous match having been drawn, 1 try each. The match will long be remembered for the wonderful play of F. H. Fox. If it be a merit in a half-back to be always in possession of the ball then Fox can claim that merit in the highest degree, for it seemed as if he, and he alone, was the player to get possession. For quickness and snapping of the ball his play in this match has never been surpassed. With Allan Rotherham as his companion, and opposed by F. Bonsor, of Bradford, and J. Mills, of Swinton, the little Somerset man shone out conspicuously for the ubiquity by which he seemed always to be able to obtain possession of the ball. His play was the feature of the match.

In addition to their County fixtures the Somerset men also paid a visit to London to meet the two crack clubs, Blackheath and London-Scottish. They lost to Blackheath by the narrow margin of a try to nil, but defeated the London-Scottish by the large score of 3 goals and 1 try to nil. So remarkable a performance was followed by the honour of the invitation to take part in the Charity Festival at the Oval, the match being arranged with Middlesex. The West-countrymen gave a grand exhibition of football and were defeated by the narrow margin of a try, the actual score being Middlesex 1 goal and 2 tries to Somerset's 1 goal and 1 try. Somerset lost a forward early in the second half, after which Middlesex scored twice. Their goal was a penalty one.

The season of 1888-89 saw a slight diminution in the strength of Somerset. Devon and Gloucester were again defeated, Devon by the substantial score of 4 goals and 3 tries to nil; but Gloucester made a better fight, being defeated by a goal only, and thus gave promise of the reversal of the tables at an early date. Lancashire were defeated at Manchester by a goal to nothing, but at Wakefield the Yorkshiremen completely outplayed Somerset, scoring 2 goals and 3 tries to a try. Lockwood for Yorkshire was in very fine form, and to him more than any other player did Somerset owe her defeat. Blackheath, twice, and London-Scottish were also met, with the result of two defeats and one victory. The New Zealanders had no difficulty in polishing off a weak team of the County by scoring 4 goals and 5 tries to a goal and a try. Reviewing this season, it was evident that though the Somerset record was excellent there were not wanting signs that the County team was retrograding. These prognostications were borne out by the results of the succeeding season, when with five lost games and two drawn Somerset could not lay claim to a single victory. Three of the matches were, however, lost by narrow margins. Blackheath succeeded in winning by 1 goal to a try, whilst Gloucester and Yorkshire, respectively, scored 1 try to *nil*. The Yorkshire match was a very close contest, and will be memorable for the successful efforts of the Somerset Executive to cope with the frost and thus to render the ground at Wellington fit for play.

In 1890–91, the County Championship scheme was formally adopted, and it was generally anticipated that Somersetshire would be returned as group winner in the South-Western division. Though the Somerset men were successful in defeating Middlesex and Devon, they were doomed to be disappointed, and being defeated by Gloucester, after having played a drawn game, were compelled to relinquish the honour of champion of the South-west—a position which they had held for several seasons.

The characteristic of Somerset football is the thorough sportsmanship of the followers of the game. No County, considering the few clubs in membership with the Union, and the scattered nature of the population, combined with the difficulty of railway communication, has attained so high a position in the football world. The performances against Yorkshire, Middlesex, and Lancashire have affixed the hall stamp of merit on the teams playing in the seasons of 1886–7–8–9. Eager to fulfil their engagements, they have journeyed to Lancashire, Yorkshire, and London, to keep their fixtures with those distant centres, and have invariably been able to place a representative team in the field. Such enthusiasm and zeal on behalf of County football are in strong contrast with the apathy and languor of the Southern counties, in the Metropolitan district. Much of the enthusiasm displayed, and the punctuality exhibited in the fulfilment of engagements entered upon, are due to the energy and business management of their admirable secretary, F. H. Fox, who, in

F. H. FOX.
(From a Photograph by Vanderweyde, Regent Street, W.)

H. FOX.
(From a Photograph by Maull and Fox, Piccadilly.)

S. M. J. WOODS.
(From a Photograph by E. Hawkins & Co., Brighton.)

F. E. HANCOCK.
(From a Photograph by W. D. Brighton, Cardiff.)

P. F. HANCOCK.
(From a Photograph by the Stereoscopic Company, Regent Street, W.)

addition to having rendered valuable service in the field, has been a model official.

At the present time, no less than three Somerset players have seats upon the Rugby Union Committee. Harry Vassall, the famous Oxford captain, and possibly the best football general that ever appeared on the field of play, assisted Somerset County on several occasions. He last played for the County v. Devon, in 1880-81, when he obtained the only 3 tries scored by Somerset. The West-country is famed for its big men, but even in a County which can boast of its "John Ridd," the mighty Vassall was an object of interest and wonder, and in his passage to and from the field of play he used to be followed by a small crowd of boys, intent on gazing on the massive limbs of the Ajax of the football field. Another prominent Somerset man—prominent both in the field of play and in the council chamber of the Union — is H. G. Fuller, of Bath, and now the representative of Cambridge University on the Executive. Fuller was captain of the team in 1875 and 1876. He first played for Somerset in 1877-78, and in 1878-79 obtained his blue at Cambridge as half-back, but in 1879-80 he played forward for his 'Varsity. He took part in the North v. South match in 1881-82, and obtained his England cap in 1881-82, appearing against Ireland and Scotland. In the season 1882-83, he played in all three International matches, and also against Wales in 1883-84. In that year he left England and did not return till 1886, when he continued playing for Somerset for two or three years. He was a very fine forward, possessing both pace and weight; but in his latter years was inclined to play wing forward. His bald head was a familiar object in the football field, and the writer can remember overhearing a spectator remark: "How well that old gentleman does play!" It may be that such prominence was distasteful to the sensitive mind of the stalwart Cantab, or that his modesty prompted him to screen himself from public view, and so he invented and patented an "ear-cap."

F. H. Fox is the last of the trio of committee-men. He succeeded his cousin, the late H. Fox, in 1888. He captained England against Scotland in 1890.

Besides the above, the following Somerset men have gained International honours, viz.:—F. E. Hancock (Wales), P. F. Hancock, S. M. J. Woods, and E. L. Strong. S. M. J. Woods, as a forward, has a style peculiarly his own. If given a "roving commission," Woods is one of the most dangerous of forwards. His strength, pace, and dash cause his individual play to be of a most determined character, and though he cannot be termed a scrummager, he has been selected for England on account of the extraordinary pieces of play he is continually bringing off. His tackling is wonderfully sure and exceedingly severe, and in International matches, notably against Wales in 1891 and against Scotland in 1890 and 1892, he has frequently been brought out as an extra three-quarter to strengthen the defence when England have been pressed on their goal-line. His cricket abilities are well known, and he enjoys, with A. N. Hornby and A. E. Stoddart, the fame of being equally prominent at cricket and football. His best individual performances in big matches have been for Somerset against Yorkshire in 1892; and for England against Wales in 1891; against Scotland in 1892; and for the Rest of England v. Yorkshire in the same year. E. L. Strong will best be known as a member of the "Vassall" Oxford team, and his connection with Somerset was limited to playing against Gloucestershire in 1881-82. His football career is more particularly connected with Oxford football. But the Hancocks are essentially Somerset men, and it is with Somerset particularly that they are known in football circles.

P. F. Hancock, known familiarly as the "Baby," is one of a family of ten brothers, of whom five have played for Somerset County. He was never at any public school, and learnt his football in playing for the local club of Wiveliscombe, which through the exertions of the Hancock brothers was for many years about the strongest in Somerset. He and his brothers used to play football constantly in a large garden, where they had rare keen games, though perhaps not very scientific. He has played for Somerset regularly from 1882-92. He has also appeared in the ranks of the Blackheath Club, beginning in 1884, but has not been able to play regularly in consequence of the distance. In order to play with the great Kent Club,

Hancock frequently travelled from Somerset to London and back (170 miles each way) in the day, and has been known to walk home a distance of ten miles after the double journey. He obtained the England cap in 1886-87, appearing against Wales and Ireland. He formed one of the Rest of England team against Yorkshire in 1889 and again in 1890, in which last year he also played against Wales at Dewsbury. He was, too, one of the team that took part in the late tour to the Cape. As a forward, though not very fast, he is a clever dribbler, and difficult to stop. His height and weight make him a most useful man in the line-out. Woe betide the man he falls on; but, with all his weight and strength, he is a most gentlemanly player, without the slightest suspicion of roughness. Unlike most big men, he can last through a long and hard-fought match, being always in good condition, owing principally to the constant exercise taken in stag-hunting, and in following the beagles.

F. E. Hancock, an elder brother of P. F., first played for Somerset as a forward, in 1879, but soon afterwards took the position of three-quarter-back, and was captain of the county for two seasons. He went to Cardiff in 1883, and was elected captain of the Cardiff Club in 1885. He was the main instrument in introducing the four three-quarter system into Wales, and under his leadership the Cardiff team were almost invincible. He was a brilliant runner, wonderful dodger, and an excellent captain. He gained his Welsh cap playing against Ireland in 1884, against England and Scotland in 1885, and also played in 1886. He is best known in connection with Welsh football.

In connection with the Hancock brotherhood, it may be remarked that not only have five Hancocks played for the county (all brothers), but that three Smiths (brothers), also three Glasses (all brothers), and three Foxes (two brothers and a cousin), have appeared in the county teams. Another remarkable fact is the number of years that several of the members of the team have played for the county. This is a wonderful testimony to the healthy, vigorous effect of the quiet life and the country air of the West. But may there not from it be deduced the probable cause of the decline in the county

G G

fortunes? May it not be that, now the old hands are declining in their skill, there is not being found the young blood to take their places? But, whatever may be the cause of the present cloud of ill-success that has descended upon Somerset football, it is to be hoped that a speedy resuscitation may take place, and that the county may regain that position in the football world which the sportsmanship and energy of its executive entitle it to hold.

CHAPTER XXIV.

FOREIGN TOURS.

IN most branches of sport it is the fashion nowadays to indulge in tours in foreign countries, and the first step in this direction as regards Rugby football was taken by Messrs. Shaw and Shrewsbury in the spring and summer of 1888. During the previous winter those two cricketers had been managers of a cricket team in Australia, and whilst there conceived the idea of taking an English Rugby football team to play matches in the Southern Colonies. They approached the Committee of the Rugby Union for their sanction and patronage. The Committee, true to the high traditions of sport that have always guided their deliberations, declined to award their patronage to a team which was manifestly being organised and conducted for the benefit of individual promoters, and which was not under the control and management of some recognised athletic body. At the same time they saw no reason to interfere with the project as long as the promoters and players did not infringe the principles of amateurism, which had been so firmly adhered to by the Rugby Union. This attitude of *laissez faire* had a material influence upon the composition of the team, which, though fairly strong, would have been materially strengthened by the presence of more International players had the tour been under the auspices of the Rugby Union Committee. As it was, Messrs. Shaw and Shrewsbury secured the services of twenty players, all, with one exception, hailing from the North of England, and including four International players, four who had gained the distinction of playing in the North and South matches, and eight who had represented their respective counties. As G. Brann, A. E. Stoddart, and C. A. Smith, who were already in

Australia with the cricket team, were also available, the combination was sufficiently powerful to give the Colonials a fair idea of the football strength of the Mother Country, and, as the results of the tour testify, the achievements of the players were such as to worthily uphold the honour of England, for in the thirty-five matches played under Rugby rules, twenty-seven were won, six drawn, and only two lost. One objectionable feature of the tour was the arrangement of matches under Victorian rules. This was done with a view of exhibiting the English players in those districts where the Victorian game was played, and thus stamped the tour as an exhibition, and as a means of making money for the promoters rather than as the visit of an English International team desirous of measuring its strength against fellow-sportsmen in Australia and New Zealand. Had the tour been under the management of the Rugby Union no matches under alien rules would have been arranged or permitted. Under Victorian rules eighteen matches were played, of which eleven were lost, one drawn, and six won—a fairly satisfactory result, considering that the Englishmen were entirely strange to the rules, and especially nonplussed by their ignorance of the tricky practices and combination so essential to success in the Victorian Code. The hero of the tour was A. E. Stoddart, who, picking up the Victorian game with wonderful rapidity, was an object of wonder to the Colonials by his marvellous exhibition of skill in the games under both codes. Harry Eagles, of Salford, earned the distinction of being the only member of the team who played in every match. A sad gloom was cast upon the tour by the death of R. L. Seddon, the captain of the team, who was drowned whilst sculling on the River Hunter, at Maitland. His place as captain was filled for the remainder of the tour by A. E. Stoddart. Everywhere the Englishmen were received with kindness and hospitality, and all thoroughly enjoyed the tour. They met the strongest teams in New Zealand, and their visit materially improved the football in the Colonies; and the lessons learnt in passing and other tactics caused them to experience considerable difficulty in winning the later fixtures. They left England March 8th, 1888, and arrived home on November 11th of the same year.

SHAW AND SHREWBURY'S AUSTRALIAN TEAM, JUNE 25, 1888.

J. ANDERTON. T. KENT. W. BUMBY. A. SHREWBURY. H. BROOKS. J. LAWLOR. T. BANKS. A. PAUL.
A. N. LAING. J. SMITH. W. H. THOMAS. C. MATHERS. A. PENKETH. W. BURNETT. R. L. SEDDONS.
H. C. SPEAKMAN. S. WILLIAMS. J. NOLAN. A. E. STODDART. J. T. HASLAM. R. BURNETT. H. EAGLES.
A. J. STUART. J. G. McSHANE.

The tour will be ever memorable for the disqualification of J. P. Clowes, of Halifax, who, previous to the sailing of the team, was declared to be a professional by the Committee of the Rugby Union—a decision afterwards endorsed at a special general meeting convened at the instance of Captain Bell, of the Halifax Club, to obtain a reversal or remission of the sentence. As the case is remarkable as disclosing the agreement made between Messrs. Shaw and Shrewsbury and the members of the team, it may not be out of place to refer to it in detail.

The Yorkshire Cup competition is answerable for this exposure of professionalism, as it has also been for many others. The match Dewsbury v. Halifax at Dewsbury, on March 3rd, 1888, was the occasion leading to the arraignment of Clowes. Mr. Turner, the agent in England of Messrs. Shaw and Shrewsbury, had approached Lockwood, Stuart, and Stadden, of the Dewsbury Club. Lockwood and Stuart had signed agreements to go, and a similar agreement had been sent to Stadden. Lockwood afterwards withdrew from his agreement, and Stadden placed the agreement forwarded to him in the hands of the Dewsbury officials, who were now in a position to lay a trap for the Halifax Club. They had not forgotten the Jones incident in 1883, when Halifax had successfully appealed, and caused the match to be replayed; and the opportunity of returning a Roland for an Oliver was not allowed to pass by. Dewsbury left Stuart out of their team, and entered the contest in the delightful position of standing upon velvet. They might win, but they could not lose. Fortunately for the interests of the Rugby game Dewsbury lost the match; they then disclosed the negotiations that had passed between Messrs. Turner and Stadden. Stuart, like Stadden, was a Welshman, and had received £15 from Mr. Turner for his outfit and preliminary expenses. This he had told to Stadden, and so the Dewsbury Club charged Clowes with having received the same sum for the same purposes. Clowes acknowledged in an open manly manner that such was the case, and he admitted having spent the money in providing himself with clothes and other articles necessary for the trip. The Yorkshire Committee found: "1. That J. P. Clowes, of the Halifax Club, having received £15 from Mr. Turner of Nottingham for an outfit in connection with a football tour in Australia, has thereby received money consideration for playing football, and, in the opinion of this committee, is a professional football player according to the Union rules as to professionalism adopted in October, 1886. 2. That the Halifax Club have played Clowes in ignorance of his receipt of this money, and the committee therefore order that the match be replayed, on Wednesday, on the Bradford ground." It may be interesting to remark that Halifax won the match, and were eventually the winners of the Cup for that season.

The Yorkshire Committee then communicated with the Committee of the Rugby Union, and a special meeting of the latter was held at Leeds on Wednesday March 7th, when the following resolution was adopted:— "The Rugby Football Union has decided, on the evidence before them, that J. P. Clowes is a professional within the meaning of their laws. On the same evidence they have formed a very strong opinion that others composing the Australian team have also infringed those laws, and they will require from them such explanation as they may think fit on their return to England." On the return of the team each player was required to make an affidavit that he had received no pecuniary benefit from the tour, and then the matter ended.

The power and influence of the Rugby Union were never more strongly exemplified than in the action of Messrs. Shaw and Shrewsbury in not playing Clowes in Australia. They feared that his presence in the team might lead to the Unions in the Colonies, affiliated to the Rugby Union, declining to play matches with their team, and also that the mere fact of Clowes playing might disqualify the other members on their return.

THE TEAM.

Backs: J. T. Haslam (Batley, Yorkshire, and North); A. Paul (Swinton). *Three-quarter Backs*: H. C. Speakman (Runcorn, Cheshire); H. Brooks (Edinburgh University, Durham); J. Anderton (Salford, North); A. E. Stoddart (Blackheath, Middlesex, England). *Half-Backs*: W. Bumby (Swinton, Lancashire); J. Nolan (Rochdale Hornets, Lancashire); W. Burnett (Hawick). *Forwards*: C. Mathers (Bramley, Yorkshire, North); S. Williams (Salford, Lancashire, North); T. Banks (Swinton, Lancashire); R. L. Seddon (Swinton, Lancashire, England); H. Eagles (Swinton, Lancashire, England); A. J. Stuart (Dewsbury, Yorkshire); W. H. Thomas (Cambridge University, Wales); J. P. Clowes (Halifax, Yorkshire); T. Kent (Salford, Lancashire, England); A. J. Penketh (Douglas, Isle of Man); R. Burnett (Hawick); A. J. Laing (Hawick); J. Smith (Edinburgh University), Umpire.

The New Zealand Native Football Team.

A noteworthy feature of the season 1888-9 was the visit of a team from New Zealand, composed of colonists, half-castes, and Maoris. Taking the latter title, it was generally designated during the tour as the "Maori" team, though the legitimate appellation was that of "The New Zealand Native Football Representatives." Ere quitting New Zealand, the team received the sanction and support of the Rugby Union, the list of fixtures being arranged for them by G. Rowland Hill. The "boys," as J. R. Scott almost invariably called them, were under the management and control of J. R. Scott and T. Eyton, the former gentleman taking the more prominent part in the guidance of the team, and to his energy and enthusiasm the team owe a great share of the success and popularity they attained during their stay in England. Commencing against Surrey on October 3rd, and playing the concluding match against the Southern Counties at Leyton on March 27th, they contrived in the space of twenty-five weeks to play no less than seventy-four matches, of which they won forty-nine, drew five, and lost twenty —a truly satisfactory result, considering the hard work entailed upon the team through the extraordinary number of matches, and the quality of some of the teams opposed to them. The record would probably have been more largely in their favour had they contented themselves with playing fewer matches, but the expenses connected with the tour were so great that it was absolutely necessary for them to play extra matches in order to obtain the necessary funds to enable the tour to be a financial success. That the tour was carried out on strictly amateur lines may be accepted from the fact that the Rugby Union practically had control of the finances, for previously to the commencement of the matches G. R. Hill, instructed by the committee, required an undertaking that the accounts should be submitted to the Rugby Union if so desired.

It is to be regretted that in 1891 Keogh, the halfback, was declared to be a professional by the New Zealand Unions. In the early matches the New Zealanders appeared on the field in their native mats and headdresses, and uttered their well-known cry

NEW ZEALAND NATIVE FOOTBALL TEAM, 1888–1889.

(From a Photograph by H. A. Chapman, 235, High Street, Swansea.)

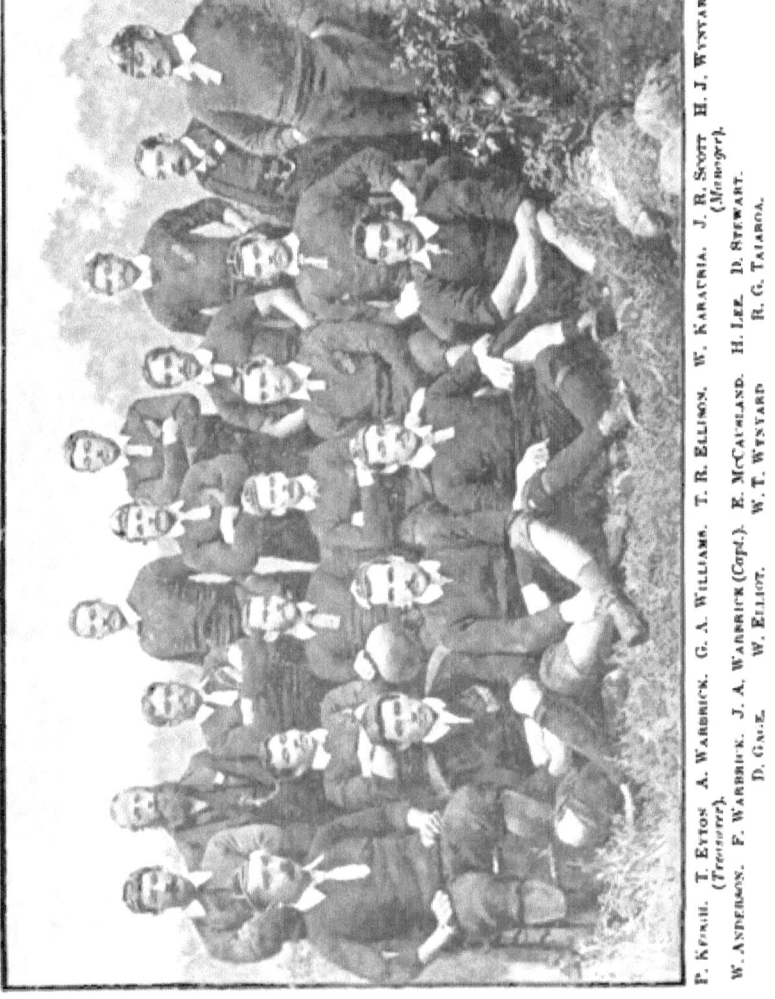

J. A. Warth. G. H. Wynyard.

P. Keogh. T. Eyton. A. Warbrick. G. A. Williams. T. R. Ellison. W. Karauria. J. R. Scott. H. J. Wynyard.
(Treasurer). (Manager).
W. Anderson. F. Warbrick. J. A. Warbrick (Capt.). E. McCausland. H. Lee. D. Stewart.
D. Gage. W. Elliot. W. T. Wynyard. R. G. Taiaroa.

of "Ake, ake, kia, kaha." ("For ever be strong and bold"); and undoubtedly curiosity had much to do with the attendance at the games. Later, when the real merit of their play was recognised, they discarded these advertising spectacles, and depended upon their genuine exhibition of football to attract spectators. At first their strength and scrummaging powers were the most noticeable features, but as the tour proceeded they improved in their play, and especially in passing. Their backs were strong and speedy, and in E. McCausland they had a most reliable place-kick, whilst Keogh at half-back was quite first-class. They adopted the system of eight forwards and three half-backs, and rarely did their eight stalwart forwards fail to hold their own against their opponents.

Their most noticeable victories were against Ireland, Swansea, Newport, Yorkshire (2nd team), Gloucestershire, Somersetshire, Blackheath, Halifax, and Manchester, whilst they suffered their most severe defeats from Middlesex, Halifax, and Yorkshire. The games with Hull, Wakefield, Swinton, Cardiff, Bradford, and Huddersfield were very closely contested. Of the three International matches, they won one—against Ireland (4 goals 1 try to a goal and a try)—and lost to Wales and England. For the latter match they had specially reserved themselves; and though defeated by a goal and four tries to nothing, the score does not give evidence of the gallant fight they made, nor how for some time they threatened to lower the colours of the England team. In this gallant attempt they would have received the chivalrous recognition of all English sportsmen had they not, through some of their players leaving the field, marred their excellent play by a most childish and unsportsmanlike protest against the decision of the referee, G. Rowland Hill. The Rugby Union at once showed their opinion of this conduct by requiring an apology. This step was, as may well be imagined, most distasteful to the Union, but the principles of the game have always been of the first importance in the minds of the Union Committee. It might seem ungracious to treat visitors in this manner, especially as a prohibition of the Union meant a collapse of the tour, but the fundamental principles underlying the office of the referee, viz., that his decision on matters of fact are indisputable, and that his person is inviolable from either violence or insult, have been upheld consistently by the committee.

The majority of the matches were played in the North of England, and principally in Yorkshire and Lancashire, where the players were more enthusiastically welcomed by the followers of the game, and where the receipts at the matches were considerably higher than in other parts of the country. By making Manchester and Leeds their headquarters for a lengthened period, they were enabled to play many matches without having to expend great sums in travelling expenses.

A tendency to rough play, and the objectionable practice, indulged in by certain players, of cavilling at the decisions of the referees (and in this their captain, Joe Warbrick, set a very bad example to the team), were the only features to mar a most successful tour. Their visit was thoroughly enjoyed and appreciated by the football-loving population of the North. The Southerners were not so appreciative of the style of play and manners of the Natives. Undoubtedly they were a strong combination, and their wonderful physique was a great factor in their many victories, and in the successful manner in which they went through the most numerous list of matches ever undertaken by a single team.

New Zealand Team.

Backs: J. A. Warbrick (Captain) (11st. 12lb.), County Hawke's Bay; W. Warbrick (12st. 3lb.), Matata; D. Gage (11st.), Poneke, Wellington; E. M'Causland (11st.), Gordon, Auckland; C. Madigan (12st. 2lb.), Grafton, Auckland; W. Wynyard (11st. 4lb.), North Shore; F. Warbrick (11st. 3lb.), County Hawke's Bay. *Half-Backs*: P. Keogh (11st. 4lb.); C. Goldsmith; W. Elliott (11st. 12lb.), Grafton, Auckland; Ihimaira ("Smiler"), (13st. 13lb.), County Hawke's Bay; G. Wynyard (12st. 10lb.), North Shore. *Forwards*: J. R. Ellison (12st. 3lb.), Poneke, Wellington; R. Maynard (12st. 9lb.), North Shore; W. Anderson (12st. 2lb.), Thames; Taare (11st. 10lb.), County Hawke's Bay; H. Lee (13st. 11lb.), Riverton; A. Webster (13st. 12lb.), Hokianga; R. Tairoa (11st. 10lb.), Dunedin; W. Karauria (12st. 13lb.), County Hawke's Bay; Arthur Warbrick (13st. 4lb.), Matata; Alfred Warbrick (11st. 12lb.), County Hawke's Bay; G. A. Williams (14st. 7lb.), Poneke, Wellington; D. Stewart (14st. 10lb.), Thames; T. Reune (13st. 2lb.), Nelson; W. Nehua (14st. 2lb.), Nelson; J. R. Scott, Manager; T. Eyton, Treasurer.

The above classification of the positions of the players is only general, as they were changed so frequently—notably W. Nehua, who played full-back, three-quarter, and forward—that an exact classification cannot be attempted.

The South African Tour.

The visit of Major Wharton's cricket team to the Cape undoubtedly gave the first impetus to the idea of inviting a team of English football players to make a tour in South Africa. As in England, so there are the two games of Association and Rugby played in Africa, though in the early days there was an inclination to favour a game which was a mixture of Rugby and Association. Fortunately this game was not successful in obtaining permanent hold, and at the present day the only codes recognised are the Association and Rugby Union. The latter seems to have gained the affections of spectators and players, and is undoubtedly the rule amongst the African clubs, already boasting of a Union, cups, and competitions. Of late years the clubs have greatly developed in strength, but, as is the case in all new ventures, the clubs and players lacked the knowledge and experience of the older organisations and players of the Mother Country. It was therefore thought to be advisable in the interest of the game—both in improving the play, and also in giving a healthy stimulus to football—to invite the Rugby Union to send over a team of Rugby Union players to contend against the picked teams of South Africa. Mr. Harold, the hon. secretary of the Western Province Rugby Football Union, was the initiator of the project; and Mr. J. Richards, of Cape Town (well remembered in connection with the Old Leysian Football Club), who was visiting England, was requested to conduct the negotiations. The Rugby Union looked with favour upon the project, but, as in duty bound, were exceedingly cautious in making arrangements. That the visit of a team from England would be of benefit to African football was admitted, but there were many points to be considered ere the Union would definitely pledge themselves to the scheme. They could not run the risk of repeating the experiences of the Australian tour, and so the first stipulation imposed was that the matches should be played under the laws of the English Rugby Union and the regulations regarding players. In a word, the Rugby Union were true to the traditions that have always guided them, and were determined to have the control of the matches, and to absolutely guarantee that the team leaving England and

THE CAPE TEAM, 1891.

those encountered in Africa should be composed of amateurs. Then the committee were firm on the matter of guarantee. The invitation came from Africa, and the colonists offered to guarantee the expenses of the tour. The Rugby Union, whilst most courteous in their communications, required the guarantee to be placed upon a business footing. No general assurance could be entertained. If there should be a loss on the tour, the Rugby Union would be responsible for the deficiency, and would have to answer to the clubs at a general meeting for such deficiency. Mr. Rowland Hill is by disposition far too cautious to allow of the merest chance of such a contingency, and it was accordingly intimated to the Cape representatives that the expenses must be absolutely guaranteed. The difficulty was satisfactorily removed by Mr. Cecil Rhodes, Prime Minister of the Cape, who himself accepted the responsibility.

The length of the tour was fixed at fifty days, and the strength of the team was much debated. At first there was some idea of leaving the choice to Cape men conversant with the relative strength of English and Colonial players; but the views of G. R. Hill, that if a team were sent out at all it should be a powerful one, coinciding with the expression of opinion from the Cape that a strong combination should be selected, caused the Rugby Union to take the selection of the players entirely into their own hands. Edwin Ash, a past secretary of the Union, and well known in connection with the Richmond Athletic Club, was elected as secretary and manager; and W. E. Maclagan, the famous Scottish International and London Scottish player, was appointed captain. The team was selected by a sub-committee consisting of Messrs. G. Rowland Hill, R. S. Whalley, H. Vassall, A. Budd, and J. H. S. McArthur. A fairly strong team was selected, including no less than eight Internationals, and it would be giving a very fair estimate of its strength to describe it as being somewhat on a par with an average North or South team.

The team sailed from Southampton in the *Dunottar Castle*, on September 20th, 1891, their captain, W. E. Maclagan, taking with him a handsome silver cup presented by Sir Donald Currie, and entrusted to W. E. Maclagan to be presented by him to the colonial club doing the best against the English team; the cup to be held by the winning club until the next ensuing season, and then to be competed for by the clubs of South Africa.

The tour was a decided success, and the English team had every reason to be proud of the unbroken record of victories. Nineteen matches were played, and they were all won—a performance unrivalled in the history of touring teams, whether cricket or football. Only one try, and that in the first match at Cape Town, was scored against them. The performance is the more noteworthy when the amount of travelling that had to be undertaken, and the fêting of the team, are taken into consideration. Their reception wherever they went was most kind, enthusiastic, and hearty. Their spare time was filled up—in the most agreeable manner possible—with dances, concerts, dinners, entertainments of every description, shooting parties and excursions. All this told against condition, and nothing but superior science in the game gave them the victory on several occasions. The passing entirely nonplussed the colonial teams; they could not understand it in the least. Screwing the scrummages and other similar tricks beat them forward. R. L. Aston's play was a revelation to the opposing teams. His record of 30 tries is a wonderful evidence of his superiority over the colonial backs.

The South Africans played a very hard game, especially forward, and on several occasions taxed the powers of the English forwards to the utmost, but they failed in the science of the game. Screwing the scrum, passing, and working the ball generally, were their weakest points. At tackling, kicking, and saving they were very good indeed. Fondness for individual distinction was perhaps the most important factor in their defeats. Forwards and backs alike were very loth to part with the ball when once they had possession of it. Towards the end of the tour they had very much improved, and in the course of a year or two will in all probability play a first-class game.

The best teams were undoubtedly the Western Provinces, played at Cape Town; the Griqualand West (to whom the "Currie" Cup was given), at Kimberley; and (which was really with but one exception the same team) the Kimberley Club, also at Kimberley. The

ENGLAND V. CAPE COLONY. AT CAPE TOWN.

ENGLAND v. SOUTH AFRICA, AT KIMBERLEY.

"THE KICK-OFF."

games played against the combinations of South Africa were very closely contested. These combinations were met three times, viz., at Cape Town, Port Elizabeth, and Kimberley. The hardest game of the tour was the second South African match at Kimberley, which was won by the Englishmen by 1 goal—kicked by Mitchell from a mark at the half-way flag—to *nil*.

The best players in the South African team were generally those who had received their football training in the Mother Country; of these the most prominent were H. H. Castens, an old Oxford 'Varsity and South of England player, and a hard-working forward; he had the best knowledge of the game of any player in Africa, and also refereed on several occasions. (Refereeing was rather weak, and Castens was decidedly the best of the officials.) A. Richards, the Old Leysian, played a really first-class game at half-back, and his style was equal to that of our English half-backs. B. Duff was a good full-back, cool sure kick, and a very good tackler. C. Versfeld was also a fairly good left wing three-quarter, and gained the only try scored against the Englishmen. Guthrie was also a good half-back, playing a splendid defensive game. While amongst others who may be mentioned as being good players were Boyes, Vigne, M. Versfeld, H. M. Hepper (late of the Leeds St. John's Club, and who also played for Yorkshire), Heathe, and E. Castens.

The character of the grounds was much against the play of the Englishmen. On most of the grounds the grass was almost entirely burnt off by the sun, this being especially the case at Kimberley, which was very bad, there being absolutely no grass at all. The Johannesberg ground was much the same as that at Kimberley, only not quite so hard. At Newlands, Cape Town, where the first match was played, there was a considerable amount of grass; but the best ground was at Port Elizabeth, where the game took place on a properly-levelled cricket ground.

The team arrived in England by the *Garth Castle* on September 28th, all having pleasant reminiscences of the tour. The visit of the Englishmen has undoubtedly been of benefit to football in Africa. As the early teams of cricketers fostered and developed that game in Australia, so the team of footballers to the Cape have initiated the colonists of Africa into the fine points and science of the Rugby game.

The following were the members of the team :—

W. E. Maclagan (Captain), London Scottish, Scottish International.
Edward Bromet, St. Thomas's Hospital, Cambridge University.
P. R. Clauss, Fettes Lorettonian, Oxford University, Scottish International.
R. L. Aston, Blackheath, Cambridge University, International.
W. Wotherspoon, Fettes Lorettonian, Cambridge University, Scottish International.
A. Rotherham, Cambridge University, South of England.
H. Marshall, Blackheath, Cambridge University.
P. F. Hancock, Blackheath, Somerset, International.
R. G. Macmillan, London Scottish, Scottish International.
W. E. Bromet, Oxford University, Yorkshire, International.
T. Whittaker, Lancashire.
R. Thompson, Cambridge University.
C. P. Simpson, Richmond, Cambridge University.
W. H. Thorman, Blackheath, Cambridge University.
J. Hammond, Blackheath, Cambridge University, South of England.
J. H. Gould, Old Leysians, South of England.
A. A. Surtees, Harlequins, Cambridge University, Middlesex, South of England.
W. Jackson, Cambridge University.
W. G. Mitchell, Middlesex, International.
E. Mayfield, Old Leysians, Cambridge University.
B. G. Roscoe, Manchester.

Matches played, 19; won, 19; lost, 0. Points scored: for, 224; against, 1; tries, 89, of which 50 were converted; dropped goals, 7, of which one was a penalty goal; placed penalty goals, 6; one goal placed from a mark.

W. Wotherspoon dropped 2 goals (one being a penalty).
R. L. Aston dropped 1 goal.
P. R. Clauss dropped 1 goal.
W. G. Mitchell dropped 2 goals (one from a mark).
H. Marshall dropped 1 goal (from a mark).
A. Rotherham placed 39 goals (two penalty, one from a mark).
W. G. Mitchell placed 7 goals (one penalty).
W. Wotherspoon placed 6 goals (three penalty).
R. L. Aston placed 5 goals.

R. L. Aston scored 30 tries; E. Bromet, 9; W. E. Maclagan, 8; H. Marshall, 8; T. Whittaker, 7; R. Thompson, 7; P. R. Clauss, 6; W. Wotherspoon, 5; R. G. Macmillan, 3; B. G. Roscoe, 3; A. Rotherham, 2; E. Mayfield, 1.

NUMBER OF MATCHES PLAYED BY THE MEMBERS OF THE TEAM.

J. Hammond		A. A. Surtees	
R. G. Macmillan		E. Bromet	13.
W. G. Mitchell	19.	P. R. Clauss	12.
R. L. Aston		J. H. Gould	11.
W. E. Maclagan		C. P. Simpson	
R. Thompson	18.	H. Marshall	10.
W. E. Bromet		W. Wotherspoon	8.
P. F. Hancock		W. H. Thorman	6.
T. Whittaker	16.	B. G. Roscoe	
A. Rotherham		W. Jackson	5.
E. Mayfield	14.		

www.ingramcontent.com/pod-product-compliance
Lightning Source LLC
Chambersburg PA
CBHW051156300426
44116CB00006B/329